The Great Waterloo Controversy

The Great Waterloo Controversy

The Story of the 52nd Foot at History's Greatest Battle

Gareth Glover

Frontline Books

First published in Great Britain in 2020 by
Frontline Books
An imprint of
Pen & Sword Books Ltd
Yorkshire – Philadelphia

Copyright © Gareth Glover 2020

ISBN 978 1 52678 885 6

The right of Gareth Glover to be identified as Author of this work has been asserted by him in accordance with the Copyright, Designs and Patents Act 1988.

A CIP catalogue record for this book is
available from the British Library.

All rights reserved. No part of this book may be reproduced or transmitted in any form or by any means, electronic or mechanical including photocopying, recording or by any information storage and retrieval system, without permission from the Publisher in writing.

Typeset by Mac Style
Printed and bound in the UK by TJ Books Limited,
Padstow, Cornwall.

Pen & Sword Books Limited incorporates the imprints of Atlas, Archaeology, Aviation, Discovery, Family History, Fiction, History, Maritime, Military, Military Classics, Politics, Select, Transport, True Crime, Air World, Frontline Publishing, Leo Cooper, Remember When, Seaforth Publishing, The Praetorian Press, Wharncliffe Local History, Wharncliffe Transport, Wharncliffe True Crime and White Owl.

For a complete list of Pen & Sword titles please contact

PEN & SWORD BOOKS LIMITED
47 Church Street, Barnsley, South Yorkshire, S70 2AS, England
E-mail: enquiries@pen-and-sword.co.uk
Website: www.pen-and-sword.co.uk

Or

PEN AND SWORD BOOKS
1950 Lawrence Rd, Havertown, PA 19083, USA
E-mail: Uspen-and-sword@casematepublishers.com
Website: www.penandswordbooks.com

For more information on our books, please email: info@frontline-books.com, write to us at the above address, or visit:
www.frontline-books.com

Contents

Foreword		viii
Acknowledgements		xi
Chapter 1	The Establishment of a Reputation	1
Chapter 2	The 'Ogre' Returns	8
Chapter 3	Preparing for War	17
Chapter 4	The Campaign Begins – 16 June	31
Chapter 5	Retreat to Waterloo – 17 June	40
Chapter 6	Battle Begins 11.30–16.00 Hours	49
Chapter 7	The Great Cavalry Attacks 16.00–18.00 Hours	61
Chapter 8	The Crisis 19.30–20.30 Hours	85
Chapter 9	The Centre Attack 19.30–20.00 Hours	95
Chapter 10	To Maitland's Left, Defeating the Second Attack 19.45–20.15 Hours	111
Chapter 11	Defeating the Third Attack – The Second Column 19.45 to 20.00 Hours	123
Chapter 12	The Support	147
Chapter 13	The Chase 20.00 to 20.45 Hours	156
Chapter 14	The Cavalry Assault 20.15–22:00 Hours	182
Chapter 15	The Dying Embers of the Day 21.00 to 22.00 Hours	189
Chapter 16	The Morning After – 19 June	203
Chapter 17	The March on Paris 19 June–5 July	218
Chapter 18	The Rancour of Jealousy	233
Chapter 19	Investigating the Claims	240
Chapter 20	Overall Conclusion	266

Appendix I: Company Numbers 269

Appendix II: Named Casualties of the 52nd Foot at Waterloo 272

Appendix III: Known Desertions from 52nd Foot December 1814–December 1815 281

Appendix IV: Soldiers on Command etc. in June 1815 285

Appendix V: Comparison of Battalion Returns April–July 1815 Adam's and Maitland's Brigades 286

Appendix VI: Number of Regimental and General Courts Martial (by Company) held on members of the 1st Battalion 52nd Foot in 1815 288

Appendix VII: General Adam's Wound 294

Appendix VIII: Deployment of the Imperial Guard Battalions at Waterloo 295

Appendix IX: Private James Raw's Execution 302

Bibliography 305

PRESENTED AUGUST 8th, 1798; ALTERED TO SUIT THE REQUIREMENTS NECESSITATED BY THE UNION WITH IRELAND, 1801; CARRIED AT WATERLOO, AND FINALLY RETIRED 1818.

Foreword

The lightning Waterloo campaign of 1815, in which three great battles were fought in only three days and which culminated in the total defeat of Napoleon's last great army, has long been a source of endless debate, rancorous argument and conspiracy theories. The conflict is so shrouded in myth, conjecture and claims of betrayal, that it is not easy at times to separate fact from fiction.

For the past decade or more, a small number of dedicated historians – including Pierre de Witt, Erwin Muilwijk, Paul Dawson, Stephen Beckett, Robert Burnham, Michael Crumplin, Andrew Field, John Franklin and my good self – have delved into the archives all over Europe and beyond, to unearth literally tens of thousands of documents, which had been lost or forgotten, in an effort to help build a clear, honest, unbiased narrative of the events of that fateful campaign. Much that is completely new to us has been discovered, a number of myths have been buried, but a few contentious issues remain stubbornly unresolved.

In many cases, these contentious issues have been regularly reignited by partisan 're-appraisals' which have unashamedly set out to prove their own chosen stance on the issue, no matter what the evidence actually shows. Indeed, many are guilty of selective editing of material and unquestioning use of original documents that conveniently support their claims, without subjecting them to the same stringent tests that they use on those that do not support their theory.

When even written with the best intentions, ex-members of a particular regiment or corps cannot help but bring a heavy baggage to the task, often possessing an understandably intense regimental pride and loyalty and a wish to celebrate their greatest achievements. All laudable intentions, but these factors make it very difficult, if not nigh on impossible, to view all of the evidence, good or bad, and to produce a balanced, honest view of their achievements and of their failures. No human comes without some biases, but a cold, objective weighing up of all of the available contradictory evidence in such circumstances, can only, I would submit, be achieved by someone who has no personal interest in the outcome, other than a desire for a balanced, thoroughly honest assessment of all the relevant facts without any bias.

As a historian, I am also painfully aware that less than one thousandth of the documentation produced during any given period, actually still survives to this day, even in such an era as the early nineteenth century, when the system only functioned at all by the production and exchange of vast quantities of paper documents. Often the most vital evidence, or the key to a specific question is not to be found, having been lost through the vagaries of time. It can be incredibly frustrating and much of our time as historians is taken up, piecing snippets of evidence together, in an attempt to work out what the missing material said. What it is not, almost certainly, is evidence of a cover up, or an attempt to mislead by purposely removing incriminating evidence.

Conspiracy theories are therefore extremely easy to manufacture, the simple claim that the evidence has been 'removed' rather than more accurately 'lost' is enough to cast doubt and engender suspicion, add a few selective comments to hint at nefarious dealings and there you have it. Unfortunately, once the seed has been sown, it is often hard to disprove it, despite much circumstantial evidence against it, because the seed has been planted and of course, the vital solid evidence is 'mysteriously' unavailable. This is not good history.

One of the most enduring arguments regarding Napoleon's defeat at Waterloo and the one which is fought over with perhaps the most vitriol and passion on both sides, is that of the defeat of the Imperial Guard at around 20.00 hours on the evening of 18 June 1815. It is rightly seen as a decisive moment, when Napoleon launched a final all-out attack with his finest troops, his world-renowned Imperial Guard, only to see them defeated and chased from the field of battle. The sight of the failure of his 'Immortals'[1] shocked his army to the core and morale, already shaken by the sound of the Prussians arriving and attacking their flank, collapsed disastrously and caused them to turn and flee en masse, ending Napoleon's dreams of re-establishing his glorious empire for ever.

The argument centres on which regiments delivered the coup de grace and how it was actually administered and here the evidence is often fragmentary, incomplete and shrouded by the taint of regimental bias. Even how the French Imperial Guard attacked is still debated, with many eyewitnesses contradicting each other. When it comes to individual regiments arguing over the relative merits of each to a claim of the laurels of defeating the Imperial Guard, the waters become very murky indeed, with claim and counter-claim being made and with little impartial fact finding in evidence.

It is into this maelstrom that I stride, not by any means oblivious to the heated claims and sensibilities of the contending parties, but determined to re-examine the dozens of witness statements, many recently discovered, including the only full account written at the time by an officer of the 52nd Foot, which has never been published or indeed properly studied before. I will assess the reliability of the witnesses, given their military experience, ability to see what they describe and even the length of time after events that they described them.

Given the impossibility of getting three eyewitnesses to a terrible road traffic accident to agree on the details within twelve hours of the incident, it is a daunting task to try to establish the sequence of events as seen through a haze of smoke, as the light of the day was beginning to wane, when their concentration was

---

1. The term Immortals was actually a term of derision, invented by Napoleon's 'ordinary' line infantry. They hated the fact that they were paid more, lived better and were held in reserve in most battles and rarely used, as too valuable to lose.

fully occupied on their own immediate circumstances and caring about their self-preservation, whilst friends fell besides them at every moment. Because many of these witnesses recorded their memories of these events some twenty or even forty years after the event and often after discussing it at great length with fellow survivors, great care must be taken to identify the vein of truth running through their time worn and inevitably greatly embellished accounts.

This work is unapologetically not simply another account of the entire campaign. This work concentrates solely on the exploits of the Light Brigade in the campaign and therefore only mentions aspects of the campaign in which they were not involved in the briefest terms.

For the reader who wants to explore the entire campaign in detail, this is not the work for you. Detailed descriptions of the Battle of Quatre Bras, the retreat via Genappe and d'Erlon's attack and the counter charge by the British heavy cavalry are not included here, but what you will find within is the most thoroughly researched study as to the quality and discipline of the Light Brigade and particularly the 52nd Foot in the Waterloo campaign and the most thorough examination of the 'Crisis' of the battle ever produced.

This work will look specifically at the 52nd (Oxfordshire) Regiment of Foot, which was one of the strongest regiments in the army and rightly became one of the most renowned regiments of the Duke of Wellington's army in the Peninsular War and during the ensuing Waterloo campaign. Trained as light infantry and personally commanded by the highly-regarded General John Moore until his death at Corunna, its reputation was second to none. It was commanded at Waterloo by another well-respected officer, Colonel Sir John Colborne. I will look at the regiment's training, how prepared it was for the campaign, how it performed and also briefly look at what it did during the subsequent three years, forming part of the Army of Occupation in France until 1818.

I will fully investigate its role at Waterloo, hailing its achievements, but also not hiding its failures and I will assess fairly its contribution to the great victory. I will also investigate the claims that it was robbed of its laurels and who, if anyone, was to blame for that.

This volume will be published simultaneously with a sister volume containing all of the known eyewitness statements from the 52nd Foot from 1815 to 1818 during the Waterloo campaign and the subsequent Army of Occupation in full. This volume will be published by Ken Trotman Publishing and will be entitled *The Waterloo Campaign and the Army of Occupation 1815–18, Eyewitness Accounts of the 52nd (Oxfordshire) Regiment of Foot*.

It is intended to give the first in-depth investigation and analysis of a single regiment in the Waterloo campaign and to establish a very honest assessment of its achievements. You, as the reader, can judge, having read all of this evidence, and can form your own opinion.

Gareth Glover
Cardiff 2020

Acknowledgements

Any project of this scale requires a great deal of help and advice and I have a great number of people that I must thank. Firstly I must mention Nicholas Haynes, who initially brought the Journal of Lieutenant Charles Holman to my attention and helped garner support for the project within the regiments and Mrs Christine Pullen, curator and the staff of The Royal Green Jackets (Rifles) Museum at Peninsula Barracks in Winchester, who kindly allowed me to photograph the journal so that I could transcribe it at leisure and helped me with a number of other queries. I must also thank the staff at Hampshire Archives in Winchester, who helped me find a number of interesting documents in their files transferred from the Green Jackets.

Jenny Lelkes the Readers Services Officer at the National Army Museum was also very kind in providing copies of a number of documents.

I must add a special thank you to Peggy Ainsworth, the Archivist at the Museum of the Oxfordshire Soldier, who kindly allowed me to check every file they owned during two day-long visits, in which I discovered a large number of very useful documents, some of which did not even appear on their rather ancient list of holdings or were mis-identified. She also very kindly (and cheerfully) supplied copies of a very large number of these documents.

Another special thank you must be added for Josephine Dixon and Alison Rosie at the National Register of Archives of Scotland who identified the whereabouts of the contemporary Adam's letters and personally valiantly liaised for some months with the owner in an effort to gain access to them. Their efforts were beyond the call of duty and were very gratefully received, however, frustratingly the owner still feels unable to release them into the public domain and has chosen not to allow me access to them.

I must also offer my heartfelt thanks to my good friend Robert Burnham who offered sage advice from his home in Hawaii and kept finding new sources to check out via the internet. His and Ron McGuigan's learned advice on the conundrum of company numbers helped to formulate my thoughts and formed a large part of my findings which will be found in Appendix 1. I must also mention Ian Yonge, a fellow 'Waterloo Association' man, who kindly guided me towards a copy of the incredibly rare, short biography by Lieutenant Yonge of John Colborne and also to the short history of the 52nd published by Colborne's daughter. Many others have helped me with advice along the way and I do apologise profusely if I have forgotten to mention anybody specifically, but all of your help was gratefully received and has helped to make it the work I have produced, although I of course take all responsibility for any errors or omissions.

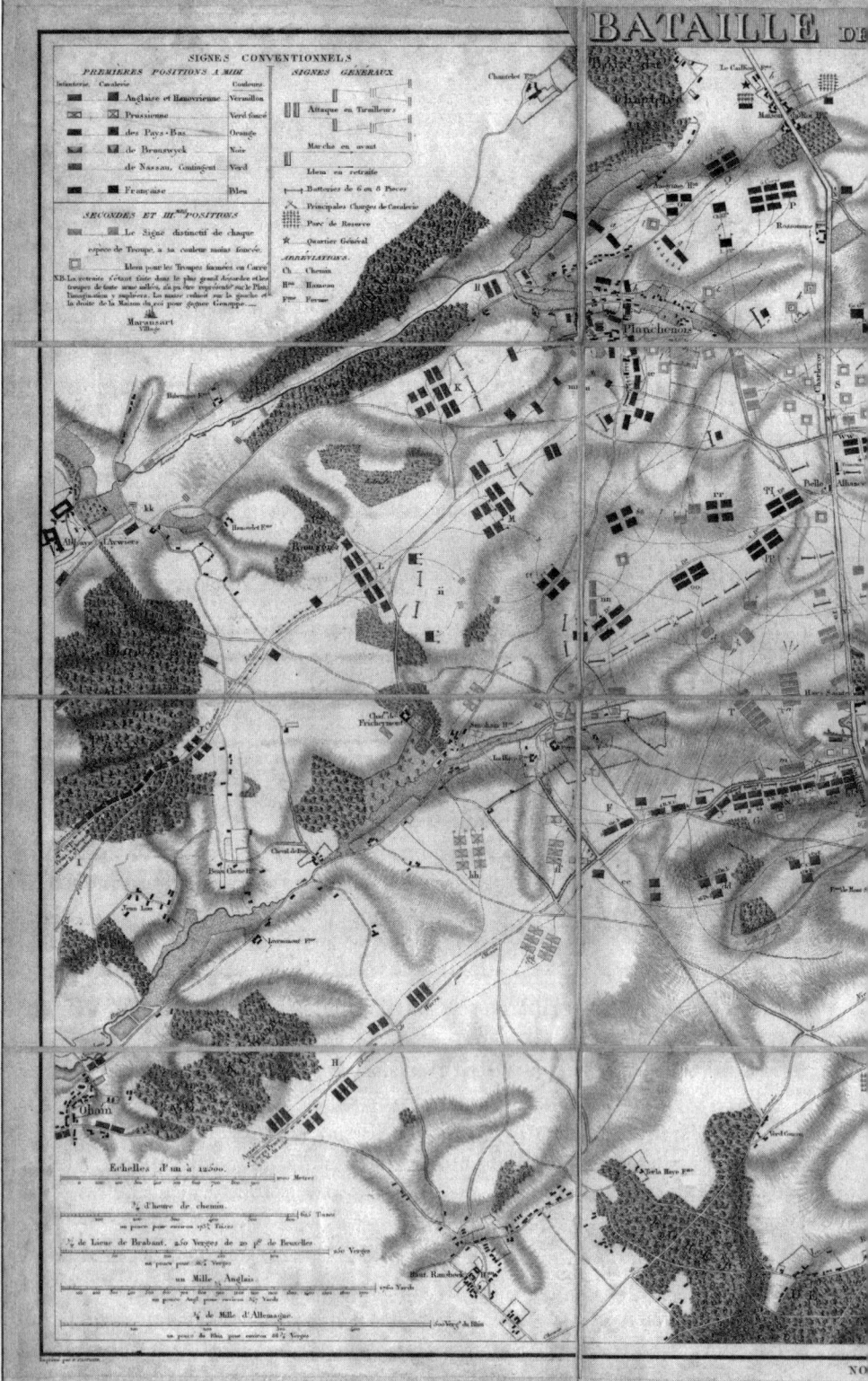

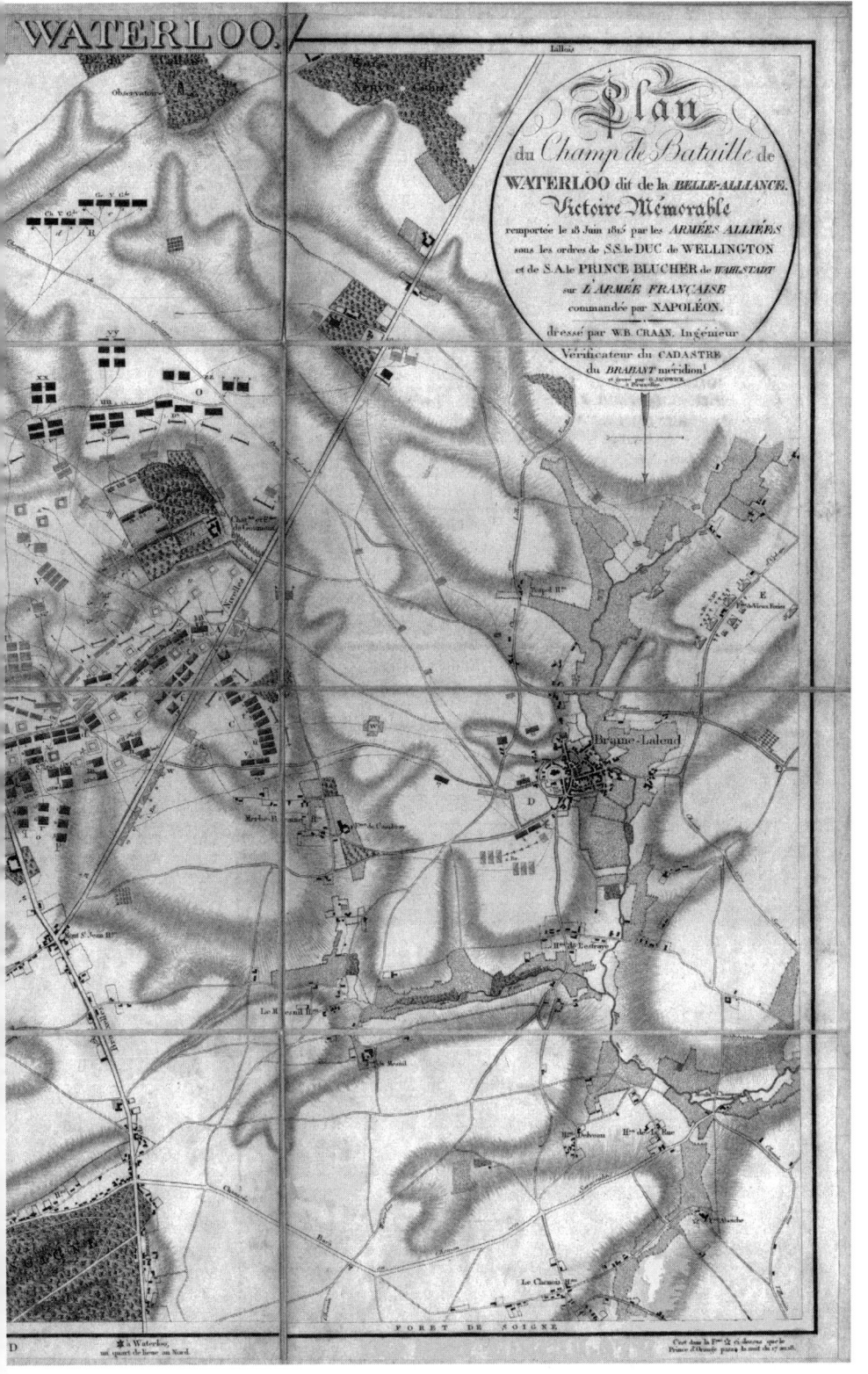

Chapter 1

The Establishment of a Reputation

It is strange to relate, but the 52nd (Oxfordshire) Regiment started life as Colonel Lambton's Regiment in 1755 numbered as the 54th Regiment of Foot. However, with the disbandment of Colonel Shirley's 50th Regiment and Colonel Peperell's 51st Regiment of Foot, within a year, the regiment had been renumbered as the 52nd, which it subsequently retained. The regiment had been fully recruited by early 1756 and it spent a number of years in garrisons throughout England and Ireland, before it was posted abroad for the first time in 1765, serving in Canada until the outbreak of the American War of Independence in 1775.

The 52nd was sent to join a force under the command of General Gage at Boston and here it was to meet the 43rd Regiment of Foot for the first time, a regiment they were to be closely linked with throughout the next century, until they eventually amalgamated in 1881 to form the 'Oxford and Buckinghamshire Light Infantry'. The regiments both participated in the actions of Lexington and at Bunker Hill, a bayonet charge by the two battalions capturing the rebel trenches, but with heavy loss. The regiment was also involved in the capture of New York in 1776 and the victories of Brandywine River and Germantown in 1777, but by now the ranks were so depleted, that they were ordered to return to England to recruit.

In 1782 King George III ordered that regiments were to be given a regional affiliation, with the theoretical aim of recruiting mainly from their designated region, the 52nd Foot becoming the 'Oxfordshire Regiment'.

The following year, the regiment was sent to India, taking part in the Siege of Cannanore [Kannur] in 1783 and of Dindigul and Palgautcherry [Palakkad] in renewed fighting in 1790. In 1792, the regiment successfully stormed the mountain fortress of Savendroog [Savandurga] and helped in the capture of Pondicherry from the French in 1793. It also participated in the campaign to capture Ceylon [modern day Sri Lanka] from the Dutch in 1795–6, before finally sailing back to Britain in July 1798 after fifteen years abroad.

Whilst in garrison in Barking and then Ashford, the regiment received some 2,000 volunteers from the militia, when a second battalion was formed, and Major General John Moore was appointed colonel of the 2nd Battalion.

In 1800, both battalions served in an abortive expedition to Ferrol in Spain and then proceeded to Gibraltar and later Lisbon, to protect Portugal from Spanish aggression. Whilst on campaign, the colonel of the regiment, General Cyrus Trapaud, died and John Moore was appointed colonel in his place on 8 May 1801.

With the regiment returning to England in June 1801, they were stationed in Kent until November 1802, when both battalions were assembled at Chatham. In January 1803 the 1st Battalion of the 52nd Foot was designated as 'Light Infantry'[1] whilst the 2nd Battalion was renumbered as the 96th Regiment.

An Experimental Corps of Riflemen, dressed in green, had been established in 1800 and this corps had served in the Ferrol campaign and a detachment had also served as marines at the naval battle of Copenhagen in 1801. In 1802 the corps was formally accepted into the line, having been given the title of the 95th Regiment of Rifles.

The 52nd was moved to a training camp at Shorncliffe in July 1803, where an earth ramped redoubt had been constructed in 1794 by Colonel William Twiss of the Royal Engineers[2] and barracks built within. It had already been used as a training ground since 1795[3] and had been identified as the perfect spot to site an 'Army of Observation' ready to deal with any invasion force landing in Kent. Moore's brigade then consisted of the 4th, 59th, 52nd and 95th Foot, the latter two battalions, along with the light companies of the 4th and 59th, began to practise 'Light infantry' tactics. A few days later the 43rd Foot, then stationed in the Channel Islands, was also designated as 'Light Infantry', but it was not until June 1804 before they joined the training at Shorncliffe and replaced the 4th and 59th in the 'Light Brigade' under the overall command of Lieutenant General John Moore.

Ensign George Barlow of the 52nd described the beautiful scene overlooking the English Channel in a letter to his uncle:

> Shorncliffe is situated at nearly the most southern extremity of the County of Kent; from whence we command one of the finest views of land & Straits that perhaps was ever beheld. On one side we view Beachy Head, a considerable portion of Kent & the greatest part of the County of Sussex, Dover on the left. Every day of my life I behold the French shore; on a clear day houses and other white objects on which the sun may happen to shine, are sometimes to be distinguished with the naked eye & are commonly to be seen at all times with the telescope.[4] Yesterday from Folkestone Telegraph[5] with a fine glass, I beheld Boulogne, Ambelteuse, & several towns on the immense line of coast we daily see. The different tints of produce on the opposite hills, trees, privateers at anchor close to the beach, or getting under

---

1. It was not however the first regiment to be designated as Light Infantry as the 90th Foot had been raised as Light Infantry as early as 1794. Philip Haythornthwaite in his The Armies of Wellington, p 94 (London 1984) claims that the 52nd were not officially designated as Light Infantry until 1809, but it was clearly assigned as Light Infantry in the 1803 Army List.
2. Summerfield, Sir John Moore and the Universal Soldier, p 137.
3. ibid, p 134.
4. For those that may doubt this statement, Jonathan Leach of the 95th Rifles wrote regarding his time at Shorncliffe in June 1803 'We had no difficulty seeing the immense mass of white tents on the French coast, when the day happened to be clear.' Quoted from Sir John Moore and the Universal Soldier, pp 144.
5. The telegraph station was situated on the top of Folkestone cliff.

sail, together with our men of war cruising before their harbours in proud defiance, presented a spectacle at once so grand, that I should scarcely have believed such a report, unless I had not seen it myself.[6]

Another rifle corps had been established on the Isle of Wight in 1797, mainly composed of Germans, and designated as the 5th Battalion 60th Foot. It had been trained as light infantry and its commander, Colonel Baron von Rottenburg, developed regulations and a light infantry training manual for them, which was eagerly adopted by John Moore, to train his newly organised brigade. Ensign Charles Shaw recalled that:

> No officer was allowed to do duty in the 52nd, until he was completely drilled in every branch of his duty. The regimental regulation was six months at six hours a day; and, at the end of this period, every subaltern was perfected as a private and non-commissioned officer. It resulted that none of the juniors of the regiment ever displayed that ignorance which is the cause of the want of much moral respect on the part of the soldier.[7]

We will see that this was not completely true at Waterloo. Whereas the 95th, who dressed in green, carried the more accurate but slower loading rifles and fought more often as skirmishers in pairs, than in large linear formations, the 52nd along with the 43rd were to be armed with a musket and to remain in the red uniforms of the line regiments, being fully trained to perform the battlefield manoeuvres of a line regiment, but also trained to act independently and perform the role of skirmishers, giving them an elite status within the army.

All three regiments were regularly sent out across the rolling landscape of Kent to practise their manoeuvres. The 43rd and 52nd could form line, square and column and operate in these formations as well as any troops, but the battalion commanders were also encouraged to educate their men and to instil a far less rigid discipline, allowing them to think, rather than act purely as automatons. The training was constant and given greater impetus by the ever-present threat of a French invasion force landing on the Kent coastline at any moment.

Light Infantry were ordered to perform all manoeuvres at 'quick time' except when firing and advancing or retiring, when they would do so at ordinary pace. When in skirmish order they would react to the bugle calls, a bugler being allocated to each company. Like Line battalions they also consisted of ten companies each but did not designate the flank companies as grenadier and light, as all were light. They were simply designated as companies, numbered 1–10, all being the same.[8]

During 1804, Lieutenant General Moore was created a Knight of the Order of the Bath, when the officers of the 52nd Regiment presented him with a diamond

---

6. Glover, A Light Infantryman with Wellington: The letters of Captain George Ulrich Barlow 52nd and 69th Foot 1808–15, pp 23–4.
7. Charles Shaw Personal Memoirs and Correspondence of Colonel Charles Shaw Volume 1, London 1837 pp 6–7.
8. See Appendix 1 regarding the confusion of Muster and Field company numbers.

encrusted star in celebration. The light troops were seen to be glamorous by the public and their recruitment was consequently easier than for the regular line regiments. Soon there were so many recruits that both the 52nd and 43rd were able to form second battalions during 1804 and the 95th did so in 1805.

The brigade was eventually split up in 1806, with the 1st Battalion 52nd proceeding to Sicily and Sweden with Moore, whilst the 1/43rd, 2/52nd and 1/95th went to Copenhagen in 1807, where they served for the first time under Sir Arthur Wellesley, the future Duke of Wellington. The 1/43rd, 1st & 2nd 52nd and 1st & 2nd 95th then served together in the 1808 campaign in Portugal and in the subsequent march into Spain under the command of Sir John Moore. They then fought in the eventual retreat to Corunna, where of course Moore was killed. On Moore's death Lieutenant General Sir Hildebrand Oates took command of the 52nd as its colonel, a position he held until 1822.

The success of these troops led to further regiments being retrained and designated as light infantry; the 68th (Durham) and 85th (Bucks Volunteers) doing so in 1808 and the 51st (Yorkshire West Riding) and 71st (Glasgow Highland) in 1809.

Just after this campaign ended, Britain sent a huge armada of ships, carrying an army of over forty thousand men to Walcheren, which included elements of the 2/43rd, 2/52nd[9] and the 2/95th. The campaign was disastrous, the army led by the Earl of Chatham was dilatory in its operations and soon got bogged down on the pestilential islands in the mouth of the Scheldt. No more than a couple of hundred men died in the fighting, whereas thousands died of fever (undoubtedly a form of malaria) and thousands more were incapacitated for years to come. The expedition soon ended, and the troops returned to Britain.

Major General William Stewart of the 95th Rifles commanded the brigade at Shorncliffe in 1809 and he retained the same intense training programme. A newly arrived Ensign George Barlow of the 52nd Foot wrote of Stewart's regime:

> He takes care to keep us in good discipline; every third or fourth day he takes us out in heavy marching order, with our knapsacks, canteens, haversacks, in short equipped as if on actual service and marched us all over the county to keep our legs in practise & to make us accustomed to those long, laborious & rapid marches such always fall to the lot of the Light Bobs. He is constantly manoeuvring us, makes us ascend the steepest hills in double quick time & full trot, lay down and fire on our bellies & a thousand similar diverting tricks. In short, he makes us go wherever a human being can possibly set his foot. I do not grudge all this, as I wish to be perfect in every department of my duty whatsoever and this reflection even makes things agreeable to me, which are very irksome to others.[10]

The 52nd Foot was now a very prestigious infantry regiment in which to serve, second only to the Guards regiments, its renown having grown significantly

---

9. Five companies of the 2/52nd went to Walcheren.
10. Glover, A Light Infantryman with Wellington, p 17.

during the previous few years, due not only to the 'Light Infantry' training programme, but also from the renown of Sir John Moore who had originally been a Glasgow boy. Ensign George Barlow went so far as to call the 52nd a Scottish regiment!

> The 52nd ought properly to be termed a Scotch Regiment. The officers are almost entirely of that nation; a few Irish and a still fewer number of English, make up our regiment. Moore's name attracted all the Scotch nation into this corps; all my acquaintances in this battalion are Scotch with a very few exceptions. All the officers of the regiment behave to one another more like brothers, than any set of men I ever beheld who were utterly unconnected with one another. They are all young without any single exception, even of the colonel & majors & though young in years, are veterans in experience, all of them having seen so much service.[11]

Barlow also makes it clear that Sir John Moore had used the fame of his regiment to accept only the sons of the wealthiest families, making it the most privileged officer corps after that of the Guards regiments.

> The officers are equally as select as the commander, they chiefly consist of men of large fortune & the first connections in the kingdom, who have entered the regiment through a love of arms and are determined to continue in it as a profession. The fame of Sir J[ohn] Moore invited the best families to place their sons & relatives in his corps.[12] Although young in years, they are old in experience and I do not hesitate to say, that there is not a single considered who is not only acquainted with the common routine of his duty, but has not also a more extended knowledge of his profession than most of their acquaintances in other corps of the same standing. This as I have said before, is entirely the work of General Moore, who was determined that his officers should be soldiers in reality, so that the subaltern officers are as well acquainted with their common duty as their commander.[13]

The Light Brigade, consisting of the three first battalions of the regiments, proceeded to Portugal again in June 1809 under the command of Brevet Colonel Robert Craufurd. Its first claim to fame in this new campaign was not in battle, but a forced march undertaken to reach the front before the expected battle at Talavera commenced, which failed gloriously. The troops marched somewhere in the region of fifty miles (claims to the exact distance vary) in around 26 hours but arrived only to find the battle had ended. Such a march in the scorching summer

---

11. ibid, p 19.
12. This is an interesting comment and one little touched on by the histories of the regiment. It is true that many of the names of officers in the regiment at this time indicate that they were the sons of landed gentry and a few more were the sons of dukes etc, but it is quite a claim that Sir John Moore had selected these junior officers because of their wealth and position in society and requires further investigation.
13. Glover, A Light Infantryman with Wellington, p 22.

sun, whilst carrying a heavy pack weighing between fifty and sixty pounds and a musket, was rightly deemed an extraordinary feat.

In 1810, Lieutenant General Arthur Wellesley, incorporated two battalions of Portuguese Cacadores[14] and 'A' Troop Royal Horse Artillery, when the Light Brigade was re-designated a division. The division fought at the action on the Coa, at the victory at Busaco and formed part of the defending force maintaining the lines of Torres Vedras. They were also very active in numerous actions in the pursuit of the French army when it was forced to retire into Spain in early 1811.

In March of that year the 2nd Battalion of the 52nd Foot arrived in Portugal and joined the Light Division and both battalions of the regiment were present at the Battle of Fuentes d'Onoro and later that year Lieutenant Colonel John Colborne joined the 52nd.

In January 1812 both battalions took part in the storming of the fortress of Ciudad Rodrigo where General Craufurd was killed and the following month, the 2nd Battalion, having transferred 504 men into the First Battalion, returned to England to recruit.

The Light Division was subsequently heavily involved in the storming of the fortress of Badajoz, where both the 43rd and 52nd suffered very heavy casualties. The division then fought at the Battle of Salamanca and headed the subsequent advance on Madrid and remained in the vicinity until the end of October 1812, when the army was forced to endure a difficult retreat to the Portuguese frontier.

During 1813, the Light Division headed the advance across northern Spain, seeing action at the battles of Vitoria and the Pyrenees, the crossing of the Bidassoa into France and the battles of Nivelle and Nive. The following year, its advance into southern France continued, with actions at Orthes, Tarbes and at Toulouse, when the war ended with the capture of Paris by the allies and the abdication of the Emperor Napoleon. The 1st Battalion sailed back to Britain in April 1814 and went into garrison at Hythe and Chatham.

Meanwhile, at the end of 1813, the 2nd Battalion of the 52nd had proceeded to Holland in a campaign designed to drive the French out of the Low Countries and to restore Dutch independence. The campaign was not a success and an assault on the fortress of Bergen op Zoom went drastically wrong with thousands being made prisoner. The war soon ended, but the 2nd Battalion was to remain in the newly formed Kingdom of the Netherlands, which comprised both modern Holland, Luxembourg and Belgium.

As can be seen from this brief summary of events, the 52nd Foot were involved in almost all the major actions fought by the British Army in Europe between 1808 and 1814 and its reputation as a fighting unit, particularly when commanded by John Colborne, was second to none. Between the actions of Vimiero in 1808 and Toulouse in 1814 the two battalions of the 52nd lost on the Iberian peninsula 11 officers, 8 sergeants and 161 rank and file killed; 76 officers 57 sergeants, 10 buglers and 986 rank and file wounded; and 123 rank and file missing, totalling

---

14. The 1st and 3rd Cacadores were assigned to the Light Division.

1,431 casualties during those six years of war. This of course, does not take into account the many hundreds, who also died of diseases and fevers.[15]

Unfortunately, the war against the United States of America, known as the War of 1812, still raged and the British Government ordered large numbers of troops to proceed to America in an effort to bring the war to an end. The 43rd had been sent directly to America from Bordeaux in April 1814, but the 52nd had initially sailed home and probably assumed with great relief, that they would escape this war.

With all of the excitement in Europe over, the 1st Battalion of the regiment probably expected to settle down to garrison life and those men on fixed terms of seven years, or until the war ended, undoubtedly looked forward to their discharge with a modest pension. The 1st Battalion 52nd however, was one of those destined still to sail for America, delaying the discharge of those soldiers who were time served. On 4 January 1815, the battalion embarked on transports at Portsmouth to be shipped to Cork, where a large force was being assembled as reinforcements.

---

15. Figures extracted from an appendix entitled General Return of the killed, wounded, and missing, of the 52nd Regiment during the war, or from August 1808 to June 1814, subtracting the Waterloo figures, which are included in the appendix despite the title. Reference Historical Record of the Fifty-Second Regiment (Oxfordshire Light Infantry) from the year 1755 to the year 1858, William Moorsom, London 1860 p 454.

Chapter 2

The 'Ogre' Returns

News of Napoleon's escape from the Mediterranean island of Elba on 26 February 1815 and of his subsequent landing at Golfe Juan between Cannes and Antibes three days later, was greeted with shock and incredulity throughout Europe. Indeed, many even thought it was comical and sheer madness, pitting himself and his tiny force of no more than 1,000 men against the might of Royalist France. Many wiser heads saw the dangers and it seems that many soldiers, including those of the 52nd Foot, saw an inevitable renewal of war. Many were even looking forward to it, after enduring nearly a year of the dullness of garrison life. By 20 March, Napoleon had marched into Paris, his army swelled by thousands of soldiers who flocked to his banner. King Louis XVIII was forced to flee to Belgium, whilst Napoleon re-ascended his throne as Emperor of France in a bloodless coup.

The 2nd Battalion of the 52nd was still in Belgium and, ever since November 1814, had been garrisoning Ypres, an ancient walled city, lying almost directly on the French/Belgian border, unfortunately the defensive walls of which had been partly dismantled.

Lieutenant Charles Shaw of the 52nd recorded how the regiment had won over the locals:

> We marched to Ypres, which town we were informed, boasted the best society in Brabant. We had not been long there, before it was determined to give a ball to the inhabitants. It was thought necessary in the regiment to make the lieges of Ypres know what a fine set of fellows we were; so, before going to the ball, it was agreed among ourselves, that our conversation to the ladies should be of the amiable qualities of our brother officers.
>
> We spoke with such effect that a ball was given in return for ours, and the houses of all the inhabitants were thus opened to us amiable young men.[1]

Shaw was also highly amused at a local custom, which occurred at carnival season:

> There is a curious custom at this place, which afforded us much amusement, but of its origin I have not the remotest conception. A cat is taken to the top of the high steeple in the square; about twenty blown bladders are then attached to its body, when it is flung into the street below. The poor creature sails quietly and slowly through the air, mewing piteously all the while. As it approaches the earth, all hands are extended ready to seize it, for the lucky person is free from municipal taxes during the ensuing year. The cat's claws

---
1. Shaw p 38–9.

and feet are left at liberty, and it sometimes happens that the happy man who is to pay no taxes, gets well scratched for his pains.'[2]

The British force in Belgium was however very weak, despite General Henry Clinton's regular correspondence with Horse Guards regarding the small number of active troops in many of the battalions in Belgium, including the 52nd.

Sir Henry Clinton had been sent to Belgium in August 1814 as Inspecting Officer of all the forces in the Kingdom of the Netherlands, reporting to their commander, the youthful Prince of Orange, whose military experience was limited to a couple of years in Spain, attached to the Duke of Wellington's Staff. Clinton had written to Major General Sir Henry Torrens, the Military Secretary at Horse Guards, on 4 October 1814, highlighting the weakness of the British battalions:

> I am just retired to this place after making the inspection of the army under the command of the Hereditary Prince. Much is wanting to place the several corps of which it is composed in order. The defects are very different in different corps. The general complaint of the commanders of the English regiments is the want of men and in some few, that of officers; they do not feel the same interest in what has the appearance of detachments, which they would in the command of a battalion of 5 or 600 men. I do not say that this might be the case, but so it is. It is not easy to give useful lessons of field movements to regimental and still less to company officers, when the companies do not exceed 10 or 12 files. The British force in this country would be in a preferable shape, if it consisted of a less[er] number of stronger battalions. The following regiments, 25th, 33rd, 37th, 52nd, 44th, 78th & 81st, turned out very short of 300 rank & file; and the 30th of 309, had only one captain present. Most of these regiments have at their several depots, as I understand, considerable numbers. The expense of sending them to their 2nd battalions in their present situation would not be great, and in a short time they would become very effective and serviceable corps. Even in the view of preparing drafts for the several first battalions, should that measure become necessary, it would be advantageous, for the men would sooner become good soldiers.[3]

However, being at peace in Europe, little was done to augment the battalions in Belgium and indeed, when General Clinton inspected the battalion again at Ypres on 6 January 1815, he reported the battalion as only consisting of 1 field officer,[4] 3 captains, 10 subaltern officers,[5] 16 sergeants, 12 buglers[6] and only

---

2. ibid, p 39.
3. Glover, The Correspondence of Sir Henry Clinton in the Waterloo Campaign, Volume 1, Gareth Glover, Godmanchester 2015, p 82.
4. A field officer in the British Army was and still is, an officer higher in rank than a company officer (Captain) and below that of a General. The ranks included in this group of officers includes Major, Lieutenant Colonel, Colonel and Brigadier.
5. Subaltern officers comprise the junior officers of a battalion, namely Ensigns and Lieutenants during the Napoleonic Wars.
6. Clinton throughout gives the numbers of drummers in each battalion, but in the 52nd and 95th the bugle was used to convey orders, not the drum.

212 rank & file. He was also not very pleased with its appearance including the tendency of the troops to bring down the visors on their caps which restricted their visibility and also the poor organisation of the ammunition pouches. He was particularly critical of Colonel Edward Gibbs[7] commanding the 52nd Foot, for a lack of improvement since his last inspection and his poor manoeuvring skills.

> This battalion has gained nothing since I saw it in the autumn, the pouches which are good, being for the most part supplied with the wooden boxes[8] and the ammunition kept in the bottom of the pouch, there is some difficulty in getting at it; this would be extremely objectionable in the course of services, it is to be hoped that no prejudice, ignorances [sic] or apathy will prevent a better contrivance for carrying ammunition, being adopted. I was disappointed to see even these caps disfigured as in other ill commanded regiments. Colonel Gibbs is more indebted to the system established before he commanded the regiment than any exertion of his moderate abilities.[9]

Henry Clinton explained his unflattering remarks two days later in a report to the Brigade commander, Major General Kenneth Mackenzie. Put simply, he expected better from such a renowned regiment, but that presently it was no better than any other battalion in Belgium.

> Although from the superior system established in the 52nd Regiment; and the general excellent composition of its officers, it has a great advantage over most corps. I had not the same reason to make this remark as I have had on former occasions. In such a corps no fault, no instance of the slightest inattention should be observable upon the most minute examination, the commanding officer himself appeared to require some little practise in moving the battalion.[10]

Even as late as 21 March, when Napoleon's escape and his reinstallation as Emperor of France was known, General Clinton was still writing to Henry Torrens in London over his concerns regarding having only such weak battalions.

> It must be recollected that several of the battalions composing the army in this country have hardly sufficient numbers to take the field, most of them are below 400, so that after deducting the ordinary non effectives in the field they become mere skeletons. The battalions which from their present order,

---

7. Henry Clinton was very critical of Gibbs, but it must be said in his defence, that he was a very experienced officer, who had fought gallantly throughout a great deal of the Peninsular War, being mentioned in Wellington's despatches after both the sieges of Ciudad Rodrigo and Badajoz. It is most likely that Gibbs had been influenced by the Duke of Wellington's inclination not to worry too much what the men looked like, as long as they were well prepared for the fight. However, his poor manoeuvring skills are a surprise.
8. Some regiments inserted unofficial wooden frames into the men's backpack to ensure that they retained their shape and looked smarter. The wood frame was heavy however and added significantly to the already significant weight carried by the soldiers. Clinton was determined to have them removed.
9. Glover, The Correspondence of Sir Henry Clinton in the Waterloo Campaign, Volume 1, p 115.
10. ibid, p 118.

would in the shortest time bring forward a draft, are the 30th, 33rd, 35th, 44th, 52nd and 69th, the 95th are also in a state to bear reinforcing.

In the number I have named as the amount of the infantry, I have included the sick &c &c but the number of men fit for duty after deducting the two brigades of British and only one of Hanoverians would not exceed 17,000.[11]

Indeed, the official Returns in March 1815, show the battalion with only 229 rank and file effective, with a further 29 sick and 12 on command (acting mostly as officer's servants).[12]

In a further letter of the same date to Lieutenant General Sir Harry Calvert, Adjutant General to the Forces, at Horse Guards, Clinton informed him of the current situation and particularly highlighted the weakness of the 2nd Battalion 52nd Foot.

The measures which have been taken here have been to reinforce the frontier towns whose works are to be repaired and to put the remainder of the army into convenient quarters for its assembly in the neighbourhood of Ath, if there is to be war we are in want of most of the materials for composing an army not excluding the article of soldiers. Some of our 2nd battalions are in tolerable order and in a state soon to become efficient if their ranks were only filled. The best are the 30th, 33rd, 35th, 44th, 52nd and 69th, the 52nd is a mere skeleton. I hope those whom you will send from England will bring with them brown arms and improved pouches, by the way, let me mention to you that General Adam is now very desirous of employment and there is a brigade without a general, it will be very useful to begin at last with appointing experienced and zealous officers to insure a good ton.[13], [14]

The 2nd Battalion of the 52nd would therefore appear to be very short of men and in need of some improvement before any hostile operations commenced.

During March, an undated report looked at the current garrisons in the border fortresses and suggested how numbers could be increased from the troops presently in Belgium. Ypres would see the 73rd (Highland) Regiment of Foot and 100 cavalrymen added.

Towns	Capacity Cav/Inf	Total	Present Garrison	Total	Proposed Increase	Total
Ypres	822/1000	1822	52nd Regt (270) 69th Regt (526) 2nd Hussars [KGL] (602)	796	73rd Regt (558) Royal Cavalry (100)	1454

---

11. Glover, The Correspondence of Sir Henry Clinton in the Waterloo Campaign, Volume 1, Gareth Glover, Godmanchester 2015, p 165.
12. Readers are referred to Andrew Bamford's fantastic series of tables summarising the Returns by battalion, now published on the Napoleon-Series website.
13. A word used in Regency Britain to indicate a showing or style.
14. Glover, The Correspondence of Sir Henry Clinton in the Waterloo Campaign, Volume 1, Gareth Glover, Godmanchester 2015, p 166.

What of the 1st Battalion, which we last saw arriving at the Cove of Cork[15] on 20 January 1815, as part of a large reinforcement under the command of General Sir Rowland Hill, for the army still fighting the United States of America?

Twice the huge fleet ventured into the North Atlantic, only to be struck by heavy storms, forcing the fleet to disperse and run back to the protection of Cove or other ports along the south coast of England. Such interference with the passage, divine or not, had a profound impact on the future of the first battalion, as on its return a second time to Cork, it received the news that peace had been signed between Britain and the United States and that its orders for America had consequently been rescinded. It was then ordered to proceed to Plymouth, where the transports arrived on 22 March. Here the men learnt of Napoleon's return and they were ordered to proceed to Belgium promptly. The battalion sailed from Plymouth on 27 March and disembarked at Ostend on 31 March.[16]

Having landed, there was some confusion over the battalion's route, General Henry Clinton wrote in his diary on 28 March, whilst visiting Brussels:

> From the total want of some such management, the 52nd Regiment upon its arrival at Ostend (though its presence was much wanted at Courtrai & General Vandeleur received notice of its march upon that place) was ordered at Ostend, to march to Nieuport. There have been for the last fortnight almost incessant hard gales of wind with heavy rains so that it must have been with great danger that vessels of the size of ordinary transports could put into Ostend.[17]

The Weekly State of the Infantry Forces in Flanders under the Command of General His Royal Highness the Prince of Orange, Headquarters, Brussels 1st April 1815[18] gave the following numbers in each battalion:

---

15. Now more correctly spelt Cobh.
16. This is in accordance with the regimental record, although John Colborne wrote to General Henry Clinton on 24 March that 'The reinforcements are arriving, the 52nd and 95th are at Ostend.' The Correspondence of Sir Henry Clinton in the Waterloo Campaign, Volume 1 p 173. It is likely that their arrival was delayed by storms.
17. ibid, p 181.
18. ibid, p 192.

	Officers				Sergeants					Trumpeters					Rank & File							
	Field Officers	Captains	Subalterns	Staff	Present Sick	Absent Sick	Command	PoW	Total	Present	Present Sick	Command	PoW	Total	Present	Present Sick	Absent Sick	Command	PoW	Total		
2nd Battalion 52nd Foot	1	4	12	4	22	2			24	13				13	232	34	2	2		270	Lt. Colonel Gibbs[19]	At Leuze
1st Battalion 52nd Foot	1	6	28	6	55				55	23				23	824					824	Major Rowan In Command	On march to Brussels

19. Lt. Colonel Edward Gibbs.

In fact, the report should have shown that the 2nd Battalion was on the march to Leuze that day, as General Clinton records in his diary on 1 April that:

> This day, the [2nd Battalion] 52nd & 95th Regiments composing General Adam's Brigade marched from Tournai to Leuze, he had formed them in the streets in Tournai where having arrived very unexpectedly from Courtrai they had not got under cover, fortunately the weather is fine & warm.[20]

The 1st Battalion marched towards Brussels by easy stages, but via a circuitous route, which unnecessarily tired the troops. General Clinton wrote to Major General Sir Hudson Lowe, Quarter Master General of the Army in the Netherlands, to complain that:

> It is very disadvantageous to troops to be marched into the country transport by transport, without letting them collect. It would be much better that the officer commanding a brigade or his representative should see these in order before they leave the place where they are now ordered to assemble. The 1st Battalion of the 52nd as they have been directed not to proceed by the direct road are marching about the country, the change of route we must of course already be liable to, but the battalions should not be affected themselves.[21]

In a further letter to Sir Hudson Lowe of the same date, Clinton showed his frustration with the slow arrival of the 1st Battalion in the vicinity of his headquarters at Ath:

> When are we to expect the remainder of the first battalion of the 52nd Regiment, they may easily march from Ghent to this place even by Oudenarde and Grammont in 3 marches, what other troops have arrived from England?[22]

His last question betrays Clinton's urgent desire for reinforcements to strengthen his very weak army. Nevertheless, the first battalion finally arrived in Brussels on 4 April. On the very same day, General Frederick Adam, commanding the Light Brigade, wrote to Henry Clinton regarding the 2nd Battalion and highlighting the severe scarcity of some necessary equipment for the coming campaign, but he was able to confirm that the companies were finally quartered together, although the battalion was inevitably spread across a number of small villages:

> The 52nd are not complete either in pack saddles or horses. Each of these battalions have a wagon for their sick. The brigade is complete in wagons for the carriage of ammunition, but the covers are not yet furnished by the commissary nor are all the tarpaulins completed. The 52nd have not yet received their camp kettles & nor have they got entrenching tools. The 52nd are now so quartered that the companies are together.

---

20. Glover, The Correspondence of Sir Henry Clinton in the Waterloo Campaign, Volume 1, p 188.
21. ibid, p 218.
22. ibid, p 229.

2 companies at Ligne
4 between Moulbaix and Bliquy
4 In hovels [at] St Amand & Villers near [the] chaussee
The whole regiment is very well put up.[23]

Three days later the 1st Battalion marched on towards Grammont,[24] where it was joined by the 2nd Battalion for the express purpose of carrying out the order to transfer all of the able men from the 2nd into the 1st Battalion.

The poor health of the battalions at this time is indicated in the Regimental Returns, which show that Privates John Longstaff and William Baglin had died of natural causes at Grammont on 13th and 24th of March respectively, whilst Private Robert Gray died of natural causes at Villers St Amand on 31 March.[25]

The order written at Horse Guards on 27 March 1815 to the Prince of Orange and signed by Major General Sir Henry Torrens, the Adjutant General stated that:

> I have it in command from the Commander-in-Chief to acquaint your Royal Highness, that the 1st Battalion, 52nd Regiment, having proceeded to join the army in Flanders, it is His Royal Highness's wish that, when perfectly convenient to the public service, the effectives of the second battalion should be transferred to the 1st, and that the officers and non-commissioned officers of the former should be ordered home.[26]

In consequence of this order, all of the serviceable men of the 2nd Battalion, totalling 9 sergeants and 224 rank and file were transferred to the 1st Battalion. A number of officers also transferred, including Lieutenant Charles Shaw from the 2nd to the 1st Battalion.

However, the 1st Battalion actually ended up, on paper at least, weaker than before the transfer had occurred. It is unclear whether it had been intended, as the official order does not mention it, but the prince had also ordered that all unserviceable men in the 1st Battalion should transfer to the 2nd Battalion. At first, such an order appears to be sensible, but the numbers transferred out of the 1st Battalion as unfit for active service was actually greater than those transferred in, actually reducing the numbers in the battalion, which was clearly not the intention of the order. In fact, an incredible 26 sergeants, 8 buglers and 284 other ranks transferred to the 2nd Battalion as unfit. Such a large number of men, who only three months previously had been deemed fit to sail on active service to America, seems very high indeed. There is clear evidence from contemporary correspondence that many soldiers were war weary and did not relish the thought of yet another campaign, this time against Napoleon himself. Having survived so long, perhaps understandably, there was a little more reluctance to participate in yet another bloody campaign. Such numbers transferring out of the battalion on active service, particularly the

---
23. ibid, p 225.
24. Also known as Geraardsbergen.
25. Reference WO25/1850 Casualty Returns 1st Battalion 52nd Foot 1809–16.
26. Moorsom, Historical Record of the Fifty-Second Regiment, p 242.

exceedingly high number of sergeants, would give some credence to the possibility that a significant number of them had seen enough and felt that it was time for others to take their chances. Certainly, the number of sick in the battalion cannot warrant such numbers suddenly becoming unfit for service.

When the transfers were complete, the 2nd Battalion immediately marched for Ostend via Courtrai [Kortrijk] to board the transports conveying them back to Britain. They landed at Dover on 20 April and proceeded to Canterbury.

In the April Return, the 1st Battalion mustered 1,029 men present, 973 being fit for duty, 44 returned sick and 12 on command, tending the officers as personal servants.

Chapter 3

Preparing for War

The first battalion of the 52nd had now replaced the second battalion in the Light Brigade commanded by Major General Adam and it had taken over its cantonments in the vicinity of Villers St Amand. On 14 April, General Henry Clinton formally reviewed the battalion and he was far from impressed. He recorded the battalion strength on parade as 1 field officer, 9 captains, 30 subalterns, 50 sergeants, 21 drummers (he wrote drummers in all of his inspection reports, here he presumably meant buglers) and 904 rank and file.

> Lt Colonel [Blank][1] the only field officer present does not seem quite equal to the command of this strong battalion, the men are generally a fine and serviceable body, ...[2] Though there are 9 captains there was hardly an officer who would account for any deficiency, but they are so used to be applauded that anything like inquiry excites only surprise or even displeasure. The arms however, are not in the order in which they certainly ought to be, the ammunition is in most part loose in the boxes with which the pouches that lately now are furnished. This regiment has not been provided with camp kettles or bill hooks. The caps are put out of shape as I have observed in many of the English regiments, they are however complete in shoes & linen and the excellent manner of packing & putting on the knapsacks is well attended to. The commanding officer excused the awkward manner in which this regiment moved by saying they had been for 5 months on board ship. There are no less than 22 extra drummers & musicians, a fault which I recommended to General Adam to have corrected.[3]

This report was harsh, given that so many men had been so recently transferred between the two battalions and that officers and men had had little time to get to know one another. It was also true that the men of the first battalion had been at sea on and off for months or on the march and were therefore certainly in dire need of practice at field exercises. Clinton however, was not a man to pull his punches, and his damning indictment that 'altogether this regiment lately the pattern of the English army has now more the appearance of the remains of a good system than the present possession of it', must really have stung. The lack of camp kettles and bill hooks was a major concern as without them they would

---

1. The April Return shows that the 52nd was then commanded by Major Charles Rowan who was a lieutenant colonel in the army.
2. The missing phrase is given below in the next paragraph.
3. Glover, The Correspondence of Sir Henry Clinton in the Waterloo Campaign, Volume 1, p 256.

be unable to operate on campaign and the extra musicians, presumably forming a regimental band – a piece of foppery many well-to-do regiments were in the habit of forming – was clearly to end immediately. It certainly was a short, sharp, shock and made the battalion prick up and immediately set to, to put everything to rights, which was undoubtedly Clinton's intention.

A letter written two days later by John Colborne – who was still working for the Prince of Orange – to General Clinton, was clearly meant to defend his old regiment against this critical report and to excuse the poor showing of Lieutenant Colonel Rowan and indeed the drill of the men. Recognising the accuracy of the report, however, Colborne also requested that the battalion could be cantoned together in a large town, to allow them to rectify its faults at drill by facilitating constant practice in the weeks available before the planned invasion of France by the allies in the middle of May.

> My dear Sir,
> I find the quarters of the 52nd Regiment are so scattered that it will be inappropriate to take advantage of the next three weeks leisure before the advance of the army, to get the battalion into that order which is so necessary at the commencement of a campaign. I must mention to you that since the battalion disembarked at Plymouth from the south of France it has had no time for drill nor can it have yet recovered from the effects of the peninsular service & at Chatham the duty was so severe, little could be done during the winter months and certainly after being three months on board transports and the manner in which they were marched off from Ostend, some time should be given to the commanding officer to make it the best and the most effective battalion in this army. I shall be much obliged to you if you can give the 52nd some village or town, where the companies are more together, and that the commanding officer can work hard whilst we remain in cantonments.[4]

General Henry Clinton replied positively, stating that although, the most that could be achieved was cantonments suitable to keep each company together, that this would prove sufficient if the current officers showed the same spirit and determination as the officers of the 52nd had evinced in the peninsula. He also looked forward to Colborne seeing the situation for himself.

> My dear Colborne,
> I have received this morning your letters of the 16th and 17th with respect to the quarters of the 52nd Regiment, it has been a great inconvenience to put them into such scattered quarters and I have most readily adopted every suggestion of General Adam for getting them more together. I hope at this time they are so disposed of, that the companies in themselves are sufficiently collected to be under the eyes of their commanders, and with a battalion of your strength, unless a town be given to it that is the most that can be expected. Indeed from what I have seen of the 52nd Regiment provided the company commanders are what they were a few years back; really competent

---

4. Glover, The Correspondence of Sir Henry Clinton in the Waterloo Campaign, Volume 1, p 262.

to the instruction of their men and zealous in the performance of their duty, what the regiment most wants at this time it may as well remain disposed of as it is at present. If it collected together in a town however when you come and shall have made yourself thoroughly acquainted with the state, if you should think anything further can be done for the advantage of such a battalion I shall be glad to afford you every facility in my power.[5]

The Duke of Wellington had been ordered to take command of the Allied army in Belgium and he arrived in Brussels from Vienna on 5 April, where he had been attending the congress. By 11 April he had issued a General Order completely reforming the army, and assigning the 2nd Division, commanded by General Henry Clinton, to General Hill's 2nd Corps.[6]

Lieutenant General Sir Henry Clinton's Second Division

3rd (British) Brigade of Major General Frederick Adam
1st Battalion 52nd Foot   Brevet Colonel Sir John Colborne
1st Battalion 71st Foot   Brevet Colonel Thomas Reynell
2nd Battalion 95th Foot   Brevet Lieutenant Colonel Amos Norcott
3rd Battalion 95th Foot (2 companies) Brevet Lt Colonel John Ross

1st (KGL) Brigade of Brevet Colonel George Du Plat
1st Line Battalion   Major Friedrich Wilhelm von Robertson
2nd Line Battalion   Major Georg Muller
3rd Line Battalion   Lieutenant Colonel Friedrich von Wissell
4th Line Battalion   Major Friedrich Reh

3rd (Hanoverian) Brigade of Brevet Colonel Hugh Halkett
Brevervorde Landwehr Batt   Lt Colonel Friedrich von Schulenberg
Osnabruck Battalion   Major Count Louis von Munster
Quakenbruck Battalion   Major Clamor von Bussche-Hunefeld
Salzgitter Landwehr Batt   Major Friedrich von Hammerstein

Artillery of Lieutenant Colonel Charles Gold
Captain Samuel Bolton's Foot Battery
Brevet Major Augustus Sympher's Horse Troop KGL

Attached during the Battle of Waterloo

4th (British) Brigade of Colonel Mitchell
3rd Battalion 14th Foot   Lieutenant Colonel Francis Tidy
23rd Foot   Colonel Sir Henry Ellis
51st Foot   Lieutenant Colonel Hugh Mitchell

---

5. ibid, p 265.
6. Wellington, Supplementary Despatches, Correspondence and Memoranda of Field Marshal Arthur Duke of Wellington KG, Vol. 10 p 63.

Lieutenant Shaw records a certain lack of discipline in the 1st Battalion of the 52nd at this time, because the men had received some back pay and he states that drunkenness was rife, he also compares Sir John Colborne's humanity against Colonel Rowan's rigidity and interestingly, he comes out very much in favour of the latter:

> The men of the 1st Battalion received about this time, a good deal of money that was due to them, and there was, in consequence, a great deal of drunkenness. Every morning, we had numerous [regimental] court martials and floggings, but without much effect, for after the men had received a few lashes, and promised good behaviour, Sir John [Colborne] took them down… during Sir John's absence we were commanded by that most excellent officer Colonel Rowan…[who] is likewise an enemy of flogging; but having, for the first two days, inflicted every lash to which the prisoners were sentenced, he put an end both to crime and punishment. I always made a point of following Rowan's system, as I saw there was mercy in the end in making this degrading punishment most serious and painful.[7]

Now, Colborne was not officially attached to the 52nd until May 1815, although he retained his colonelcy and it is certain that he was not with the regiment until then, but the overall impression given by Shaw remains valid and is backed up by further reports of the regiment in 1816, see Appendix No.6 for further details.

There are hints however, that even the officers of the 52nd Foot were sometimes guilty of thinking themselves beyond the rules. On 17 May Colonel Du Plat presided over a court martial held at Ath on the conduct of Lieutenant George Scott of the 52nd Foot. He was charged with:

> Neglect of duty when in command of a detachment on its route from Ostend to Audenarde by leaving or absenting himself from the said detachment when at or near Ghent, on or about the morning of the 25th April last, thereby impeding the public service and causing great irregularity in the march of the said detachment which by devolving to the charge of Corporal Hinton[8] of the 52nd Regiment was moved to Brussels instead of the proper place of its destination. [9]

Lieutenant Scott was found guilty and formally reprimanded by the Duke of Wellington. The Duke emphasised that he wished:

> to impress upon the minds of the officers of the army that the most minute parts of their duty are not trifles and that the omission to perform any of them must be attended by the most serious public inconvenience and even misfortunes.[10]

---

7. Shaw, p 41.
8. Corporal Thomas Hinton of Lieutenant Colonel R Campbell's Company was not at Waterloo and was reduced to Private on 9 July 1815. Why he missed the battle and was reduced is unclear.
9. Quoted from The Duke of Wellington's General Order dated 24 May 1815.
10. ibid.

On 19 April General Clinton suddenly received notice at 04.00 hours that the Duke of Wellington would review Colonel Du Plat's Brigade of the King's German Legion and General Adam's Light Brigade near Ath at 17.00 hours that day. The review took some two hours, after which the troops marched back to their cantonments and the Duke of Wellington, Lord Hill and all their Staff, dined with Sir Henry afterwards. It must be presumed that the review went off successfully as no reports of it have emerged.

Three days later Frederick Adam wrote to Clinton regarding Lord Hill's desire to have the 1/52nd brought together in one cantonment, Hill having suggested Lessines. General Adam was keen to ensure it happened but was more relaxed regarding bringing the brigade together for exercises:

> I received your note & instruction yesterday which shall be attended to forthwith. Lord Hill proposed Lessines for the 52nd as a quarter in order to bring them together & said he would arrange [this] with you. It is an object to get them if possible into one place for some time & perhaps you might arrange it while in Brussels. The separation of the brigade is of little consequence as there is no military object requiring them united. I remain dear Sir, yours very faithfully, Frederick Adam.[11]

The following day, 23 April, Henry Clinton wrote to Lord Hill with the news that the 71st (Highland) Regiment (Light Infantry) was due to arrive to join his division and on arrival he would put them in Lessines for a few days to organise themselves. As the Prince of Orange no longer commanded the entire army, his additional staff was disbanded, and its officers could return to their regiments. This meant that John Colborne would soon be back in command of the battalion. Clinton suggested that the 52nd should then move to Lessines so that the battalion could benefit from a period of intense drill under its old commander:

> My dear Lord,
> If the whole of the 71st Regiment should be arrived at Ghent, it was to march this day & to arrive on the 25th in the neighbourhood of Ath, I should wish if you have no objection, to let the 71st go to Lessines & to be together therefore a few days, where I will inspect them & make my report to you. Colonel Colborne will be able to take the command of the 52nd about the end of this week & then I think the 52nd would benefit from being sent to Lessines, the 71st will in that case occupy the present quarters of the 52nd.[12]

On the 25th, Henry Clinton wrote to Major General Sir Edward Barnes, the Adjutant General of the Army, to inform him that he had granted General Adam permission to carry out a live firing to test the new muskets which a number of men of the 52nd had recently been issued with:

---

11. Glover, The Correspondence of Sir Henry Clinton in the Waterloo Campaign, Volume 1, p 270.
12. ibid, p 271.

Major General Adam having represented that the arms of the 52nd are for the most part new and expressed a desire to fire a few rounds in order to ascertain that they will fire, I have approved of his doing so. H Clinton.[13]

The 71st Foot arrived at Frasnes on 26 April and the following day, Henry Clinton ordered a change of cantonments, with the 52nd moving to Lessines as planned. He recorded in his diary entry for Thursday 27 April: 'The 71st marched to Leuze, the 52nd to Lessines and 2nd Battalion 95th to Frasnes.'[14] In a further diary entry on 4 May, Clinton recorded that the 52nd had carried out some combined drills with a battalion of the King's German Legion:

> The 52nd Regiment from Lessines met the other battalion of the German Legion[15] & manoeuvred in the meadow of Poperinge. The troops had no sooner quitted the ground than the meadow was immediately inundated by the opening of the sluices.[16]

William Leeke, a relative of Sir John Colborne, had initially been thwarted in his desire to join the 52nd Foot by the rather inconvenient end of the Peninsular War and then of the war in America. Whilst considering an opportunity to join a cavalry regiment which was due to sail to India, he was saved by the announcement of Napoleon's return to power and encouraged to join the 52nd in Belgium by Sir John, who suggested travelling out to Belgium as a Volunteer[17] but, having previously deposited the money with the Army Agents for an ensigncy in the 52nd, which could then occur at the earliest opportunity. Leeke reached the regiment at Lessines on 11 May and was entered into a company as a Volunteer, although news arrived soon after to confirm that he had been gazetted as an Ensign dated 4 May 1815. As the most junior officer in the battalion, Leeke was put to, to immediately learn his drill, although he had to admit that he did not complete it until after the campaign was over: 'During the five weeks between my joining at Lessines and our start for Waterloo, I went through some portion of my drill.'[18]

According to Leeke, Sir John Colborne arrived to take command of the battalion around 14 May. Colborne continued to prepare the battalion for active service and Sir Henry Clinton, in a letter dated 17 May, to Sir Edward Barnes, backed Colborne's decision to return the large camp kettles supplied for each

---

13. ibid, p 274.
14. ibid, p 274.
15. It is unclear which battalion of the King's German Legion this refers to.
16. Glover, The Correspondence of Sir Henry Clinton in the Waterloo Campaign, Volume 2, p 25.
17. Volunteers were young gentlemen, who usually could not afford to purchase a commission and therefore joined the regiment, hoping for an opportunity to impress the commanding officer with their valour and on the death of an officer, that they might be given an ensigncy without purchase. Volunteers carried a musket and fought in the ranks, but were allowed to mess with the officers, although many officers refused to mess with a Volunteer. It is not clear that Leeke received very much formal training before he fought at Waterloo.
18. Leeke's Lord Seaton's Regiment at Waterloo, Volume 1, London 1866 p 7.

six men. Their use had been discontinued in the army serving in Spain in 1813, but they had been re-issued to the troops in Holland in 1814. They would, in its stead, utilise the individual small kettle which every soldier of the battalion was issued with. This significantly reduced the weight carried by the soldiers on the march and Clinton recommended that the rest of the army did the same. He did, however, also report that a court martial was to be held on a private of the 52nd:

> Sir,
> I enclose two letters which I have just received from Colonel Sir John Colborne, that marked No.1 applying for permission to return into store the camp kettles for the use of 5 or 6 men conceiving of the small kettles in the possession of every non-commissioned officer and soldier as sufficient, has been approved by Major General Adam and I wish to recommend his application to the consideration of the commander of the army.
> The letter of this date contains a report that a soldier of the 52nd Regiment is to be tried by the general court martial assembled at this place and encloses the charge. HC.[19]

Barnes replied, three days later, that the Duke approved of this plan regarding the large camp kettles, also confirming that the General Court Martial on the soldier of the 52nd would be arranged. The Court Martial was almost certainly for Private James Hickman, who had deserted on 7 January 1815, when the battalion had just arrived in Ireland whilst awaiting its convoy to North America. Regimental records show that he rejoined the battalion in Belgium on 12 May 1815. Unfortunately, the results of the Court Martial are not recorded, but he did fight at Waterloo and was wounded.

On 18 May, Henry Clinton wrote to General Adam that he wished to have the entire division, except for the 52nd, practise its manoeuvres:

> I propose if we can manage it, leading the division out together with the exception of the 52nd. The 71st & indeed the 2nd Battalion of the 95th require a great deal of good practice, both made the same fault in closing their intervals, the change of front of the 95th was not at all what I should have expected from that battalion & the diminution of front was as faulty as so simple an operation can be.[20]

It is not clear from the letter but it could be presumed that the 52nd had improved so rapidly in its drill under the direction of Sir John Colborne, that it was deemed unnecessary to make the battalion practise with the other battalions of the brigade; this, as will be seen, was not the case, however.

Lieutenant Charles Holman of the 52nd Foot, who was returning from his home in Exeter following an extended period of leave, landed at Ostend on 13 May. Whilst proceeding to join the battalion at Lessines, he met Lieutenant

---
19. Glover, The Correspondence of Sir Henry Clinton in the Waterloo Campaign, Volume 2, p 44.
20. ibid, p 46.

George Campbell of the regiment at Bruges, who had been ordered to Ostend to receive new trousers for the regiment. Finally arriving at Lessines on 20 May, Holman found that he knew virtually none of the junior officers of the battalion: 'Arrived at 1pm and felt rather annoyed at meeting several of the officers and not knowing one present.'[21] The following day, he confirmed his awkwardness at meeting so many strangers in his regiment:

> At 5 dined at and became a member of their mess. Although I possess a tolerable share of self-opinion, yet I felt rather awkward at first, amidst upwards of fifty young men whom I had never before seen, however this soon blew off.[22]

Charles Holman being a stranger in the regiment, despite being gazetted into the 52nd Foot as an ensign in September 1812, should not be a surprise. He was attached to the Portuguese Army from November 1811 right through to the Battle of Toulouse in April 1814 and would therefore have only occasionally encountered the 52nd on campaign. He was, however, an experienced officer having served with Portuguese troops at the battles of Salamanca, the Pyrenees, Nivelle, the Nive, Orthes and Toulouse.

Recording the daily routine in his diary, Charles Holman noted in a block that spanned from 22 May right up until 9 June, that they had interminable drills every day and regular reviews.

> Parades and drills every morning at 6 and evening at 6, marched several times to Elignee St Ann [Ellignies-Saint-Anne] 5 leagues, to be reviewed by Sir H[enry] Clinton, where we always joined the rest of our brigade, comprised of the 71st L[ight] Inf[antry]. 2nd and 3rd Battalions 95th Rifle Corps under Major General Adam and the rest of the division consisting of a brigade of the German Legion and two brigades of Hanoverian Landwehr.[23] After our reviews, we generally returned the next day thro[ugh] Ath to our old quarters at Lessines. [24]

One firing practice by companies near the River Dender nearly ended in tragedy however. Ensign Leeke records that:

> At Lessines, on one occasion when the regiment was at ball practice not far from the bank of the Dender, and were firing volleys by companies at targets set close to a very thick wood, we were all astonished and horrified, and our firing put a stop to, by the appearance, round the side of the wood, of a man and woman with uplifted arms and horror stricken countenances, No one had the least idea that there was any habitation in the wood; but it turned

---

21. Holman Lt, Journal for 1815, Royal Green Jackets Museum, Winchester.
22. ibid.
23. Colonel Du Plat's 1st KGL Brigade and Colonel Halkett's 3rd Hanoverian Brigade constituted the rest of the division, no evidence has been found that there was another Hanoverian brigade attached.
24. Holman Lt, Journal for 1815, Royal Green Jackets Museum, Winchester.

out that these poor people occupied a cottage somewhere within it. No wonder that they were alarmed, for, before they could get round the skirts of the wood, several volleys had been fired into it by the ten companies, each consisting of about one hundred men.[25]

On 26 May Henry Clinton recorded in his diary that he had manoeuvred Adam's and Du Plat's Brigades on the pastures at Quevaucamps, but that he was not happy with any of their manoeuvres, including the 52nd. He also had them set up their blankets as tents, using their muskets as the poles, it being determined by the Duke of Wellington, that the army was not to be encumbered with tents, which would require extra carts and horses to transport them.

> I attempted to execute some manoeuvres with the 2nd Division, the simple move of entering an alignment by wheeling up to it, though previously practised in battalions, was very ill executed & the march in line, by General Adam's Brigade & that of the German Legion as bad. After exercise the troops encamped under their blankets and in the afternoon marched back to their quarters.[26]

Ensign Leeke and his fellow officers were far from enamoured with the drills at Qevaucamps:

> Towards the latter end of May, Sir Henry Clinton's Division, of which Adam's Light Brigade, in which the 52nd was, formed a part, proceeded to occupy the country beyond Ath towards the French fortress of Conde and they assembled for division drill in a large domain, surrounded by extensive plantations, in the neighbourhood of Qaevres-au-camps [Quevaucamps]. Here they practised the formation of an encampment by means of blanket tents, which appeared to be a most troublesome affair, and did not meet with much favour on the part of officers or men. We remained there only a few days, and then returned to our former cantonments.[27]

On 3 June General Clinton was, however, still recording his dissatisfaction with the manoeuvring of the 52nd, presuming that its poor showing was due to its regular use as skirmishers rather than as line troops:

> The 2nd Division executed some manoeuvres on the pasturage de Quevaucamps, the 52nd has many of the vices of a battalion which has been accustomed to move about, the 71st is only good. Neither of these regiments nor the 95th understand the first principles of accuracy in line with any number beyond their own battalion.[28]

Indeed, Clinton was so unhappy with the divisional manoeuvres, that the following day he sent out a long letter to each of his brigade commanders, reiterating large

---

25. Leeke, p 8.
26. Glover, The Correspondence of Sir Henry Clinton in the Waterloo Campaign, Volume 2, p 54.
27. Leeke, pp 9–10.
28. Glover, The Correspondence of Sir Henry Clinton in the Waterloo Campaign, Volume 2, p 62.

parts of the drill book as regards manoeuvres as a brigade. To such senior and experienced officers, this undoubtedly did not go down well but, clearly, he felt that it was necessary.

The troops did get some rest periods amongst all of the training and the officers regularly attended a race meeting at Grammont each week. Charles Holman recorded: 'At Grammont, about 5 miles from us, there was horse races about once a week which we used to see'.[29] Ensign Leeke also recorded that they often enjoyed riding their horses about the country:

Each day, between thirty and forty horses were usually paraded, and we used to have some excellent steeple-chasing or rather brook-leaping in the meadows adjoining the town. I recollect particularly Whichcote,[30] now

---

29. Holman Lt, Journal for 1815, Royal Green Jackets Museum, Winchester.
30. Lieutenant George Whichcote, 52nd Foot.

General Whichcote, as the most determined rider on those occasions; it was really a very pleasant and happy time.[31]

On the 7 of June, there was also the famous Review of the entire British cavalry and horse artillery at Schendlebeke by the Duke of Wellington, Prince of Orange, Field Marshal Blücher, the Duc de Berri[32] and many others. Many army officers, including a number from the 52nd rode over to watch the grand spectacle. Charles Holman went, and he recorded that:

> On the 7th June about 1 mile from Grammont there was the finest review of English cavalry and flying artillery ever seen. There were upwards of 7,000 cavalry and six brigades of artillery. There was Prince Blucher, the Duque de Berri, Marshals Marmont and Victor, Sir Sidney Smith[33] and many other general officers of different nations present, with near three hundred British infantry officers mounted, all following the Duque [sic] of Wellington thro[ugh] the lines, it was the finest sight I ever witnessed. The troops defiled to their cantonments as did all the Big Wigs, to a grand dinner given by the Earl of Uxbridge. Returned at 6 to Lessines much gratified with the review.[34]

William Leeke was not so enamoured with the occasion, remembering mostly that he had been thoroughly drenched and most uncomfortable.

> This took place near Grammont, about eight or nine miles from Lessines. There were about 7,000 men present. There were no particular incidents; but we were exposed to a most drenching rain for some time. The Prince of Orange and his brother,[35] who were on a break[36] with some young Englishmen, were placed by them, well wrapped up in greatcoats and tolerably well exposed to the storm, on the box of the break, the seat of honour, whilst their young friends got a much better berth themselves under the body of the vehicle.[37]

Unfortunately, the weather over the ensuing days turned particularly bad, the roads becoming a sea of mud. In order to preserve the shoes of the battalion, the 52nd were excused from numerous other days of manoeuvres because of the distance they had to march. Clinton confirmed to General Adam on 11 June that:

> The state of the roads certainly is against any unnecessary marching & if the 52nd cannot arrive at the general position for it near the exercising ground, but at the expense in shoes you apprehend, I think its march had better be postponed, the rest ... go on.[38]

---

31. Leeke, p 8.
32. Charles Ferdinand de Bourbon, Duc de Berri was the nephew of King Louis XVIII.
33. Admiral Sir Sidney Smith was residing at Brussels when the campaign began.
34. Holman Lt, Journal for 1815, Royal Green Jackets Museum, Winchester.
35. His brother was Prince Frederick of Orange.
36. A break was an open horse drawn carriage with four wheels and usually without doors, designed for pleasure excursions, carrying 6 or 8 people comfortably.
37. Leeke, p 9.
38. Glover, The Correspondence of Sir Henry Clinton in the Waterloo Campaign, Volume 2, p 73.

Extract from the State of the 2nd Division of Infantry under the Command of Lieutenant General Sir Henry Clinton GCB Headquarters Beloeil, 11 June 1815.

Regiment	Officers						Sergeants					Drummers					Rank & File					
	Colonels	Lt Colonels	Majors	Captains	Subalterns	Staff	Present	Present Sick	Absent Sick	Command	Total	Present	Present sick	Absent sick	Command	Total	Present	Present sick	Absent Sick	Command	Prisoners of War	Total
52nd Regiment	0	1	1	10	41	6	64	1	1	3	69	22	0	0	0	22	998	20	13	7	0	1038[39]

Regiment	Horses			Alterations							Horses			
	Present	Sick	Command	Total	Men joined	Men dead	Men Deserted	Men Discharged	Men Given	Men Discharged	Men Promoted	Men Reduced	Joined	Dead	Sold	Cast	Transferred
52nd Regiment	82	0	0	82	0	0	0	1	0	0	2	0	1	0	0	0	0

39. The Official Return dated 25 May 1815 gives a total effective in the battalion as 986, with a further 35 sick, 11 on command and 2 having deserted, giving a total of 1034 – which is only 4 out with this return, therefore we can be pretty certain that the number of men on the battlefield of Waterloo was around 990 and certainly under 1,000.

Certainly, comments about the heavy rain also predominate the diary entries of Charles Holman, but despite the weather, the regiment did move to Ellignies-Saint-Anne to avoid such long marches from Lessines:

> 11th June – Hard rain, which prevented our parades, constant reports of our moving, however nothing certain known and at night gave up all idea of moving.
>
> 12th June – At 7am parade as usual, at 12 noon, received an order to pack up and at 2 marched thro[ugh] Ath to Elignee St Ann [Ellignies-Saint-Anne] 5 leagues, arrived before dark and each company took its old quarters for the night, as did I also with the 8th Company.
>
> 13th June – There was no parade of the regiment this morning, in consequence of the hard rain, the 71st were out and got a nice wetting, employed in making a more equal distribution of the quarters, as it was determined not to return to Lessines, to be obliged to march out to this place every week, fatiguing the men and wearing out their shoes merely to show us.[40]

Despite the poor weather, the 52nd marched to Qevaucamps and manoeuvred with the whole division on 14 June and were thoroughly soaked through for its efforts. It is clear that Charles Holman did not enjoy the experience. More worrying, were the increasing number of rumours of Napoleon having arrived with the army and the increased threat of a French attack.

> 14th June – Paraded at 6 am and marched to the plain called Quivochamp [Quevaucamps] on the road and about 6 miles from Conde [-sur-l'Escaut]. Here we found our division assembled and a regiment of Lunenburg Hussars under Major Korkenbourg,[41] continued manoeuvring until 11 o'clock, when it rained so hard that we returned to quarters wet with rain and annoyed at being marched so far merely for the amusement of Lady C and daughter.[42] Report of Bonaparte's arrival at Maubeuge with two Corps d'Armee, great movement observed among the enemy's troops on this part of their frontiers. Ordered to be on the Qui vive [on the alert] and to turn out at the sound of the first bugle and baggage to the rear.[43]

On 15 June, General Henry Clinton wrote to General Adam regarding his report that the three days' rations that had been issued to the 52nd Foot, had to be condemned as wet through. He was not very sympathetic, stating that:

> I do not think it shows much attention to the interest of the publick [sic], to condemn as spoiled, the whole of 3 days food, because the regiment having that quantity in possession had been exposed to a few showers of rain, none

---
40. Holman Lt, Journal for 1815, Royal Green Jackets Museum, Winchester.
41. Major George Krauchenberg previously of 3rd Hussars KGL.
42. This undoubtedly refers to Lady Caroline Capel (sister of Lord Uxbridge) and one of her daughters.
43. Holman Lt, Journal for 1815, Royal Green Jackets Museum, Winchester.

of them heavy. I believe if this was at the cost of individuals, with no better means [of] restoring it, than those which may be resorted to by almost every soldier of the 52nd though within present quarters, a very small portion would have been found unfit for food.[44]

That same day, General Clinton was also considering moving the troops and General Adam confirmed the new cantonments he had arranged. The 52nd were to remain in its present cantonments:

52nd Regiment	Ellignies-Sainte-Anne
71st	Blicquy, Chapelle-a-Oie, Bury - 1 Company
2nd Battalion 95th	Tourpes – 4 Companies Aubechies – 2 Companies
3rd Battalion 95th	Tourpes[45]

However, events were to rapidly overtake this planned change of cantonments. As early as 13 June, Henry Clinton had written home to his brother, General William Clinton, stating what he knew of the latest intelligence, which included the fact that:

Bonaparte is at Solre le Chateau, it is said he will attack on the 15th.[46]

---

44. Glover, The Correspondence of Sir Henry Clinton in the Waterloo Campaign, Volume 2, p 85.
45. ibid, p 61.
46. ibid, p 83.

Chapter 4

The Campaign Begins – 16 June

The 15th of June passed quietly for Henry Clinton's Division, which was stationed so far to the west of Napoleon's dawn attack on the Prussian positions around Charleroi, that they remained blissfully ignorant that the war had actually begun that day.

The Duke of Wellington, at Brussels, did not receive news of the invasion himself until 18.00 hours[1] and it was nearer midnight before he felt sure that this was not a feint and ordered his army to begin marching on its pre-arranged forward assembly point at Nivelles.[2]

We have already seen that Henry Clinton was busy that day discussing changes of cantonments and complaining about the food ruined by the 52nd, by getting it wet. Meanwhile Charles Holman wrote in his journal:

> 15th June – At 8am the regiment marched to Quivochamp [Quevaucamps] to parade, I was put on guard and escaped plenty of manoeuvring and a good wetting. A great many reports as to the commencement of the campaign, at night heard that the enemy had been feeling their way and driven back the Prussians with great loss.[3]

Holman was understandably pleased to avoid a drenching and his comment regarding rumours that the Prussians had been attacked and driven back was, as we know, only too true. At the time, however, it was simply the latest in a long stream of wild rumours and counter-rumours and when no orders to march arrived that evening, it was almost certainly written off as just another false report and they turned in for a good night's rest. The brigade had suffered so much manoeuvring in the rain because of General Clinton, as he wrote in his own diary:

> I went at 7[am] to see General Adam's Brigade at exercise, [but] he had countermanded them, I directed them however to return, but the exercise did not commence till past eleven, before which time it had begun to rain & continued to do so in showers all the day.[4]

---

1. Thorough investigation of the evidence by such authorities as John Hussey has proven beyond doubt that Wellington was not informed officially by the Prussians of the attack at Charleroi until 6pm. Claims by various historians over the last two centuries that Wellington knew of the attack as early as 9am have been wholly disproved.
2. It is clear from all of the available evidence that in the event of a French attack, Blücher would assemble his army in the area around Sombreffe and Wellington would assemble his army at Nivelles. It was only on the morning of 16 June, that Wellington realised the significance of Quatre Bras and he then ordered troops to march there.
3. Holman Lt, Journal for 1815, Royal Green Jackets Museum, Winchester.
4. Glover, The Correspondence of Sir Henry Clinton in the Waterloo Campaign, Volume 2, p 85.

The evidence that General Adam had indeed cancelled the manoeuvres on 15 June, can be found in his Brigade Orders of 14 June:

> B[rigade] O[rder]
> The Brigade will assemble tomorrow at 7 o'clock as heretofore. The 52nd will furnish the officer and the 71st the sergeant to go in charge of the sick. The hospital of the 71st and 95th Regiments will be collected at Leuze and move to Ath, under the direction of the officer of the 52nd Regiment.
>
> A[dditional] B[rigade] O[rder]
> No.1 <u>The order for the brigade to assemble tomorrow morning at 7 o'clock is countermanded.</u>
> No.2 The letter party of the 95th Regiment at La Petite Rosaire is to be withdrawn this evening.
> No.3 The 52nd Regiment will furnish a corporal and one private as a letter party at Ligne, and a private as an orderly to the DAAG [Deputy Assistant Adjutant General]. This corporal and the two privates will be at the Chateau La Catoise tomorrow morning at 7 o'clock, to receive orders from the brigade major.[5]

That night Wellington and his senior officers attended a ball at the Duke and Duchess of Richmond's residence on the Rue de la Blanchisserie in Brussels, a modest affair in a single storey, converted coach showroom attached to their house, which had been hastily draped to hide its modest origins. It was certainly not the high ceilinged, light and airy miniature palace with a balcony for the orchestra and hung with glittering chandeliers of later invention.

We know that a number of officers of the 2nd Corps were invited to the ball, the three lists we have of those invited do differ at times, but all seem to agree that the invitations included General Sir Rowland Hill and his aides de camp Captain Orlando Bridgeman, Captain Digby Mackworth and Major Chatham Horace Churchill, but not it would seem Major Egerton; General Sir Henry Clinton and his wife Susan and his aides de camp Captain Francis Dawkins and Captain John Gurwood were also included; as was General Sir Frederick Adam and his aide de camp Captain Yorke of the 52nd and Colonel Charles Rowan of the 52nd, but not, it would seem, Colonel Sir John Colborne despite the fact that he was a personal friend of the Richmond family. [6]

This does not mean of course that they all attended the ball. In fact, it appears that none of the generals Hill, Clinton or Adam attended, as the rumours of a French attack had led them to judge it better to remain at their posts, nor did Susan Clinton attend. As regards Hill's aides de camps, it is certain that both Orlando Bridgeman and Digby Mackworth had received permission to attend the ball and

---

5. Glover, The Correspondence of Sir Henry Clinton in the Waterloo Campaign, Volume 2, p 281.
6. Honourable Mrs Swinton A Sketch of the Life of Georgiana, Lady de Ros, London 1893 pp 124–132. It is possible that the list of commanding officers provided to them still showed Rowan commanding, but then Colborne was not invited as a member of the Prince of Orange's Staff either.

did so, leaving only Major Churchill on duty with Lord Hill. It is believed that John Gurwood, an ex-52nd man now in the 10th Hussars, did attend the ball as he was closely involved in making all of the arrangements with the Duchess and was there to ensure it all went off well; Francis Dawkins presumably stayed on duty with Henry Clinton. It is thought unlikely that either Yorke or Rowan attended the ball either. The reason why John Colborne was not invited is not known, but suggestions that he was invited but refused to leave his regiment can be largely discounted, as he is not on any of the three versions of the invitation list, and as can be seen above, many who did not attend are still listed. His recent change of role also fails to explain it as both the Prince of Orange's Staff were certainly invited, whilst many commanding officers were also invited. He had been back in command a full month, so even the suggestion that the invitations were sent out before Colborne resumed command of the battalion and that his was sent to the Prince of Orange but was not forwarded on, is impossible, as Captain Verner of the 7th Hussars records that the Duchess gave him the invitations for the cavalry on 6 June, which he personally gave to individual officers after the Schendelbeke Review, on 7 June.[7] The failure to invite Colborne was almost certainly nothing more than a simple oversight.

The Duke of Wellington had sent out his initial orders to the army, simply to assemble and be ready to march. These were written and despatched from Brussels by around 19.00 hours, but the difficulties of riding through the waterlogged country lanes in the dark, made delivering the orders to Corps headquarters at Grammont a very difficult, if not dangerous, task. Even by the most direct route, via back roads, Brussels to Grammont is some 27 miles (42km) away and we know that Lord Hill received these orders between 02.30 and 03.00 hours in the morning of 16 June. This would mean that the despatch rider achieved a rate of a little under 3½ miles per hour (5.5kmph), which given the difficult circumstances is not unreasonable. Having read the order, Hill had to write orders for each of his divisional commanders and forward them on to their respective headquarters. Clinton had his headquarters at Ath, some 13 miles (21km) away and we know that Henry Clinton received the order at 05.30 hours, the aide de camp achieving this in about 2½ hours, at a very respectable rate of just over 5 miles per hour (8 kmph).

The order simply read:

Grammont 16 June 1815

Sir,

In consequence of instructions from headquarters I am directed by Lord Hill to request you will collect the 2nd Division immediately upon the receipt of this order at Ath and adjacent and be in readiness to move at a moment's notice. I have the honour to be your obedient, humble servant Charles Broke, Lieutenant Colonel A.Q.M.G.[8]

---

7. Verner R Reminiscences of William Verner (1782–1871) 7th Hussars, London 1965.
8. Glover, The Correspondence of Sir Henry Clinton in the Waterloo Campaign, Volume 2, p 90.

The note is untimed, but a further order sent by Broke to Clinton, to forward an order to Baron Estorff's Cavalry Brigade on the frontier, is annotated by Clinton as 'Received at 5:30 am'. It is presumed that the same courier would have carried both messages.

Henry Clinton then had to write orders to each of his battalions to assemble and move to Ath at the earliest opportunity. The 52nd was based at Ellignies-Saint-Anne, a further 7½ miles away (12km), they could not have received these orders before 07.30 hours at the very earliest.

As for General Hill's aides de camp at Brussels, they had initially heard rumours of the invasion at around 18.00 hours, but they learnt that everyone was still determined to go to the Ball as no orders to march had been issued. However, soon after they arrived, it became clear that the orders to march were just going out and they immediately made their excuses and departed for Hill's headquarters. Captain Orlando Bridgeman recorded in a letter that:

> On Thursday the 15th I left Grammont to come to a ball given at this place by the Duchess of Richmond, about six o'clock that evening when walking in the park, I heard that we were going to move immediately, but on enquiry I found that everybody meant to stay out the ball, I therefore determined to do so myself. About half past eleven it was said that the French army was advancing & I found that orders were immediately going off to Lord Hill to move his corps, I therefore determined to stay no longer, & consequently I went off to Grammont, & reached it on Friday morning, the headquarters of our corps were that day at Enghien.[9]

Luckily, the 52nd had previously received orders at 05.00 hours to assemble at 08.00 hours for another field day at Quevaucamps, which meant that the regiment was forming up ready to march off, when the order to march immediately to Ath was received. This ties in exactly with the journal entry of Charles Holman: 'At 5am received orders to assemble at 8am for a field day, while we were forming, we received an order to march immediately to Ath.[10]

This is entirely consistent with General Adam's Brigade Order of 15 June, which stated: 'The brigade will assemble tomorrow morning [the 16th] at 10 am in the usual formation on the Partir de Paturage.'

We know that the pasturage referred to was at Quevaucamps, which was about 4 miles (6km) from Ellignies-Saint-Anne and it would take about 1½ hours to march there, therefore a parade at 8 am would fit perfectly with these timings.

Lieutenant William Ogilvy recorded with eminent pride, the strength of his company as a proof of how strong the regiment was this day:

> I happen to have preserved the parade state of the company on the 16th of June, on which morning I dare say you will remember we turned out for one of Sir H Clinton's field days. Cross, not being very well, did not come out,

---

9. Glover, Waterloo Archive Volume IV, p. 25.
10. Holman Lt, Journal for 1815, Royal Green Jackets Museum, Winchester.

and, by the time I had inspected the company, a cavalry man was seen on a jaded horse coming up the road, and, it was soon known that he brought an order for the division to march on Enghien &c. In the agreeable excitement at the news, Winterbottom [the Adjutant] did not collect the [company] states. The state is interesting from shewing the splendid condition of the corps then. The company, 87 rank and file, under arms, five tailors left at Lessines employed on the soldiers' clothing,[11] and only one man sick; officers' servants, batmen, band, &c making a total of 104 rank and file. I have no doubt the other companies were equally strong. What a noble battalion it was![12]

Ensign Leeke however, states that they were on company parade at 10.00 hours when Clinton's aide de camp – presumably Francis Dawkins – arrived with the order to march. This seems very late in the day, especially when he agrees with Holman that they were forming up to march to Qevaucamps for a field day.

Given that the 52nd were already mustering to march off when the order arrived and Ath was only some 7½ miles (12 km) away, which should take no more than three hours, it is surprising to find that the 52nd did not arrive at Ath until 13.00 hours, a full five hours later, as Lieutenant Holman recorded: 'At 1pm arrived at Ath, received orders to proceed with all possible dispatch.'[13]

This is confirmed by General Clinton who wrote to his wife at Brussels, whilst on the march, timing his message at 15.30 hours. In it he confirms that: 'We did not get clear of Ath till about one o'clock'.[14] But in two further letters describing the campaign to General Thomas Graham and his brother William Clinton, he writes: 'as it happened, [they] had not passed that place till 3 in the afternoon.'[15]

How do we make sense of these apparent discrepancies? Henry Clinton mentions receiving a further order to march to Enghien, which is some 13 miles (21km) away at 09.30 hours: 'It was not until the 16th at 9½ in the morning that I received orders to march to Enghien.'[16]

This order is entirely consistent with Wellington's later orders of 23.00 hours written on 15 June, which began to order the troops to close towards Nivelles. These messengers were on the road some four hours after the initial orders to assemble at Ath had been dispatched and they arrived consistently with Henry Clinton, four hours later. This ordered Hill's corps: 'To move from Ath and Grammont ... and to continue their movements upon Enghien'. [17]

11. Note by Leeke: The men at Lessines, amounting to between forty and fifty, probably joined us at Enghien or Nivelles. Siborne states, that the 52nd had 1038 men at Waterloo, which number would agree with this company's parade state.
12. Lieutenant Ogilivie's letter quoted in Leeke, p21.
13. Holman Lt, Journal for 1815, Royal Green Jackets Museum, Winchester.
14. Glover, The Correspondence of Sir Henry Clinton in the Waterloo Campaign, Volume 2, p 90.
15. ibid, p 119.
16. ibid, p 119.
17. Movements of the Army, After Orders 10pm, Gurwood, The Dispatches of the Duke of Wellington, Volume 12, p 474.

The receipt of this order, helps to explain the apparent discrepancy in the timings of the orders received, as stated by Holman and Leeke. When Holman speaks of the order being received prior to 08.00 hours, he is referring to the first order, to assemble at Ath, whereas Leeke's memory of receiving an order at 10.00 must refer to the second order, to march on Enghien, which we know was received by Clinton at 09.30 hours. As they had formed for field exercises, the men had not packed up their camp. It is therefore presumed that the intervening two hours was used to pack up the regimental camp and send off the baggage. This would also conveniently explain the late hour of their arrival at Ath. This scenario also ties in perfectly with Lieutenant Hart's statement that: 'On the 16th at ten o'clock we received the orders to march to Enghien'.[18]

Henry Clinton was eager to begin the march to Enghien as soon as possible, but his division had been very spread far and wide and took a great deal of time to assemble at Ath.

Halkett's entire Hanoverian Brigade and two battalions of Du Plat's King's German Legion Brigade (1st & 2nd Line) were formed at Ath quite quickly, being cantoned in the neighbourhood. However, two further King's German Legion battalions (3rd & 4th Line) were encamped at some distance and would be seriously delayed. Frustratingly, the British Light Brigade was stationed further from Ath and the 2/95th which was at Mons had to march the furthest of all, a distance of 16 miles (26km). They couldn't be expected to arrive at Ath until 14.00 hours.

Realising the urgency of the orders, Henry Clinton decided to order the Hanoverian Brigade, the half of the KGL Brigade and his two artillery batteries to march at around 13.00 hours for Enghien, sending orders for the other two KGL battalions to meet them on the march near Meslin L'Evecque, which they succeeded in doing, allowing the two complete brigades to arrive at Enghien between 16.00 and 17.00 hours.

Whilst on the march to Enghien, Henry Clinton had received a further order at around 15.00 hours, ordering his division to continue its march to Braine le Comte immediately, which was another 9 miles (15km) or so.

However, his troops found the road at Enghien very congested with cavalry and artillery and they were forced to delay for some time. They then marched on to Braine le Comte despite the oppressive heat, but it was not until 21.00 hours before the leading elements of the division arrived and nearer midnight before the Light Brigade, at the rear, finally tramped in.[19]

The rest of the Light Brigade had been ordered to await the arrival of 2/95th at Ath and then to march as rapidly as possible to catch the rest of the division. It appears that the Light Brigade only caught up to the rest of the division at Enghien. Ensign Leeke states that the 52nd:

---

18. Hart letter dated 20 June 1815. NAM 1981–11–84.
19. Leeke says midnight, whereas Hart who wrote only four days later, says 23.00 hours.

were ordered to move on Ath and Enghien; we reached the latter place a little after two o'clock. There we halted for two or three hours, and the men cooked their ration beef. During this time, we distinctly heard the cannonade of Quatre Bras, although it was twenty-two miles from us.... When we first heard the cannonade at Quatre Bras, one of the old soldiers exclaimed, 'there they go shaking their blankets again.' The sound of a distant cannonade is not unlike that arising from the shaking of a carpet or a blanket.[20]

Leeke's memory is at fault here, as his timing is certainly off, given that those that recorded events on or soon after the day, make its arrival at Enghien between 16.00 and 17.00 hours. Leeke is also the only eyewitness that claims that they halted for such a long period at Enghien and that they had time to cook, but the other witnesses do agree that there was some delay to allow the cavalry to pass. Lieutenant John Hart told his father that: 'we received orders to march to Enghien and we were there for about ten minutes when we heard ... that we were to march directly for Braine le Comte.'[21]

He does not however, state how long they remained at Enghien. Lieutenant Holman, however, wrote in his journal: 'We halted on the road at 6 for half an hour and received a ration of gin and bread, continued our march within hearing of the warlike musick [sic] which ceased at dark.'[22]

It is almost certainly this stop, which Leeke mistakenly recalled as a stop of some 3 hours with the troops cooking their rations. Other troops who were passing were jealous of the 52nd, Private Thomas Jeremiah of the 23rd Foot recalled that: 'we passed the 52nd Regiment who were serving their men out with one ration of spirits. We marched by them in gloomy silence cursing our quartermaster for not having provided us with the same dose.'[23]

Henry Clinton had already received yet another order whilst on the march to Braine le Comte, to continue the march to Nivelles, which was yet another 10 miles (16km) further on.

As darkness had fallen, Clinton ordered two hours' rest for the troops in the town of Braine le Comte and a ration of rum for every man to fortify them. They would need it to survive the night that was to come. Poor Charles Holman was still on duty and had to oversee the pickets, whilst the rest of the battalion tried to grab some sleep: 'At 11pm arrived at Braine le Comte, 9 leagues, under heavy rain, bivouacked in an orchard within the town, still on guard as the order to march was so sudden as to prevent my being relieved.'[24]

The leading elements of the division began marching again soon after midnight, just after the Light Brigade had arrived. Ensign Leeke was lucky

---

20. Leeke, p 10.
21. Hart letter dated 20 June 1815. NAM 1981-11-84.
22. Holman Lt, Journal for 1815, Royal Green Jackets Museum, Winchester.
23. Glover's Waterloo Archive, Volume IV pp 183.
24. Holman Lt, Journal for 1815, Royal Green Jackets Museum, Winchester.

enough to discover an inn nearby and found a novel way to gain some food and a warm dry bed for an hour or two:

> The lower room of an adjacent auberge I found crowded with men of the brigade waiting for their turn to purchase something to eat; I was directed to a room upstairs, where I found some bread and cheese on the table, and two 71st officers lying their full length on two beds fast asleep. After eating some bread and cheese, I took the liberty of lying down by the side of one of them, although they were perfect strangers to me, judging that, according to the laws of war, the one half of the bed fairly belonged to me. I could not sleep, so, after lying there about an hour and getting a good rest, I left my friends of the 71st not at all aware of the honour I had conferred upon them. [25]

The 52nd was ordered to form up again for the onward march at 02.00 hours and marched off at 02.30 hours, minus a prisoner under Holman's guard: 'At 2am the regiment turned out to march, during which time Pat Wall,[26] a prisoner in charge of the guard deserted to the enemy, at ½ past marched to Nivelles 2 leagues.'[27]

A night march is always difficult, but marching in the dark through a dense forest, while their feet sank in the clay-like mud which sucked their shoes off and as they struggled to pass abandoned carts which blocked the lanes, it felt like it would never end. Frequent rest stops and even a rousing interlude of marching behind the regimental band helped to keep the men of the 52nd going, as did a few mishaps:

> I remember one good halt after leaving Enghien, which we made from about eight till half-past nine. There was also another halt on the 16ᵗh [17th], which took place in a large open wood. As we moved off again, the band struck up a march, the horse in a sutler's light covered cart, frightened by the band, dashed off amongst the trees, and the last I saw of the occurrence was that the body of the cart separated from the wheels and axletree and shafts, with which the horse ran off, leaving the poor woman inside the body of the cart. I think she could not have been much hurt; but it would probably be some considerable time before she and her husband, if she had one, would be able to join the division again.[28]

---

25. Leeke, pp 11–12. How these could be officers of the 71st who were marching with the 52nd is not explained.
26. The history of Private Patrick Wall of Captain Love's company is a complicated one. The regimental records show that he had deserted on 11 May 1815 but had rejoined on 25 May, hence he was a prisoner presumably awaiting a court martial. He absconded in the night of the 16 June and he did not return until 23 June. According to the regimental muster book, he has a 'W' against his name, which denotes that he fought at Waterloo and would have been awarded a Waterloo medal. However, the Waterloo Medal Roll does not list a Patrick Wall and it almost certain that he did receive a medal. He was absent during the battle and must have been mistakenly marked on the muster roll as a Waterloo man. He was subsequently court martialled and discharged on 24 August 1815 after he 'volunteered' to continue to serve abroad for life.
27. Holman Lt, Journal for 1815, Royal Green Jackets Museum, Winchester.
28. Leeke, p 11.

The march did eventually end, but only at 05.00 hours for the leading elements of the division and past 07.00 hours before the 52nd and the other British regiments finally arrived. Having at last arrived, there was no ceremony, no establishing encampments, the men simply found a free space in the sodden fields allocated to them and just slumped to the ground, rapidly falling into the sleep of the dead.

The men of the 52nd had been roused at 06.00 hours the previous day and in the ensuing twenty-six hours they had marched in excess of forty miles in pretty horrendous conditions, with stifling heat during the day and heavy rain during the night, while only getting about two hours sleep and a tot or two of rum as their only sustenance to keep them through the long night march. The hard marching had taken its toll, but Privates John McCardle and Thomas Rielly of Captain Cross's company had discovered a wine cellar in the town and were so drunk that they fell out 'sick' on the night march and one did not return until after the Battle of Waterloo.[29]

They were now very close to the seat of war and they had no idea what the new day, which was already dawning, would bring.

---

29. Private Thomas Rielly was marked on the Return as having fallen out on the march on 16 June but is recorded as being back on duty at 03.00 hours on 18 June 1815 and continued serving with the regiment. Private James McCardle is also shown as having fallen out on the march on 16 June, he missed Waterloo, and he was invalided to England on 24 October 1816 and discharged to pension on 21 November 1816. Leeke relates that a number of men returned after the battle but were not court martialled, the dishonour of not being a Waterloo man being punishment enough for them, in Colonel Colborne's view.

Chapter 5

Retreat to Waterloo – 17 June

Clinton's Division had missed the first day of serious fighting whilst they marched interminably to join Wellington's army. Napoleon had launched his attack at dawn on 15 June at Charleroi and had succeeded in driving the Prussians back from the bridges across the River Sambre before they could destroy them. Pushing northwards and north-eastwards in two large columns, Napoleon's troops had ended the first day of operations with his left wing facing a small Dutch force at a vital crossroads called Quatre Bras, and his right wing facing a sizeable force of Prussians near Ligny.

Napoleon had assumed correctly that the Duke of Wellington would be more cautious in deploying his army and he felt sure that Marshal Ney, commanding his left wing, could drive off the few troops at Quatre Bras and push a division along the main chaussee towards Brussels, whilst the rest of his force would turn to the east and take the Prussians at Ligny in the flank and rear.

Napoleon had also assumed correctly that the Prussian commander, Field Marshal Blücher, would be the more rash in his approach and would offer battle at the earliest opportunity. By late morning Napoleon's right wing, under the command of Marshal Grouchy found that they were facing superior numbers at Ligny and it soon developed into a very bloody and hard fought battle, which was only settled by a final devastating attack from Napoleon's Imperial Guard, which broke Prussian resistance, but did not destroy the Prussian army, which withdrew to fight another day.

Meanwhile, Marshal Ney's advanced forces were wholeheartedly committed to take the crossroads at Quatre Bras but were prevented from gaining the victory by the arrival of the leading elements of Wellington's army which had been rushed to the vital crossroads. This battle ended in somewhat of a stalemate with the forces of both sides in the same positions they had occupied that morning, allowing Wellington to claim the victory as he held the battlefield at the end of the day. The march of General Clinton's Division throughout 16 and early hours of the 17 June was required to bring these troops from the western edge of Wellington's initial deployment area to the very eastern edge of his cantonments where Napoleon had launched his attack. As has been seen, it was only after a very long and trying night march that the 52nd and the remainder of his division had finally arrived at Nivelles, only 6 miles (10km) from the battlefield.

Early that morning, everyone in Wellington's army from the commander down, expected to renew the fight at Quatre Bras on the 17th. However, by 09.00 hours, the Duke of Wellington had learnt of the Prussian defeat and Blücher's retreat to

Wavre, which was perfectly situated 12½ miles (20km) to the east of Wellington's previously chosen spot, where he would offer battle in front of Brussels. It was on the Brussels chaussee near the village of Mont St Jean, and from his position Blücher's forces could easily join up with Wellington. There was no other option for Wellington, than to retreat to his pre-planned position 3 miles (4.5km) south of the village of Waterloo and await Napoleon's attack there.

Ensign Leeke recalls that morning that the 52nd were just beyond Nivelles, where the officers' servants prepared a hasty breakfast, but he also hints at future woes:

> We reached Nivelles about seven o'clock; the narrow streets were full of cavalry horses tied to the doors and windows of the houses. The morning had become fine, and the 52nd got into a large orchard. Here we got our breakfast, and here about thirty of the officers of the 52nd, I being amongst the number, saw their baggage for the last time.[1]

Leeke appears to be in error here again, the 52nd along with the rest of the 2nd Division apparently actually halted in the town of Nivelles that morning, expecting the order to march on to Quatre Bras, to join the remainder of Wellington's army. His mistaken memory of an orchard would appear to link this to Braine le Comte. Lieutenant Charles Holman recorded in his diary:

> Marched to Nivelles 2 leagues, halted here to cook and unloaded our baggage, found here in the town a great number of men who were wounded (in a gallant affair near Quatre Bras) belonging to the 1st and 5th Divisions.[2]

The officers of the 52nd had remained relatively fresh on the long march, as they were nearly all mounted, a very unusual situation for a line regiment, but again indicating the personal wealth of many of the officers.

> Sir John Colborne always strongly advocated the importance of infantry officers, when on active service, having riding horses, and used to say, that if, from insufficiency of income, they found it difficult to manage this, still they should stint themselves in wine, and in everything else, in order to keep a horse if possible. As mounted officers they were more useful, under very many circumstances; they were less tired at the end of a day's march, and more ready for any duty which might be required of them; they could be more effective in bringing up stragglers on a long and weary march; some of them might be usefully employed when extra staff officers were required. I think, on the long march of upwards of fifty miles, which we had from Quevres-au-camps [Quevaucamps] to Waterloo, all but two of the officers of the 52nd were mounted.[3]

---

1. Leeke, p 12.
2. Holman Lt, Journal for 1815, Royal Green Jackets Museum, Winchester.
3. Leeke, p 7.

Initial orders received by Henry Clinton at 08.00 hours, confirmed the assumption that it would soon join the army, when he was ordered to march to the crossroads: 'It was not before 8 that my division could be collected there [Nivelles] & then we received orders to the village called Les 4 Bras.'[4]

Henry Clinton ordered his division to march on Quatre Bras, leading with Du Plat's Brigade. Meanwhile he took the opportunity to ride ahead the six miles (10km) to view the battlefield of the previous day, but he unfortunately does not record any of his thoughts regarding it. Around 09.00 hours, however, Clinton received orders to halt the march and he ordered Du Plat's troops to halt: 'We had passed Nivelles about a league [three miles] when I met an order to halt at that place.'[5]

Nearer 9:30 am Henry Clinton received revised orders to retire towards Wellington's chosen position near Waterloo via Nivelles:

INSTRUCTIONS TO GENERAL LORD HILL FOR THE MOVEMENT OF THE ARMY ON THE 17TH

17th June 1815

The 2nd Division of British infantry to march from Nivelles on Waterloo at 10 o'clock.

The brigades of the 4th Division, now at Nivelles, to march from that place on Waterloo at 10 o'clock. Those brigades of the 4th Division at Braine le Comte, and on the road from Braine le Comte to Nivelles, to collect and halt at Braine le Comte this day.

All the baggage on the road from Braine le Comte to Nivelles to return immediately to Braine le Comte, and to proceed immediately from thence to Hal and Bruxelles.

The spare musket ammunition to be immediately parked behind Genappe.

The corps under the command of Prince Frederick of Orange will move from Enghien this evening, and take up a position in front of Hal, occupying Braine le Chateau with two battalions.

Colonel Estorff will fall back with his brigade on Hal and place himself under the orders of Prince Frederick.[6]

This would mean that Wellington's troops would be retiring along two major highways (or chaussees) which converged on the proposed battlefield, greatly easing the problems of congestion. It did however, mean that the leading troops of his division, which had now arrived virtually in sight of the Quatre Bras battlefield, would have to retrace their steps. It was a march of just over 7 miles (11.5km), a relative breeze after the previous day's march, but now with the real threat of French cavalry intercepting their march.

---

4. Glover, The Correspondence of Sir Henry Clinton in the Waterloo Campaign, Volume 2, p 87.
5. ibid, p 119.
6. Gurwood, The Duke of Wellington's Dispatches, Volume 12.

Clinton ordered the convoys of stores to move out first and allowed time for the Dutch medical staff to evacuate the wounded from the hospital they had established at Nivelles to Braine l'Alleud, before marching themselves. Charles Holman confirmed this in his journal: 'Our baggage was ordered immediately to load and move to the rear and after baggage, artillery &c left the town.'[7]

The division therefore had time to prepare what food the men had before they marched. Not Du Plat's Brigade, which had to march back to Nivelles. It was also unfortunate for Captain Diggle's company,[8] as it was its turn to be the advanced guard and they had to put out pickets to the front instead of taking any rest. Lieutenant John Hart was one of them: 'The next morning, No.1 [Diggle's] company, in which I was, was ordered on picquet and remained there about five hours.'[9]

It was early afternoon when the 2nd Division eventually began its march towards Mont St Jean, with the cavalry and horse artillery protecting its flanks:

> Shortly after leaving Nivelles, we found ourselves marching in a parallel line with British artillery and cavalry, we being on the road and they moving for some distance along the fields on either side .... We moved very slowly, the men being wearied with their long march, and by the heavy load which each had to carry; this consisted of the knapsack, containing the kit and blanket, (the greatcoats had been sent to England) the musket and bayonet, and 120 rounds of ball-cartridge, sixty rounds of the latter being in the knapsack;[10] this was a wise precaution adopted by the commanding officer.[11]

The far more experienced Lieutenant Charles Holman recorded that French cavalry began to appear soon after they left Nivelles and that the battalion halted on the sides of the chaussee a number of times, to give the waggons carrying the wounded and stores time to withdraw safely. He doesn't mention it, but incessant rains began to fall heavily again that afternoon.

> We marched thro[ugh] it [Nivelles] on the road to Bruxelles. As soon as we were about 2 miles out of the town, we heard a sharp fire of musquetry and presently we caught sight of our old friends [the French] following slowly our skirmishers, who were retiring in good order about one mile on our right flank. We halted on the side of the road several times to allow our wounded &c to pass and to cover the road.[12]

As to the regimental baggage, that had been sent on to Brussels under the charge of Ensign Shaw, much to his consternation: 'On the afternoon of the 17th, I was,

---

7. Holman Lt, Journal for 1815, Royal Green Jackets Museum, Winchester.
8. Captain Charles Diggle 52nd Foot.
9. Lieutenant John Hart's letter dated 20 June 1815.
10. It was normal for each man to carry 60 rounds, but Leeke states that Colonel Colborne had made them carry 120 rounds.
11. Leeke, p 12.
12. Holman Lt, Journal for 1815, Royal Green Jackets Museum, Winchester.

much to my grief, put on baggage guard, with orders to proceed instantly to Brussels.'[13]

These regular halts were required to ensure that the French did not capture any of the waggons which were still trundling slowly in convoy along the chaussee:

> About midway between Nivelles and Hougoumont, the 52nd halted for rather more than two hours, 200 yards to the left of the road. I heard Sir John Colborne asking if any of the officers could lend him the cape of a boat-cloak, as he wished to lie down for a couple of hours, and try and get some sleep; I had a very large boat-cloak with a cape and hood to it, I unhooked the cape and hood and handed them to him. He wore them over his uniform during the whole of the Battle of Waterloo.[14]

Their efforts were only partially successful however, as we have clear evidence that some of the supply wagons were captured by French cavalry on the Nivelles road:

> I was taken prisoner on the 17 June near Nivelles with the loss of nine wagons loaded with provisions for the regiment I am attached to. I am happy to inform you that no blame is attributed to me whatever. I received a letter from the officer commanding the 1st Royals [1st Foot] about twelve o'clock on Thursday [Friday] evening the 16th to proceed to Nivelles without loss of time, which orders I readily complied with and when within ten miles of the town I was given to understand that the British army was retiring, supposed[ly] upon Waterloo. Scarce had the British troops left Nivelles but the enemy was in the town. I found it impossible to retreat with the wagons as the advance of the enemy was [so] rapid, the commissariat lost on that day I believe, lost nearly one hundred carts & wagons. I am pleased to have it in my power to inform you that I made my escape the same evening.[15]

Lieutenant Edward Byam of the 15th Hussars also recalls French cavalry appearing on the Nivelles Chaussee: 'near Lillois, here, some French hussars cut into the Nivelles road and took many wagons, laden with our wounded.'[16]

Leeke recalls that as they re-entered the chaussee in front of a Netherlands regiment, they found the road lined with men, women and children from every conceivable regiment, resting, unable to carry on. They were exhausted and miserable, being drenched from the heavy rain that was now falling:

> Whilst we were halted on this occasion, several waggons, with those wounded at Quatre Bras, passed along the main road towards Waterloo and Brussels. After our halt we came on to the road again just ahead of a

---

13. Shaw, p 52.
14. Leeke, p 13.
15. Storekeeper James Robinson's letter to Sir Henry Clinton dated 31 August 1815, Waterloo Archive Volume VI, p 59.
16. Glover, The Waterloo Archive Volume I, pp 84.

regiment of Dutch Belgians and formed open column of companies from subdivisions as each company reached it, so that our allies had to halt till we were all on the road. Each side of the road was now lined with soldiers of different regiments, and with some women and drummer boys, who had fallen out from fatigue. From this time until some time after we had reached the entrance to Hougoumont, no less than five mounted officers were sent, one after the other, to bring up stragglers belonging to the 52nd.[17]

As the regiment neared the farm and chateau of Hougoumont, the regiment halted to form up against the French cavalry and both sides brought some artillery into play. The supply waggons broke into a panic however, and a number were captured, although many were recaptured by a charge from some British dragoons. Lieutenant Holman recalled that: 'About 3pm our fellows made a stand and the enemy then were obliged to. They brought up some artillery as did we also and there commenced a lively cannonade.'[18]

Ensign Leeke became aware of the French for the first time at this halt: 'Shortly after this we halted, still in open column of companies, and loaded. Two French staff officers rode down to within 200 yards of us to reconnoitre, and one of them I saw writing down what he observed.'[19]

Privates Francis Bass of Captain Shedden's company and Terence O'Neal of Lieutenant Colonel Rowan's company were sick and fell out of the march,[20] while Privates Charles Gregg (or Grieg) of Captain McNair's company and Patrick Coffey of Captain P. Campbell's company also fell out of the march, but then used the opportunity to desert, only returning to the regiment in Paris on 17 July.[21] They continued marching along the chaussee until they had passed Hougoumont farm to their right at about 16.00 hours. Here, they turned left along a track that took them northward, towards the village of Merbe Braine. Henry Clinton recorded that:

> The enemy followed our cavalry & brought on a cannonade, which occasioned a sad panic in the baggage, a great part of which fled to Brussels. In the evening of the 17th the Duke of Wellington ordered some change to be made on the left [British right], throwing it back towards the forest & leaving only a Dutch regiment for the protection of Braine l'Alleud, the Dutch division on my right was near the forest. About half a mile in front of our position & to the

---

17. Leeke, p 13.
18. Holman Lt, Journal for 1815, Royal Green Jackets Museum, Winchester.
19. Leeke p 14.
20. Privates Francis Bass and Terence O'Neal fell out sick, they did not serve at Waterloo and did not receive a medal, but the records indicate that they were both court martialled and acquitted, indicating that their sickness was genuine.
21. Private McCardle was sentenced to 200 lashes, but this was commuted to an unstated period of confinement. Private Charles Gregg/Greig however was court martialled on 7 October 1815 and was discharged from the regiment having agreed to 'serve abroad for life'.

left of the Nivelles road is a large solidly built farm with extensive buildings & around its enclosures & some open wood, called Hougoumont.[22]

The regiment had finally arrived at its cantonment for the night and despite the rain, the men attempted to light fires and to prepare whatever meagre morsels of their rations which they still possessed. Charles Holman wrote that:

> At 4pm we moved off the road and formed line in front of Braine l'Alleud and [the] rear of Hougoumont under very heavy rain, saw several fine charges of cavalry. The skirmishing continued until after dark, during which time we changed our position three times, after lighting our fires to make ourselves comfortable at last [we] halted in line with our front to Braine l'Alleud.[23]

Captain Digby Mackworth, General Hill's aide de camp confirms the timing:

> It was about 4 o'clock that the retreat terminated, and the troops are now getting a little rest, of which they are in the greatest need; having been marching almost ever since they set out at daybreak yesterday, with little or nothing to eat, by bad roads, and in torrents of rain.[24]

Where the British Brigade actually stopped was described by General Adam to William Siborne as: 'The 3rd [British] Brigade ... bivouacked on the night of the 17th *en potence*[25] to the main line of the troops. Merbe Braine was a little in front of its left.'[26]

Lieutenant Colonel Thomas Reynell of the 71st Foot agrees that they stood *en potence* to the main ridge:

> On the night of the 17th, that previous to the battle, the 71st Regiment bivouacked in a fallow field on the extreme right, and, together with the other regiments of Major General Adam's Brigade, [was] placed *en potence* to the British line.[27]

George Gawler who had been a lieutenant in the 52nd at Waterloo states its position as: 'Major General Adam's Brigade, of which the 52nd formed a part, bivouacked on the night of the 17th-18th June nearly on the summit of a height between the Nivelles chaussee and Merbe Braine, 400 or 500 yards east of the latter village.'[28]

Ensign Leeke recalls being sent into the village of Merbe Braine to find straw, which the officers could use to sit on and keep them out of the saturated mud, but he did not find it easy to find any:

---

22. Glover, The Waterloo Archives Volume 1, p 150.
23. Holman Lt, Journal for 1815, Royal Green Jackets Museum, Winchester.
24. Glover, Waterloo Archive Volume IV, p 22.
25. En potence in military terms means thrown forward or back from the main line, ie in order to guard a flank.
26. Siborne, The Waterloo Letters p 275.
27. ibid, p 296.
28. ibid, p 287.

Whilst we were halted near Hougoumont, a heavy clap of thunder from the direction of Mont Plaisir startled us all; my first idea was that the French artillery in that direction were opening upon us. [William] Siborne [the historian] speaks of there having been much thunder and lightning during the evening and night of the 17th of June, but that was the only clap of thunder I heard; there was much rain during the night. Just after this, when it was decided to what part of the ground we should move, Lord Seaton directed me to ride and see if the regiment could get through a hedge about two hundred yards off, in the direction of the village of Merbe Braine; it was a stiff hedge cut down to stakes nearly five feet high, with gaps here and there through which a single file might pass, and I was somewhat afraid if I reported that the regiment might pass through it, I might get into a scrape, if the column should be brought up by it. I reported it passable, and we marched through it without any great difficulty, and took up our position in a ploughed field, just in advance of Merbe Braine, looking towards Hougoumont, and at about two miles to the eastward of the town of Braine-la-leud [Braine l'Alleud].

I was ordered with a fatigue party to go into the village to bring straw for the company. As we passed along the street we saw lying in the middle of the road, opposite to one of the cottages, the dead body of one of the 95th Rifles; I supposed he had been plundering and had been killed by one of the inhabitants. I proceeded with my fatigue party to the principal farm, where I found our general of brigade, Adam, who had taken up his quarters there. We could find no straw in the barn, and so, as 'necessitas non habet leges,' [necessity is above the law] we took the straw from the roof of the barn itself, which had been recently thatched. On my return to the bivouac, our servants made a bed of straw on the wet ploughed field, and all four of us, McNair, Hall, Yonge, and I, lay down and, being covered with our boat cloaks, tried to go to sleep; it was very hot and there was heavy rain, and the straw conducted the rain into the inside of my stock,[29] so that I was soon glad to get up.[30]

They were not, however, to be left in peace for the night, as they were required to move position at about 22.00 hours. Ensign Leeke was not going to get much sleep:

I think it was a little after ten o'clock when we were ordered to fall in again, as we were going to move, and each man was to take his straw with him. I don't know where the others were, but I found myself to be for a short time the only officer with the company. We moved in file, left in front, and I was very proud of my command, when Colonel Charles Rowan rode up to me, as No. 9 formed up into line on the left of No. 10, and said to me, 'Leeke, dress

---

29. The leather stock around his neck.
30. Leeke, p 15.

your company in a line with that distant fire.' Our line then faced the French position and was about 400 yards in rear of the crest of the British position, and about 500 yards from Merbe Braine. Here, having formed open column of companies, we piled arms and remained for the night.

My friend Yonge shared my boat cloak and straw with me, and we consequently both of us got very wet. The horses were picketed near us, and very soon some half-dozen of them got loose and galloped away towards Hougoumont and the French position, and then came back again at speed towards the horses they had left, nearly passing over us, and only being prevented from doing so by our jumping up; they galloped about in this way the whole night, and thus made this wretched night still more wretched. I fell asleep several times, then dreamt we were advancing and closing with the enemy, then started up again, then thought of home and all my beloved ones there; again I dozed off, then came our horses like a furious charge of cavalry, and we had to start up and scare them off; and this kind of thing went on till the night had passed, and the morning of the 18th broke upon us.[31]

Captain Orlando Bridgeman, another of General Hill's aides de camp, felt sorry for the troops but he had no intention of sharing their plight:

Our corps kept marching on through Braine le Comte, Nivelles & arrived at the position [at Waterloo] late on that night, having had no rations at all… Our army bivouacked that night, many of them with empty stomachs, from the utter impossibility of getting up the stores, it rained the whole night through, our staff got into houses near Waterloo, & laid down about eleven.[32]

Ensign Jack Barnett of the 71st Foot described the terrible conditions they found on their arrival:

By this time, it was 10 o'clock, fatigued to death & too late to build huts or light fires. I was sent out with a party for wood & water, before I could find which, it was 12 o'clock.

I came into the regiment & threw myself down on the ground at the first place I came to, without even a greatcoat & raining very hard.[33]

The misery for the troops that night is probably most succinctly described by Private William Smith who was also of the 71st Foot, lying next to the 52nd, who wrote: 'that night betwixt the 17th and 18th was one of the dreadfullest [sic] nights of rain ever I was aware, the water running out of the shoes on my feet.'[34]

---

31. ibid, pp 15–16.
32. Glover, Waterloo Archive Volume IV, pp 25–6.
33. ibid, p 151.
34. ibid, p 113.

Chapter 6

Battle Begins 11.30–16.00 Hours

The troops were woken before daylight and ordered to stand to with their arms ready primed, as a precaution against a sudden dawn attack. Few had really slept well in the constant rain and everyone was saturated through and numbed by the early morning chill. Lieutenant Charles Holman wrote that there had been: 'Continual rains the whole night and when we got up in the morning almost everyone left his impression in the mud where he had slept.'[1]

Exhausted, famished, dripping wet and mind-numbingly cold but also fearing an attack, the men slowly hauled themselves upright and stood shivering in the chilly waterlogged fields, waiting impatiently for some senior officer to pronounce that they could see a white horse at a mile, the official indicator that the enemy could no longer launch a surprise attack in the early morning gloom. It meant that the men could be stood down and that they could instead set to, rekindling the warming fires to dry their saturated clothes and to cook any morsels of food that they still possessed. Many of those who had nothing to eat or drink, quietly slipped off into the nearby cottages, searching for any scraps that had been left there by their owners as they hurried away, taking their families far away from the fighting. We have recently read that Ensign Jack Barnett of the 71st had sunk to the ground, having been so exhausted that:

> I fell asleep directly & never even woke till the 'Assembly' blew & woke with my side in a puddle of water. I got up with my teeth chattering, but begged a smoke from a man in my company, out of an old dirty pipe, who had a little tobacco, this warmed me & made me once more fit for a march.[2]

General Hill and his Staff were up and out at just after 03.00 hours, riding around the position chosen for the battlefield and checking that all of their orders had been carried out fully. Satisfied, they had the luxury of returning to an inn for some breakfast, with Captain Bridgeman recording that: 'On Sunday the 18th we were all on our horses at twenty minutes before three in the morning & everything was quiet, we rode all round the position; & returned to eat something about ten.'[3]

William Gavin of the neighbouring 71st Foot wrote of the discomfort but also of their huge success in finding food:

---
1. Holman Lt, Journal for 1815, Royal Green Jackets Museum, Winchester.
2. Glover, Waterloo Archive Volume VI, p 151.
3. Glover, ibid, p 26.

> The men were ordered to dry their clothes and accoutrements and put their firelocks in order, and the writer was sent with a party to a farmhouse, to seize on all the cattle that could be found about it. This was soon performed. Cows, bullocks, pigs, sheep and fowls were put into requisition and brought to camp. Butchers set to work, fires made by pulling down houses for the wood, camp kettles hung on, and everything in a fair way for cooking, when the word 'fall in' put everything to the route. Men accoutring, cannon roaring, bugles sounding and drums beating, which put a stop, to our cooking for that day. Our brigade were ordered to advance to the brow of a hill and lie down in column.[4]

His statement is confirmed by Second Lieutenant Richard Cocks Eyre of the 2/95th who recorded that:

> At about seven o'clock however to our great satisfaction the skirmishers were called in, and as a reward for our nocturnal labours, we had leave from General Adam who commanded our (Light) Brigade to plunder three farm houses which were near us![5] The idea of a fire was a most consoling one! Chairs, tables, sofas, cradles, churns, barrels and all manner of combustibles were soon cracking in the flames, our fellows then proceeded to the slaughter of all the living stock the yard contained, and in less than an hour we had as delicious a breakfast of beef, pork, veal, duck, chicken, potatoes and other delicacies as I ever made an attack upon. This repast was just finished and our fellows had got themselves thoroughly dry when we were ordered to fall in and proceed as fast as possible with the 52nd and 71st Regiments (which comprised our brigade) to the front to protect three brigades of artillery which were ordered out to the edge of the hill on which the British and Belgic armies had taken up their position.[6]

It is doubtful whether any of the 52nd shared in this feast, as none have recorded doing so. Wellington was known for his strict enforcement of the rules against soldiers plundering during the Peninsular War, but there is ample evidence that during the Waterloo campaign, that these rules were relaxed by senior officers, without Wellington's knowledge because of the complete failure of the commissariat service during the whirlwind campaign. In his desperation to feed his division, Commissary Tupper Carey took advantage of some Dutch wagons he had discovered, full of biscuit, to supply his own troops:

---

4. Glover, The Diary of William Gavin, 1806–15, pp 129–130.
5. An interesting comment, given the usual assertion by modern historians that Wellington maintained such a tight discipline on the troops that only the French, Belgian and Prussian forces looted. It is clear from a number of sources that in his Belgian campaign Wellington was unable to exert the same level of discipline on the troops, presumably because of the massive change in his Staff, and that both plundering and excessive baggage was actually a problem with the British troops as well, once campaigning began in Belgium. There is some reason to believe however, that the tight control reasserted itself on the march to Paris because of a fear of aggravating the population and the British troops seem to have behaved themselves.
6. Glover, Waterloo Archive Volume III, p 115.

I started again for Waterloo, after having in vain inquired for my groom and second horse. I passed through the sad relics on the road of the preceding night's adventure, and arrived about eight o'clock on the ground occupied by the division, hoping that the baggage and provisions expected by roads different from that from Brussels would have made their appearance and put us at ease in regard to provisions and other comforts; but there were no tidings of them. Some meat and biscuits had been given to the men for these three days' march, 16th, 17th and 18th, but, with their usual improvidence it is very likely little remained for the last day's consumption. Spirits they had none, and they therefore fought the battle without any artificial stimulant to their courage.

While on the field an individual came up to me and inquired if I spoke French, and having answered in the affirmative, he told me he had in his charge, a little distance off, several wagon loads of biscuit for the Dutch troops, but as he could not find them, and as the drivers were afraid of remaining any longer where they were, and threatened to throw their loads on the side of the road and save their horses and wagons, he did not know what to do with them. I demurred for a moment as to what I should do, the temptation being great, but finding the man very urgent and knowing that no one would derive any benefit from the biscuit if left on the ground, I desired him to bring it up to the division. This was done without delay. The heads of the casks in which the article was contained were then knocked out in an instant and the contents soon found a vanishing point down the throats of those who needed it...Our troops were permitted to cook while all remained quiet, but as the onset was momentarily expected on the troops in our front, the chance of succeeding was very precarious.

It so happened that those whose meat was preparing for soup had at last to throw the liquor away, for at about eleven o'clock the men were ordered to fall in and stand to their arms, and very shortly afterwards we heard the commencement of the skirmishing which was soon followed by the first attack on Hougoumont, a little before midday. The cannonade speedily became violent, but the balls did not reach us. The General,[7] seeing me still with the division, called me to him and told me that I was no longer required on the field, but requested me to endeavour to find them out when the action was over and if possible bring up supplies. I remained a little longer looking on, until the troops received orders to change ground, and I then joined other commissariat officers similarly situated as I was. We retired a short distance to the rear watching the progress of the action, but as it spread from right to left the whole position became enveloped in a dense smoke, and nothing could be perceived. We thought it therefore advisable to ride to the fork where the two chaussees met leading to Brussels, to enable us more

---

7. Sir Henry Clinton.

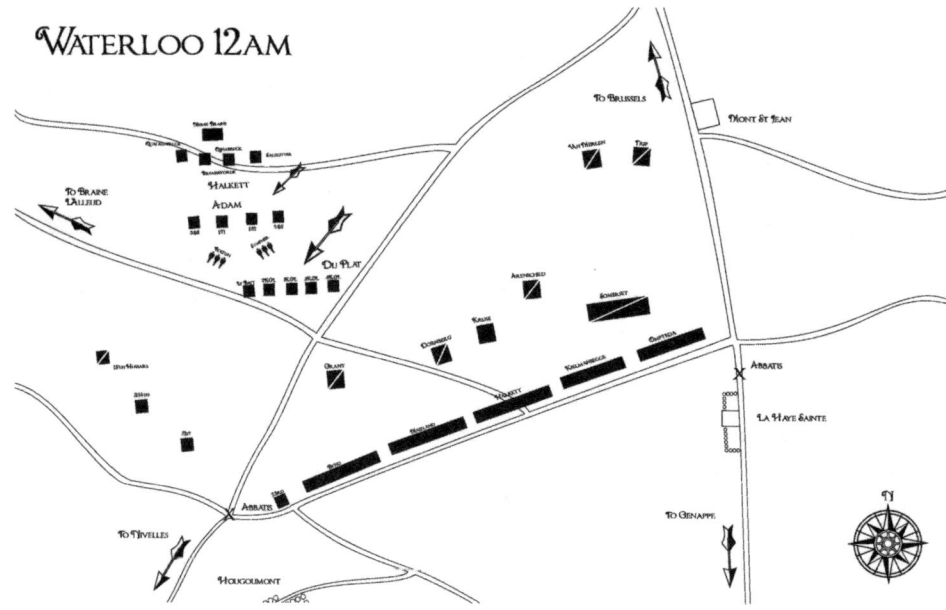

readily to learn what was passing, and, in case either of success or disaster, to be prepared to do our duty or to follow in the retreat.[8]

Ensign William Leeke recalled finding a fire to warm himself at and fell asleep for three hours, only to be woken by his servant announcing breakfast, although the scanty morsels on offer could hardly be deemed sufficient to bear the name.

> Some little time after we were all stirring, I wandered off a short distance to a fire belonging to the 71st, at which one or two officers were standing; I was very glad to get the opportunity of warming and drying myself. I found a plank, of about my own length, near the fire; where it came from I have no idea, but I took the liberty, as no one was using it, of laying myself at full length on it before the fire; I very soon fell asleep and must have slept three hours, which much refreshed me, when my servant came to tell me some breakfast was going on amongst the officers of Captain McNair's company, the company to which I belonged. Our breakfast consisted of a biscuit each and some soup, which was in one of the servants' mess tins; I was, unintentionally on his part, done out of my drink of broth by one of the officers exclaiming, just as I put my lips to the tin, 'Come, Master Leeke, I think you have had your share of that.' This half-mouthful of broth and a biscuit were all I tasted that day until after nine o'clock, when I got a lump of bread about as big as my fist from a French loaf.[9]

It would appear that Private Patrick Kibby of Captain Love's Company, acting as a servant to Lieutenant Colonel Charles Rowan, deserted during the battle,

---

8. Glover, The Waterloo Archive Volume VI, p 236.
9. Leeke, p 19.

taking Colonel Rowan's horse with him. Meanwhile, Ensign Shaw had arrived at Brussels and having arranged for the baggage to be parked safely, he immediately set out again for Waterloo, hoping to rejoin the regiment before the battle commenced, he was to be disappointed:

> I arrived there on the morning of the 18th; and, having deposited all my baggage in the court of my old quarters, proceeded straightway to the field of battle. I arrived at the village of Waterloo about 9 o'clock, and on application to the aide de camp of General Clinton,[10] was instantly ordered back to my duty. Thus were all my aspirations and wishes to take part in the glories of that day entirely defeated, it was no fault of mine. I did all I could, to 'share in the triumph', but was unsuccessful.[11]

Leeke also noted that Captain Diggle's company had been ordered into the village of Merbe Braine along with two or three companies of the 95th Foot:

> Early on the 18th, Captain Diggle's company No. 1 of the 52nd, was sent with two or three companies of the 95th into the enclosures of the village of Merbe Braine, facing Braine-la-leud [Braine l'Alleud]; they were withdrawn sometime before the action commenced.[12]

Lieutenant George Gawler of the 52nd confirms the deployment of Diggle's company to Merbe Braine as he was with them.

> After daylight on the morning of the 18th June some companies of the brigade were sent to occupy Merbe Braine. The 52nd gave its right company, to which I belonged. This company was posted in the garden of a small country house, of which the westernmost hedge was the limit, on that side, of the enclosures of Merbe Braine.
> On the summit of the rise towards Braine-la-Leud two or three battalion columns were in sight, which proved to be Dutch or Belgic.[13]

Lieutenant John Hart of the same company also confirms their deployment as skirmishers but does not mention Merbe Braine:

> The next morning, No.1 company, in which I was, was ordered on picquet and remained there about five hours when we heard the French were moving to attack our left, we immediately joined the regiment and marched to the field, which was between the town of Braine le Leud [Braine l'Alleud] and the high road leading to Brussels, which they wanted to gain.[14]

These troops at Merbe Braine were undoubtedly sent there with the intention of preparing the village as a defensive bastion. The position also secured their communications with the Netherlands division commanded by General Chasse,

---

10. Captain Francis Dawkins of the 1st Foot Guards.
11. Shaw, p 52.
12. Leeke, p 19.
13. Letter to William Siborne, The Waterloo Letters, p 288.
14. Lieutenant John Hart's letter dated 20 June 1815.

which held the much larger town of Braine l'Alleud for similar reasons. The position of this village precluded its use in the battle, as it was over 500 metres behind the allied front line. A number of roads and tracks emanated from the village and led northward through the Forest of Soignes and these undoubtedly would have been needed in the event of the army being forced to retreat through the forest. The village would act as a bastion protecting the line of retreat and would hopefully delay the pursuing French troops, allowing them the time to safely debouch through the woods. However, no sappers were sent to secure Merbe Braine, whilst those ordered to Braine l'Alleud failed to arrive and eventually the Duke of Wellington abandoned any attempt to defend it and had the companies of the Light Brigade sent back to their regiments.

Charles Holman, an old peninsular hand, did not write of his sufferings however, they were just something he had to expect and endure. He was much more matter of fact:

> At 10am got under arms after having finished our cooking and marched to take up a position with our left on the Nivelles road and our right stretching towards the church of Braine La Leud [l'Alleud], where we formed line and laid down.[15]

William Leeke agrees that they got under arms about 10.00 hours, but he was more enamoured by receiving a warm smile from General 'Daddy' Hill as the men affectionately called him:

> About ten o'clock, Lord Hill, with his staff, came galloping along, about fifty yards in the rear of the 52nd, through the high corn;[16] he was riding towards the extreme right of our position; as he passed me, I recollect he gave me one of his pleasant smiles. Shortly after this we got under arms.[17]

He states that they did not move until 11.00 hours.

> About eleven o'clock the 52nd moved from the ground on which it had bivouacked, about 300 yards more to the rear. The right wing of the regiment was in column of subdivisions, about twenty yards in front of the steep bank between it and Merbe Braine; the left wing was in line to the left of the front sub-division of the right wing, with an interval of a few paces between the wings. Captain Siborne, in his first plan of the field of Waterloo, places the

---

15. Holman Lt, Journal for 1815, Royal Green Jackets Museum, Winchester.
16. There does seem to be some variance in the heights of the corn at Quatre Bras and at Waterloo. It is stated by virtually every soldier who has left us any memories of the Battle of Quatre Bras that the corn grew beyond head height which made the visibility for anyone who was not riding a horse very restricted. At Waterloo, even given that some areas of cultivation were trampled down by the masses of troops, it is very noticeable that almost no one states that the corn was above their heads or indeed that their visibility was severely hampered by the corn. Indeed, virtually everyone who mentions the corn at Waterloo describes it as being waist high. The reasoning for this could be different crop varietals or even a different micro-climate, but Leeke is almost alone in describing the corn at Waterloo as head high.
17. Leeke, p 20.

52nd, when in reserve, 200 yards more in advance, and 100 yards more to the eastward than they were.[18]

At about this time, Lieutenant William Ogilvy recalls being called with a party of men under the command of Colonel William Rowan to proceed to the left, with entrenching tools; its destination can only be guessed at, but they were soon recalled as the cannonade began.

> One additional circumstance, which I have not seen anywhere mentioned, occurred shortly before the action. An order came for a working party from the brigade with intrenching tools; it was accordingly paraded; William Rowan, now General Sir William Rowan, commanded it, and it chanced to be my turn for that duty also. When ready, I heard the Brigade Major direct Rowan to march on a single tree, far to our left, where he would receive further orders. The party, however, had proceeded but a very short way, when the French attack on Hougoumont commenced, and we were immediately recalled. I have since had very little doubt that the purpose was to have used the working party to strengthen the post of La Haye Sainte, had time allowed, and it was unfortunate it was not thought of a few hours sooner.[19]

The Return shown previously dated 11 June 1815 was the last official muster recorded before the Battle of Waterloo, which shows the battalion with 998 men in the field.[20] This number is the nearest we have to an official figure for those actually at the battle, but having lost a few men on the lengthy marches and a few more being sent off to escort the baggage to Brussels, the battalion must have numbered less than 990 officers and men on the day. Following the losses incurred by the Guard battalions at Quatre Bras, it is very likely that the 52nd was the strongest British battalion at the commencement of the battle. This clearly shows that Captain William Chalmers' statement, cannot be anywhere near correct, when he states that 'The strength of the 52nd Lt Infantry was 1,148 including all ranks on going into action.'[21]

Even Captain William Rowan, who forwarded Chalmers' letter to Siborne, explained that this figure was way too high: 'I think he must mean that we had 1,148 of all ranks in the country, having shortly before received all the effective men of our 2nd Battalion; from that number must be deducted the sick, batmen etc etc which left about 1,000 bayonets when in squares.[22]

---

18. Leeke, pp 21–2.
19. Letter of William Ogilvy, quoted in Leeke, pp 20–21.
20. William Siborne undoubtedly used this return to provide a figure for the battalion at Waterloo as he shows 1,038 present, which just happens to be the total figure of the battalion on this same return, but includes those sick and those 'on command' who would not have been at the battle. This would indicate that Siborne's return, showing the effective strengths of all of the allied battalions at Waterloo is likely to be overstated by some 5 per cent. See Siborne's History of the Waterloo Campaign pp 531–4.
21. Glover, Letters from the Battle of Waterloo, p 180.
22. ibid, p 182.

Ensigns William Leeke and William Nettles were ordered to carry the two stands of Colours, despite the fact that it was not their turn for the duty. By an error of Major William Chalmers, despite Leeke carrying the Regimental Colour, as he was the junior ensign, was placed in the right wing of the regiment with companies numbered 1 to 5, rather than with the left wing which consisted of companies 6–10, as he should have been. This, he believed, probably occurred because the Colours were mere shreds, but the error was not rectified and Ensign Nettles carrying the King's Colour was eventually killed in that position, where Leeke should have stood. Leeke later became a cleric, this incident may well have had some influence on his calling.

> Nettles and I were warned by Winterbottom, the adjutant, that we were to carry the Colours; on our taking them over from the sergeants, we both agreed that it was not our turn to carry the Colours, and wondered why we had been told off to them. I recollect observing, that it would suit me very well, that I had not been long enough in the regiment (I had only joined five weeks before) to be of any other use, but that I could carry a Colour. Major William Chalmers rode up to us and said, 'The regiment is going to act in separate wings; I am going to command the right wing, and one of you gentlemen will go to my wing', and addressing me, he added, 'You, sir, will go to the right wing.' Now I was anxious, as I did not know so much of the other officers as I did of those belonging to my own company, No. 9, to be in the left wing with them, which I knew was the proper wing for the Regimental Colour, carried by me as the junior ensign of the two. I therefore ventured to tell Major Chalmers that mine was the Regimental Colour which should be with the left wing, but he did not choose to rectify the immaterial mistake, which nobody else, probably, discovered at the time, for our Colours, which had been with the regiment and the Light Division all through the Peninsular war, were little more than bare poles. Immediately afterwards, poor Nettles and I separated, not to meet again; he was killed by a cannon shot, about seven o'clock in the evening.[23]

Leeke goes on to state that there was some possibility of confusion over William Chalmers: 'There were two brevet majors by the name of William Chalmers in the 52nd; the one at Waterloo, being a dark man, was always called "Black Will", the other, "White Will"'.[24]

He is mistaken here. There were indeed two Captain William Chalmers in the regiment in 1815, but only the one at Waterloo was a major in the Army. The second William Chalmers, or 'White Will', was a junior captain in the 2nd Battalion in England.

It would seem likely that the movement forward occurred nearer to 11.00 hours as the firing, signifying the commencement of the battle, appears to have begun soon afterwards. Whilst lying down in this position in the rear of Wellington's

---

23. Leeke, p 20.
24. Leeke, p 21.

ridge a few cannon shots denoted the commencement of the action and it soon rose to a crescendo as hundreds of French and allied cannon bellowed forth. General Adam stated in a letter to William Siborne that: 'The first position taken up by the 3rd Brigade was nearly that marked on the plan, formed by battalions in columns of companies at quarter distance, In this position the brigade remained in reserve with piled arms.'[25]

Almost all of the other eyewitnesses agree that they were in battalion columns (the 52nd because of its size in two columns of wings[26]), lying down in an effort to avoid the worst of the cannonade, but men were still occasionally struck whilst lying on the ground, never to rise again.

To a man, throughout the army, those with a pocket watch, took them out and made a mental note of the time of the start of the battle, but unfortunately watches were not synchronised, and every version gives a different time. According to William Leeke, the cannonade commenced:

> Exactly at twelve o'clock, by Chalmers's watch, the battle was begun by a cannon shot fired from the French position at the Duke of Wellington, who, with a numerous assemblage of general and other staff officers, had taken post about a third of a mile in our front on the high ground in rear of the north eastern corner of the enclosure of Hougoumont, from whence he could see the greater part of the French position. Such an assemblage was sure to attract the attention of the enemy, and unnecessarily to bring on itself the opening cannonade. It was said the Duke told some of the generals they were 'rather too thick upon the ground'.[27]

Captain John Hart of the 52nd also thought that the cannonade began around 12.00 hours: 'About 12 o'clock we arrived on the ground when there commenced a most tremendous cannonade and the balls fell just amongst our regiment.[28] He also admitted that he had to pull himself together and give himself a stern talking to: 'Curious sensation before I went into the heat of battle and all I could do would not hinder me from bobbing, though the balls flew 100 yards over my head, but that was only for a little while, as I soon got accustomed to them.'[29]

Charles Holman also thought the action began around about 12.00 hours, his experienced eye also noted a French movement to probe the allied right wing towards Braine l'Alleud:

> The artillery were just beginning to announce the feat and as we were directly behind them, we lost a great many men from the ricochet [sic] shot. About 12 the firing seemed to increase and was soon followed by heavy musquetry on our left. Observed the enemy stretching his left to Mon Plaisir and saw

---

25. Letter of General Frederick Adam to William Siborne, The Waterloo Letters p 275.
26. Battalions were normally of ten companies which could be split into two wings of five companies when required.
27. Leeke, p 23.
28. Lieutenant John Hart's letter dated 20 June 1815.
29. Lieutenant John Hart's letter dated 20 June 1815.

several fine charges of cavalry close to it. The enemy appeared to have entire possession of it, on which they brought up some artillery and still attempted to stretch their left towards Braine l'Alleud but were continually driven back by the skirmishers of the 51st L[ight] I[nfantry][30, 31]

This movement on the extreme right of the allied position was also noticed by Colonel John Colborne who, 'Desirous of seeing the commencement of the action, I rode with Colonel Rowan to a commanding eminence. My attention was directed to the French lancers, which showed themselves near the crossroad leading to Braine-la-Leud [Braine l'Alleud] and cheering.'[32]

After enjoying a hearty breakfast, no doubt, General Hill's Staff rode back to the front. Captain Orlando Bridgeman thought the cannon began firing at 11:30, noting: 'we then went out again, about half past eleven the enemy showed some columns of cavalry & infantry upon which our guns opened, from that time the action increased.'[33]

However, according to Captain Oldfield of the Royal Engineers, the first shot was at 11.20 hours: 'First shot fired 11.20 according to Diggle (52nd), others say 11 a.m.'[34] Lieutenant Gawler agrees:

> While in this garden we heard the first cannon shot of the battle, fired in the direction of Hougoumont. An officer [Diggle?] near me pulled out his watch and said it was 'Twenty minutes past 11 o'clock.' Soon after this, it might be about 12 o'clock, we were ordered to rejoin the brigade. When we cleared the enclosures of the village it was seen standing in open column in about the position B. The brigade almost immediately advanced, the 52nd halted in close or quarter distance columns of wings at about C. I feel much confidence as to the ground, as near that point its outline is remarkable. The crop about us was very low.[35]

The battalion lay down a few hundred yards behind the allied ridge line in a position to protect the allied artillery along the ridge line if necessary. However, it was not a completely safe location, as some of the cannon balls fired at the allied batteries flew over the ridge, whilst others were fired specifically to arc over the ridge crest and land amongst the masses of infantry, which Napoleon assumed the Duke of Wellington would be holding in reserve, just behind the ridge line. Ensign Leeke recalls that he saw the effects of the first cannon balls he had ever faced and that a number of casualties were suffered by the regiment whilst in this position:

> Whilst we were in reserve above the village of Merbe Braine, the regiment suffered several casualties from the shot and shell which passed over the

---

30. The 2nd Yorkshire West Riding Regiment.
31. Holman Lt, Journal for 1815, Royal Green Jackets Museum, Winchester.
32. Colborne's letter to Siborne, The Waterloo Letters, p 282.
33. Glover, Waterloo Archive Volume IV, p 26.
34. ibid, p 211.
35. Siborne, The Waterloo Letters p 287.

British position in our front. I think the first occurred to Major Chalmers. The regiment was lying down; I was forced to remain with the Colour in rear of the centre subdivision of the right wing, but several of the officers were standing in a group round Chalmers's horse when a ricochet shot came lobbing in amongst them, but fortunately did no other injury than that of breaking the horse's leg; Chalmers drew a pistol from his holster and put the animal out of his misery. Most of our casualties at this time were occasioned by shells bursting over us, but we saw many cannon-shot ploughing up the ground near us; I had been already regarding several of them with great respect, when my Colour Sergeant, Rhodes,[36] who took great care of me and showed me much kindness all the day, said, pointing to a shot passing through the standing corn, on the right of the column, 'There, Mr Leeke, is a cannon shot, if you never saw one before. Sir!' Sergeant Houseley,[37] whilst standing in rear of the column, narrowly escaped having a round shot through him, by stooping just as he saw it in a line with him at some little distance; this was quite allowable when his comrades were lying down at their ease.[38] One of my narrow escapes occurred whilst we were lying here in reserve; I had my head against my Colour sergeant's knapsack, and was trying, but in vain, to get some sleep, when all at once there was a great rattle against the mess tins, which, fitting one within the other, were strapped to the back of every man's knapsack; a piece of shell about the size and about as thick as the half of the palm of one's hand, had struck, and lodged in the inner tin; we both sat up, and he extracted the inner tin and the piece of shell, saying, as he pitched them both away, 'If that had hit either you or me on the head Sir, I think it would have settled our business for us.'[39]

Lieutenant George Hall of the 52nd, speaking of the casualties which occurred at this time, wrote of one lucky man:

A young lad, (Kearns[40]) of our company was struck by a cannon shot and was borne off motionless and white as a sheet. Those about me and myself concluded he was dying. Two or three days afterwards I could scarcely believe my eyes, when I saw him walk into the bivouac. The shot had carried away his pouch so cleanly, that he suffered no injury beyond the temporary shock and fright.[41]

Captain William Eeles of the 95th Rifles confirms that the brigade, being behind the guns, did suffer from the artillery fire, but states that the 3/95th being on the

---

36. The Waterloo Prize Money Roll and Medal Roll shows Jeremiah Rhodes as a sergeant in Captain Robert Campbell's company. It would appear that Leeke is in error as to his rank at Waterloo.
37. The Waterloo Prize Money Roll and the Waterloo Medal Roll shows Benjamin Housley as a corporal in Captain Diggle's company. It would appear that Leeke is in error as to his rank at Waterloo.
38. It was not the done thing for officers or men to duck when stood up in line.
39. Leeke, pp 23–4.
40. This would appear to be Private Timothy Kyrnes on the Waterloo Prize Roll and incorrectly shown as Timothy Lyrnes on the Waterloo Medal Roll, in Captain McNair's company.
41. Quoted in Leeke, pp 24–5.

right in some enclosures, did not lose a man.[42] Certainly the 2/95th on the left of the brigade was suffering, as Captain Logan recalled:

> About 12 o'clock on the 18th June the action commenced. Our brigade (General Adam's) was formed in columns of battalions in rear of our guns; here we were cruelly mauled with shot & shell. About five minutes after we went into action I succeeded to the command of the battalion in consequence from three field officers being severely wounded.[43]

William Leeke estimated that they remained in this position in reserve for three hours:

> The 52nd remained about three hours in reserve just above Merbe Braine, and during that time three [he only lists two] of the principal attacks of the French took place on our position. The first of these was made on the post of Hougoumont, ... [and] a grand attack which the Emperor caused to be made about half-past one or two on ... the [left of the] Allied position, by the whole of Count d'Erlon's corps.[44]

Leeke underestimated the time they spent in this position, even if they only arrived there at 11.00 hours as he states. It was not until just before 16.00 hours that they were ordered to advance into the front line as will be seen. However, he does give us a realistic idea of the losses suffered by the regiment from cannon fire whilst in this position:

> On our leaving this ground I looked back and saw we had left two poor fellows in 52nd uniform lying dead under a tree, and [I] could scarcely refrain from shedding tears at the melancholy sight; one of them was the assistant sergeant major, a man greatly respected in the regiment. We lost, whilst in reserve, these two men killed, and I think about ten or twelve men wounded, who were taken to Merbe Braine.[45, 46]

---

42. Siborne, The Waterloo Letters p 303.
43. Glover, Waterloo Archive Volume I, p 217.
44. Leeke, p 25.
45. Leeke, p 24.
46. The wounded were actually ordered to be taken to the church of Braine l'Alleud.

Chapter 7

The Great Cavalry Attacks 16.00–18.00 Hours

The battle had raged for some four and a half hours, whilst the men of the 52nd Foot and the rest of the Light Brigade simply lay down to avoid the cannon balls, many so exhausted that they fell asleep, whilst awaiting their moment.

The heavy fighting continued around Hougoumont chateau and Napoleon's great attack with d'Erlon's entire corps on Wellington's left flank had been defeated with heavy losses on both sides. Marshal Ney now looked to launch a huge cavalry attack on the allied centre-right (the allied right actually extending as far as Braine l'Alleud), assuming that the intense cannonade had severely weakened Wellington's troops, which could not be seen, but were undoubtedly stationed just beyond the ridge to protect the allied artillery lining the crest of the ridge.

Napoleon later claimed that he had no idea that Marshal Ney was about to launch almost 10,000 French cavalry at the allied ridge, in an attempt to replicate the stunning victory at the Battle of Eylau.[1] This requires us to believe however, that although stationed less than 500 metres south of La Belle Alliance, that he was completely unaware that thousands of his cavalry were marching across the chaussee from his right wing, to form up with thousands more taken from his left wing and were then launched in waves at the allied ridge without his knowledge, until it was too late. That is very hard to believe. The fact that he then made no counter-orders to stop the attacks and even allowed further cavalry units to be drawn into subsequent attacks over the best part of the next two hours, proves that he knew and fully approved of it, until it failed!

For over four hours, the French cannonade along the allied centre had been relentless and casualties in the rear of the allied ridge had mounted slowly but steadily, however the allied troops were far from disorganised or demoralised.

Having become aware of the obvious build-up of very large numbers of cavalry in his front, Wellington ordered his troops to form a chequerboard of squares behind the ridge line, close enough to the summit to protect the guns on the crest with their musket fire and for the gunners to retreat into them for their protection.[2]

---

1. At the Battle of Eylau in 1807, Napoleon's forces were on the verge of defeat, when he launched Marshal Murat's reserve of 11,000 cavalry at the Russians. The charge broke through two lines of infantry, overran the Russian artillery and drove off a large cavalry counter-attack.
2. It is commonly stated that all of the artillery were ordered to do this, but it is clear from the evidence, that many artillery units had not received or failed to act on these orders, leading to the Duke of

Ney launched his cavalry in lines, in wave upon wave against the allied ridge. The allied artillery initially caused heavy casualties on the French cavalry formations as they trotted across the muddy shallow valley which divided the two armies. As the cavalry rode closer to the guns, they were now struck by cannister shot, but still they rode on. As they reached the allied guns, some of the artillerymen took refuge in the squares or under their cannon, a few remained at their guns and drove the cavalry off, but many others removed themselves and their guns far to the rear.

Many historians criticise the French cavalry for failing to disable the allied cannon whilst they were temporarily in their possession. They argue that armed with a mallet and iron spikes or nails, they could have hammered them into the touchhole of the cannon, rendering it useless until the hole could be bored out again in a workshop. The problem with this criticism, is that no cavalry of any nation, to my knowledge, carried mallets and nails for this purpose and I have been unable to identify one occasion during the entire twenty-three years of this worldwide conflict, where any cavalryman ever 'spiked' a cannon. The simple reason for this being, that no cavalryman would willingly dismount so near to the enemy and even if they did, they were unlikely to survive being fired on at close range from the nearby squares whilst they attempted to disable it.

The Duke of Wellington has never written about what he thought when he saw the masses of cavalry being prepared, but as an avid student of military history, he would have been fully aware of the devastating success of the French cavalry at Eylau and undoubtedly would have considered measures to counter such an attack.

He organised the regiments of his front line into a chequerboard of squares, carefully laid out to avoid the face of each square firing directly at another. He also looked to his light cavalry, who were positioned to counter-attack the French cavalry after they had been greatly thinned by musket fire and disorganised from having to funnel between the squares.

The Light Brigade had been moved in columns to a position near the Nivelle road and of here the men witnessed the first attacks of the French cavalry. Just after the first waves of French cavalry crested the allied ridge, the Duke ordered Adam's Brigade to advance past the squares and then, once formed in line four deep, to drive off some infantry. As there was insufficient room to deploy, the 52nd advanced in a second line forming a sort of reserve. Having driven off the infantry, they then proceeded to pass over the allied ridge line onto the forward slope. Here, they encountered French cavalry and immediately formed into squares, the 52nd forming two squares of wings. General Frederick Adam confirmed this sequence of movements in a letter to William Siborne:

> The brigade remained in reserve with piled arms until the enemy's cavalry gained the crest of the position running from the [rear of] Hougoumont

---

Wellington being very dissatisfied with the performance of much of the artillery, particularly during the cavalry attacks.

towards La Haye Sainte. When this was perceived the men stood to their arms, as we expected the cavalry of the enemy would break the small Brunswick battalions which were down the slope. The contrary occurred and the Brunswickers stood firm, and the enemy's cavalry retired. Shortly after this the 3rd Brigade was ordered to advance; which it did in the order in which it was formed, to the Nivelles road, on the edge of which it remained for some time exposed to a fire of artillery, by which a considerable number of men were disabled.

After crossing the Nivelles road, the Duke of Wellington personally directed that the brigade should form line four deep 'and drive those fellows away', meaning some French infantry. There was not space to form the 52nd in line with the 71st and 95th, and the 52nd consequently was a sort of reserve to the brigade. The enemy's infantry were very soon disposed of, and the brigade continued to advance to where the cavalry of the enemy, being prepared to attack, the brigade was formed in columns and then in squares.[3]

This advance, by general consensus, must have occurred shortly after 16.00 hours, although eyewitnesses are unsurprisingly all over the place with their timings. Lieutenant Charles Holman wrote soon after the battle, that:

At 2 [we] received an order to form square,[4] which we instantly did and advanced towards Hougoumont. The instant we had mounted a small height in front, the finest sight ever seen, presented itself to our view, fourteen squares of different nations formed and the French cavalry most gallantly charging along the whole front faces of the squares between the artillery, without being able to break them and the squares in their turns giving a most murderous fire of musquetry, they retired almost immediately, when our artillerymen, who had saved themselves under the guns, gave them a fire the instant they turned their backs. We advanced and passed in front of the artillery and saw an amazing body of cuirassiers formed in our front.[5]

Ensign Leeke thought that the advance into the front line occurred an hour or so later, but he also mistakenly stated that they advanced in squares, whereas we know that they advanced in four deep line – indeed he corrects his own statement later:

About three o'clock or a little after, the whole regiment formed open column of companies to the left, and proceeded about a quarter of a mile along the right of the road from Braine la leud [Braine l'Alleud], in an eastern direction, nearly to the angle formed by the junction of that road with that running from Nivelles to Brussels and formed square on No 10 [Captain

---

3. Siborne, The Waterloo Letters, p 276.
4. They only formed squares once on the forward slope as will be shown.
5. Holman Lt, Journal for 1815, Royal Green Jackets Museum, Winchester.

Shedden's] company. We there saw the grand charge of the French cavalry, before described, all along the British position, a quarter of a mile in our front, and numbers of our guns deserted.[6] Colonel Charles Rowan addressed the regiment, and said, he did not think 'those fellows would come near us, but that if they did we would give them a warm reception.' Sir John Colborne was somewhere away in front at that time. Almost immediately after the formation of the square, the 52nd advanced in square, up to, and over the British position.[7] Some little time before it crossed the position, Cottingham,[8] who was the first officer wounded, was struck by a spent cannonball on the right ankle. He had a trick of continually exclaiming 'By Jove!' and was often joked about it. I had a little joke against him on the subject, as on our march up from Ostend, in describing to me an attack by a German regiment of cavalry on a body of French, he concluded by saying, 'By Jove, they cut them up like sparrows.' When he received this very severe contusion, he was immediately supported by one of the sergeants, and hopped about on his other foot, crying out 'Oh, by Jove, by Jove!' One could hardly help smiling at the exclamation. This shot must have been fired from the extreme left of the French army, at the troops of Mitchell's or Du Plat's Brigade, stationed on the higher ground in rear of Hougoumont, and have first taken the ground near them. It passed over, or through the lengthened out right face of the 52nd square and spent its strength on poor Cottingham's ankle. I was marching about five or six feet behind him; and first of all thought it was a shell, but, on looking at it, I found it to be a roundshot, from one of the French twelve-pounder batteries.[9]

On the position we passed over the spot on which one of the Brunswick squares had stood and found lying there many of their killed and badly wounded men. They had suffered most severely from roundshot and shells. It was one of the most shocking sights we saw even on that most blood-stained battlefield. One poor fellow, whose thigh was completely taken off high up, by the explosion of a shell at the moment it struck him, and who was black in the face, raised himself and caught hold of the hand of one of our men, and then fell dead. Another, who had not long to live, shook the

---

6. There is very strong evidence to support the view that despite the Duke of Wellington's orders for the gunners to retire to the squares during the cavalry charges, that a number of batteries either did not get this order or ignored it. Reading the witness statements of a number of those in the batteries deployed along the ridge just before the cavalry charged, it becomes clear that a number retired on mass, either with or without their guns to the rear of the cavalry who were stationed behind the infantry squares, some claim this was because they were short of ammunition, but this is questionable, as records show that they did not fire any more rounds than other batteries, who do not appear to have vacated the ridge. This would appear to be the basis of the Duke's critical letter written to Earl Mulgrave on 21 December 1815.
7. Leeke is mistaken, it advanced in four deep line and formed squares after crossing over the ridge to the front, he confirms his own error later in his statement.
8. Lieutenant Thomas Cottingham of the 52nd Foot.
9. Poor Cottingham's injury, although causing some mirth for Leeke, was actually quite serious and he was listed as 'severely wounded'.

hand of another 52nd man, as we were passing to the front, and cried 'Brave Anglais.' Close to this was a Brunswick square, prepared to receive cavalry, with the front rank kneeling, as steady as a rock;[10] but whether it was the square these wounded men belonged to, which had been removed out of its exposed position, or another square, I know not. We must have passed here near to the right square of Maitland's Brigade of Guards, but we saw nothing of them.[11] Our advance was just at the close of the first attack of the French cavalry on the Allied squares.[12]

Lieutenant George Gawler recalled the initial move forward but put it down to a desire to get out of the worst of the cannonade rather than as preparation for an advance. He also honestly admits that he was far too busy to take any notice of what the rest of the brigade were doing, they actually moved together. He correctly thought that the advance beyond the allied ridge began shortly after 16.00 hours.

> In consequence of this annoyance from the cannonade, the 52nd went over the rise [not the main ridge] to the ground D or *D,[13] I think the former... I do not know positively what became of the other regiments of the brigade during this interval, but suppose them to have remained at short distances from the 52nd. The crops about the spot D were very high.
>
> I cannot speak with confidence to the precise time, but calculating from other occurrences of which the times are fixed, I think it must have been after four o'clock when the 52nd left the point D. It then proceeded in wing square by the track a a a.[14]

The brigade had marched beyond the allied squares and now continued over the allied ridge line, past the remaining allied cannon lining the crest, into the valley in front, driving the French infantry away. However, as they crested the ridge in columns of wings, they became a prime target for the French artillery, who were starved of much to aim at and did not waste this golden opportunity.

---

10. It is interesting to note that Leeke refers to the Brunswickers as standing like rocks. These Brunswick troops are the same that Mercer describes as: 'very boys whom I had but yesterday seen throwing away their arms and fleeing' and 'I glanced at the Brunswickers, and that glance told me it would not do'. This has coloured British perceptions of the Brunswickers ever since. It is however very interesting to gauge the British attitudes at the time just before Waterloo, when they are described very differently. A random selection from the author's Waterloo Archive Volume VII reveals that, 'The Brunswicks did well' wrote Captain Taylor of the10th Hussars; 'the Brunswick infantry are some of the finest troops that ever were' agreed Ensign St John 1st Foot Guards; 'The gallant and noble conduct of the Brunswickers was the admiration of everyone', said Lieutenant Colonel Colquitt 1st Foot Guards; and, 'a finer body of men I never beheld' concurred Captain Oldfield of the Royal Engineers.
11. The Guards were certainly there somewhere, such throw away remarks by Leeke do tend to show that his judgement on the actions of the Guards is very biased.
12. Leeke, p 29.
13. The letters refer to points on a copy of Siborne's map depicting the 52nd's position at various times. It is reproduced in this volume on pages 66/67.
14. Siborne, The Waterloo Letters, pp 288–9.

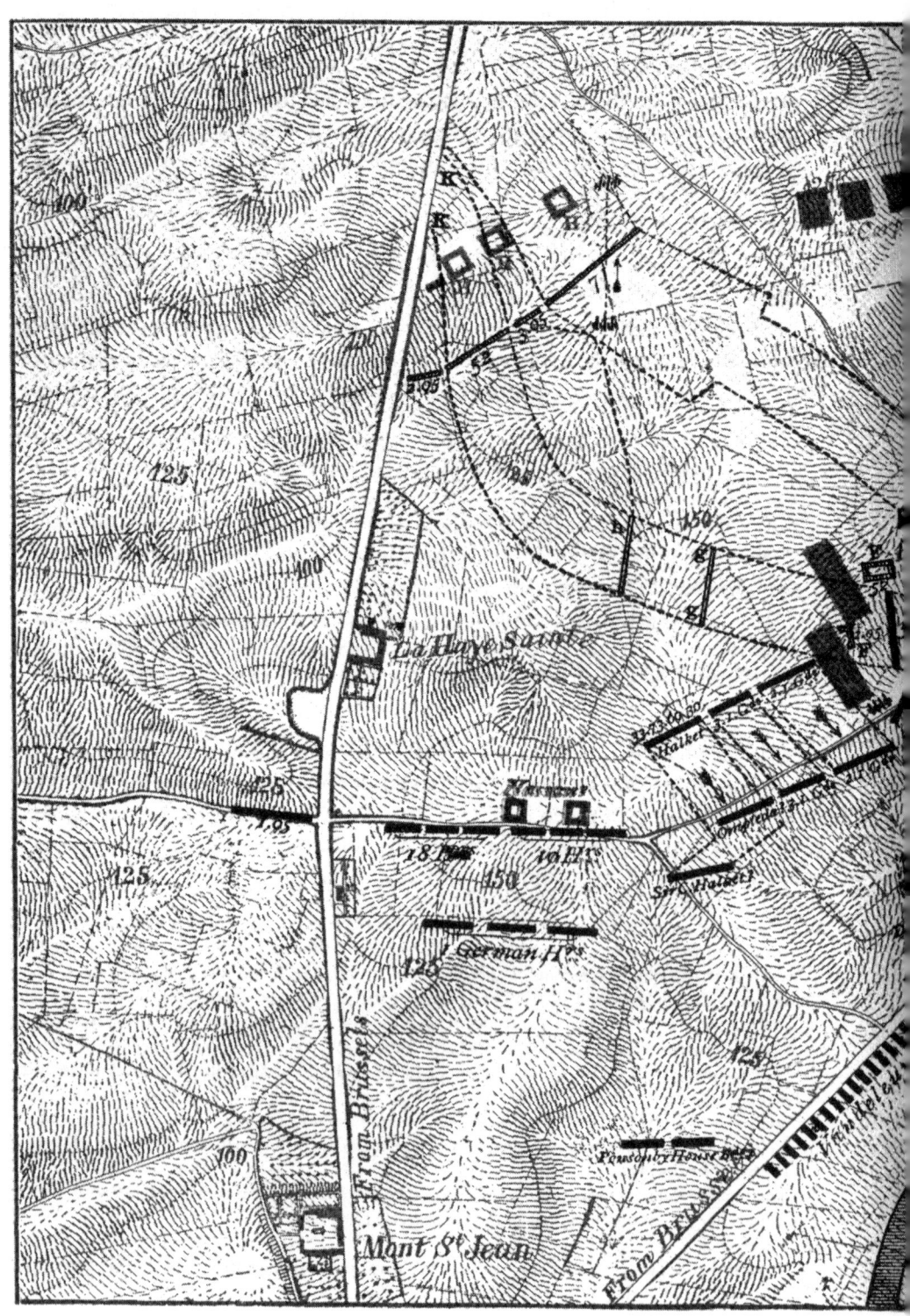

The Great Cavalry Attacks 16.00–18.00 Hours 67

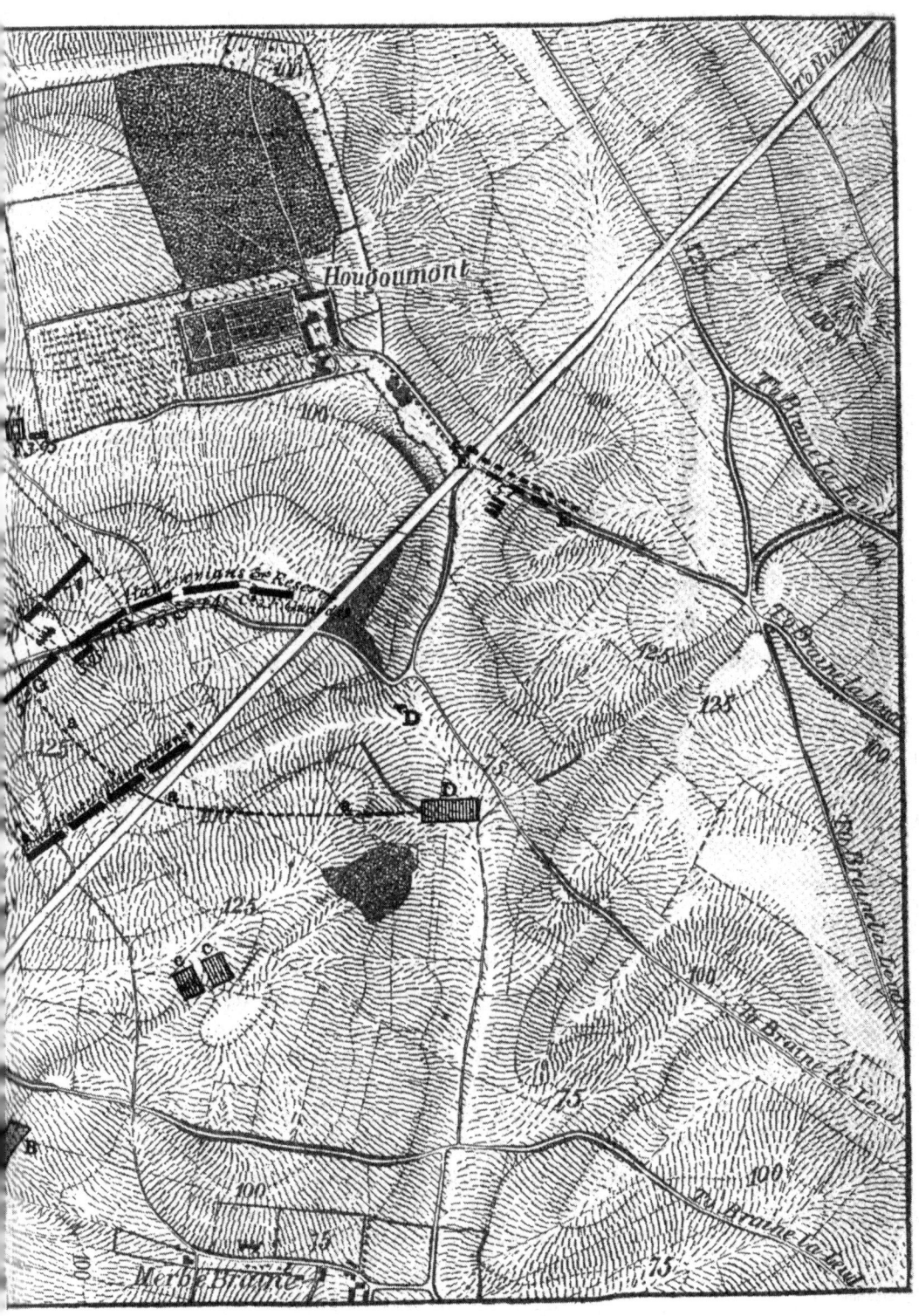

Lieutenant Colonel John Colborne had been absent for quite some time, presumably viewing the battle further to the front. He returned to the battalion just as they began the march forward to clear the enemy skirmishers:

> I returned to the 52nd Regiment, which was on the march in column, and advancing towards the cross road [the ridge line] that connects the high road from Genappe to Waterloo, and the road from Nivelles to Waterloo. The 52nd continued its march to the valley which separated the right central part of our position from the enemy, and halted about five hundred yards in front of the cross road [on the ridge line]. I rode up the opposite ascent and observed two guns pointed, and firing at our column. I returned, and called out to Captain Shedden, the officer leading the column, and desired him to tell me whether he could see these guns.[15]

Whether Shedden could see the guns or not, the brigade certainly suffered from the French artillery as it crossed the ridge line and advanced down the outer face. Private Lewis of the 2/95th described the mayhem:

> My front-rank man was wounded by a part of a shell through the foot & he dropt [sic] as we was advancing. I covered the next man I saw and had not walked twenty steps before a musket shot came sideways and took his nose clean off, & then I covered another man which was the third; just after that the man that stood next to me on my left hand had his left arm shot off by a nine pound shot just above his elbow & he turned round and caught hold of me with his right hand & the blood ran all over my trousers, we was advancing so he dropt directly.[16]

Captain William Eeles of the 3/95th recalled that the 71st found itself very close to a large body of formed French infantry near Hougoumont orchard and had to sustain a heavy musketry duel before they drove them off, only then to be assailed by cuirassiers:

> The brigade advanced to the front. There was at this time a tremendous cannonade both from the English and French batteries, and the smoke was so dense that I cannot venture any description of the appearance of the field…The brigade continued to advance through the smoke until it passed beyond the crest of the British position; on the smoke clearing away, the 71st Regiment, with whom my company of the 3rd Battalion 95th Regiment was then acting, found itself while in column very close to and in front of a large body of the enemy's infantry, formed in line, and dressed in grey greatcoats. The 71st immediately formed line, and I placed my company of rifles [3/95th] on the right of that regiment. I can only here observe that the French and 71st were closer than I ever before saw any regular formed adverse bodies, and much nearer than troops usually engage. The French

---

15. ibid, pp 282–3.
16. Glover, Waterloo Archive Volume I, p 159.

opened a very heavy fire on the 71st, who, nevertheless, completed their formation in the most regular and gallant style. I formed my company on their right, and in line. During this operation the 71st and the company of the [3/]95th suffered severely but immediately on being formed succeeded in repulsing the enemy, who retired almost unobserved in the smoke. Finding, however, notwithstanding the retreat of the French, that many men, both in the 71st and the company of the [3/]95th, were still falling, I moved my company forward, and found a considerable number of the enemy in a dell in a rye field, from which place they were firing on the 71st. The company I commanded immediately attacked and drove them back to their position on the hill.

While we were so employed I observed a large body of the enemy's cavalry advancing to attack us. We had just time to get back and form in rear of the 71st square, when the enemy attacked that regiment with much impetuosity and determination. The charge was received with the utmost coolness and gallantry by the 71st. The cavalry were repulsed in this instance, and in all their other attacks, without occasioning the least loss or disorder to the square of the 71st. During one of these charges of the enemy's cuirassiers on the right angle of the front face of the 71st square, I moved my company from the rear to the right, in line with the rear face of the square, and placing myself in front of it, kept every man from firing until the cuirassiers approached within thirty or forty yards of the square, when I fired a volley from my company which had the effect, added to the fire of the 71st, of bringing so many horses and men at the same moment to the ground, that it became quite impossible for the enemy to continue their charge. I certainly believe that half of the enemy were at the instant on the ground; some few men and horses were killed, more wounded, but by far the greater part were thrown down over the dying and wounded. These last after a short time began to get up and run back to their supports, some on horseback, but most of them dismounted. I mention this merely to prove how perfectly impossible it is for cavalry to arrive in sufficient force against infantry, so as to be at all dangerous, if the infantry will only be steady, and give their fire all at once.

After these various attacks of cavalry had failed, everything remained for some time in a state of comparative quiet, and the brigade remained in squares, with the 71st in square near the enclosure of Hougoumont, the 52nd in square of wings in the centre of the brigade and the six companies of the 2nd Battalion of the 95th in square on the left of the 52nd. In this manner the brigade remained for a considerable time, much exposed to the fire of the enemy's batteries, and suffered considerably, particularly the 71st Regiment, with which regiment my company of the 3rd Battalion [95th] was formed, and, I believe, during this time, the late Colonel Fullerton's Company of the 3rd Battalion was acting with the 52nd Regiment.[17]

---

17. Siborne, The Waterloo Letters, pp 304–5.

As it descended from the crest towards the French infantry, General Adam became aware of the large force of cuirassiers a little off to its right. Once the infantry had been driven off, the front of the brigade halted in echelon and rapidly formed squares ready to receive cavalry, the 71st on the right (supported by a company of the 3/95th) near the orchard of Hougoumont and the 2/95th well to the left and only half way down the slope. The 52nd, who were following behind as a form of reserve in two columns of wings, was marched into the gap between the two squares and immediately formed their own two squares in echelon to plug the gap (supported by a company of the 3/95th).

> The cavalry of the enemy, being prepared to attack, the brigade was formed in columns and then in squares. The interval between the 71st and 95th was larger than desirable, and when the cavalry were just reaching the 71st Sir John Colborne brought down the 52nd to fill up the space and [threw] in a most oblique fire on the cavalry, which were in the act of attacking the 71st Regiment.[18]

Colonel Colborne confirms that he brought the two squares up into the gap:

> I formed two squares on the appearance of the masses of heavy cavalry to our right, but nearer to the 71st Regiment than to the 52nd. Several shells fell near the left angle of our more advanced square, and the left side of it was grazed by a sharp fire. Lieutenant Colonel Charles Rowan was anxious to take the command of the left square in which Colonel Chalmers was, but on my acquainting him that I should superintend both the squares he remained, at my request, with me. The front and right faces of this square opened fire on the French cuirassiers advancing towards us, and the French cavalry halted and retired and appeared in disorder.[19]

William Leeke remembered vividly forming the two squares, his square being virtually on the trackway which runs to La Belle Alliance:

> Immediately on descending the slope of the position towards the enemy, the regiment, almost concealed by the tall rye, which was then for the first time trampled down,[20] formed two squares. I remember that when we formed these two squares, we were not far from the north-eastern point of the Hougoumont enclosure and on the narrow white road which, passing within 100 yards of that point, crosses the interval between the British and French positions in the direction of La Belle Alliance. The squares of Adam's Brigade advanced till the 71st were nearly half way down the enclosure of Hougoumont, and about 300 yards from it; the right square of the 52nd was nearly 150 yards down the line of the enclosure and about 400 yards from it, the left square of the 2nd being on its left, and more up the British position, whilst the square of the 2nd battalion of the 95th Rifles, was the left square

---

18. ibid, p 276.
19. Siborne, The Waterloo Letters, p 283.
20. It is very noticeable that no one else comments on the height of the vegetation here.

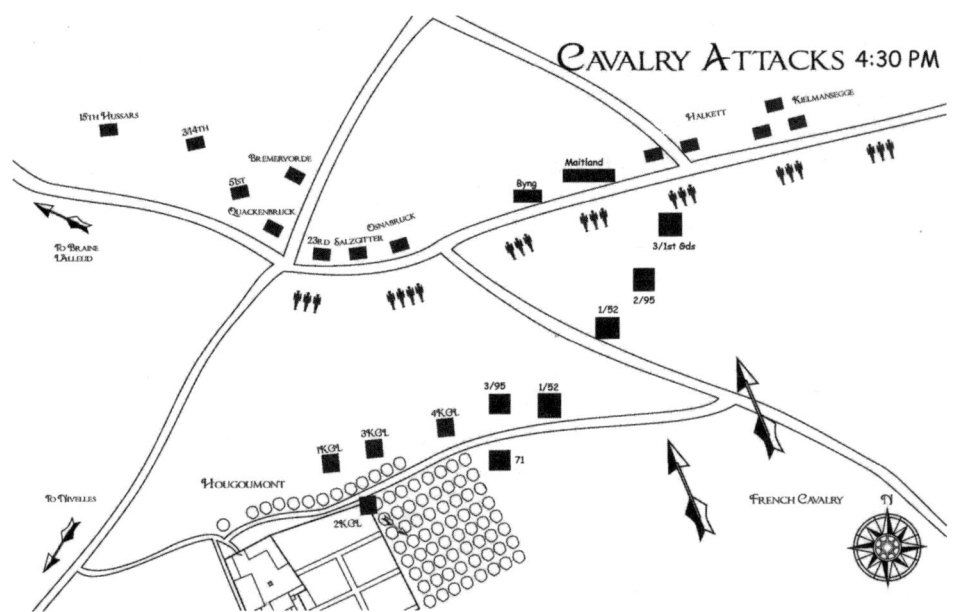

of the whole brigade, and was still further up the position. Of the 71st and 95th squares I only know that they suffered very severely from the fire of the French artillery; and they appeared, as the French General Foy said of the squares of this brigade, to be rooted to the ground, so steady were they, under the tremendous fire to which they were exposed.

The old officers, who had served during the whole of the Peninsular war, stated that they were never exposed to such a cannonade as that which the 52nd squares had to undergo on this occasion for two hours and a half, from the French artillery planted about half a mile in their front. Our own artillery, on, or just under the crest of our position, were also firing over our heads the whole time, either at the enemy's troops or at their guns. Some shrapnel shells burst short and wounded some of the 52nd men; but the firing of these shells was discontinued, on our sending notice of what they were doing to the artillery above us. In the right square of the 52nd, and I suppose it was the same in all the squares of our brigade, there was one incessant roar of round-shot and shells passing over or close to us on either flank; occasionally they made gaps in the square. The only interval that occurred in the cannonade, was when we were charged by the French cavalry, for they, of course, could not fire on our squares for fear of injuring their own squadrons, so that the charges of cavalry were a great relief to us all I believe, at least, I know they were so to me.[21]

Charles Holman agreed, but thought that the 71st was much closer to the orchard, the cavalry were beaten off by the musketry of the squares:

---

21. Leeke, pp 30–31.

The whole brigade were [sic] in squares, the right square the 71st, were with their right face, fifty paces from the garden of Hougoumont. We advanced within 200 paces of this mass of cavalry, in a few minutes they made a most desperate charge on us, but were suffered to approach within 25 paces, when they received a fire which nearly annihilated their advanced squadrons. They attempted it twice after but were each time repulsed.[22]

General Frederick Adam found that the 71st was indeed too close to Hougoumont and it was moved further away and into a sort of trough to help to protect them:

After the cavalry attacks had been disposed of, and subsequently when the enemy's infantry were again about attacking Hougoumont, the right of the brigade was judged to be too near the enclosures of that place, and had it remained, would have been exposed to being taken in flank from thence. It was therefore, at the suggestion of Sir J Colborne, retired, and again brought a little further back in order to be screened from the fire of the enemy's artillery by the fall of the slope.[23]

George Gawler confirms the details of this deployment and of the cavalry attacks, particularly on the 71st:

On crossing the summit the 2nd Battalion 95th was seen, as if taking up its ground, in square at F ... and shortly after the 71st was visible in square at F, very near to the easternmost hedge of Hougoumont. The two companies of the 3rd Battalion 95th with the 71st. Adam's Brigade remained in this position F F F F, I think for at least an hour, until nearly six o clock. During the whole of this time, no other Allied troops were seen by us in front of the position, unless it might be some light cavalry in rear of the north hedge of Hougoumont. On the French position scarcely any troops were visible. Their artillery only certified that they were there. The great hollow about La Haye Sainte, however, was evidently occupied in force, from the boldness with which the French skirmishers pushed out of it, at times almost to the summit of the British position. From this hollow the square of the 2nd 95th was, I believe, charged by cavalry. I saw a large body of cuirassiers move down the easternmost hedge of Hougoumont and charge the 71st. After breaking upon its square they rushed on in apparent infatuation upon the right wing of the 52nd, and received the fire of its front and right faces.[24]

Ensign Leeke also observed the French cavalry and how they made their attacks on the squares:

I have a very vivid recollection of the charge of the French cavalry. Those who advanced on the right square of the 52nd were cuirassiers, having not only a steel breastplate but the same covering for the back. As I observed

---

22. Holman Lt, Journal for 1815, Royal Green Jackets Museum, Winchester.
23. Siborne, The Waterloo Letters, p 276.
24. ibid, p 289.

before, the pleasing part of the charge was that, for several minutes, perhaps ten, we were relieved from the cannonade which the French had kept up upon us, except when their cavalry charged.

They came on in very gallant style and in very steady order, first of all at the trot, then at a gallop, till they were within forty or fifty yards of the front face of the square, when, one or two horses having been brought down, in clearing the obstacle they got a somewhat new direction, which carried them to either flank of the face of the square, which direction they one and all preferred to the charging home and riding on to our bayonets. Notwithstanding their armour many of the men were laid low, many horses also were brought down, and the men had a difficulty in disentangling themselves from them. The cuirassiers passed the square, receiving the fire of all the four faces, and proceeded up to the crest of the British position. They then re-formed, and came down the slope again upon us in the same way, and again avoiding to charge home upon the rear face of the square, as they could scarcely hope to penetrate the squares.[25]

Lieutenant Colonel William Chalmers wrote about himself in the third person. He recalled that the 2/95th were under heavy fire from French skirmishers lining an earth bank to its left and the 52nd sent out a company, as skirmishers rather than weaken the square of the 2/95th:

When the army formed squares the 52nd Regiment composed two squares. The right one commanded by Sir John Colborne, the left by brevet Lieutenant Colonel Chalmers, immediately on the left of the latter were posted four [six] companies of the [2/]95th Rifles under the command of Lieutenant Colonel Fullarton (also in square) and were suffering rather severely from a corps of French sharpshooters posted behind a kind of natural banquette on their left, Colonel Fullarton's square was too weak to admit of his detaching any men to drive off the French sharpshooters and in consequence Colonel Chalmers took a detachment of the 52nd Regiment, passed the 95th square and drove off the tirailleurs. Colonel Chalmers has no recollection of any other skirmishers being thrown out during the day.[26]

Leeke states that the 3/95th were also unable to supply skirmishers at that moment and Colonel Colborne ordered the front rank of the left face of the square out skirmishing, rather than a company, which would have required the square to reform:

There being some difficulty about the 3rd battalion of the 95th Rifles sending out skirmishers to drive them in, Colborne[27] ordered the front rank of the left face of the 52nd square to do so, thus leaving that face of the square with

---

25. Leeke, pp 35.
26. Glover, Letters from the Battle of Waterloo, pp 180–181.
27. He writes Lord Seaton here, but as this is a later title, I have replaced it in the text as Colonel Colborne, his title on the day at Waterloo.

only three ranks for a short time. Captain Yorke of the 52nd, who served at Waterloo as extra aide-de-camp to General Adam commanding our brigade, had his horse killed by a cannon-shot or a shell, when riding near the 52nd squares.[28]

Captain Hamilton of the 2nd Line Battalion KGL watched the cavalry charge against the 52nd from close by:

> We observed the regiments of the first line form squares to repel cavalry, this movement was scarcely executed when the French cavalry made a dashing charge. They were received with a severe and galling fire that did much execution. They did not however retire immediately but finding they could make no impression on the 52nd which received their charge. They galloped down the line of squares, perhaps in the idea of finding some corps in confusion, but they were at every point repulsed with the greatest steadiness. They finally came in confusion and our cavalry observing the opportunity, cut in amongst them and completed the havoc previously made by the infantry.[29]

The brigade stood in this position for some two hours but as the cavalry attacks eased the cannonade grew much heavier, and Captain Joseph Logan of the 2/95th recalled that, being further up the slope, they were suffering badly, although he certainly overstated the proximity of the French artillery:

> We were now attacked in square by lancers & cuirassiers supported by 18 guns which played into our square at one hundred yards distance. We repulsed this attack but suffered cruelly, one shot knocked down nine men. We were attacked again four different times but my little battalion maintained their ground. The general [Wellington] finding we were so terribly exposed, sent me an order to fall back upon our guns.[30]

William Leeke wrote at length of the horrors of having to simply stand and bear a heavy cannonade:

> The standing to be cannonaded, and having nothing else to do, is about the most unpleasant thing that can happen to soldiers in an engagement. I frequently tried to follow, with my eye, the course of the balls from our own guns, which were firing over us. It is much more easy to see a round shot passing away from you over your head, than to catch sight of one coming through the air towards you, though this also occurs occasionally. I speak of shot fired from six, eight, nine, or twelve-pounder guns.[31] Some

---

28. Leeke, p 37.
29. Undated letter of Lt John Hamilton NAM 2002-02-1352.
30. Glover, Waterloo Archive Volume I, p 157.
31. The British at this time were using 6 and 9 pounder cannon, the French 8 and 12 pounders of the An XI design (the cumbersome Gribeauval system having been abandoned). The French pound being lighter than the British the British 6 pounder was compatible to the French 8 pounder etc.

of the artillery above us were firing at one time, over our square, at a body of cuirassiers drawn up to their right and rear of the lower enclosure of Hougoumont; one of the round shot, which I caught sight of, made a regular gap, and occasioned some confusion in their front squadron. After this, as the officer in command of the regiment was riding up and down about twenty yards in front of the leading squadron, I saw a round shot which I thought would have struck his horse's head; it however appeared to pass about half a foot from his head, causing him to start back affrighted, and in a way calculated to have unseated his rider had he not been a superior horseman.

My position in the right square was in the rear of the centre of the front face. I have before stated that it is only very occasionally that a person can see a round shot coming from a twelve-pounder gun, or from one of smaller calibre. After we had been stationed for more than an hour so far down in front of the British position, a gleam of sunshine, falling on them, particularly attracted my attention to some brass guns in our front which appeared to be placed lower down the French slope, and nearer to us, than the others; I distinctly saw the French artilleryman go through the whole process of sponging [sic] out one of the guns and reloading it; I could see that it was pointed at our square, and when it was discharged I caught sight of the ball, which appeared to be in a direct line for me. I thought, 'Shall I move? No!' I gathered myself up, and stood firm, with the Colour in my right hand. I do not exactly know the rapidity with which cannonballs fly, but I think that two seconds elapsed from the time that I saw this shot leave the gun until it struck the front face of the square. It did not strike the four men in rear of whom I was standing, but the four poor fellows on their right. It was fired at some elevation and struck the front man about the knees, and coming to the ground under the feet of the rear man of the four, whom it most severely wounded, it rose and passing within an inch or two of the Colour pole, went over the rear face of the square without doing further injury. The two men in the first and second rank fell outward, I fear they did not survive long; the two others fell within the square. The rear man made a considerable outcry on being wounded, but on one of the officers saying kindly to him, 'man, don't make a noise', he instantly recollected himself, and was quiet. This was the only noise, except the 'By Jove!' mentioned before, which I heard from any wounded man during the battle, although I must have been within hearing distance of many hundreds of the wounded, particularly later in the day, when we passed over the killed and wounded of the French Imperial Guard. The story one used to hear in one's boyhood, of the bands of regiments playing during the raging of a battle to drown the cries of the wounded, is a myth. The men of the band and some of the buglers generally make themselves useful in action, in attending to the wounded. This cannon shot coming through the centre of the front rank of our square without touching me was, I think, my narrowest escape up to that period of the action. I should not omit to mention that it was said, after the action, that a round shot had expended its force in the solid square of the 71st Highland Light Infantry on our right front, and only stopped when it had killed or wounded seventeen men; I can easily suppose this to be possible from what I saw of the effects of the shot which passed so close to me. We stood in the right square, not on rye, or wheat trampled down, but, I think, on clover or seeds which had been recently mown ...

A company of the [3/]95th Rifles were extended in front of the brigade at one time, that they might fire into the French cuirassiers, who were drawn up some three hundred yards from us. One of the files[32] was about ten paces in front of our right square; they were both kneeling, and the front rank man was taking aim at the cuirassiers, when a shell pitched two or three feet before them; they hastily retired towards our square, when, from its not exploding, they supposed it was a round shot, and returned to the spot and knelt down, and the front rank man was just raising his rifle again to take aim, when the shell exploded, covering them with dirt, and they retired, the front rank man having evidently been wounded. It was said some little time after the action, but I did not observe it myself, that in one of the squares, probably the left, whilst Colonel Nicolay[33] or some other officer who had come down from the position, was speaking to Colonel Charles Rowan, a shell fell in the midst of the square, when on Colonel Rowan saying, 'Steady, men!' Colonel Nicolay observed, 'I never saw men steadier in my life.' The shell burst, and seven poor fellows were struck by the fragments... [34]

Lieutenant George Hall recalled the artillery fire:

A French half battery (i.e. two guns) about 600 yards distant from the farthest advance of this [left] square, made it their especial object. They hit us several times whilst we stood halted, yet the casualties were not so numerous as might have been expected. I should say the enemy fired well but not with rapidity.

While the left wing square stood under the cannonade, one of Shedden's company (Woods I think[35]) was struck down by a ball, full on the knee. He was removed into the centre of the square. I observed the limb above the knee quickly swell till it became the size of his body. The poor fellow was left upon the ground, I suppose to die there.[36]

---

32. The Riflemen were taught to operate in pairs of 'files'. One would fire and, whilst he was vulnerable reloading, his partner held his shot.
33. Colonel William Nicolay of the Royal Staff Corps.
34. Leeke, pp 32–3.
35. There was no Wood in Shedden's Company, but there was a Private John Wood of No. 3 Company who was recorded as sick and was embarked for England for discharge, he may have been thinking of him.
36. Hall quoted in Leeke, pp 34–5.

George Gawler realised that the 71st and the 2/95th were suffering a great deal more from the cannonade than the two squares of the 52nd, because of the undulations of the landscape:

> In this position the 71st suffered very heavily and with admirable steadiness from the cannonade; the 2nd Battalion 95th considerably, the 52nd but little, the difference of loss arising, I imagine, from the 71st being more advanced, and the 2nd 95th more elevated than the 52nd.[37]

The Duke of Wellington sent a message via Colonel Hervey,[38] presumably meant for Frederick Adam, but it seems that it was delivered to Colonel Colborne, stating that the brigade could return over the ridge out of the artillery fire:

> Colonel Hervey, one of the Duke of Wellington's aides-de-camp, brought an order from the Duke for the 52nd to retire up the hill. I mentioned to him that if the Duke had ordered us to retire with reference to our exposed position, that we were protected by the ground in front. 'Very well,' he replied, 'I will mention this.' However, soon after I had received this order, I heard a great noise and clamour in the direction of Hougoumont, and observed the Nassau regiments,[39] I believe, running in disorder out of the wood; and supposing that Hougoumont would be abandoned and our flank would be exposed, I formed columns from squares, and wheeled into two lines, and this formation being completed, we faced about and retired in two lines through the Belgian Guns under the command of Colonel Gaeld [Gold], and as we were ascending the hill a French Colonel of the Cuirassiers galloped out of the French ranks, holloaing out '*Vive le Roi*,' repeatedly, and rode up to me, addressed and said, '*Ce — Napoleon est la avec les Gardes. Voila l'attaque qui se fait.*' ['Napoleon is coming here with his Guard']. This officer remained with me for some time.[40]

This statement does raise quite a few issues. It was true that the 52nd was largely obscured from the French bombardment and therefore only receiving light casualties, but the other battalions were in far more exposed positions and undoubtedly were suffering heavily. It would seem that John Colborne had paid

---

37. Siborne, The Waterloo Letters, p 290.
38. Colonel Hervey of the 14th Light Dragoons was an Assistant Quartermaster General at Waterloo, he became Military Secretary to Wellington following Delancey's fatal wounding. He was not his aide de camp.
39. A number of officers of the 52nd mention the sudden retreat of some Nassauers from Hougoumont wood at this time, but this is difficult to accept given the known facts. Colborne says Nassau regiments whereas there was only one battalion of Nassau troops at Hougoumont. Two companies of this battalion had been placed in the wood before the battle, but the entire wood was in the hands of the French by 12 noon and these two companies are widely reported as having fled to the rear then. The remaining companies of Nassau troops remained in the walled garden and appear to have remained there throughout the battle. So who the 52nd saw retiring at around 6 pm is uncertain, but was unlikely to be Nassau troops.
40. Siborne, The Waterloo Letters, p 283.

little attention or had any concern for the situation of the rest of the brigade. I venture to suggest that Private John Lewis of the 2/95th would not have agreed:

> Our large guns was firing over our heads & the enemy's large guns & small arms was firing at the British lines in our rear & I declare to God with our guns & the French guns firing over our heads, my pen cannot explain anything like it. It was not 400 yards from the French lines to our British lines & we was about 150 yards in front of ours, so we was about 250 yards from the French & sometimes not one hundred yards so I leave you to judge if I haden [sic] a narrow escape for my life. As I just said, we was extended in front, Boney's Imperial Horse Guards all clothed in armour[41] made a charge at us, we saw them coming & we all closed in & formed a square just as they come within 10 yards of us & they found they could do no good with us, they fired with their carbines on us & come to the right about directly & at that moment the man on my right hand was shot through the body & the blood run out of his belly & back like a pig stuck in the throat, he drop on his side, I spoke to him, he just said 'Lewis I am done' & died directly.
>
> All this time we kept up a constant fire at the Imperial Guards [cuirassiers], they retreated but they often came to the right about & fired and as I was loading my rifle one of their shots came & struck my rifle not two inches above my left hand as I was ramming down the ball with my right hand & broke the stock & bent the barrel in such a manner that I could not get the ball down. Just at this time we extended again & my rifle was of no good to me, a nine pound shot came and cut the sergeant of our company right in two, he was not above three file from me so I threw down my rifle and went and took his rifle as it was not hurt. At this time we had lost both our colonels, major, and the two oldest captains & only a young captain to take command of us... [42]
>
> Seeing we had lost so many men & all our commanding officers my heart began to fail, & Boney's Guards [cuirassiers] then made another charge on us, but we made them retreat as before & while we was in square the second time the Duke of Wellington and all his Staff came up to us in the midst of all the fire & saw we had lost all our commanding officers. He himself gave the word of command, the words he said to our regiment was this, '95th unfix your swords,[43] left face & extend yourselves once more, we shall soon have them over the other hill' & then he rode away on our right & how he escaped being shot God only knows, for all this time the shots were flying like hail stones.[44]

---

41. These were cuirassiers, having never encountered them in Spain, many British soldiers mistakenly presumed that they formed a part of the Imperial Guard.
42. Captain Logan commanded the battalion after his seniors had all been wounded.
43. The 95th had an enormous 'sword bayonet' which allowed them to stand in line with infantry carrying the standard 'Brown Bess' musket.
44. Glover, Waterloo Archive Volume I, p 159.

As regards the retreat of the Nassau regiments (plural), there was only one Nassau battalion in Hougoumont and three quarters of it was within the chateau complex and remained there throughout. The two hundred Nassau troops who had been positioned in the woods had been driven out many hours previously and indeed most people who say they saw the Nassauers flee from the wood, do so at around 12.30 hours not at 18.00. We do know that the 3rd Foot Guards was struggling to retain its hold on the orchard at around 16.00 hours and that as well as Adam's Brigade being brought forward, Du Plat's King's German Legion Brigade had been brought up into the fields behind Hougoumont in direct support of the defenders. Indeed, the 2nd Line Battalion KGL had even been sent into the orchard to help to maintain it in allied hands against renewed French assaults. The Hanoverian Brigade had also been brought forward but had been kept in reserve on the ridge line behind Hougoumont. It is strange that none of the 52nd officers mention seeing anything of Du Plat's men on the forward slope, but this was most likely because they did not have time to look in that direction.

It is also odd that Colonel Colborne mistakenly assumes that the artillery on the ridge line behind them was Belgian, when there were no Belgian troops of any sort in the vicinity and that he had forgotten that Colonel Gaeld was actually Colonel Gold, a British officer of the Royal Artillery, who commanded Clinton's divisional artillery, consisting of Captain Bolton's British Foot Battery and Major Augustus Sympher's Horse Artillery Troop of the King's German Legion.

Charles Holman however, also believed that the pressure on Hougoumont was what caused the brigade to retire to the allied ridge although he does not mention having seen large numbers of men fleeing from there. He does however mention Du Plat's men moving forward to support Hougoumont although at a later time than it actually occurred: 'The enemy having got possession of the orchard at Hougoumont, we were obliged to retire to the top of the hill and part of our division was sent to drive them from it.'[45]

This is also supported by the evidence of Ensign Jack Barnett of the 71st, who saw Germans pushed out of the wood/orchard temporarily: The Germans at this time gave way in the wood, consequently we were obliged to retreat in this manner, for 2 or 3 hundred yards, the Germans were again reinforced.[46]

Colonel Colborne wrote a further memorandum to Siborne which gives a much fuller account than his previous statements:[47]

> Assuming that the three regiments, the 52nd, 71st and 95th, passed the cross road which runs a few hundred yards in the rear of La Haye Sainte, and forms an acute angle with the Nivelles road, at ½ past 3 or 4 o'clock; the 52nd halted in the low ground three or four hundred yards in front of that road, and about 700 yards from the nearest angle of Hougoumont,

---

45. Holman Lt, Journal for 1815, Royal Green Jackets Museum, Winchester.
46. Glover, Waterloo Archive Volume VI, p 151.
47. This account can be found in the last folio (34708) of Siborne's papers in the British Library and therefore is likely to date from around 1843–4.

remaining there an hour. The 52nd being a strong regiment, formed two squares, the 71st formed square two hundred yards to the right of the 52nd, and on the approach of the French cavalry towards the 71st, the [3/]95th apparently not more than two companies, formed close to the rear of the 52nd. Colonel Nicolay of the Staff Corps and several officers ran into the squares of the 52nd. Two guns were on the high bank or ridge in front of the 52nd, apparently about 200 yards from the squares, but were only to be seen by the mounted officers. A mounted officer who had ascertained the exact position of these guns, called out from the commencement of the ascent to a captain of the 52nd, to say whether he could see the guns from his part of the square. These guns and a howitzer fired constantly over the squares, the right and front faces of the right square of the 52nd opened a fire obliquely on the French cuirassiers who made a movement to the rear of Hougoumont toward the 71st. The remainder of Clinton's Division were formed to the rear of the right of the 71st Regiment. The Duke of Wellington sent a message to the 52nd by Colonel Hervey, to retire up the hill about ½ past 5 o'clock, but Colonel Hervey was requested to inform the Duke that the regiment was not in danger from the guns in front, if the order was given from the apparent vicinity of the guns.

However on the Nassau Regiment or some of the allied troops[48] running rapidly out of the wood of Hougoumont towards our line, the 52nd prepared to retire and formed two lines, the right subdivisions forming one line and the left subdivisions the other, and retired leisurely up the hill towards the cross road which they had passed an hour before.[49] While they were retiring a field officer of cuirassiers galloped out of the enemy's column and came in full speed down the hill towards the 52nd, hallooing lustily '*Vive le Roi*' as he approached. This officer mentioned the point where Napoleon was and that the Imperial Guards were on the march to make a grand attack. The 52nd halted in two lines ten yards behind the cross road where the ground sloped towards our position. The officer of the cuirassiers pointed to the exact spot where the Imperial Guards and Napoleon were. The guns under Colonel Gold on the crossroad were all silent, scarcely any firing except in the rear of La Haye Sainte and in that part of our centre. The dense columns of the French were in full march on the plateau of La Haye Sainte near the farm, and the front of the columns at this time appeared to form a right angle with the 52nd, supposing the left of the line of the 52nd to be produced.[50]

It appears by this time that Colborne had been corrected in his identification of the divisional artillery commander as Gold rather than Gaeld. During this movement to the rear, the brigade formed in squares continued to represent an

---

48. Clearly his identity of these troops as Nassau troops was now not so firm.
49. It is usually stated that it formed line after it had re-crossed the allied ridge line.
50. Glover, Letters from the Battle of Waterloo, p 186.

excellent target for the French artillery until they reached the cover of the ridge line. Major William Rowan was one of the casualties, as was his servant:

> The Duke of Wellington sent an order for the regiment to move back again; it was during this change of position that a discharge of grape from the said battery, struck me on the right arm and a shot passed through my horse's head, causing the animal to fall heavily, by which I was much stunned. About the same time my faithful servant, who had accompanied me to the peninsula, had both of his feet carried away by a single shot.[51]

William Leeke also recalled that the order to retire had been originally deemed unnecessary by Colonel Colborne, but that there was soon a need to retire beyond the crest after the Nassau troops fled from Hougoumont orchard. This passage indicates a clear example of his wish to coordinate his statement with his colonel's. His version shows little indication that he was actually an eyewitness to the events described. However, he puts the time of the incident a bit later:

> About half-past six o'clock, the Duke of Wellington sent an order by his aide-de-camp, Colonel Hervey, to the commanding officer, that the 52nd should retire; but he replied that, if it was necessary, he could remain, for although the squares appeared very much exposed, the shot generally passed over them. Immediately afterwards, however, when the Nassau troops were driven back in the enclosures of Hougoumont, the 52nd squares were ordered to retire up and over the position. Whilst this movement was taking place, the fire of the French artillery was more furious than ever, and several casualties occurred. In the left square Colonel William Rowan was wounded in the elbow by a shot which passed through his horse's neck and killed it, bringing its rider very heavily to the ground.[52]

Another casualty was Ensign William Nettles, who was killed outright by a cannon ball. He was to be the only officer fatality which the 52nd suffered in the battle. As the regiments retired in squares four ranks deep, the Colours which normally stood in the front line, would then be in the rear. When poor Nettles was struck, it would appear that no one noticed or at least no one did anything about it as they all sought the safety of shelter behind the crest of the ridge. The King's Colour was apparently left under his body and completely forgotten in the confusion. It is unclear that anyone even noticed its loss. Only Leeke mentions this incident at all, most perhaps choosing to brush over such an embarrassing incident. This does show Leeke to be an honest witness, mentioning things that the regiment would certainly prefer to have permanently covered up, but that certainly does not mean that we can trust his version of events implicitly as some choose to do, given the many years that had passed before he recorded his memories leading

---

51. Mss Personal Reminiscences of Captain William Rowan, Museum of the Oxfordshire Soldier. Ref SOFO 2178.
52. Leeke, pp 37–8.

to inevitable lapses of memory including false memories. Of course, we must not forget the cause for which he was certainly the chief proponent:

> Poor Nettles, who carried the King's Colour, was killed just before reaching the summit of the position, by a cannon shot through his body; and it was said that his Colour sergeant was killed at or about the same time; and, in some unaccountable way, the Colour was left under the body of poor Nettles till the next morning, when it was discovered by a sergeant of Captain Mercer's troop of horse artillery.[53] The other two sergeants attached to that colour, I presume, were in front of it when retiring in square, and poor Nettles, if he kept his relative position, would be just in front of the rear rank of what had been the front face of the square before it faced about to retire.
>
> As we neared the summit of our position, it seemed as if the whole of the French artillery was firing round shot at our devoted squares. Almost every shot which took effect, brought death or some dreadful wound to the person struck. It certainly was a pleasant relief from 'one of the most murderous cannonades ever recorded in the annals of war', when, on passing the crest of the position, we found ourselves, at forty paces from it, out of fire on its reverse slope.[54]

The cannonade was heavy but certainly paled into insignificance against those endured at the Battles of Borodino and Leipsig amongst many. William Leeke's assertion that they retired in square is also possibly backed up by Charles Holman's journal, which stated that:

> We then formed line four deep and halted a little, at this instant a French colonel who commanded a regiment of the cuirassiers deserted and came to Sir J[ohn] Colbourne [sic] and informed him of an attack to be made with all their force on our left.[55] He was immediately sent to Lord W[ellington] who was luckily near our left, this I think must have been about ½ past 5.[56]

Holman's comment on changing formation into four deep line would appear to have occurred once the regiment had retired over the ridge. His timing is however certainly too early.

One question regarding this period of the battle has yet to be satisfactorily answered. Why had Wellington placed the two brigades of the Second Division on the forward slope of the allied ridge for some two hours? The answer would seem to be twofold.

---

53. It is strange that Mercer's manuscript journal of the campaign (rather than the heavily edited version published by his son) makes no comment regarding anyone from his troop discovering the Colour. It is quite possible that Leeke is mistaken as regards to which artillery unit the sergeant belonged to, simply assuming he was from Mercer's as they were directly in front of them when they returned behind the allied ridge. My thanks to my friend Robert Pocock for this information.
54. Leeke, p 38.
55. As the 52nd were on the right of the line, I presume he means the French left.
56. Holman Lt, Journal for 1815, Royal Green Jackets Museum, Winchester.

The deployment of Adam's and Du Plat's Brigades close to Hougoumont was clearly done with the intention of bolstering the defence of the chateau complex. This particularly applies to the orchard adjoining it, which was certainly very close to being lost at this time, with the 3rd Foot Guards being pushed right back to the 'hollow way' at the northern edge of the orchard. The fact that elements of both brigades came under an intense musketry from French skirmishers in the orchard makes it clear that they had virtually wrested control of it from the British Guards, despite their heroic defence. It required the addition of the entire 2nd Line Battalion of the KGL to support the Guards to stabilise the critical situation. Wellington's determination to retain his hold on Hougoumont is often criticised, but its defence does not form part of this narrative.

The second reason is one that has largely been overlooked by historians but was vital to the success of the allied infantry against the massed ranks of the cavalry. The French cavalry had clearly been sent forward en masse, with the aim of recreating the success of Eylau, by smashing through what they undoubtedly perceived would be the disordered allied troops, whose squares, Ney assumed, would not stand firm after the terrible cannonade they had endured for some four hours or so. Wellington must also have worried about the solidity of some of his untried allies and the frequent glimpses of him riding from square to square to urge on their defence makes it clear how concerned he must have been at this moment. If one square had broken and ran, the morale of his entire army could have been compromised. With this in mind it is clear that the brigades were ordered onto the forward slope to protect the allied ridge and to disrupt the cavalry attacks. The huge unbroken lines of cuirassiers so beautifully painted by Dumoulin in his Waterloo panorama certainly occurred during the first attacks against the allied ridge, until broken by the solid squares behind the ridge line. Wellington could not be sure how many such waves of these terrific cavalry attacks some of his units would stand. The deployment of Adam's Brigade on the forward slope was undoubtedly intended to place some of his most trusted and experienced troops in a way that was specifically designed to frustrate and disrupt these attacks, significantly lessening their impact on the squares to the rear of the ridge. The four solid squares deployed from the corner of Hougoumont orchard in echelon across the slope ensured that the long lines of French cavalry had already spent their energy crashing against these forward squares. The cavalry had to filter between this forward line of squares, which ensured that they now only reached the allied ridge in isolated packets, all cohesion and discipline having been largely dissipated before they arrived at the allied squares beyond. This is often not appreciated.

However, when Wellington ordered Adam's Brigade onto the forward slope, he also ordered the 3/1st Foot Guards to do the same and they remained on the outer slope until 18.00 hours, when they were also ordered to retire and to rejoin 1/1st Foot Guards behind the ridge.

If looked at in the terms of heavy waves crashing onto a shoreline and causing severe coastal erosion, then the brigade's deployment on the forward slope was not in the form of a groyne (as some have incorrectly described it), but more akin to a coastal defence system known as 'moving defences seaward', whereby artificial obstructions such as small islands are constructed to dissipate the raw power of the waves before they reach the coastline in their rear. This action was vital to the overall success of the allied squares against the cavalry but is often completely overlooked or misunderstood by historians. At best it is almost viewed as an irrelevance, whereas it was almost certainly as vital a service as the later much celebrated defeat of the French Imperial Guard.

Chapter 8

The Crisis 19.30–20.30 Hours

Napoleon had seen that the cavalry charges had failed to break Wellington's centre and the cream of his horsemen were now exhausted and little more than a spent force. His line infantry on both wings had also been deployed in major attacks and had failed signally to break through. His remaining options were diminishing rapidly. In Napoleon's estimation, Wellington's army must be thoroughly exhausted and worn down and this was the perfect moment to launch a final blistering attack by his elite, the Imperial Guard, to carve a path through the weakened allied centre, causing it to collapse and rout, as they had done so often before, including against the Prussians at Ligny only two days before.

Unfortunately for Napoleon, his calculations were not to be as straightforward as that, as from 16.00 hours, he no longer only had Wellington's army to contend with. Marshal Blücher's Prussians had not been routed at the Battle of Ligny. They had retired and then regrouped at Wavre in order to be able to cooperate with Wellington, who had only stood to offer battle at the previously selected position near Waterloo because he had been promised Blücher's support. This support had in truth arrived much later than anticipated due to the poor state of the roads, but now that they had finally arrived and launched a furious assault on the village of Plancenoit, in Napoleon's right rear, the French Emperor had been forced to deploy a significant number of troops to hold the Prussians back. These included Lobau's Corps, the 5,000 men of the Young Guard and he eventually had to deploy two battalions of his Old Guard there to finally stabilise the situation.

Napoleon's options were now very limited indeed, he could either order a full retreat in order to fight another day, or he could launch one final attack on Wellington's army, which he was certain was near to collapse. Defeating Wellington's forces would allow him to turn his entire remaining force against the Prussians, whom he was confident of beating. Ever the adventurer, knowing how badly any defeat would play out in Paris and how fragile was the morale of his army, riven as it was with doubt and fears of treachery, he characteristically chose to roll the dice one last time hoping for a double six.

Napoleon ordered his remaining Old and Middle Guard units to launch an attack on Wellington's right centre, confident of victory.

Time however was extremely tight for him. The morale of the French army was visibly ebbing away, as the noise of the Prussian assault on Plancenoit announced to every soldier that the recent joy at the announcement of the arrival of French troops under Marshal Grouchy had been at best a terrible mistake, at worst treachery.

The attack of the Imperial Guard is with certainty, the most debated moment in the entire Battle of Waterloo. It exercises historians more than any other, because the French accounts do not appear to agree between themselves and certainly do not agree with the Allied accounts, which are undoubtedly heavily tainted by partisan regimental claims. Indeed, a survey of the histories of the battle produced by twenty of the most acclaimed historians of the past two centuries, reveals that it is impossible to find two versions of the attack of the Imperial Guard that match exactly. They even disagree as to which units were involved or even the basic sequence of events[1]. It has therefore proven imperative, for this new attempt to make sense of the whole matter, to ensure that every scrap of evidence, from all sides, is analysed and thoroughly scrutinised as to its veracity. Any such undertaking must also take careful note of when each version of the events was written, taking into account the inevitable distortions of the human memory that occur with time, which includes the dangers of false memories. The accounts written much later in life also inevitably suffer from the influence of early histories of the campaign, which subliminally alter the memories of eyewitnesses, by suggestion. William Siborne had published his *History of the Waterloo Campaign* by 1844 and it is clear that his version of events immediately began to influence later writers who tried to make their memories fit with the 'established version'. It is therefore a path fraught with dangers and one that this historian has attempted to tread with great care, but we must still try to make sense of it all, in the ultimate search for the truth.

The French Version

To properly understand what occurred during the attack of the Imperial Guard, we have first to examine what the French sources say happened. We know with certainty that the entire Young Guard was engaged at Plancenoit, therefore Napoleon only had 14 (or 15) battalions of Middle and Old Guard which he could utilise. The identity of these units is as follows:

Old Guard
1st Grenadiers 2 battalions
2nd Grenadiers 2 battalions
1st Chasseurs 2 battalions
2nd Chasseurs 2 battalions

Middle Guard
3rd Grenadiers 2 battalions
4th Grenadiers 1 battalion
3rd Chasseurs 2 battalions
4th Chasseurs 1 or 2 battalions (see below)

---

1. This issue is too complicated to discuss in this chapter and will therefore be tackled separately in Appendix 8

Some historians argue that in 1815, the Middle Guard was not officially reinstated and therefore all of these units were deemed as Old Guard, but it is clear, whether reinstated or not, that the French Army still continued to refer to them as Middle and Old Guard in 1815.

There is also some confusion regarding the 4th Chasseurs, who certainly fought at Ligny on 16 June with two battalions, however one source, General Petit, states that following the heavy casualties that they suffered at Ligny, they were amalgamated into one battalion for Waterloo.[2] Petit is usually considered a good reliable source, although he was not an actual eyewitness to most of its proceedings as he was with his two battalions which were situated at Rossomme, half a mile (0.8 km) from the French front line, for most of the attack of the Imperial Guard. When there is no corroborating evidence, we must therefore be circumspect in accepting his statement as fact. The official returns give losses for the Old and Middle Guard at Ligny as 1st Grenadiers 43, 2nd Grenadiers 152, 3rd Grenadiers 107, 4th Grenadiers 29, 1st Chasseurs 32 and 4th Chasseurs 229, no other units recorded any losses at all.[3] As you can see, the figures are in each case for the regiment of two battalions, it does not apportion the numbers of casualties per individual battalion. From this however, it can be seen, that the 4th Chasseurs did lose the most casualties, but the total of 229 casualties has to be split over the two battalions, which averages a loss of 115 per battalion. The regiment mustered 1,071 officers and men before Ligny,[4] meaning that even with the casualties deducted, each battalion still averaged around 421 men. Given that few of the other Old or Middle Guard battalions greatly exceeded 500 men each, it seems very unlikely that it would have been deemed necessary to amalgamate the two battalions, as the joint battalion at 841 men would have been the strongest battalion of the Guard at the battle by far which, I suggest, would have caused a few comments – these are conspicuous by their absence. I therefore believe that the 4th Chasseurs still acted as two separate battalions at Waterloo, which makes a total of 15 battalions available.

We also know that 1/1st Chasseurs were ordered to remain at Imperial headquarters – Le Caillou. Two battalions of the Old Guard had also been sent to Plancenoit to stabilise the situation there and were unavailable for the main attack, these were the 2/2nd Grenadiers and 1/2nd Chasseurs.[5]

This left 12 battalions available for the attack against Wellington, of which Napoleon retained a further two battalions as a reserve at Rossomme, these were the two battalions of the 1st Grenadiers. This reduced the total number of battalions available for the attack to ten battalions.

---

2. Petit, pp 325.
3. Figures kindly supplied by Paul Dawson.
4. Figures from Andrew Field's Grouchy's Waterloo p 279.
5. The correct identity of the Grenadier battalion is a topic of debate, I have explained in Appendix 8 why I am certain that it was 2/2nd Grenadiers.

The Sequence of the Attacks

Napoleon knew that he had very little time in which to gain a victory, otherwise certain defeat was staring him in the face. So how was the advance organised? The Middle Guard was stationed a few hundred yards or so nearer to the battlefield than the Old Guard and hence would be able to deploy first. Normally the entire seven battalions of the Middle Guard would deploy with the Grenadiers leading from the right as the senior battalions and with the Chasseurs echeloned back to the left. Many historians therefore claim that is exactly how they deployed. However, numerous French eyewitnesses do not agree with this supposition, so let us examine their evidence.

Firstly, it is argued that the Grenadiers, as the senior battalions, would have been to the front, not the Chasseurs, and therefore would have arrived first, but General Petit clearly states that:

> It was the custom of the Old [and Middle] Guard always to march the left at the head; the Chasseurs therefore always marched before the Grenadiers, and the last regiments were the Grenadiers. So the 4th Regiment of Chasseurs marched first, then the 3rd, then the 2nd. It was the same with the Grenadiers.[6]

Napoleon is not always the most reliable of witnesses, particularly when he was seeking to place all the blame for a disaster on some poor subordinate. However, at times he can be more honest and forthright about his failures, and the Guard attack would appear to be one such occasion, as his statement could only bring criticism upon himself and is therefore more likely to be his honest view of matters:

> Some regiments drew back, I noticed this ... Realizing, that I still needed another quarter of an hour to rally my whole Guard, I put myself at the head of four battalions and advanced to the left, in front of La Haie [sic] Sainte....It was important that the Guard should be in action all at once, but the eight other battalions were still in the rear...I ordered General Friant to go with these four battalions of the Middle Guard to meet the enemy's attack. The four battalions repulsed everybody that they encountered ... Ten minutes later, the other battalions of the Guard arrived.[7]

Napoleon claims that as soon as the four battalions of the 3rd and 4th Chasseurs were organised, he launched them without waiting for the Grenadiers to come up. General Friant was actually in charge of all the Grenadiers of the Old and Middle Guard, so it may sound odd to send him with the Chasseurs, but Napoleon's rush to send the first battalions forward may have caused him to overlook such niceties, indeed Petit states that Friant was put in charge of the entire attack. General Gourgaud closely follows Napoleon's statement, but goes further, describing how:

---

6. Petit p 322.
7. Napoleon (De Chair) p 535.

The Emperor... marched with the four first battalions to the left of La Haye Sainte. ...A quarter of an hour after, the other eight battalions arrived on the brink of the ravine. One battalion in order of battle, having two in close column on its flanks. Two of these brigades thus ranged and marching at battalion distance, formed a first line, behind which the third brigade was posted in reserve.[8]

He concurs with Napoleon's statement that the initial advance was made with only four battalions and that eight further battalions drew up some fifteen minutes later. He further indicates that these latter eight battalions were deployed in three brigades. Two brigades formed of three battalions in formation of *l'ordre mixte*[9] and two battalions remaining in reserve, which must refer to the two battalions of the 1st Grenadiers which had originally been left at Rossomme, but now moved up to La Belle Alliance.

However, it must be said that Marshal Ney, who was prominently involved in this attack records that: 'A short time afterwards, I saw four regiments of the Middle Guard advancing, led on by the Emperor.'[10]

Now here, Ney says four regiments rather than battalions (i.e. both the 3rd & 4th Chasseurs and 3rd & 4th Grenadiers), but this would mean that most of the Guard (up to 7 of the 10 battalions available for the attack) were brought forward together and consequently Napoleon's statement regarding the poor coordination of the attack would therefore be wrong. Ney is supported by General Petit, but he was not an eyewitness to the initial attack. Ney's statement does appear to be out of kilter with everybody else, however, and I believe that he may been mistaken and meant four battalions rather than regiments. I will explain why shortly.

General Pelet who was in the attack commanding the 2nd Chasseurs states:

The 3rd and 4th Regiments of Chasseurs during the attack, agree that these regiments had received only a few musket shots and a few cannon balls that were fired from their left. Michel [overall Commander of the Chasseurs of the Guard] and Mallet [Commander of the 3rd Chasseurs] fell dead with the first divisions. General Friant [He commanded the Chasseur attack] was seriously injured. These four battalions heroically endured a terrible fire. Battalion commanders Angelet [2nd Battalion 3rd Chasseurs], Cardinal [1st Battalion 3rd Chasseurs] Agnes [1st Battalion 4th Chasseurs] fell dead[11] with a large number of officers and half of the Chasseurs.[12]

This clearly indicates that the Chasseurs were acting alone, naming only senior officers of Chasseurs as casualties, and importantly, he goes further:

---

8. Gourgaud pp 106–7.
9. The formation had the centre battalion in line to maximise its firepower, whilst the battalions on each flank were formed in solid column to give the formation strength and to protect against cavalry attacking the flank.
10. Marshal Ney's own memorial of the campaign.
11. Angelet was wounded, the other two were killed.
12. Pelet, Carnet de la Sabretache p 50.

> All agree that the regiments of Grenadiers were several hundred feet behind and could not take part in this attack. We are forced to admit that this heroic attack went very badly. ... Firstly, we did not wait for the arrival of the Grenadiers... we did not wait for the end of the deployment executed under fire from the enemy, to make a simultaneous attack. All attacks were isolated and disconnected.[13]

This confirms that the Chasseurs went off without waiting for the Grenadiers and General Gourgaud concurs, stating that the Chasseurs fought manfully, whilst awaiting the arrival of the Old Guard to clinch a stunning victory:

> Meanwhile the four battalions of the Middle Guard were engaged with the enemy; they repulsed all before them [so that] upon the arrival of the Old Guard we should be masters of the whole field of battle.[14]

Interestingly, General Foy wrote on 23 June that the Chasseurs had formed squares and talks about them as if they were alone in their actions, he also specifically mentions the 4th Chasseurs, but does not make any mention that the two battalions had been amalgamated:

> The Third and Fourth Regiments of Chasseurs were ordered to move forward and form into squares by battalion to the left of the roadway in the direction of La Haye Sainte, the Fourth Regiment of Chasseurs suffered at the Battle of Ligny, which despite these losses did not advance with less resolution.[15]

Meanwhile Corporal Pierre Alexander Tousaint le Cat of the 3rd Chasseurs states that: 'We attacked the English positions ... and were supported moments later by the brave Grenadiers marching along the road against La Haye Sainte'. [16]

These comments would appear to be conclusive and in perfect agreement with Napoleon's own statement, that the four battalions of Chasseurs were the first to form up and that General Friant was ordered to take them forward in the attack, some 5 to 10 minutes before the Middle Guard Grenadiers and the Grenadiers and Chasseurs of the Old Guard could form up. These four battalions marched up the allied ridge with the 2nd Battalion 4th Chasseurs arriving at the point described as: 'where there is a ridge of land separating the shallow valleys of La Haye Sainte and Hougoumont'. This tongue of land, forming a small plateau, is very evident on maps of the battlefield, protruding southward between two sections of sunken roadway and close to the juncture of three trackways. Without doubt, this description refers to the plateau which is now the base on which the Lion Mound was later constructed. From this plateau, running to the south towards La Belle Alliance, is a low ridge line which forms a watershed, with the land falling away quite noticeably both towards La Haye Sainte to the east and Hougoumont to the west and therefore making it impossible to see the one from the other.

---

13. ibid.
14. Gourgaud, p 107.
15. Kindly supplied by Paul Dawson.
16. Kindly supplied by Paul Dawson.

French sources rarely describe how exactly these four battalions marched forward, except that they almost universally state that they were in columns of battalion squares and that they endeavoured to deploy when within about 100 yards of the allied ridge where they came under intense fire from the British infantry of Colin Halkett's and Peregrine Maitland's Brigades.

Paradoxically, almost every English Guards' officer who has described this attack, states that the French attacked in columns rather than squares with a frontage of two companies wide (or in grand divisions). As the British were used to their own battalions consisting of ten companies of 60–80 men each, whereas the French Imperial Guard consisted of only four companies of about 130 men each, each face of the French squares consisting of a full company, would appear to them to consist of two companies. Hence, they could easily be describing a compact square rather than a solid column.

If we now look to the statements of the 1st Battalion 3rd Grenadiers and 4th Grenadiers, the belief that the Grenadiers advanced some short time after the Chasseurs is corroborated by General Poret de Morvan who commanded the 3rd Grenadiers, who wrote in the third person:

> Already in the first line of the Imperial Guard, the brave Generals Friant [commanding the Chasseur attack] and Michel [commanding the Chasseurs] had been wounded... and Colonel Malet [commanding 1st Battalion 3rd Chasseurs] was killed....the column, led by Poret de Morvan [3rd Grenadiers], who ascended the plateau to the pas de charge under a terrible fire, <u>came to revive the first line</u>'.[17]

I have underlined this final phrase, which serves to confirm that the Grenadiers came up after the Chasseurs, effectively as a second wave to the attack. This struck the allied line further to the east (on the other side of the tongue of land) and was therefore invisible to most of the British troops who had fought the Chasseur attack.

Chef de Battalion Guillemin of the 1st Battalion 3rd Grenadiers says they arrived 'on the plateau that dominated the battlefield'[18] which would be in the area of the tongue of land. This is also confirmed by Colonel Crabbe who records that: 'I found the Marshal [Ney] in the middle of the 3rd Grenadiers on the plateau ... At his side was General Friant ... and ... Colonel Poret de Morvan.' [19]

Meanwhile, an officer of the 4th Grenadiers, writing in 1823 states that: 'We advanced at the pas de charge with our bayonets, our flank against La Haye Sainte'.[20]

This would indicate that the single battalion regiment of the 4th Grenadiers was to the right of the 1/3rd Grenadiers and therefore out of their normal order, this again could indicate the haste in which they were propelled forward to support the Chasseurs.

---

17. Paul Dawson Waterloo p 363.
18. Field, Waterloo p 196.
19. ibid.
20. Kindly supplied by Paul Dawson.

This does mean that the attack of the Chasseurs and the battalions of Grenadiers must be viewed as two separate attacks with five to ten minutes between them. In fact, it would appear that the Chasseur attack was virtually over when the Grenadier attack went in. However, because the 2nd Battalion 3rd Grenadiers was sent elsewhere, this attack was made by two battalions only, not in *'l'ordre mixte'* as originally intended with the 3 battalions, as in Gourgaud's statement.

There is thankfully little contention amongst historians regarding the role of the detached Grenadier battalion, the 2nd Battalion 3rd Grenadiers. This battalion was apparently sent 'a long cannon shot' to the left of the main chaussee to protect the left flank of the Chasseurs attack. General Friant, as an example of this, stated that 'the 2nd Battalion of the 3rd Grenadiers was detached to the left and remained there.'[21]

It seems that this battalion was also used by Napoleon as his vantage point from which to watch the attack unfold. General Petit confirms that Napoleon was there: 'the 2nd Battalion of the 3rd Regiment of Grenadiers, where the Emperor was to be found, had held its ground'.[22] We will return to the story of this battalion later.

When the five remaining battalions of the Old Guard finally arrived, they were brought forward of La Belle Alliance and formed in the low ground between the two ridges. The 1st Battalion 2nd Grenadiers stood near La Haye Sainte, whilst the 2nd Battalion 1st Chasseurs under General Cambronne and the 1st Battalion 2nd Chasseurs were placed in the centre, closer to the 2nd Battalion of the 3rd Regiment of Grenadiers.

A number of historians claim that these three battalions simply remained there as a reserve and were not employed until the allied infantry and cavalry attacked them. But that is not what the French say themselves and it may well be the key to understanding the various claims by the British infantry regiments involved, particularly the Foot Guards versus the 52nd Foot argument.

With regard to the 1st Battalion of the 2nd Grenadiers, it appears to have remained in the vicinity of La Haye Sainte as a reserve to the Grenadier attack already mentioned. This is exactly what its own commander, General Christiani, states himself. The battalion appears to have helped extricate the remnants of the two Grenadier battalions that did attack the allied ridge, and both De Mauduit and General Guyot state that at one stage the French Guard heavy cavalry also attacked to extricate Colonel Martenot of 1st Battalion 2nd Grenadiers and Poret de Morvan with the 1st Battalion 3rd Grenadier from a cavalry attack.

On seeing the defeat of the Chasseur attack and its retreat from the ridge, we know that General Cambronne marched his battalion of Chasseurs to join the 2nd Battalion 3rd Grenadiers. General Petit states that: 'During all these misfortunes, the 2nd Battalion of the 3rd Regiment of Grenadiers, where the Emperor was to be found, had held its ground. General Cambronne arrived at the same position with the 2nd Battalion of the 1st Regiment of Chasseurs.'[23]

---

21. Kindly supplied by Paul Dawson.
22. Petit, pp 325–6.
23. Petit, p 325.

General Friant concurs, stating that:

> The 2nd Battalion of the 3rd Grenadiers was detached to the left and remained there, although he was heavily attacked, General Cambronne, a colonel of the 1st Chasseurs, came to his aid with the 2nd battalion of his regiment.[24]

Another unknown French officer agrees: 'The 2nd Battalion of the 1st Chasseurs commanded by General Cambronne, went on his part to support.'[25]

De Mauduit goes further stating that both battalions of the Chasseurs of the Old Guard went to join the 2/3rd Grenadiers: 'General Cambronne moved rapidly forward with the 1st Battalion of his regiment, ... and he was followed by the ... 2nd Battalion of the 2nd Chasseurs.'[26]

The French also claim that this little ad-hoc brigade, consisting of the 2nd Battalion 3rd Grenadiers, the 2nd Battalion 1st Chasseurs and the 1st Battalion 2nd Chasseurs, formed up to attack. General Friant states that:

> The 2nd Battalion of the 3rd Grenadiers detached to the left ... General Cambronne ... came to his aid with the 2nd Battalion of his regiment ... General Roguet tried in vain to take the offensive, the great disproportion of forces and cruel losses already experienced, and constantly increasing, did not allow for more, it was necessary to retreat but not without a fight, the enemy still saw before him the Imperial Guard.[27]

An unknown officer also records that:

> The 2nd Battalion of the 3rd Grenadiers detached on the left...The 2nd Battalion of the 1st Chasseurs commanded by General Cambronne, went on his part to support and cover the retreat and the flank of the other battalions of the Guard.[28]

Even if these French battalions had advanced simply to cover the retreat of the Chasseurs, it would have appeared to the allies as an advance. De Mauduit confirms that:

> General Cambronne moved rapidly forward with the 1st [sic] Battalion of his regiment ... and he was followed by the 2nd Battalion of the 3rd Grenadiers and 2nd Battalion of the 2nd Chasseurs ... With this small reinforcement the Emperor would still try the offensive.[29]

Captain de Steurs of the 2nd Battalion 2nd Chasseurs indicates that they had tried to protect the Chasseurs to allow them to reform, but that it failed:

---

24. Kindly supplied by Paul Dawson.
25. Paul Dawson p 405.
26. Kindly supplied by Paul Dawson.
27. Paul Dawson p 394.
28. ibid, p 405.
29. ibid, 396.

> After the flight of the debris of the four battalions of the Middle Guard ... it was not possible to rally them behind the small reserve which we, the Imperial Guard, formed.[30]

How far this movement in advance went, is very difficult to ascertain, but given that its advance did cause consternation on the allied ridge as will be seen later, it is not inconceivable that they began to ascend the allied ridge, as a final attempt to break through the allied lines. Indeed, a number of Frenchmen who were in this final attack actually claim to have reached the plateau which now forms the base of the Lion Mound. I quote their later claims here, but I doubt very much that they got so far, or that they were so far to the east on this advance. Chasseur Chaude Jacquet of the 1st Chasseurs wrote on 28 November 1832: 'The square was on the plateau overlooking the two valleys, at the confluence of three roads near to where General Michel was killed.'[31] Also, Corporal Pierre Salle of the 2nd Battalion 2nd Chasseurs wrote on 14 July 1842: 'We formed in square ... we stood where the lion mound is.'

The advance of these three battalions, added to infantry of the line sent from Foy's troops in support, would have appeared very much to the allied troops to be a third and very significant attack. In a letter he wrote on 23 June 1815 General Foy confirms that his troops were involved:

> We were ordered with the divisions of Bachelu and Foy to ascend the plateau in squares. We almost reached the English, when we received a rapid fire of grapeshot and musketry. It was a hail of death.

In summary, we therefore have a clear sequence of events from the French sources, that the attacks of the Imperial Guard were disjointed and uncoordinated and that the ten battalions advanced in squares behind each other, not in solid columns. Napoleon initially launched forward the four battalions of Middle Guard Chasseurs and that they proceeded towards the allied ridge a little to the west of the watershed (to the left of the Lion Mound) and as they neared the ridge line the squares deployed in echelon to the left. A few minutes later, the Grenadiers of the Middle Guard proceeded forward to support the initial attack but, although originally consisting of 3 battalions, one was ordered to a position near Hougoumont, where Napoleon apparently based himself to view the attacks. The other two battalions marched up the allied ridge to the east of the watershed (to the right of the Lion Mound), the 4th Grenadiers passing close to La Haye Sainte. Being either side of the watershed, these two attacks could not see each other. Finally, when the initial Chasseur attack began to fail, the two Old Guard Chasseur battalions stationed in reserve to the west, joined the Grenadier battalion sheltering Napoleon and these three battalions, quite possibly along with further battalions from Reille's Corps, sought to cover their retreat by advancing and quite possibly hoping to succeed where the Chasseurs had failed.

Armed with this evidence, we now need to examine what happened in the views of those on the allied ridge.

---

30. ibid, p 399.
31. Kindly supplied by Paul Dawson.

Chapter 9

The Centre Attack 19.30–20.00 Hours

As has already been seen, there is little agreement amongst historians regarding the attack of the Imperial Guard, but most do agree that the Chasseurs approached the allied ridge in a column of battalion squares to the west of the watershed, marked today by the position of the Lion Mound, and that they arrived at the point of the ridge defended by the troops of Maitland's Guards Brigade, but that is about as far as this consensus goes. So, let us analyse what the various eyewitnesses say of the attack which arrived in front of Maitland's 1st Brigade, consisting of the 2nd and 3rd Battalions of the 1st Foot Guards.

One issue needs to be highlighted, however, before we try to decipher these accounts. Within days of the battle, the 1st Foot Guards was being lauded in parliament in London for overthrowing the Grenadiers of the Imperial Guard and an over-excited Prince Regent immediately announced that the 1st Foot Guards were to be known henceforth as the 'Grenadier Guards' in recognition of its great feat. Because of this, Guards officers were understandably very keen to identify their assailants as Grenadiers of the Guard and this must be borne in mind, as the identification of their assailants may well have been strongly influenced by these circumstances.

Quite rightly, many historians have pointed out that it is pretty certain that the 1st Foot Guards faced elements of the Middle Guard and it is very probable that they defeated Chasseurs and not Grenadiers. So how could this confusion have occurred?

We must first take note of the problems with identification. The French fought as usual in their greatcoats with their white belts over them, making distinctions between units very difficult even at close range. However Imperial Guard units could be relatively easily distinguished from the soldiers of the line regiments, as they wore a blue greatcoat rather than the standard grey or brown. It was also easier to identify Middle and Old Guard uniforms from the Young Guard as they generally wore bearskins rather than shakos, although a few Guard units did fight in shakos because of a shortage of bearskins. They also did not wear their plumes – the Grenadiers being solid red, whereas the Chasseurs wore red over green – in battle (I have only found one source that claims that they did, but they were normally kept safe in their knapsacks for formal parades). They wore small rosettes in their stead, again making identification problematical. Indeed, the only quick and easy method of identifying the difference, was that the Grenadiers had a brass plaque on the front of their bearskins, which the Chasseurs did not. However, in the heat of battle, in the half light, with the swirling smoke and with no prior knowledge of Imperial Guard uniforms, having never met them in combat before, I believe that most British eyewitnesses simply saw a bearskin through the smoke and presumed that they were Old Guard Grenadiers.

Colonel Colborne mentions receiving a warning of the forthcoming attack from a French turncoat around 18.30 hours, but it is evident from many witnesses that the Duke of Wellington was very well aware of developments, as he could clearly see the Guard battalions being formed up in the valley in front of La Belle Alliance and he hurriedly made a number of changes to his dispositions. The Duke ordered the two battalions of the 1st Foot Guards to form line four ranks deep and to take shelter by lying down behind the track which ran along the crest of the ridge. This formation reduced its frontage significantly, so the battalions were ordered to close up to the left, leaving room for General Adam's Brigade to fit in close to its right. The Guards appear to have been to the left of a small rise, described as a knoll, and Adam's Brigade to the right of this feature. This knoll can easily be identified in Siborne's maps of the position as the point where the track along the crest of the ridge was joined by the track from the ridge to La Belle Alliance.

Captain George Bowles of the Coldstream Guards, who was with the small detachment of that regiment still on the ridge with the Colours, described how:

> The cannonade continued tremendous till about half-past six o'clock, when Napoleon again assembled *la Vieille* [Old] Garde, harangued them, and putting himself at their head, led them forward in different columns against our battalions still formed in squares.[1]

It is clear however, that the Guards were already formed in line four ranks deep at this time. Lieutenant Colonel James Stanhope of the 3/1st Guards wrote that:[2]

> When the last desperate effort was made by three columns of Imperial Guards. The Grenadiers of it, accompanied by Bonaparte to the bottom of the hill, came to our share, the right column to that of the 52nd etc.

His reference to three columns is mentioned in a few other accounts, including that written by General Maitland, who describes this third column as partly consisting of French line infantry and cavalry, which were presumably ready to exploit any breakthrough by the two columns of Guard infantry. Writing to the Duke of York, who was colonel of the regiment, he was a little more effusive:

> The most gratifying event of the whole day was the desperate attack, made about seven o'clock by the Imperial Guard, headed by Buonaparte in person. His Grenadiers attacked the [1st] Guards, and had soon cause to find they would not sup in Brussels, as the Emperor had told them.[3]

Major General Maitland also wrote expansively on the attack:

---

1. Glover, A Guards Officer in the Peninsula and at Waterloo, p 99.
2. Glover, Eyewitness to the Peninsular War and the Battle of Waterloo, p 191.
3. Glover, Waterloo Archive Volume I, p 133.

The Centre Attack 19.30–20.00 Hours

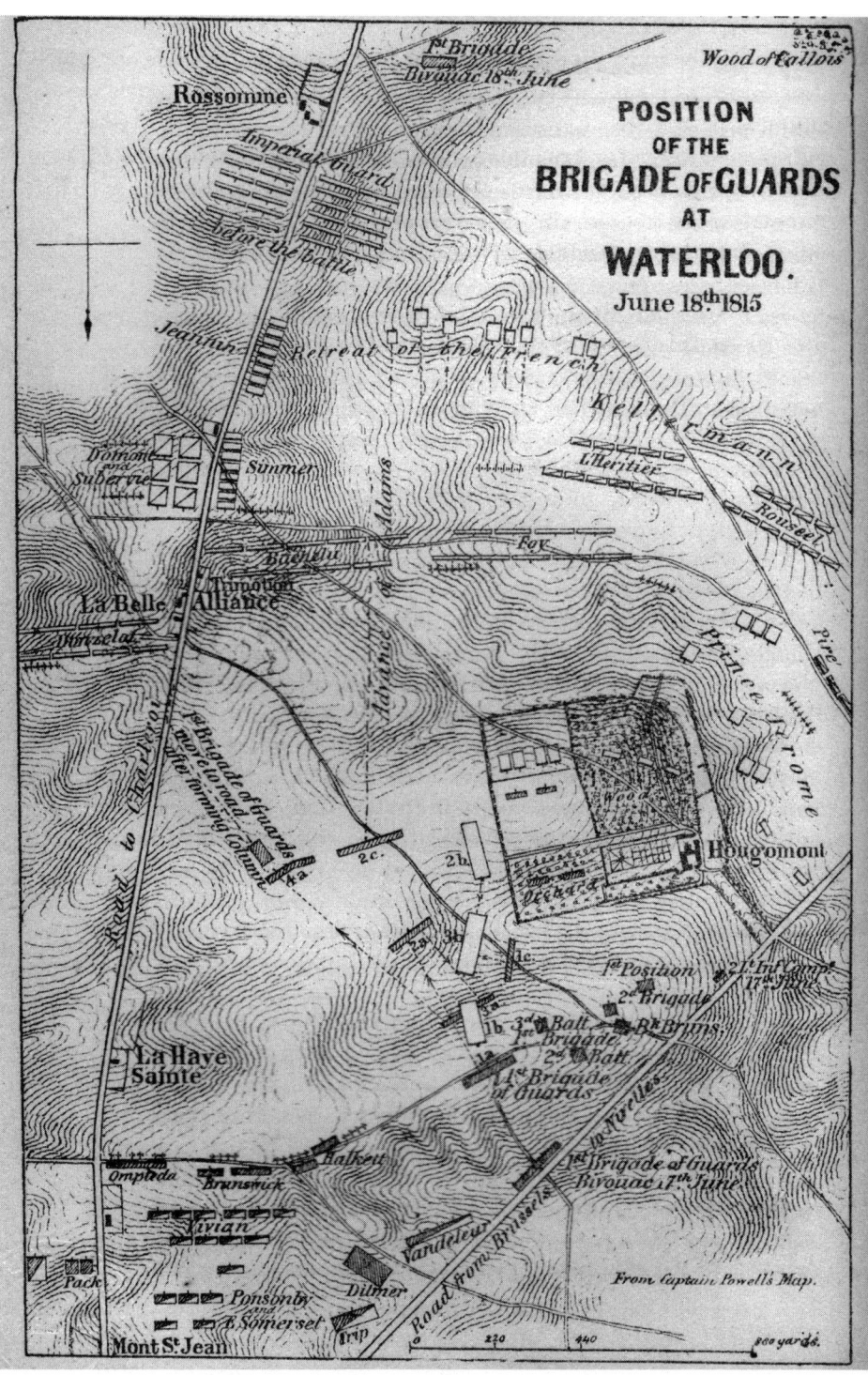

Map of the Guard's movements from Hamilton's History of the 1st Foot Guards, based on Captain Powell's drawings.

About seven o'clock pm, the Duke of Wellington, aware of the enemy's preparations for a new attack, desired me to form the 1st Brigade of Guards in line four files [ranks] deep, His Grace expecting that the French cavalry would take part in the affair.

The formation of the brigade was scarcely completed, before the advance of the enemy became apparent. The forces employed by the enemy in this service consisted of two strong columns of infantry, a third corps, consisting of both cavalry and infantry, being in reserve.

The attacking columns were alike composed of the infantry of the Imperial Guard, the Grenadiers forming one column, the Chasseurs of that corps the other.

As the attacking force moved forward it separated, the chasseurs inclined to their left. The grenadiers ascended the acclivity towards our position in a more direct course, leaving La Haye Sainte on their right, and moving towards that part of the eminence occupied by the 1st Brigade of Guards. Numerous pieces of ordnance were distributed on the flanks of this column.

The brigade suffered by the enemy's artillery, but it withheld its fire for the nearer approach of the column. The latter, after advancing steadily up the slope, halted about twenty paces from the front rank of the brigade. The diminished range of the enemy's artillery was now felt most severely in our ranks; the men fell in great numbers before the discharges of grapeshot, and the fire of the musketry distributed among the guns.

The smoke of the artillery happily did not envelop the hostile column or serve to conceal it from our aim...The fire of the brigade opened with terrible effect. The enemy's column, crippled and broken, retreated with utmost rapidity, leaving only a heap of dead and dying men to mark the ground which it had occupied.

The brigade pressed on the retreating column and was in some measure separated from the general line of our position. The enemy's second attacking column advanced towards that part of our position which had been vacated by the Second Brigade of Guards, when it moved to Hougoumont [where Adam's now was] ... the enemy column had already advanced across the line of extension on the right of the brigade. The brigade began to change front towards its right.

The Light Brigade under Sir F Adam ... opened its fire on the enemy's column.[4]

General Maitland makes some interesting comments which need to be discussed. He confirms that the third body of troops consisted of cavalry and infantry, not Imperial Guardsmen, this would indicate that this consisted of troops from Reille's Corps and cavalry which Napoleon had ordered to move forward to support the Guard attack. He also recognises that French artillery accompanied the columns of the Guard in their advance, but his statement that they came

---

4. Siborne, The Waterloo Letters pp 242–3.

within twenty yards of the British Guards would appear to be an exaggeration, given that none of the Guards describe losing huge numbers of men to enemy cannon fire at what would have been such a murderous range. He also claims that having destroyed the column in its front it turned to its right to face the other oncoming Imperial Guard column which was now on its right flank. This claim is inconsistent with the statements of most eyewitnesses in the 1st Foot Guards and we will discuss this further shortly.

General Byng also wrote in his despatch:

> I had also to witness the gallantry with which they met the last attack made by the Grenadiers of the Imperial Guard, ordered on by Buonaparte himself, the destructive fire they poured in, and the subsequent charge, which, together, completely routed the enemy.[5]

Lieutenant Colonel Alexander Lord Saltoun of 3/1st Guards returned to the battalion from Hougoumont in the late afternoon, to soon find himself in command of the brigade as all ten officers senior to himself had been killed or wounded. He subsequently wrote to his wife claiming all of the success of defeating the Guard for his regiment and making it out to be little more than a picnic:

> About ½ past six,[6] Napoleon made his last desperate attack at the head of his Old Imperial Guards upon our brigade. It was a thing I always wished for and the result was exactly what I have often said it would be. To do them justice they came on like men but our boys went at them like Britons and drove them off the field in less than ten minutes.[7]

By contrast, there are those, such as Captain Lord Charles Fitzroy of the 1st Foot Guards, serving as Deputy Assistant Adjutant General, who was in the area, being assigned to Clinton's Second Division at the time, who assert that Adam's Brigade had nothing to do with the defeat of the Guard at all:

> The Guards advancing and bringing their right shoulders forward brought them on the left of Adam's Brigade with a wide interval. The whole advancing brought the Guards in immediate contact with the Imperial Guards; an honour which others (Adams Brigade) claimed but had no more right than a ship in sight when another ship engages and captures an enemy.[8]

An unidentified officer of the 1st Foot Guards also claimed all the laurels for the Guards together with a brigade of Dutch troops under General Chasse (to be discussed later) which were to its left, but of course led by Saltoun, a Guards officer:

---

5. Glover, The Waterloo Archive Volume IV, p 144.
6. The attack by the Middle Guard occurred later, at around 19.30 to 20.00 hours.
7. Glover, Waterloo Archive Volume VI p 109.
8. Glover, Letters from the Battle of Waterloo, p 178.

At eight o'clock, the enemy moved forward his Old Guard, who were received by the First Brigade of Guards, and a Dutch Brigade, with Saltoun at their head, with such a fire, that they took to their heels.[9]

However, far more of the eyewitnesses from the 1st Foot Guards claim to have seen only the two large columns, one of which they defeated, and they readily admit that the latter was defeated by Adam's Brigade. Lieutenant Colonel John Reeve of 3/1st Guards helps to set the scene:

> When the French Imperial Guard made their attack about 7 o'clock pm the 1st Brigade of Guards were lying down in a line of four deep resting upon their arms and as far as my recollection carries me, occupied the position which I have marked upon the plan,[10] being covered by some broken and gently rising ground in their front. They had been thus situated for about the space of 20 minutes previously to the enemy's last attack, all firing in their immediate front having ceased. The enemy, advanced in two parallel close columns of infantry of the Imperial Guard in a front of Grand Divisions preceded by a very strong line of sharpshooters[11] who came on in a most gallant and determined manner, shouting and keeping up a most destructive fire. On the enemy's columns arriving within about 30 paces of our line they halted, but from the warm reception they met with, instead of deploying they commenced firing several file deep evidently in confusion; at that moment we charged them – they began to waver; went to the right about and fled in all directions.[12]

An anonymous officer of the Guards also recalled that:

> The head of an immense column of the Old Guard appeared trampling down the corn fields in our front: they advanced to within one hundred and fifty yards of our brigade, without attempting to deploy or fire a shot. Our wings threw themselves immediately forward, and kept up such a murderous fire, that the enemy retired, losing half their numbers, who, without any exaggeration, literally lay in sections.[13]

The fact that the column was of a considerable size, and the estimated casualties found in the following statements, would appear to refute claims that the British Guards only fought one battalion of the Imperial Guard. The envelopment of the head of the column by the wings is also of great interest, the Guard Brigade even in four ranks, still stretched much further than the front of the column, before it fully deployed. Lieutenant Charles Ellis of 3/1st Guards adds:

---

9. Eaton, A Near Observer, volume 1, p 71.
10. Not extant.
11. Few mention skirmishers in front of the squares.
12. Glover, Letters from the Battle of Waterloo, p 160.
13. Eaton, A Near Observer Volume 1 p 69.

The Centre Attack 19.30–20.00 Hours

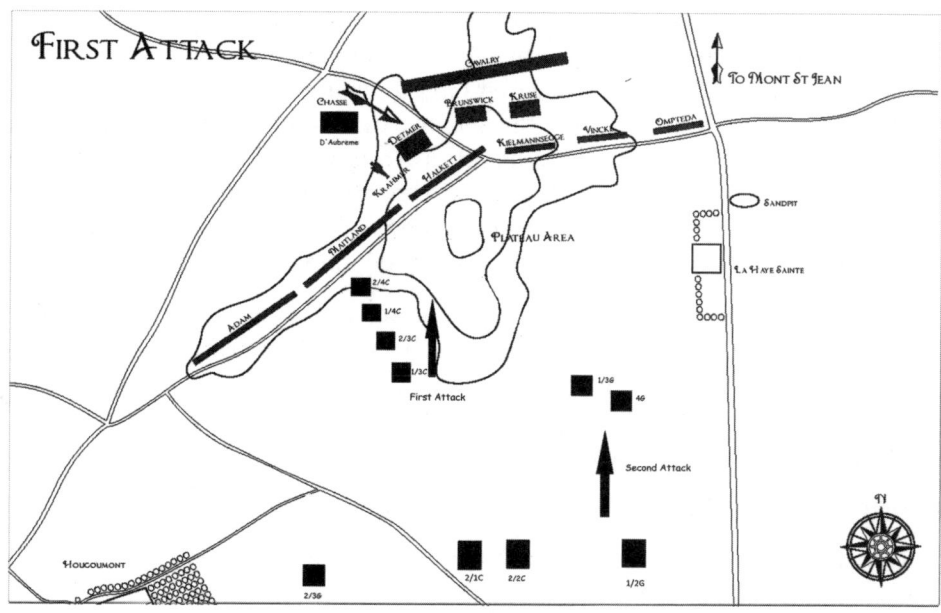

The first attack of the Imperial Guards was (I believe) composed of the Old Guard; and this first attack was repulsed, and I may add, the attacking column almost destroyed, by the First Brigade; no other corps having anything whatever to do with that attack.[14]

Although his identity of the Old Guard was incorrect, he went further in a subsequent letter claiming that the attack on the Guards was much larger than subsequent ones:

> I believe the first attack of the Imperial Guards to have been composed, of a very much larger force than four battalions, moreover the attack was decidedly in column and not in line, upon this point I have no doubt, for I have never heard it stated otherwise by any officer, besides which the French rarely, if ever, attacked in any other formation. The column presented a front of about 200 men which might have led to the mistake, and after receiving about ten rounds of a close and well directed fire, they began firing from the rear of this column and killing themselves, and at this moment (as described to me) the column seemed to burst, if I may use such an expression. The French officers were observed to be very active in trying to form a line, and it was then the brigade charged them, and with complete success. I have mentioned these minor circumstances as proof of the attack having been made in column.[15]

Given that the faces of each side of the Imperial Guard squares were comprised of a full company in three ranks deep, they cannot have exceeded 70 men wide.

---

14. Glover, Letters from the Battle of Waterloo, p 161.
15. ibid, p 162.

If Ellis was correct, then the squares in the column must have begun to deploy to the left in echelon, therefore appearing as if forming into line.

Lieutenant Charles Lascelles of 2/1st Guards, confirms that his battalion was on the right of the brigade, being the senior battalion of the brigade, and that they had the 2/95th to its right, although the company of the Coldstream and 3rd Foot Guards protecting their Colour parties was presumably in-between. He also states that the French approached in column, but then began to open out; was this the squares behind one another deploying into echelon?

> The Imperial Guard came up in close column, and began to open out into line, but did not complete the manoeuvre. If I remember right the [2/]95th Rifles (part of General Adam's Brigade) were on the right of the 2nd Battalion, between it and Hougoumont. I beg leave to state that I was in the 2nd Battalion 1st Foot Guards during the campaign of 1815.[16]

Ensign Joseph St John of 2/1st Foot Guards, wrote of the attack:

> They opened another tremendous cannonade for some time, we then heard musket balls whizzing over our heads and our division alone took ground to the left just on the ridge of a hill, where the French Imperial Guards were, we were then ordered to lay down till the Imperial Guards came up close. The prisoners of them all say that Bonaparte came up to them and said his last hope was in them and that if they broke our front the plunder of Brussels should be their reward. When we laid down, the Imperial Guards thought we were gone and they came up very fast, the moment they came near we jumped up and poured in such a volley upon them that they could not stand it and from that time there was a complete defeat of the French, it was a second Leipzig[17] with [the] slaughter.[18]

This confirms that the 2nd Battalion were involved in the fighting, however, Colour Sergeant Charles Wood, 3/1st Foot Guards, makes it clear that his battalion stood the brunt of the fighting:

> He [Napoleon] then sent against us his Grenadier Imperial Guards; they came within 100 yards of us and ported arms to charge; but we advanced upon them in quick time, and opened a brisk file fire by two [the third and fourth ranks could not fire] ranks, they allowed us to come within about 30 yards of them, they stood till then, looking at us, as if panic struck, and did not fire, they then, as we approached, faced about and fled for their lives, in all directions. They did not like the thought of the British bayonets, for we had just commenced the charge, they ran very fast, but many of them fell, while we pursued, and with them one stand of Colours; and I have the

---

16. Glover, Letters from the Battle of Waterloo, p 164.
17. The Battle of Leipzig (or Battle of the Nations) was fought between 16–19 October 1813 and involved over 600,000 soldiers leading to 100,000 casualties, but over a wide area. The fighting at Waterloo was more intense on a local scale.
18. Glover, The Waterloo Archive Volume VI, p 107.

honour to wear a colonel's sword of the French Imperial Guard. Though not mentioned in the dispatch (they all fought so well), yet it was our Third Battalion of the First Guards, and the rifle battalion of the KGL, that first completely turned the day in our favour. It was at this moment of the charge that I prayed thus, 'Lord, stretch forth thine arm' and this I did unceasingly, until the enemy was driven. When the Imperial Guards, the dependence of Bonaparte, ran, his defence departed from him, and his whole line, as has been stated, became confusion.[19]

Lieutenant Henry Powell of the 2/1st Foot Guards explained how the brigade formed unconventionally into four-deep line and drove the first column of the Imperial Guard away, but finding a second Guard column advancing on its right, he is honest enough to admit that the British guardsmen were forced to hurriedly retire to the ridge line. This again proves that the entire 1st Brigade of the Guards was involved[20] whilst this retiring to the ridge line also explains how the 52nd could later march across its front without encountering them.

The Duke ordered the 1st Brigade of Guards to take ground to its left and form line four deep, which poor Frank d'Oyley[21] did by wheeling up the sides of the square putting the Grenadiers and my company [No 1] in the centre of our line.

There ran along this part of the position a cart road, one side of which was a ditch and bank, in and under which the brigade sheltered themselves during the cannonade ...

A close column of Grenadiers (about seventies in front) of la Moyenne Garde [Middle Guard], about 6,000 strong, led, as we have since heard, by Marshal Ney, were seen ascending the rise au pas de charge shouting 'Vive l'Empereur' they continued to advance till within fifty or sixty paces of our front, when the brigade were ordered to stand up. Whether it was from the sudden and unexpected appearance of a corps so near them, which must have seemed as starting out of the ground, or the tremendously heavy fire we threw into them, la Garde ... suddenly stopped.

In less than a minute above 300 were down. They now wavered, and several of the rear divisions began to draw out as if to deploy, whilst some of the men in their rear beginning to fire over the heads of those in front was so evident a proof of their confusion, that Lord Saltoun, ...holloaed out 'Now's the time my boys'.[22] Immediately the brigade sprang forward. La Garde turned and gave us little opportunity of trying the steel. We charged down the hill till we had passed the end of the orchard of Hougoumont, when our right flank became exposed to another heavy column... who were advancing in support of

---

19. ibid, p 129.
20. Some historians incorrectly claim that only the 3/1st Guards was involved.
21. Lieutenant Colonel Sir Francis d'Oyly who was killed soon after.
22. Such phrases, such as 'Up Guards and at them!' are more often attributed to the Duke of Wellington.

the former column. This circumstance, besides that our charge was isolated, obliged the brigade to retire towards their original position.²³

It is interesting that this column was estimated at 6,000 or more and, as will be seen, the column engaged by the Light Brigade is estimated at no less than 10,000, when the entire ten battalions of the Imperial Guard which advanced to attack the allied ridge numbered little more than 6,000 all told. Clearly both estimates are therefore greatly exaggerated. This might have occurred because the Imperial Guard were in open squares, whereas the British eyewitnesses generally believed that they were in solid column, which would cause them to over-estimate their numbers by a factor of up to three. Powell wrote again on 20 June 1815, when it was apparent that his views of the action had not changed significantly that:

> He [Napoleon] brought up his Garde Imperiale, quite opposite our brigade, which had formed in [four deep] line, on their advancing. We were all lying under shelter of a small bank, as they cover[e]d their advance with a most terrible fire of grape, and musketry, Buonaparte led them himself to the rise of the hill, and told them 'that was the way to Brussels'. We allowed them to come within about a hundred yards, when we open[e]d so destructive a fire, that there were soon above three hundred of them, on the ground and they began to waver, we immediately charged, but they ran as fast as possible … After this we were again annoy[e]d with grape, and musketry which obliged us to retire.²⁴

Here we have another eyewitness admitting that they retired after defeating the Imperial Guard column. Lieutenant Colonel Stanhope had returned from his fruitless search for horses to remove some abandoned pieces of artillery, just in time to witness the culmination of the Imperial Guard attacks; he records that:

> It is hard to say which [column] was cleaned away the soonest. Our men poured in a fire standing four deep, the men who had fired then went to the fourth rank to load and thus without interruption a destructive hail was kept up against which nothing could stand and the hill was heaped with their dead.²⁵

Lieutenant Thomas Henry Davies of 3/1st Foot Guards also claims that the first column was driven off with heavy loss:

> When the French Imperial Guards advanced to the attack, the same manoeuvre was repeated by the British Guards [the battalion opened from the centre of the rear face of the square and the two flank faces bringing their right and left shoulders forward until in line with the front face, thus forming an irregular line of four deep] and the French Guards, whose attack

---

23. Siborne, The Waterloo Letters, p 254.
24. Ms Letter dated 20 June 1815, due to be published in The Waterloo Archive Volume IX, in 2020.
25. Glover, Eyewitness to the Peninsular War and the Battle of Waterloo, p 191.

was made in column, were broken and driven back with great slaughter, the field being literally covered with their dead.[26]

Ensign John Dirom of 3/1st Foot Guards described the confusion within the Imperial Guard columns, note the plural, this again indicates that the various battalion squares had at least attempted to deploy:

> When the Imperial Guard came in sight, the men were desired to stand up and cautioned at the same time not to fire without orders. The Imperial Guard advanced in close column with ported arms, the officers of the leading divisions in front waving their swords. The French columns showed no appearance of having suffered on their advance but seemed as regularly formed as if at a field day.
>
> When they got within a short distance, we were ordered to make ready, present and fire. The effect of our volley was evidently most deadly. The French columns appeared staggered, and, if I may use the expression, convulsed. Part seemed inclined to advance, part halted and fired, and others, more particularly towards the centre and rear of the columns, seemed to be turning round.[27]

This is confirmed by Ensign Thomas Swinburne of 3/1st Foot Guards in his letter to William Siborne, although he incorrectly remembers the Guard attack being the cause of the battalion retiring from its position on the forward slope, whereas there was actually about an hour between these two events:

> About the period you allude to, we retired up a rising ground and the men were ordered to [go] back and lie down behind a grassy bank, which I believe was a division of the fields [actually it was the bank of the trackway running along the ridge]. We had retired in line and the French Guards had deployed and followed us up closely. On their gaining the crown of the hill (if I may so call it), there was a call for skirmishers to check the French advance. I went forward with a few men pretty close to the French, who continued advancing to the spot where our battalion was lying. I got back to the company I had the command of, shortly before we were ordered to rise and fire a volley and charge. This the French received and I think they were not more than 15 yards from us; they were so close that some of our men fired from the charging position (I mean without bringing the musket to the shoulder). The fire was very destructive, as there was a hedge of bodies lying and over which we passed in the charge after them down the slope.[28]

Ensign Rees Gronow of 1/1st Foot Guards, who had made his way to Belgium without orders, but was allowed to serve at Waterloo with the 3/1st Guards also recorded that:

---

26. Siborne, The Waterloo Letters, p 257.
27. ibid, pp 257–8.
28. Glover, Letters from the Battle of Waterloo, p 167.

> After they had pounded away at us for about half an hour they deployed and up came the whole mass of the Imperial infantry of the Guard led on by the Emperor in person. We had now before us probably about 20,000 [sic!] of the best soldiers in France the heroes of many memorable victories we saw the bearskin caps rising higher and higher as they ascended the ridge of ground which separated us and advanced nearer and nearer to our lines. It was at this moment that the Duke of Wellington gave his famous order for our bayonet charge as he rode along the line these are the precise words he made use of 'Guards get up and charge'. We were instantly on our legs and after so many hours of inaction and irritation at maintaining a purely defensive attitude all the time suffering the loss of comrades and friends the spirit which animated officers and men may easily be imagined. After firing a volley as soon as the enemy were within shot [range] we rushed on with fixed bayonets and that hearty hurrah peculiar to British soldiers. It appeared that our men deliberately and with calculation singled out their victims for as they came upon the Imperial Guard our line broke and the fighting became irregular. The impetuosity of our men seemed almost to paralyze their enemies I witnessed several of the Imperial Guard who were run through the body apparently without any resistance on their parts. I observed a big Welshman of the name of Hughes[29] who was six feet seven inches in height run through with his bayonet and knock down with the butt end of his firelock I should think a dozen at least of his opponents. This terrible contest did not last more than ten minutes for the Imperial Guard was soon in full retreat leaving all their guns and many prisoners in our hands.[30]

Gronow was a good story-teller and the numbers of Imperial Guard involved had probably grown over the years of his telling his yarns. His reference to its line breaking and descending into irregular fighting, would explain how the Guards were in confusion when the second column approached its right flank. Major Chatham Churchill of the 1st Foot Guards, aide de camp to Lord Hill also records how:

> Under cover of this cannonade advanced Bonaparte at the head of his Imperial Guard. Cavalry in a column on the left flank, the Grenadiers of the Guard on their right flank. They advanced most steadily up to our line in the great mass. They halted & commenced firing, their troops were literally mowed down. The fire was so great, nothing could stand. Our guns were moved close up to the flank of their column foudroyer [to strike down] with grape into it.[31]

Ensign Richard Master of 3/1st Guards remembered it all happening at once, as if against a single column:

---

29. This would appear to be Private William Hughes 3rd Battalion 1st Foot Guards, who was invalided out of the army soon after Waterloo.
30. Gronow, Reminiscences of Captain Gronow, pp 101–2.
31. Glover, The Waterloo Archive Volume VI, p 5.

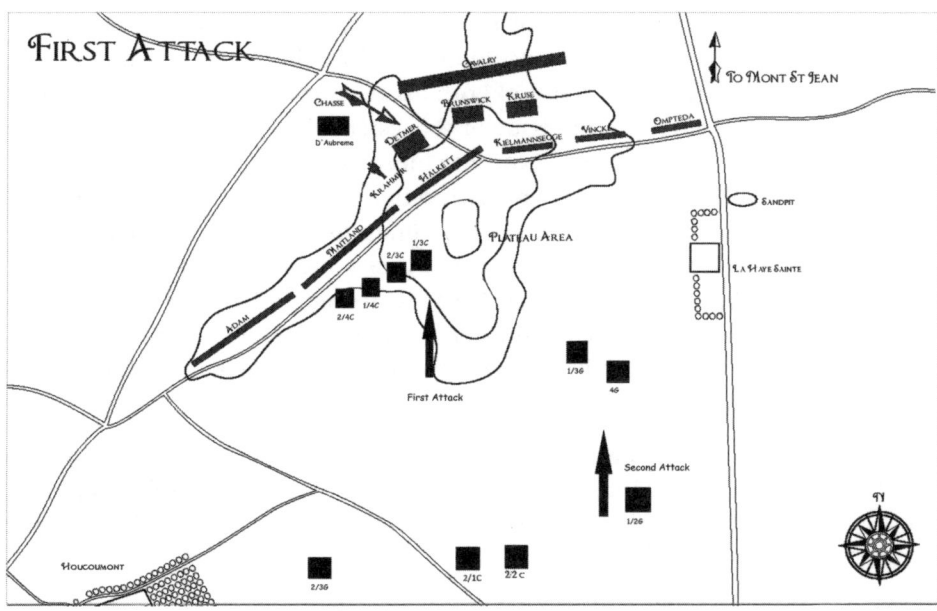

Towards the end of the battle, comes to us the Duke of Wellington almost alone, for all his adc's being killed or disabled, he calls out to us, 'Now Guard, at them again'. We rose immediately & what did we behold; a large mass creeping up the declivity 'En battalion serree' [battalions behind each other in column], fine stout men with fur grenadier caps screaming out '*Vive l'Empereur*', '*En avant*' we quickly formed line 4 deep on the ridge, first rank kneeling & 2nd rank firing, 3rd & 4th handing & loading or picking up stray ammunition, as I did; for some men had not a cartridge left & lucky for us, French cartridges from the dead served us, whilst our bullets were too large for French muskets. Thus, we gave this column of Grenadiers de la Garde Imperial so hot a reception in front, that they came to a standstill.[32]

His description of the French formation is interesting, but particularly his admission that some of the men were out of ammunition. Ensign Robert Batty of 3/1st Foot Guards, who later wrote his own history of the battle, wrote that:

Upon the cavalry being repulsed, the Duke himself ordered our Second Battalion to form with the 3rd Battalion and after advancing to the brow of the hill, to lie down and shelter ourselves from the fire. Here we remained, I imagine, near an hour. It was now about seven o'clock, the French infantry had in vain been brought up against our line and as a last resource, Buonaparte resolved upon attacking our part of the position with his veteran Imperial Guard, promising them the plunder of Brussels. Their artillery covered them and they advanced solid column, to where we lay. The Duke, who riding behind us, watched their approach and at length,

---

32. ibid, p 150.

when within an hundred yards of us exclaimed, 'Up Guards and at them again.' Never was there a prouder moment than this for our country or ourselves. The Household troops of both nations were now for the first time brought in contact and on the issue of their struggle, the greatest of stakes was placed. The enemy did not expect to meet us so soon, we suffered them to approach still nearer and then delivered a fire into them, which made them halt, a second like the first, carried hundreds of deaths into their mass and without suffering them [to] deploy, we gave them three British cheers and a British charge of the bayonet. This was too much for their nerves and they fled in disorder, the shape of their column was tracked by their dying and dead and not less than three hundred of them had fallen in two minutes, to rise no more.[33]

Ensign Daniel Tighe of the 2/1st Foot Guards also recalled that there were a number of columns. His drawing of its positions on a map shows three columns, but the positions he gives for the position where the British Guards were formed is clearly too far forward:

On the advance of the Imperial Guard we got the word to advance in line (to D) and poured in a rapid fire into the advancing columns of the Imperial Guard which they stood but a short time and retreated in full disorder. I conceive this advance of the Imperial G[uar]ds to be almost the time alluded to in your letter.[34]

What of eyewitnesses from other units close by? Lieutenant George Bowles with the Colours of the Coldstream Guards recorded that:

The First Brigade of Guards advanced to meet the leading division, and poured in so well directed a fire as literally to make a chasm in it. For a short time the fire of musketry was really awful, and proved too much for even these hitherto deemed invincibles; they gave way in every direction.[35]

An unknown artillery officer (possibly Sir Augustus Frazer) recalled very precisely that

The brigade [of guns], about the close of the day, was stationed on the right of our Guards, commanded by Captain Napier, after Captain Bolton's fall, when the Imperial Guards led on by Marshal Ney about half past seven o'clock, made their appearance from a corn field, in close columns of grand divisions, nearly opposite, and within a distance of fifty yards from the muzzles of the guns. Orders were given to load with cannister shot, and literally five rounds from each gun were fired with this destructive species

---

33. Ms Letter of Ensign Batty dated Bavay 21 June 1815, to be published in Waterloo Archive Volume IX in 2020.
34. Glover, Letters from the Battle of Waterloo, p 168.
35. Glover, A Guards Officer in the Peninsula and at Waterloo, p 99.

of shot, before they showed the least symptom of giving way. At the 29th round, their left gave way, and they were then attacked by the Guards, who were at this period lying down in line.[36]

First Lieutenant George Pringle of Captain Napier's (previously Bolton's) Battery was quite as exact in his description:

> Captain Bolton's battery was contiguous to the Foot Guards, with the right of whose it formed an angle of about 140 [degrees][37]
>
> The enemy advanced in heavy close column, with the intention of penetrating the situation at the right of the Foot Guards. They were within the angle formed by the battery and the Foot Guards before they went about, so that at last the right gun could not conveniently be brought to bear upon the head of the column. The battery fired case shot from the moment they appeared on the crest of the hill (about 200 yards) and during the advance along the plateau, from which they suffered severely, the column waving, at each successive discharge, like standing corn blown by the wind.[38]

First Lieutenant William Sharpin, also of Captain Napier's Battery gives some useful corroborating details:

> A few minutes before the French Imperial Guards made their appearance the Duke of Wellington rode up to our battery and hastily asked me who commanded it; I replied that Bolton did, but that he was just killed, and that it was then under Napier. His Grace then said, 'Tell him to keep a look to his left for the French will soon be with him' and then he rode off.
>
> I had scarcely communicated the Duke's message, when we saw the French bonnets just above the high corn, and within forty or fifty yards of our guns. I believe they were in close columns of Grand divisions, and upon reaching the crest of our position, they attempted to deploy into line, but the destructive fire of our guns loaded with cannister shot, and the well directed volleys from the infantry, prevented their regular formation.
>
> They remained under this fire about ten minutes, advancing a little, but finding it impossible to force our position, they gave way and went to the right about.[39]

Captain Digby Mackworth, aide de Camp to Lord Hill, was effusive in his description of the approach of the Imperial Guard:

> The cannonade continued without intermission, and about 6 [7:30?] o'clock we saw heavy columns of infantry supported by dragoons forming for a fresh attack, it was evident it would be a desperate, and we thought, probably a decisive one; everyone felt how much depended on this terrible moment.

---

36. Eaton, A Near Observer Volume 2, p 46.
37. i.e. facing somewhat away from the line of advance of the Imperial Guard.
38. Siborne, The Waterloo Letters, p 227.
39. Siborne, The Waterloo Letters, pp 228–9.

A black mass of the Grenadiers of the Imperial Guard with music playing and the great Napoleon at their head came rolling onward from the farm of '*La Belle Alliance*'; with rapid pace they descended the opposite heights, all scattered firing ceased on both sides, our little army seemed to collect within itself, the infantry deployed into line, and the artillery, charged to the muzzle with grape and canister, waited for the moment when the enemy's columns should commence the ascent of our heights; those spaces in our lines which death had opened and left vacant were covered in appearance by bodies of cavalry.[40]

---

40. Glover, The Waterloo Archive Volume IV, p 24.

Chapter 10

To Maitland's Left, Defeating the Second Attack 19.45–20.15 Hours

Halkett's Brigade was to the immediate left of the British Guards, what did it see and do? Captain George Barlow of the 69th Foot (who had fought for three years in the Peninsula with the 52nd) was a precise young man, who wrote home:

> Eight o'clock came and found the battle yet undecided, for shortly afterwards four solid masses of the Imperial Guard infantry advanced and made a most formidable attack. These fellows came up with carried arms and in the most determined manner to within seventy or eighty yards of the heights along which our infantry were placed and poured a terrible fire, two pieces of cannon accompanied them and being placed affront our brigade, which was formed en masses, raked it most severely with grapeshot as did shells from some more distant howitzers. This was indeed the crisis of this eventful day, both armies were in close contact and hot action and the cannonade really tremendous along the whole line as the entire artillery of either army were in full play to support their respective parties in an effort which was to decide the fortune of the battle.[1]

Captain Cuyler of the 69th confirmed that they were Guard troops accompanied with cannon: 'The French Imperial Guard was in line immediately in front with artillery upon its right.'[2] Ensign Edward Macready of the 30th Foot wrote soon after the battle:

> The enemy then sent a strong column of the Grenadiers of the Guard to drive us, but when they came within twenty paces, we gave them a volley and a huzza; and prepared for a charge, but they spared us the trouble, away they went, our cavalry got among them, and I pitied the '*pouvres* [sic] *diables*' [poor devils]. But I am endeavouring to do an impossibility, to describe a battle; so little did we know of it next morning (as we fought till dark) that I assure you I expected to see the enemy on the heights opposite us.[3]

However, in 1836, he wrote a statement, which he later copied to William Siborne:

---

1. Glover, The Waterloo Archive Volume IV, p 163.
2. Glover, Letters from the Battle of Waterloo, p 223
3. Glover, The Waterloo Archive Volume 1, pp 162–3.

I saw no troops of the Guard to the French right of that column which advanced on us (30th & 73rd) and which, though it came over the hill in beautiful order, was an inconceivable short time before us, turning and flying to a man at the single volley we fired, and the hurrah that followed it.[4]

He also recorded events in a lengthy journal, giving a great deal more detail:

About six o'clock I perceived some artillery trotting up our hill, which I knew by their caps to belong to the Imperial Guard. I had hardly mentioned this to a brother officer when two guns unlimbered within seventy paces of us, and by their first discharge of grape blew seven men into the centre of the square. They immediately reloaded and kept up a constant and destructive fire. It was noble to see our fellows fill up the gaps after every discharge. I was much distressed at this moment. I ordered up three of my light bobs [light infantrymen], and they had hardly taken their station when two of them fell horribly lacerated. One of them looked up in my face and uttered a sort of reproachful groan, and I involuntarily exclaimed, 'By God, I couldn't help it.' We would willingly have charged these guns, but had we deployed the cavalry that flanked them would have made an example of us...

It was near seven o'clock, and our front had sustained three attacks from fresh troops, when the Imperial Guard were seen ascending our position, in as correct order as at a review. As they rose step by step before us, and crossed the ridge, their red epaulettes and cross belts, put on over their blue greatcoats, gave them a gigantic appearance, which was increased by their high hairy caps and long red feathers, which waved with the nod of their heads as they kept time to a drum in the centre of their column. 'Now for a clawing', I muttered; and I confess, when I saw the imposing advance of these men, and thought of the character they had gained, I looked for nothing but a bayonet in my body, and I half breathed a confident sort of wish that it might not touch my vitals.

While they were moving up the slope, Halkett, as well as the noise permitted us to hear him, addressed us, and said, 'My boys, you have done everything I could have wished, and more than I could expect, but much remains to be done; at this moment we have nothing for it but a charge.' Our brave fellows replied by three cheers. The enemy halted, carried arms about forty paces from us, and fired a volley. We returned it and giving out 'Hurra!' brought down the bayonets. Our surprise was inexpressible when, pushing through the clearing smoke, we saw the backs of the Imperial Grenadiers. We halted and stared at each other as if mistrusting our eyesight. Some nine pounders from the rear of our right poured in the grape amongst them, and the slaughter was dreadful. In no part of the field did I see carcases so heaped upon each other. I could not account for their flight, nor did I ever hear an admissible reason assigned for it. It was a most providential panic. We could not pursue on account of their cavalry, and their artillery was

---

4. Siborne, The Waterloo Letters, p 330.

To Maitland's Left, Defeating the Second Attack 19.45–20.15 Hours

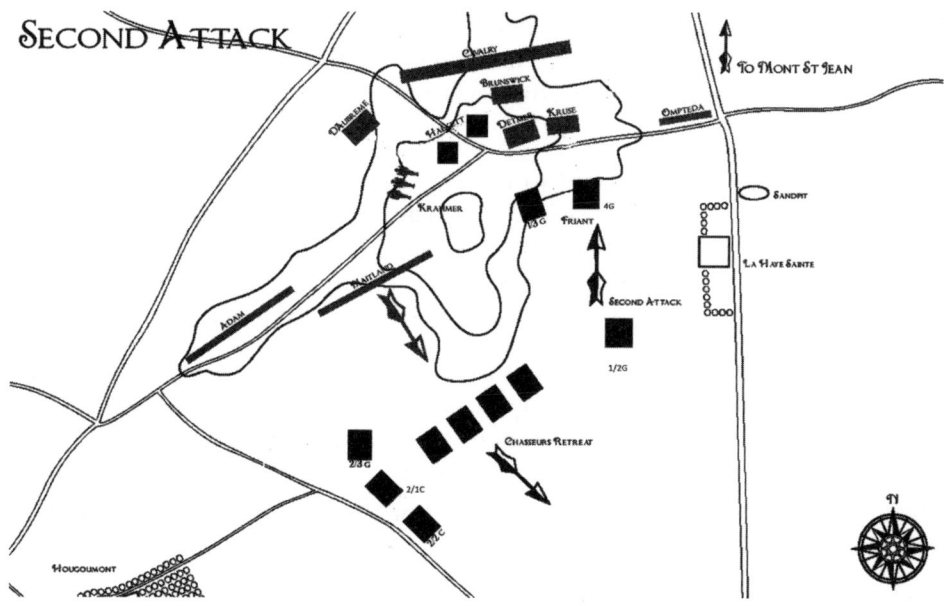

still shockingly destructive. About this time Baron Alten was wounded, and General Halkett went to take the command of the division.[5]

Major General Sir Colin Halkett records moving two of his battalions forward to bring them against a column of the Imperial Guard marching towards the British Guards:

> On the enemy advancing upon the Guards, I moved them [33rd/69th] forward towards the position of the [French] Guards, and in their front, which had the good effect of arresting their progress.[6]

Lieutenant Colonel William Elphinstone 33rd Foot, however, denies any involvement in defeating the Guard:

> About seven o'clock, when the enemy's final attack was made, [the battalion] was formed four deep, on the immediate left of the 1st Guards. At this time columns of French infantry were advancing, with guns between the heads of the columns. These, when within a short distance of our position, halted and soon after gave way.[7]

Given this evidence, it would seem that a square of the Imperial Guard came up directly towards the 30th/73rd, which was positioned to the left of the 33rd/69th and the latter seem to have done little but observe the attack on the British Guards to its right. This confirms that the Imperial Guard battalion witnessed by Macready was not one of those involved in the attack on the British

---
5. Glover, The Waterloo Archive Volume VI, pp 175–6.
6. Siborne, The Waterloo Letters p 321.
7. ibid, p 332.

Guards as this came up just to the (British) left of the plateau (current Lion Mound) and was almost certainly the 2/3rd Grenadiers. If so, we know that the 4th Grenadiers advanced to the right of this, but Macready is often used to refute this, as he claimed that:

> I saw no troops of the Guard to the French right of that column which advanced on us (30th and 73rd) and which, though it came over the hill in beautiful order, was an inconceivable short time before us, turning and flying to a man at the single volley we fired, and the hurrah that followed it ... The men I spoke to as they lay wounded were all of the '*Moyenne Garde*'.[8]

The centre of Wellington's position was indeed in a precarious state, the King's German Legion Brigade had been exhausted in maintaining the defence of La Haye Sainte and the Brunswick, Nassau and Hanoverian troops were close to breaking point, now under the intense fire of artillery which approached the allied ridge with the Imperial Guard battalions. Captain von Scriba of the Bremen Field Battalion described this movement:

> During this time period (half past seven o'clock) ... a strong square of French Guards with several guns also advanced towards us and immediately started firing at a heavy rate.[9]

Lieutenant Tschirschnitz also of the Bremen Battalion agrees that:

> At this moment, a square comprised of the French Garde Imperiale, which could be observed only now through the heavy smoke, advanced under a steady cannonade to within 50 paces of us.[10]

Major General Kruse confirmed that the French Guard reached the plateau, forcing the allied troops to fall back slightly: 'Napoleon's Guard took possession of the plateau, with our infantry withdrawing only 100 paces.'[11] Captain Weisz of the Nassau battalion described how two cannon came within two hundred yards or so and opened fire with devastating volleys of cannister shot: 'Two guns unlimbered in front of the 1st Battalion at a distance of 200 to 300 paces and started at once to cover us with case shot.'[12] Whilst Second Lieutenant Gagern described vain attempts to charge the guns, which cost the lives of many brave men: 'our battalion was ordered to make a bayonet attack against a battalion of the French Guard...we attacked two times, and were repelled each time.'[13]

The Prince of Orange ordered his Nassau troops to advance and he rode forward with them, but the Prince was soon wounded, and they were driven back. Kruse recalled that:

---

8. ibid, p 330.
9. Glover, The Waterloo Archive Volume II, p 109.
10. Franklin, Waterloo Hanoverian Correspondence, p 125.
11. Glover, The Waterloo Archive Volume II, p 176.
12. ibid, p 186.
13. ibid, p 196.

Shortly after 7 o'clock, the Prince of Orange ordered a bayonet attack on the enemy's Imperial Guard, which had been approaching in the meantime. I undertook this attack in attack column with the 2nd Battalion and the severely weakened 1st Battalion, although without success.[14]

The Duke of Wellington had ordered General Chasse to move his division of Dutch/Belgians to his centre as soon as he had become aware of the preparations for the Imperial Guard attack. This was fortuitous, as the Nassau troops, along with Kielmansegge's troops began to withdraw and the hole was temporarily plugged by the arrival of Vincke's Hanoverians and the remnants of the heavy cavalry who stood in their rear to prevent their withdrawal. The situation remained critical here, however, with the French very close to breaking through. At this desperate moment, the First Brigade of Chasse's Division under the command of Detmer arrived. Chasse realised how precarious the situation was and he ordered Krahmer's Battery to immediately deploy to the right of Halkett's Brigade and to engage the Imperial Guard column whilst he took Detmer's Brigade to the left of Halkett to fill the yawning gap in the allied front line, which the Nassau and Kielmansegge's troops had vacated. Chasse describes the situation he discovered:

> I saw the Garde Imperiale advancing, while the English [Hanoverian] troops were leaving the plateau en masse...I immediately ordered the battery of horse artillery under the command of Major van der Smissen[15] to advance, to occupy the height and to direct an emphatic fire upon the enemy column ... Having closed to within a few paces of the enemy I observed that they made a rearward movement.[16]

Captain Rochell of the 19th Militia Battalion was struck by the fragility of the allied line here at this point: 'an English [Hanoverian] division began to waver, as well as a Brunswick brigade'.

The French column began to retreat, followed closely by Detmer's Brigade. Lieutenant Van Eysinga also of the 19th Militia Battalion, recorded how: 'We forced the French back to an orchard. They took up a position there and defended themselves, like one could only expect from the noble French Guard.'[17]

Detmer's troops followed the Imperial Guard column until they arrived at the orchard of La Haye Sainte. Here the Netherlands troops reformed before moving forward again to drive them out of the orchard. It is almost certain that these were the troops seen by the 52nd near La Haye Sainte during its advance, as we will see later.

All of this evidence can appear confusing and patchy, but Lieutenant Colonel Dawson Kelly, who was serving as an Assistant Quarter Master General and as

---

14. Glover, The Waterloo Archive Volume VIII, p 219.
15. Actually commanded by Krahmer, Van Smissen commanding the two batteries which made up the divisional artillery.
16. Franklin, Waterloo Netherlands Correspondence; p 116;
17. Glover, The Waterloo Archive Volume VIII, p 198.

such had time to view the Imperial Guard attack in detail, makes very interesting comments regarding the ability of anyone to see much because of the thick smoke:

> Thus situated we remained for a short time inactive, when the last attacking column made its appearance through the fog and smoke, which throughout the day lay thick on the ground. Their advance was as usual with the French, very noisy and evidently reluctantly, the officers being in advance some yards cheering their men on. They however kept up a confused and running fire, which we did not reply to until they reached nearly on a level with us, when a well directed volley put them into confusion [from] which they did not appear to recover, but after a short interval of musketry on both sides, they turned about to a man and fled.[18]

In a further letter he rightly cautions against trusting implicitly some of the very detailed descriptions written about these events:

> The fog and smoke lay so heavy upon the ground that we could only ascertain the approach of the enemy by the noise and clashing of arms which the French usually make in their advance to attack and it has often occurred to me from the above circumstance (the heavy fog), that the accuracy and the particulars with which the Crisis has been so frequently and so minutely discussed, must have had a good deal of fancy in the narrative.[19]

Corroborating evidence as to the intensity of the fighting between the French and British Guards also comes from Captain Barton of the 12th Light Dragoons, whose troops had to pass over that ground during their subsequent advance:

> On the failure of the Enemy's last attack the brigade advanced, passing over the ground on which the struggle had taken place between the French and English Guards. The scene here was terrific from the great number of killed and wounded. Bodies were lying so close to each other that our horses could scarcely advance without trampling on them.[20]

Even Lieutenant Gawler of the 52nd Foot admits that the Imperial Guard took a significant number of casualties from the fire of the British Guards:

> In a few seconds, the headmost companies of the Imperial Guard, with rattling drums, and deafening shouts of '*Vive l'Empereur*,' crowned the very summit of the position, their dead bodies, the next day, bore unanswerable evidence to the fact. The fire of the Brigade of British Guards then opened upon them.[21]

Many of the 1st Foot Guards officers had commented on there being a second large column of the Imperial Guard, which was coming up some way behind the

---

18. Siborne, The Waterloo Letters p 340.
19. ibid, p 341.
20. ibid, p 116.
21. Gawler, p 302.

first column which they had driven off. So, what do the 1st Foot Guards say of this column?

Major General Peregrine Maitland openly admits that the second column was defeated wholly by Adam's Brigade: 'The latter [column] retreated with the utmost haste pursued by Sir F Adam's Brigade.'[22]

Lieutenant Harry Powell of the 2/1st Foot Guards confusedly has Adam's Brigade helping to drive off the column that had attacked them, before the Guards supposedly went off in pursuit of another column. This cannot be correct as the British units would have got in each other's way:

> The Duke of Wellington observing this crisis, brought up the 95th and 42nd [52nd], taking the enemy in flank, and leading them himself, quite close upon, and the column immediately dispersed.
>
> On fronting we saw another heavy column of the Chasseurs de la Garde Imperiale, we immediately started double quick to meet them, firing as hard as we could, all the time, but they had had so proper a reception just before, that they never let us come near them.[23]

Many years later he wrote to William Siborne on the same subject making his view a little bit clearer:

> Opportunely, Sir F Adam's Light Brigade …were advancing … along the northern side of the orchard at Hougoumont. As soon therefore as we had uncovered their front [ie retired out of the way] we halted and fronted.
>
> The two brigades now returned to the charge which the chasseurs did not wait for, and we continued our forward movement till we got to the bottom of the valley between the positions.
>
> Whilst we were halted in the valley the light troops and cavalry had passed us and gone in pursuit.[24]

He still thought that the Guards had been involved in the defeat of the second column, but it is clear that if they had advanced against them at this moment, they would have collided with Adam's Brigade moving at right angles to the front.

Robert Batty, however, goes so far as to downgrade the other column to a single regiment of Tirailleurs of the Young Guard, which we know cannot be right, as they were in Plancenoit:

> Seeing the fate of their companions, a regiment of Tirailleurs of the Guard, attempted to attack our flank, we instantly charged them and our cheers rendered anything further unnecessary, for they never awaited our approach.[25]

---

22. Siborne, The Waterloo Letters p 245.
23. Ms Letter dated 20 June 1815, due to be published in The Waterloo Archive Volume IX, in 2020.
24. Siborne, The Waterloo Letters pp 254–5.
25. Ms Letter of Ensign Batty dated Bavay 21 June 1815, to be published in Waterloo Archive Volume IX in 2020.

Lieutenant Charles Ellis also had the 1st Foot Guards engaging the head of the column while Adam's Brigade struck its flank:

> The second attack was composed of the Young Guard, and that was defeated jointly by the First Brigade and Adam's Brigade – while the First Brigade were engaged with the front of the column, Adam's brigade charged on the flank, and which attack I believe they sustained but a very few minutes.[26]

Ensign Richard Master, 3/1st Foot Guards, however, recognised that the second column, which had caused the 1st Guard Brigade to retire back towards the ridge, was defeated purely by Adam's Brigade:

> They were taken in flank by General Adam's Brigade & artillery, which put them 'hors de combat', these fine brave old soldiers, who when fallen or wounded kept calling out '*Vive l'Empereur*' thus the Duke sent the whole of his army down the crescent like rising ground they were on & heartedly tired of being under fire this whole day, looking on at the slaughter among them.[27]

When the Guards Brigade moved down into the valley in pursuit of the remnants of the first column, we know that they fell into some confusion, with some recalling a shout of 'cavalry.' This confusion caused the battalion to at least halt to rectify the situation, some others went further, to say that they retired back up the ridge.

Lord Saltoun disputed the orders given and effectively denied the confusion, he then stated that once reorganised, it turned to face the second column that was continuing to advance on its right flank. He claimed that they came within musket shot, but admits that they did not engage as Adam's Brigade had already defeated them:

> The next time I saw of them [the 52nd] was their attack with the rest of General Adam's Brigade on the 2nd column of the Imperial Guards...
>
> The word of command passed was 'Halt, front, form up' any other formation was impossible, and as soon as this order was understood by the men it was obeyed and everything was right again.
>
> The left shoulders were then brought forward, and we advanced against the second column of the Imperial Guards, but which body was defeated by General Adam's Brigade before we reached it, although we got near enough to fire if we had been ordered so to do.[28]

Other evidence from Guard officers shows that they did not just halt, but actually retired to the crest before reforming and it was this movement that meant that the Guards were not visible to the 52nd when they advanced, as the latter claim. Even when reformed and ready to fight again, no Guards officer claims to have

---

26. Glover, Letters from the Battle of Waterloo, p 161.
27. Glover, The Waterloo Archive Volume VII, pp 150.
28. Siborne, The Waterloo Letters, pp 248.

engaged the second column, and most are generous enough to admit that the honour for that success lay entirely with Adam's Brigade.

Digby Mackworth, aide de camp to General Sir Rowland Hill, described it all rather fancifully, however his words, purportedly written on the night of 18 June, include a very interesting first use of a phrase later falsely attributed to General Cambronne. Interestingly, the phrase (to my knowledge or anything remotely like it), does not appear in any ancient classical work and seems to be absolutely new in 1815:

> The point at which the enemy aimed was now evident; it was a re-entering angle formed by a Brigade of [British] Guards, and the Light Brigade of Lord Hill's corps, Lord Hill was there in person. The French moved on with arms sloped 'au pas de charge'; they began to ascend the hill, in a few seconds they were within a hundred paces of us, and as yet not a shot had been fired. The awful moment was now at hand, a peal of ten thousand thunders burst at once on their devoted heads, the storm swept them down as a whirlwind which rushes over the ripe corn, they paused, their advance ceased, they commenced firing from the head of their columns and attempted to extend their front; but death had already caused too much confusion among them, they crowded instinctively behind each other to avoid a fire which was intolerably dreadful; still they stood firm, '*La Garde meurt mais ne se rend pas*' [The Guard dies, but never surrenders]. For half an hour this horrible butchery continued, at last seeing all their efforts vain, all their courage useless, deserted by their Emperor, who had already flown, unsupported by their comrades, who were already beaten, the hitherto invincible Old Guard gave way and fled in every direction.

His account must of course be taken with great caution.

The evidence provided in this chapter makes it abundantly clear that the 1st Guards Brigade certainly faced a sizeable attack of around 2–3,000 men. Initially the Middle Guard Chasseurs appear to have marched forward in a column of battalions in squares. As they arrived near the ridge, just in front of the track running along the crest, there is clear evidence that they sought to deploy, the battalions moving out to their right to form an attack of battalion squares in echelon. The corroborating evidence is unfortunately very sparse as to whether they deployed skirmishers in front of the column, but the overall impression is that they did not. This is in sharp contrast to some of the statements by officers of the 52nd Foot regarding this attack – who by their own admission were not eyewitnesses and therefore carry very little weight.

The British Guards would seem to have maintained a firefight of five to ten minutes before launching a bayonet attack, which drove the Chasseurs away. Both battalions of the brigade were clearly involved in the event, despite claims from some historians that the 2/1st Foot Guards were mere spectators. It would appear to be clear, however, that the brunt of the attack was taken by the 3/1st Guards, as is shown by the casualty returns for the battle. The 2nd Battalion suffered 51 officers and men killed and 101 wounded; whereas the 3rd Battalion had losses of 84 officers and men killed and 242 wounded, or close on double. Although these losses cannot be prescribed accurately to specific time periods, it is certain that the most intensive fighting these two battalions saw that day was against the Imperial Guard and therefore it is reasonable to assume that the brunt of the Imperial Guard attack struck the 3rd Battalion, but it does show that the 2nd Battalion was also in serious action as well. It should also be borne in mind that the losses of the 3rd Battalion of 1st Foot Guards were significantly higher than those borne by the 52nd Foot during the battle, as we will see in the next chapter.

Clearly, the size of any unit's losses does not in itself prove anything, it certainly does not prove that they were either braver or less skilful in the deployment of its troops. The causes for the losses can only be attributed from evidence of its positional deployment and the active part they took in the battle, therefore only a subjective judgement can ever be drawn from these figures. Although the 1st Foot Guards were in the front line for far longer than Adam's Brigade, both were under the shelter of the ridge for extensive periods and for much of the battle were only occasionally struck by cannon balls and shells that flew beyond the crest.

Both were involved in the cavalry attacks and all but the 2nd Battalion of the 1st Foot Guards were deployed on the forward slope to disrupt these waves of cavalry and did suffer some losses from artillery fire there. All were also involved in the defeat of at least some element of the Imperial Guard attacks and both brigades claim to have lost heavily from the musketry of these elite soldiers. Neither, however, claim to have suffered excessive losses during the subsequent advance. It can therefore be seen that the highest levels of casualties were likely to have been for both brigades at two moments, during their deployment on the forward slopes against cavalry and their encounter with the Imperial Guard, therefore the higher levels of losses in the 3rd Battalion of the 1st Foot Guards would appear to support its claim to have been in a prolonged and intense firefight with a large body of the Imperial Guard in formation, not simply from fighting a weak skirmish line. The lower losses of the 2nd Battalion of the 1st Foot Guards can also largely be, although not wholly, attributed to the fact that they remained sheltered behind the ridge during the cavalry attacks and did not suffer like the others on the forward slope. This means that its involvement in the defeat of the Imperial Guard attack could well have been much more significant than the initial casualty figures might lead us to believe. All of this leads the author to the overall assessment that the attack against the 1st Foot Guards was a strong attack by some four battalions in squares and almost certainly was comprised of the 3rd and 4th Chasseurs in 3 or 4 battalions as described by both the French and the British witnesses.

If, as some historians have tried to claim, the 4th Chasseurs made a separate attack and therefore comprised the second column defeated by Adam's Brigade, then we have to accept that the Chasseur attack was completely uncoordinated – with the two regiments in separate columns which became separated by around

400 metres or more. We must also accept that the echelon attack was so badly carried out that the 4th Chasseurs in this second column arrived near to the crest of the ridge a full fifteen to twenty minutes after the 3rd Chasseurs came into contact with the 1st Foot Guards on the ridge. Why on earth would they delay so long? That would be way beyond the delay in an attack in echelon.

Almost all eyewitnesses from the 1st Foot Guards claim that it endured a firefight with the Imperial Guard for five to ten minutes, it then carried out a bayonet charge, driving the French down the forward slope. It then fell into some confusion, coinciding with the appearance of a second column having appeared on its right flank. Some witnesses claim that they remained well down the forward slope, quickly rallied and then turned to their right to face the new column. Others, however, admit that they ran back to the ridgeline and only reformed once there, hastily preparing to receive the second column. The latter version, from the evidence, must be the truth, as the 52nd could not see the Guards at all when they descended into the valley or when they marched horizontally across the front of the allied position. All the evidence leads to the fact that the British Guards must have retired to reform behind the ridgeline, those who claim otherwise must be mistaken or are lying to avoid admitting that the Guards fell into such confusion.

Being to the eastward of the second column, whilst the 52nd were manoeuvring onto the western flank of this second column, it is obvious that any view of the 1st Foot Guards would be completely obscured. When the Imperial Guard retired and Adam's Brigade began to march eastwards across the allied front, the British Guards could not possibly be still on the forward slope, otherwise they would have been seen and could well have got in its way.

In summary, for the British Guards to have continued a prolonged firefight, advanced with the bayonet, charging well down the forward slope and then hurriedly returning beyond the ridgeline, all before the head of the second column arrived on the ridgeline, means that this column was AT LEAST fifteen to twenty minutes behind the first column. This cannot, by any sensible evaluation, be the 4th Chasseurs approaching in echelon with the 3rd Chasseurs. Such an unmilitary and defective approach by the Chasseurs of the Middle Guard to the allied ridge would surely have caused at least some criticism, but such comment is conspicuous by its entire absence.

There is also very good evidence that the combined square of the 30th/73rd did encounter a unit of the Imperial Guard approaching directly on its front to the east of the plateau. This column arrived to the (allied) left of the plateau, meaning that the other square of Halkett's Brigade standing on their right, comprising the 33rd/69th, had no Guard unit in their front. Eyewitnesses from the 69th only report Imperial Guard columns to their right in front of the Guards, this would clearly indicate that the attack to their left was not seen by them because of the watershed and was a completely separate attack.

The arrival of Krahmer's Battery (sometimes mistakenly called Van Smissen's – he was the divisional artillery commander) on the right of the 30th/73rd finally destroyed the morale of the Imperial Guard square fronting them and they retired. There is also very good evidence for at least one other Imperial Guard battalion to the allied left of these units. This is denied by Ensign Macready of the 30th, but he only says that he did not think there was and could not see any. The evidence from Kielmansegge's and Vincke's troops is definite in identifying their attackers as Imperial Guard, flanked by a couple of pieces of artillery and supported by cavalry. This can be identified by French accounts as the 4th Grenadiers who had formed the right of the Grenadier advance following behind the Chasseur attack. The intense cannister fire from these cannon forced Kielmansegge's and Vincke's troops to retire and inflicted a costly defeat on an attempt to drive them back by the Prince of Orange with the Nassau Contingent. The space vacated by these troops was then filled by Detmer's Brigade from General Chasse's Division. It had been ordered to march from Braine l'Alleud to the centre of the allied position, by order of the Duke of Wellington an hour previously, when the French Guards began to form up in front of La Belle Alliance. The arrival of these troops at the very moment of the collapse of the allied centre was therefore not simply fortuitous. If Wellington had not anticipated the threat and ordered the movement prior to the attack developing, the desperate final gamble by Napoleon may well have succeeded in splitting Wellington's army in two. Detmer's fresh troops advancing with the bayonet against troops already unsteady following the devastation caused to the other Guard battalion from the close-range fire of Krahmer's battery, causing them to turn and retreat into La Haye Sainte orchard.

As the remnants of the Imperial Guard had to be ousted from the orchard before the Netherlands troops were in any position to join the allied advance, it was almost certainly these troops that were seen reforming near La Haye Sainte before attacking the orchard and were mistaken for French troops by officers of the 52nd Foot during its advance.

Remarkably, all this evidence from various allied units would seem to agree almost completely with the French version of how the attack of the Imperial Guard played out.

Chapter 11

Defeating the Third Attack – The Second Column 19.45 to 20.00 Hours

It is relatively clear from almost all of the evidence available, that two large columns consisting of battalions in squares behind each other, had approached the allied ridge to the right of the site of the Lion Mound today, while two other battalions had approached the allied line to the east of the plateau area. We have already seen that the first column was certainly defeated by the 1st Guard Brigade alone, but that the 1st Foot Guards had then retired in confusion back to the allied ridge, having been outflanked by the second Imperial Guard column.

The composition of these columns will always be open to debate and our views may well change again with future discoveries, but I hope that, so far, I have produced a very cogent argument for this scenario. This is that the British Guards had faced a column consisting of some 2–3,000 men, almost certainly consisting of the two regiments of the Chasseurs of the Middle Guard. We also know that there was a delay of some fifteen minutes between the defeat of the Middle Guard Chasseurs and the march forward of this second column of Imperial Guardsmen.

The only Imperial Guard battalion known to be stationed in reserve in the valley two or three hundred metres from the orchard of Hougoumont was initially the 2/3rd Grenadiers, (where Napoleon had apparently stationed himself). It was apparently joined by the 2/1st and 1/2nd Chasseurs which went to its support when the defeat of the Middle Guard Chasseurs became evident.

Whether simply aiming to protect the retreat of these Chasseurs, or more likely with the aim of punching a hole through the obviously disordered allied defences and rallying the defeated Chasseurs upon them, Napoleon undoubtedly ordered these three battalions forward, and they were supported by elements of Reille's Corps and the cavalry. These troops would be, by all logic, the troops which Adam's Brigade, now lining the ridge line to the west of the 1st Guards Brigade, would now face.

We have however, jumped ahead a little, having left Adam's Brigade moving back in squares into the relative shelter of the reverse slope of the allied ridge at about 18.30 hours, where at least they were out of the direct line of sight of the French artillery. Colonel Colborne commanding the 52nd wrote to William Siborne: 'On our arriving near the crossroad [track] on the summit of the hill near the Belgian Guns[1], I halted the 52nd. Many of our wounded were lying a few paces in our front.'[2]

---

1. See previously, these were British cannon not Belgian.
2. Siborne, The Waterloo Letters, p 284.

Even John Colborne is guilty here of condensing the events of over an hour into what was seemingly only a couple of minutes, but other witnesses make it clear that there was a long interlude after the brigade retired into the shelter behind the trackway running along the ridge line. Ensign Leeke however can be relied upon to give us a great amount of detail:

> It was now getting on for seven o'clock. The 52nd formed line four deep, the right wing being in the front line, and the left wing having closed up upon it.[3] The regiment stood about forty paces below the crest of the position, so that it was nearly or quite out of fire. The roar of round shot still continued, many only just clearing our head, others striking the top of the position and bounding over us, others, again, almost spent and rolling down gently towards us. One of these, when we were standing in line, came rolling down like a cricket ball, so slowly that I was putting out my foot to stop it, when my Colour Sergeant quickly begged me not to do so, and told me it might have seriously injured my foot. Exactly in front of me, when standing in line, lay, at the distance of two yards, a dead tortoise-shell kitten. It had probably been frightened out of Hougoumont, which was the nearest house to us, and about a quarter of a mile off. The circumstance led me to think of my friends at home.
>
> For some little time there was a lull in the battle all along the British line, excepting that the French artillery kept up their fire on the British artillery, almost the only force which could then be seen by them. No shells were at that time directed against the troops posted just behind the summit of the British position. Here was a most interesting scene! Everything was wild and strange, yet everything was quiet and natural. This is rather a bold paradox! Bounding our view, about forty paces in our front, was a bank not quite three feet high; there was a stunted hedge on it away to the right of our centre, but not so to the left. Under this bank and hedge to the right lay some twenty of our badly and mortally wounded men, covered by their blankets, which some of the poor fellows had got out from their knapsacks. I particularly remember at that time two poor fellows passing through the line to the rear, who, I think, must have had their arms carried away by the same cannon shot, for they were both struck exactly in the same place, about four inches below the shoulder, the wounded arm being attached to the upper part by a very small portion of skin and flesh, and being supported by the man taking hold of the hand of that arm with his other hand. About the same time, I made way also for one of the Rifles, who was seriously wounded in the head, to pass to the rear.
>
> In front of our left company were several killed and wounded horses; some of the latter were lying, some standing, but some of both were eating the trodden down wheat or rye, notwithstanding that their legs were shot

---

3. He is at variance with Sir John Colborne and other witnesses here, who also have the regiment in line four-deep, but they state that the companies were formed in line correctly numbered 1 to 10 but with half companies behind each other to form the four-deep line.

off, or that they were otherwise badly wounded. I observed a brigade of artillery, coming from our left, pass over the bank into action in a very cool and gallant style. In doing this, some of the guns went over the legs of the wounded horses, the wounded men were out of their way. It often happens in action that, in charges of cavalry and in rapid advances of artillery, wounded men are ridden or run over. It is mentioned that at the Battle of Ligny, two days before Waterloo, Blücher's horse fell, and that, before he could disentangle himself from it, the French and Prussian cavalry charged each other twice, passing over him and his horse without his being hurt. There was a peculiar smell at this time, arising from a mingling of the smell of the wheat trodden flat down with the smell of gunpowder.

Half an hour, or perhaps three quarters of an hour, had elapsed after our return to the position, when a French cuirassier officer came galloping up the slope and down the bank in our front, near to Sir John Colborne, crying, '*Vive le Roi*!' He was a chef d'escadron [major] and took that opportunity of escaping from the French left wing, that he might shew his loyalty to Louis XVIII. He told Sir John Colborne that the French Imperial Guard were about to advance and would be led by the Emperor. I think the officer of cuirassiers was sent, under the charge of a sergeant, to the Duke of Wellington. Soon after this, when it was nearly eight o'clock, the Duke rode across our front from the left of the line quite alone, and spoke to Sir John Colborne, as they were both sitting on their horses observing the enemy. The Duke's dress consisted of a blue surtout coat,[4] white kerseymere pantaloons,[5] and Hessian boots.[6]

He wore a sword with a waist belt, but no sash, and had a small extended telescope in his right hand. He rode a chestnut horse.[7] He rode across our front within fifteen paces of our centre, so that I had a complete view of him. I remember him and his cool, quiet demeanour as well as if I had seen him only yesterday. This was the first time the 52nd had seen him on the 18th. He wore no cloak, but Sir John Colborne wore then and during the whole of the action, as a short cloak, the cape and hood of my blue camlet boat cloak, which I had lent him on the afternoon of the 17th. After speaking for a short time to Sir John Colborne, the Duke rode quietly away again in the direction of the centre of the position, still unattended. We heard what the officer of cuirassiers had said to Sir John Colborne about the attack of the Imperial Guard, and not long after we heard them advancing with continued shouts

---

4. Surtout coat – a close fitting overcoat.
5. Kerseymere pantaloons or breeches were made from fine woollen cloth, they were close fitting and only extended to just below the knee where they buttoned up, they were worn with calf length riding boots.
6. Hessian boots had been made popular by German cavalrymen, they were highly polished calf length boots with curved rims and a tassle in the front at the top. Wellington had them redesigned for himself after the wars and his version became known as Wellington boots. These were later mass produced in rubber.
7. He rode his horse 'Copenhagen' all day.

of '*Vive l'Empereur*' away to our left front. The drummers were beating the 'pas de charge', which sounded, as well as I recollect, very much like this, 'the rum dum, the rum dum, the rummadum dummadum, dum, dum,' then '*Vive l'Empereur.*' This was repeated again and again, till, in about a quarter of an hour or twenty minutes, we put an end to it in the manner mentioned a little further on.[8]

Lieutenant Gawler agrees with Leeke, including how the four-deep line was formed, but he also adds a few additional remarks:

At about six o'clock Adam's Brigade was ordered to retire behind the summit or the original position GG.[9] On arriving there the 52nd at first formed quarter distance columns of wings and afterwards deployed into two lines, the left wing in rear, but closed up to one pace from the right wing. The other regiments of the brigade, I have every reason to believe, made precisely the same formation.

The order, I believe, was given by the Duke himself. At this time he passed unattended from the left to beyond our right and shortly after returned to beyond our left. In this position the 52nd's right was under good cover, it was about forty paces directly in rear of the left of a field battery,[10] which at intervals fired down the face of the hill.

The left of the 52nd was much more thrown back from the summit. A low hedge ran across its front at some distance from it. Individuals of Nos 3 and 4 Companies remember this hedge distinctly as does the Adjutant, who was generally with Sir John Colborne in front of the left centre. Sergeant Dolan[11] of No 4 Company, now a pensioner at Armagh, tore his leg so much in passing it that the Captain of his company asked if he were wounded. I have good reason to believe that the 2nd Battalion 95th Regiment was near to our left, but, if anything, rather to its rear. The 71st Regiment was certainly close to our right, so close that, as I was very distinctly informed by an officer of the 3rd Battalion 95th, the two companies of this regiment had not room to deploy between us, but remained in column in rear of the 71st.

The last great attack of the French commenced about seven o'clock. Judging from the information which I have received from others, and from my own recollections of the direction and duration of the musketry fire, I think that about the first half hour was occupied in a direct attack of the enemy, upon the tongue of ground which projects from the position, two or three hundred yards to the left of the position of the 52nd Regiment.[12]

---

8. Leeke, pp 39–42.
9. See Gawler's map pp 58–9.
10. A battery of Foot Artillery rather than Horse Artillery.
11. Regimental Records show that there was nobody named Dolan in the battalion at Waterloo. It possibly refers to Sergeant Major John Dowdall.
12. Siborne, The Waterloo Letters pp 290–1.

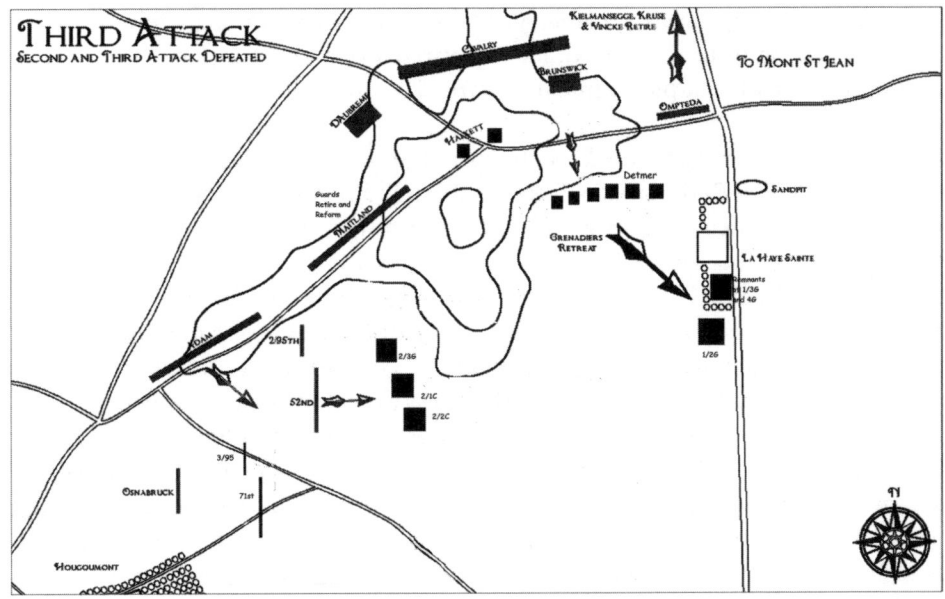

Major Hunter Blair, Brigade Major, is in complete agreement as to the delay before the Guard attack and he adds further details regarding the French cavalryman who came over to warn them, although he describes him as a hussar rather than a cuirassier:

> I feel morally persuaded that the Light Brigade, more especially the 52nd and 71st, had been a considerable time in line four deep, before the attack was made. I was in rear of the 52nd line in conversation with the late Sir Augustus Fraser, Horse Artillery, when the French hussar officer, a deserter, mentioned by Colonel Gawler, rode up to and joined us. He said we should be attacked by the French Guard within half an hour. Sir Augustus rode off to inform the Duke, then towards the left, desiring me to look to the deserter, whose information proved literally correct. The French cannonade commenced before Sir Augustus' return. I sent the French officer to the rear in charge of a sergeant of the 52nd Regiment.[13]

General Adam also recalled the French officer deserting to warn them of the attack: 'While in this position a French officer deserted and came over to where the brigade was and gave information that the Imperial Guard was forming to make an attack on that part of the position.'[14]

Lieutenant John Budgen of the 2/95th also recalls forming line four deep on the ridge:

> I fully recollect also that a very short period (say less than half an hour) before the last advance of the enemy, our line was formed four deep, our

---

13. ibid, pp 279–80.
14. ibid, p 276.

formation having been previously two deep as usual. Immediately before the formation of four deep I think we retired a very short distance from the ground we had occupied while in square.

Soon after the warning by the French deserter, the Imperial Guard could be seen occasionally through the smoke, forming up near La Belle Alliance to attack. The Guard columns then progressed to the west and then turned to advance towards the allied ridge. Ensign Leeke saw two columns which he thought followed each other up the allied ridge a few hundred metres to the left of Adam's Brigade. He noted that there appeared to be a very small gap between the columns, meaning that in his view, it was effectively one very large column. Many others viewing the columns front on unanimously state that the two columns were in echelon, but also that they approached the allied ridge parallel to each other, separated by a lateral distance of at least two hundred metres. The first column approached the area where the 1st Guard Brigade stood, whilst the second column, some fifteen minutes or so behind the first, was actually approaching the position originally held by the 2nd Guard Brigade, but now held by Adam's Brigade. Seeing that Leeke was observing these columns from the side, where the lateral displacement of the two columns at a distance might not have been readily obvious. Therefore Leeke may well be honestly relating what he thought he saw, but he was undoubtedly mistaken.[15]

He again refers to the warning of the attack. Much effort has been expended trying to identify the French officer who passed over to the allies, but his identity remains highly speculative and is of little real consequence. However, having fretted so intensely over his identity, many historians have missed or ignored the real significance of his actions. The words of the deserter are variously recorded, but the gist of them all seems to indicate that the attack was coming in that vicinity. It is unlikely that this officer knew exactly where the Imperial Guard would attack, but his indication that the attack would be made against the ridge somewhere between the plateau where the Lion Mound now stands and the orchard of Hougoumont, means that all of the theories that claim that the columns of the Imperial Guards veered heavily off course and were not meant to attack this part of the ridge are proven to be wrong. It would seem that the Guard attacks arrived on the allied ridge very close to the positions they meant to assault as would be expected of veteran troops.

He also clearly identifies that there were two distinct columns separated some few hundred yards apart laterally and he speculates that seen from the side, they might have appeared to be following each other. General Frederick Adam wrote his version of events to William Siborne. He does not make it clear, but he seems to hint that the movements he describes emanated from him:

> It was not judged expedient to [stand to] receive this attack, but to move forward the brigade and assail the enemy instead of waiting to be assailed,

---

15. Siborne, The Waterloo Letters pp 299–300.

and orders to effect it were given. The brigade was at this time formed in line four deep, from right to left 71st, 52nd, 2nd 95th; and the two companies of the 3rd 95th on right of 71st.

The first encounter with the Imperial Guard was a very sharp tussle with its tirailleurs [skirmishers], but this did not extend to our right further than the right of [the] 52nd and hardly to left of [the] 71st. When their tirailleurs were disposed of, the 52nd were right shouldered forward by Sir J Colborne, and the 71st conformed; but it being considered that the interval between the right of 71st and the enclosures of Hougoumont left the right of the brigade exposed, request was more than once made for troops from the other part of the division to occupy this space and cover the flank of the 3rd Brigade, and at length Lieutenant Colonel Halkett, with a part of his Hanoverian Militia Brigade was sent for this purpose, and as it came forward the 3rd Brigade advanced, the Imperial Guard was driven back.[16]

Sir John Colborne wrote his own account to Siborne, which broadly agreed with his brigade commander, but he emphatically denied receiving any orders to carry out the manoeuvre of marching onto the flank of the advancing column of Imperial Guardsmen. It was entirely his own decision:

> My anxious attention had been attracted to the dense columns moving on the Genappe road towards the centre of our position, and observing their rapid advance I ordered our left hand company to wheel to the left, and formed the remaining companies on that company. Colonel Charles Rowan assisted in completing this formation, with whom I had had some conversation on the intended movement, and on the necessity of menacing the flank of the French Columns.
>
> This [forward] movement placed us nearly parallel with the moving columns of the French Imperial Guards. I ordered a strong company to extend in our front, and at this moment Sir F Adam rode up, and asked me what I was going to do. I think I said, 'to make that column feel our fire'.[17] Sir F Adam then ordered me to move on, and that the 71st should follow, and [he] rode away towards the 71st.
>
> I instantly ordered the extended company of the 52nd, about 100 men under the command of Lieutenant Anderson, to advance as quickly as possible without any support except from the battalion, and to fire into the French column at any distance. Thus the 52nd formed in two lines of half companies, the rear line at ten paces distance from the front, after giving three cheers, followed the extended company, passed along the front of the Brigade of Guards in line, commanded by Sir John Byng and about 500 yards in front of them. If our line had been produced it would have formed an obtuse angle with this Brigade of Guards.

---

16. ibid, p 277.
17. Colborne talks of columns, but only attacks a column (singular), which would indicate that the other columns were further away and not attacked by the 52nd.

I observed that as soon as the French columns were sharply attacked by our skirmishers, a considerable part of the column halted and formed a line facing towards the 52nd and opened a very sharp fire on the skirmishers and on the battalion. The only skirmishers, I think, that were out on that day from our brigade were those of the 52nd which I have mentioned, but I am certain that none fired but those of the 52nd. Three or four [actually six] companies of the 95th were formed on our left rather to the rear of our line; the remainder or the brigade, the 71st, must have been at least six hundred yards to the rear when the 52nd commenced its movement towards the Imperial Guards; but I think I observed the 71st moving on, as well as the whole of Sir H Clinton's Division, when we had advanced a few hundred paces.

I have no doubt that the fire on the flank of the French column from the 52nd skirmishers, and the appearance of a general attack on its flank from Sir F Adam's Brigade and Sir H Clinton's Division generally was the cause of the first check received, or halt made by the Imperial Guards. The 52nd suffered severely from the fire of the enemy; the loss of skirmishers was severe, and the two officers of the company were wounded. The right wing of the 52nd lost nearly one hundred and fifty men during the advance; the officer carrying the Regimental Colour was killed.[18]

As usual, Colonel Colborne's version of events raises a number of issues that need to be considered. Sir John makes it clear that the companies remained in line of half companies behind each other, making a four-deep line, whilst retaining the company order with No. 1 on the right and No. 10 on the left. This, as has already been shown, is at variance with Leeke and others, who claim that the two wings of the battalion were in line behind each other, meaning that companies No.1 to 5 formed the front line in two ranks and companies No. 6 to 10 stood in two ranks behind them. If Colborne was right, then the left company which the regiment pivoted on, was Captain Shedden's No. 10 Company. It would have been Company No. 5 (with No. 10 behind them) if the battalion had been deployed in wings, but we know that No. 5 was not there. Lieutenant Anderson is named as the commanding officer of the company sent forward as skirmishers. We know that Anderson was in No. 5 Company and that his captain was absent, hence he was in command, this must mean that the company captain was either Brownrigg or Yonge, the only captains absent from Waterloo whose company we cannot readily identify. It is interesting that the company chosen to skirmish was No. 5, which does tend to indicate that the regiment was more likely to have been formed in line of wings, as Anderson would then be commanding the left-hand front ranks, whereas if formed in half companies, he would have been drawn from the very centre of the formation, which would have been very unusual. His comment that the right wing having lost around 150 men during the advance would also possibly indicate that this wing led the advance and suffered the most for it. However, Colborne would not have sent out No.5 Company as skirmishers

---

18. Siborne, The Waterloo Letters, pp 284–5.

if in four-deep line with the left wing behind the right as claimed by Leeke and Gawler as this would have made No.5 Company the pivot company for the entire realignment to the left to put the battalion facing the flank of the Imperial Guard column. Its movement in this case would have caused chaos. It therefore would appear more likely that Colborne and the other senior officers are correct in stating that the standard line formation was utilised with each half company being placed behind the other to produce a four-deep line. This meant that No.10 company was the pivot. This formation also made it easier to detach companies as occurred to No.1 company during the advance across the battlefield later on.

Colborne also states that the 52nd passed 500 yards in front of the 1st Guard Brigade, but as every eyewitness to this event states clearly that the Guard Brigade could not be seen as it was over the crest of the ridge, this can be little more than pure conjecture on his part.

The fact that the left side of the French column was able to turn to its flank and open fire without serious disruption does lend itself to the probability that the French Guards were in squares as otherwise, if in column, it would be difficult to turn just a few files from each company in line to face the flank.

He must also be correct in that the 71st on the right, having failed to copy the flanking manoeuvre until ordered to do so by General Adam a few minutes later, must undoubtedly have been a few hundred yards behind, but Colborne then suggests that the sight of the two entire brigades (Adam's and Halkett's) advancing towards them, caused the Imperial Guard to break, which seems at odds with his own previous statement that these troops were a very long way behind. If the 71st was, as he claimed, six hundred yards in the rear, then Halkett's troops would have been in excess of 1,000 yards away. With all the smoke and confusion, would the Imperial Guard have even noticed them at such distances? I would suggest not.

It is also noticeable that Colonel Colborne believed that poor Ensign Nettles was killed during this advance, but it is also interesting that he states that Nettles was carrying the Regimental Colour. This is correct as we know from Leeke's evidence, but Sir John would have known that the senior ensign carried the King's Colour with the right wing, and yet he makes no comment regarding this error.

Colborne wrote another statement for Siborne in which there are some very interesting additions:

> To establish the precise time when the battle was no longer doubtful, and the movements which were the immediate cause of hastening the Crisis, is the object of the writer, and as he is persuaded that the movement of Sir Henry Clinton's Division, and of General Adam's Brigade, and of the 52nd Regiment in particular, tended greatly to hasten the Crisis ...
>
> Fixing from 7 to ½ past 7, the critical half hour, but time passes so quickly in an action and everyone is so occupied in performing his own duty that it will be difficult to find persons agree as to time. However, it may be clearly demonstrated that while the columns of Napoleon which made the unsuccessful attack, on the point which is usually called our right

centre, and which advanced in full march towards the troops occupying our centre, the Brunswickers retiring, and the British Guards closing in; no one who was looking steadfastly at the movement of the Imperial Guards at that time, could say that the battle did not look critical, or, but that the Imperial Guards had the appearance of success, and also that our centre was on the point of being penetrated. This then we must fix as the time when no change for the better, on our side, had taken place, that we were in the greatest danger, but the moment the Imperial Guards halted and formed squares in consequence of a menaced attack on their left flank,[19] our prospects were immediately changed for the better, it was 'the Crisis', and half an hour after, when they were thrown into confusion and they retreated towards La Belle Alliance, the battle was won...

A few minutes before this an officer had occasion to look at his watch, and said 'the wounded had better be left where they are, the action must be over in half an hour' [20] it was then nearly 7 o'clock.

Therefore, at 7 we will say the 52nd wheeled, the left company nearly a quarter circle to the left, and formed the remainder on the new line, with the intention of moving on the left flank of the Imperial column, and firing into the column, to retard the movement. The 52nd thus at 7 o'clock were formed into two lines, not four deep, but each left subdivision in rear of its right, the whole forming two complete lines, the rear line keeping the wheeling distance of a subdivision from the front line. At this time the [2/]95th, apparently a small number, formed on the left of the 52nd. A strong company of the 52nd was sent to skirmish in front, and to fire into the Imperial column. At this moment General Adam came to the 52nd from the 71st, and desired the 52nd to move on. The Duke it appears at the same time, had sent Colonel Percy[21] to the 52nd to move on, the 52nd however were already in motion, its right flank totally unprotected, and marched off in two lines well formed and covered by the skirmishers commanded by Lieutenants Anderson and Campbell, who had directions to push on, and to look to the whole battalion as their support. Whether the 95th moved off with the 52nd is not certain, they certainly did not continue on the left flank the whole time of the march towards the front. The 52nd moved steadily on, the instant that the French columns felt the fire of Anderson's skirmishers they halted, appeared to be in some confusion and opened a heavy fire on the 52nd; the two officers of the skirmishers were wounded and the greater part of the men, the right of the battalion also suffered considerably. The 52nd still moved on passing the entire front of Byng's Brigade of British Guards, who were stationary and not firing, about three hundred yards or so to their

---

19. This is a new claim not repeated in any other account, or even in his own previous accounts. The evidence is pretty heavily in favour of the fact that they were in battalion squares throughout.
20. This would indicate that the regiment was about to move and therefore the unwounded men should leave the wounded where they were and remain in the ranks.
21. This is Major the Honourable Henry Percy, 14th Light Dragoons, extra aide de camp to the Duke of Wellington. He was subsequently to carry the Waterloo despatch to England.

front and forming possibly a right angle or perhaps an obtuse angle with the line of the Guards. At the moment the 52nd commenced the movement, Lord Hill was near the British Guards commanded by Maitland, and no movement on their part had then taken place. Therefore, it is imagined, that when the 52nd commenced the movement, they were shortly followed by the 71st and the whole of General Clinton's Division, the Imperial troops saw that their flank and rear were menaced by a mass of troops marching on their flank, they halted, but the moment this halt took place, our centre made a forward movement which was resisted by the attacking corps of the French.[22]

Again, Colborne's statement raises a few issues which need to be discussed. He again insists that the companies were placed in subdivisions behind each other to form a four-deep line. Intriguingly, he here adds mention of Major Percy being sent by the Duke of Wellington to make the movement on the flank of the Imperial Guard, but states that they were already in motion. This shows that although Colborne instigated the movement, it had also been thought of by the Duke of Wellington, who sent orders for it to be carried out and shows that he clearly was in the vicinity and observed everything. This makes it also very possible that Wellington genuinely thought that the movement by the 52nd had been carried out on his orders.

Colborne's statement that only the skirmishers fired seems to be at variance with many other statements where two or three of the formed companies also opened fire. Lastly, whether the 2/95th was close on its left wing throughout and when the 71st caught up will be discussed in the next chapter.

Lieutenant Charles Holman wrote a brief account of the battalion's movement onto its flank and claims that the troops did not open fire at all but drove on with the bayonet only. He is however way too early with his timing, it being around 19.45 hours:

> About 6 we observed the enemy moving amazing columns towards the left and presently we heard an incessant roar of cannon and musquetry with redoubled vigour. We immediately brought up our right shoulders and moved onto the attack of the left flank of the French. This was an amazing body of the Imperial Guards who on perceiving us, threw back their left as if on parade to receive us. We marched with sloped arms until we arrived within about 30 paces, when we gave a shout and charged. The French immediately gave way, when we made pretty havoc among them.[23]

Ensign Leeke has much to say on this subject, as one might expect of him. Writing many years later and admitting that he did not write any of his memories down until some ten years later, he is guilty of making assumptions on things he

---

22. Glover, Letters from the Battle of Waterloo, pp 185–7.
23. Holman Lt, Journal for 1815, Royal Green Jackets Museum, Winchester.

could not possibly have witnessed. I however, make no apology for reproducing it in *extenso*:

> The Imperial Guard advanced from the low ground in front of La Belle Alliance, and on the French left of the Charleroi road. At the same time a forward movement, in support of this attack, was made both by the right and left wings of the French army, whilst the troops forming the centre of their left wing under Foy, made a corresponding advance within the enclosures of Hougoumont ... Thus, when the Imperial Guard were advancing from the low ground towards the right centre of the position, the Duke could not withdraw any of his brigades of infantry from any other part of the line.[24] A mass of skirmishers was sent forward from the Imperial Guard, who were joined on their right by skirmishers from Donzelot's Division;[25] both sets of skirmishers getting, I believe, intermingled in some measure. Whether the Imperial Guard skirmishers fired into the right regiment of the 1st British Guards, that is, the 2nd Battalion, and into the left of the 2nd battalion of the [95th] Rifles, I am uncertain, but the brunt of the attack from the French skirmishers fell upon the 3rd Battalion of the 1st Guards.[26]
>
> Under these circumstances, when the leading battalion of the first column of the Imperial Guard was about 400 yards from that part of the British position occupied by Maitland's Brigade of Guards, Sir John Colborne, who had been watching [for] his opportunity, ordered No 5 Company of the 52nd, under Lieutenants Anderson, Campbell, and F W Love, to extend and move down and fire into the enemy's columns, looking to the regiment for support. The left of the skirmishers of the 52nd and the left of those of the Imperial Guard could not have passed very far from each other, for only the four deep line of the six companies of the 95th Rifles intervened, between the left of the 52nd and the right battalion of Maitland's Brigade of Guards, yet the hostile skirmishers did not meet or even see each other; probably when the 52nd skirmishers advanced from the left of the regiment, which, owing to the formation of the ground, was more forward on the British position than the troops on its left, the French skirmishers were just surmounting the more retired crest of the position in front of the British Guards, and had commenced firing into them. He then, without having received any orders from the Duke or any other superior officer, moved

---

24. This is incorrect, showing that Leeke had no information on what other troop movements were under way. Historians have always known that the cavalry brigades of Vivian and Vandeleur were ordered from the left wing to the centre of the army as the first elements of General Ziethen's Prussian corps arrived on the extreme left of the allied army. What is less well known is that the Duke of Wellington had also ordered Vincke's Hanoverian Brigade to march from the left wing to the centre. The Duke also ordered General Chasse to march with his entire division of Netherlands troops from the allied right wing at Braine l'Alleud to the centre. Many of these troops were to play an important part in the overthrow of the Imperial Guard attacks and the final advance which caused the French to rout.
25. Part of the Comte d'Erlon's Corps, which had taken and held onto La Haye Sainte and was threatening Wellington's centre.
26. This again is supposition, not being an eyewitness to these events.

forward the 52nd, in quick time, directly to its front. As we passed over the low bank and the crest of our position, we plainly saw, about 800 or 400 yards from us,[27] in the direction of La Belle Alliance, midway between the enclosures of Hougoumont and La Haye Sainte, and about a quarter of a mile from each of those places, two long columns of the Imperial Guard of France, of about equal length, advancing at right angles with the position and in the direction of Maitland's Brigade of Guards, stationed on our left. The whole number of these two columns of the French Guard appeared to us to amount to about 10,000 men [ie about 5,000 in each]. There was a small interval of apparently not more than twenty paces between the first and second column; from the left centre of our line we did not at any time see through this interval; I think they were all in close column. As the 52nd moved down towards the enemy it answered the cries of '*Vive l'Empereur,*' with three tremendous British cheers. When the left of the regiment was in a line with the leading company of the Imperial Guard, it began to mark time, and the men touched in to their left, everyone seeing the necessity for such a movement, and that, if they proceeded, they would be outflanked by the French column, which was then not quite two hundred yards from us.[28] In two or three seconds the word of command, 'Right shoulders forward', came down the line from Sir John Colborne, repeated by the mounted officers, and the officers commanding the front companies; the movement was soon completed, and the 52nd four-deep line became parallel to the left flank of the leading column of the French Guard, there being a slight dip and rise again of the ground between us and the enemy. The 52nd was alone, the other regiments of Adam's Brigade having been thrown out by the suddenness and peculiarity of the movement.[29] In this dangerous and exposed advance Sir John Colborne was on the right of the regiment, anxiously watching a large mass of the enemy's cavalry, which was seen between us and the French position. From the left centre of the 52nd line we saw a numerous body of skirmishers of the Imperial Guard running towards, and then forming about 100 yards in front of, their leading column. These appear not to have been seen by the 52nd officers on the right; possibly the head of the French column intervened. I recollect seeing a French officer strike, with the flat of his sword, a skirmisher, who was running farther to the rear than the point at which the others were forming; at that time I could see 300 yards up the slope of the British position to our left, and not a British regiment or a British soldier was in sight. ...

---

27. This is quite a variance in distances. He must mean at most 400 metres/yards as this would put it in between Hougoumont and La Haye Sainte, 800 yards/metres would put them near La Belle Alliance. In fact, it is more likely that it was even closer (200 metres) before the regiment made its forward movement onto the flank of the column.
28. This confirms that there was a 200 yard/metre displacement between the track of the Imperial Guard column and the line of advance of the 52nd Foot.
29. The 2/95th was with them almost immediately, the 71st and 3/95th took longer to catch up.

This advance of the 52nd line and its right-shoulder-forward movement was seen from the height above and was spoken of by Lord Hill as one of the most beautiful advances he had ever seen. Sir John Byng, who had succeeded to the command of the whole division of the Guards when General Cooke was wounded, and was at the time near Maitland's Brigade, said of it to one of the 52nd officers that night, 'We saw the 52nd advancing gloriously, as they always do.' The Duke of Wellington also was much pleased with it...

It is very difficult to calculate time during the progress of a battle; one officer told me that the whole action only appeared to him to last two hours, whereas it commenced exactly at twelve o'clock at noon, and lasted till a quarter after nine at night. It must have been nearly a quarter past eight when the 52nd stood parallel with the left flank of the Imperial Guard.

Our artillery on the British position, 300 yards above, had been playing upon the masses of the French Guard, but when we saw them, there appeared to be no confusion amongst them; our advance put a stop to the fire of our artillery; it was not till the 52nd skirmishers fired into them that the Imperial Guard halted, then as many files as possible, on the left of each company of their leading column, faced outwards and returned the fire; as the 52nd approached, our skirmishers fell back to the regiment, two of the three officers being severely wounded, and many of the men being either killed or wounded. The regiment opened fire upon the enemy without halting; the men fired, then partly halted to load, whilst those in the rear slipped round them in a sort of skirmishing order, though they maintained a compact line, occupying, however, nearly double the extent of ground, from front to rear, which a four-deep line usually requires.[30] The French writer, Quinet, although his account of this action contains all kinds of mistakes, speaks of this attack of the 52nd on the flank of the Imperial Guard as follows: 'Le 52e regiment Anglais en profite pour venir audacieusement se deployer sur le flanc gauche. Quand le regiment Anglais l'eut debordee tout entiere, il ouvrit son feu a brule-pourpoint qui l'ecrasait.' ['The 52nd English regiment took the opportunity to to boldly engage their left flank. When the English regiment had come alongside (overlapped) it, he opened his fire at point-blank range which was crushing.']

The mounted officers rode to the front of the line. There were Colonel Sir John Colborne, Lieutenant Colonel Charles Rowan, Major William Chalmers, Adjutant Winterbottom, and Assistant Adjutant Nixon, also our General of Brigade, Adam, who had just come up, and some of his staff, Lieutenant Campbell, 7th Fusileers, and Major Hunter Blair, 91st Regiment, Brigade-Major. Chalmers, in front of the right of No 4 company, placed his cap on the point of his sword, and, standing up in his stirrups, cheered the regiment on. Here I saw Winterbottom badly wounded in the head, and brought by his horse through the line, without his cap, the blood streaming down him; the poor fellow managed to hold on by the pommel

---

30. Others claim that only a few companies on the left fired, which was where Leeke was.

of his saddle. Captain Diggle, commanding No 1 company, had been desperately wounded just before on the left temple. Lieutenant Dawson was shot through the lungs; Anderson lost a leg. Major Love was severely wounded in the head, and afterwards, as he lay on the ground, in the foot and in two other places. Lieutenant Campbell, who had been skirmishing, came through the line severely wounded in the groin; General Adam was severely wounded in the leg, but did not quit the field. Colonel Charles Rowan was also slightly wounded; Sir John Colborne had his horse killed under him and was grazed in the hand and on the foot. Several of the other officers were very slightly hit, but were not returned as wounded; I consider that about 140 of our men were killed or wounded at this time, in the course of five or six minutes.[31] I missed Sir John Colborne for two or three minutes, and felt very anxious about him, but presently he came quickly down the front on foot, giving directions, still wearing a portion of my cloak, and wiping his mouth with his white handkerchief. As we closed towards the French Guard, they did not wait for our charge, but the leading column at first somewhat receded from us, and then broke and fled; a portion of the rear column also broke and ran; but three or four battalions of the Old Guard, forming part of this second column, retired hastily, in some degree of order, towards the rising ground in front of La Belle Alliance, with a few pieces of the artillery of the Guard, which must have been on their right flank when they advanced, as we did not see them, and those which were left by the gunners on the ground, until the French Guard had given way; indeed, had these guns been on the left flank of the columns of the Imperial Guard, when we were bringing our right shoulders forward, they might have plied our line with grape, and have caused us the most serious loss; or, possibly, had they been there. Sir John Colborne would not have ventured on the movement at all. With the exception of these battalions of the Old Guard, the whole French army, as far as the eye could reach, appeared to us to be in utter confusion.

Diggle of late years was a Major General, and silver-stick in waiting to the Queen. He was in the 52nd for several years and saw some good service. He wore a silver plate, with black silk covering it, over his wound just above the left temple. I was perfectly astonished at the depth and width of the hole in his skull, when he took off the plate one day, at Sandhurst, to shew it to me. On that occasion I doubled up my forefinger, not a very small one, and laid it against the wound, and satisfied myself that if it could have been cut off at the knuckle joint, and placed on the skin over the brain at the bottom of the wound, I could have covered it over so as to let the plate fit down close over it, and lie evenly on the surrounding portion of the skull. He kept the musket ball, and about a dozen or fourteen small portions of the skull in a box, the ball having been divided in two by the force of the blow. One of

---

31. Given that the total losses of the battalion during the entire battle were near 200, then this level of loss seems a little excessive.

our old sergeants, (Houseley[32]) whom I shall speak of afterwards, told me a few weeks ago that at Waterloo, when he was returning from conveying Corporal Hood,[33] whose heel was shot off, to the rear, which he was ordered to do on our 52nd squares retiring up the position from the neighbourhood of Hougoumont, he met Captain Diggle, who had just been wounded, and, as he passed, heard him say to the men who were with him, 'What will my poor wife do?'[34]

William Leeke was certain that the British Guards had only faced skirmishers and that the 52nd, with only very limited support, defeated the first column and the second column immediately fled. We will explore this claim further at the end of the chapter once we have seen what other eyewitnesses state.

Major's Patrick Campbell and Robert Campbell had both been on leave, but it is believed that they were still in Belgium, possibly at Brussels. Robert Campbell did not re-join the regiment until the fighting was well and truly over and his company was commanded in his absence by Captain John Cross. In the absence of Patrick Campbell, his senior Lieutenant, Charles Dawson, commanded the company, but Campbell belatedly arrived and took command of his company, apparently just before the attack of the Imperial Guard. No reasons why they were absent have been discovered, if at Brussels both would have known some days previously that the campaign had started and could have joined much earlier. Missing a battle was deemed a serious failure and both officers subsequently saw a more junior officer (Chalmers) promoted over them in their absence. Patrick Campbell wrote a short note to Siborne, but he avoided any explanation for his absence during much of the battle:

> I was unable to join my regiment until about four o'clock[35] on the memorable 18th of June. I found it drawn up in line with the [2/95th] Rifles on its left, I think about an hour after I joined we were very sharply engaged with an immense column of the enemy who appeared to me to be retreating and in confusion,[36] about this time the Duke came up to the left of the regiment and was very much exposed[37] to a sharp fire of musketry.[38]

Captain John Cross of the 52nd recalled how the regiment had advanced and then pivoted onto the flank of the Imperial Guard column and he states that the regiment fired before advancing with the bayonet:

---

32. Benjamin Housley was actually a corporal at Waterloo.
33. Corporal Robert Hood was sent to the 2nd Battalion in England in August 1815.
34. Leeke, pp 42–7.
35. It was probably nearer 19.00 hours before he arrived as he makes it clear that he joined them after it had formed four deep line on the rear slope.
36. This would seem to imply that the Imperial Guard was already in retreat when the 52nd advanced. This is at complete variance with every other account and would seem to be wrong, but it could indicate that he had seen the retreat of elements of the attack on the 1st Guard Brigade.
37. His confirmation that the Duke of Wellington was also close by and an eyewitness to the defeat of the Imperial Guard is of interest.
38. Glover, Letters from the Battle of Waterloo, p 180.

I have to state that the formation of 52nd Regiment at the period alluded to was in line, formed four deep, and rather behind the crest of the height upon which the regiment was drawn up. The enemy's attacking force at this point was formed in column either at close or quarter distance, but did not come up directly in front of the 52nd but at some distance from its left flank (a few minutes previous to this attack, a French officer who had just deserted intimated that the attack was going to commence) and as soon as the French column approached sufficiently near, the 52nd changed front to the left (so as to take the column in flank) fired, and immediately charged.[39]

Cross also wrote a fuller memorandum on the battle, where he described his role in the third party. Here he clarified that only about three companies on the left of the regiment fired before the bayonet charge:

Captain Cross commanded the left company of the 52nd Regiment when formed in double line at the Battle of Waterloo, and at the period which is now generally termed the Crisis of this battle, Captain Cross by order of Sir John Colborne, wheeled his company about the eighth of a circle to the left, in order to effect a change of position, so as to throw the front of the 52nd line on the left flank of the French attacking column, and as soon as either two or three of the companies on the left of this line had fired, Sir John Colborne ordered the line to charge, which broke the French column, and the pursuit was continued by the 52nd and a part of the [2/]95th Rifles.[40]

Cross claims that his company was the left-hand company on which the line formed, but this cannot be correct. Cross commanded No. 8 Company and no matter how the four deep line was formed it would not put his company on the left wing. Poor Captain Diggle was unable to witness much of the Crisis however:

At about seven o'clock when the attack was made on the right of the position, by columns of the Imperial Guard. The skirmishers of the regiment had just fallen back on the battalion, which was advancing to resist the attack when I was severely wounded and left the field.[41]

Lieutenant Gawler later wrote extensively in defence of his regiment's achievements at Waterloo, but did not always agree with William Leeke's claims:

The Duke had perceived the concentration of heavy columns to the right of La Belle Alliance, and to oppose a more solid resistance to their evidently approaching attack, had ordered all the infantry corps, between the two great roads, to be formed from two deep into four deep lines. Vivian's, Grant's, and the remains of the household, Ponsonby's and Dornberg's brigades of

---

39. ibid, p 183.
40. ibid, p 184.
41. ibid, p 183.

cavalry were, at the same time, brought together to the right centre, and posted in the hollows in the rear of the infantry.

Soon after these precautions were completed, but too late to afford any material information, a French officer of cuirassiers rode into the right of the 52nd as a deserter, and said that Napoleon was on the point of advancing to a desperate attack, at the head of his whole army.

A heavy cannonade from both positions announced that the columns of attack were in movement. A brigade of guns, thirty paces in advance of the right of the 52nd, (perhaps the only remaining efficient ordnance on this portion of the front) disregarding the enemy's artillery, played incessantly with unerring aim on the close, deep, approaching masses of infantry; changing as the distance diminished from round shot to canister, and finally to double charges. The columns, as they neared the summit, became impatient under this destructive cannonade, and a furious fire of musquetry opened in return from their front and left flanks; ... The artillerymen, under these close and flanking fires, could not long stand to their guns, but either lay beneath them, or retired behind the abrupt dip of the hill; two or three brave fellows now and then springing up to hastily load, fire, and drop again behind the cover ...

The fate of the crisis quivered on the beam. The two very weakened and exhausted centre brigades [Halkett's and Maitland's], good as they were in composition, could scarcely be expected to stand before the overwhelming and principally fresh force, which was desperately closing on their front and left flanks; and in their rear was no infantry that could be depended upon.

Meanwhile, the 52nd had remained entirely concealed by the abrupt reverse dip of the hill; although so much more in advance than the Guards, that the head of the Imperial column had nearly reached the prolongation of its left flank, at a distance from it of not more than one hundred yards. Until then not a bayonet appeared; the head of the commanding officer only, watching and calculating his opportunity, was visible above the summit. At this critical juncture it received the order to advance; and in a few paces, clearing the ascent, was under a furious fire from the long flank of the columns, and its left companies so closely engaged, that they had enough to do to hold their ground, until the regiment coming rapidly 'right shoulders forward' in line, to an angle of about 70° with the original position, its whole fire was brought to bear, full and close, upon the heavy masses before it. The 71st soon after supported the movement; and advancing obliquely to its left, protected the exposed right flank of the 52nd, and opened a partial fire on the enemy. The headmost Grenadiers gradually gave ground to their right and rear, still facing their assailants, and firing as the left of the 52nd closed up to the spot, many of the latter falling among the killed and wounded of the Imperial Guard. A thick white smoke enveloped the contending parties. The 52nd answered with a loud cheer the continuing shouts of '*Vive l'Empereur*,' and pressed forward to charge, still louder shouts, and a more rapid roll of musquetry marked the highest effort of the energy of the Imperial Guard, and then, at once it broke, and rushed in mingled confusion, not directly to its rear, but impelled by the flank charge, obliquely, towards the hollow road in front of La Haye Sainte, carrying with it in similar disorder all the troops on its right.[42]

He clearly states that the Duke of Wellington had ordered the entire front line of infantry to form four deep line, which concurs with other witness statements. His claim that the French deserter brought his information only as the attack began is generally refuted by all other witnesses. His statement that the Guard column was only one hundred yards/metres to its left is a much closer estimation than most others. Gawler also indicates that the regiment became embroiled in a protracted firefight with the Imperial Guards, long enough for the 71st to move up rapidly to cover the right wing of the 52nd and that this regiment even fired on the Imperial Guard before it broke, this again is at odds with most other eyewitnesses. The following year he sent a very detailed account to William Siborne:

> The enemy pushed on very heavy masses composed entirely of the Guard, the Moyenne leading rather on the western side of the projecting tongue of ground.
>
> I cannot describe positively from my own observation the formation of the enemy, for, when the right of the 52nd subsequently crossed the summit, the smoke was very dense; but it has been confidently stated in the regiment that, as seen from this side, it was in two columns, in direct echelon, the left considerably to the rear.[43] It has also been stated that at first the opening between the two columns was distinctly visible. That the flank of the enemy was much longer than the front of the 52nd Regiment seems to be established by the fact (which I have verified from the regimental books) that our loss of men was as great in the right companies as in the left.
>
> The brigade of guns in front of the 52nd's right, which had fired incessantly during the first half-hour [of the attack], was now silenced by the intensity of the opposing musketry. The extreme left of the enemy's leading masses came nearly in front of the extreme right of the Brigade of Guards, and a desperate, and as I believe most critical conflict commenced at this point. The Duke perceiving the almost overwhelming strength of the enemy in their direct attack rode in person to the 2nd 95th and ordered it to charge the flank of the Imperial column; before, however, the 95th could obey the order, Sir J Colborne, who commanded the 52nd, either

---

42. Gawler, USJ July 1833, pp 301–3.
43. This, if as stated, was the perceived view of all of the eyewitnesses, then this conforms with what the Guards and such others also say. It even conforms with the evidence from the French as to the left column being considerably to the rear and does not correspond with it being a coordinated attack in echelon with the other column. Hence it does not appear to be the 4th Chasseurs but does correspond with the 2/3rd Grenadiers being joined by Cambronne's Chasseurs, as a reserve.

from previous directions from the Duke, from catching his intention with regard to the 95th, or on his own responsibility in the excessive emergency of the moment, had given the words, 'Forward' and, after a very few paces, 'Right shoulders forward' to his regiment.

The right of the 52nd grazed the left gun of the battery in its front. The captain of No 1 Company (now Major Diggle) fell severely wounded close to its wheel. So close was the left company to the Imperial column that it was compelled to wheel back on its right, while the rest of the regiment came forward on their left. The enemy was pressing on with shouts, which rose above the noise of the firing, and his fire was so intense that, with but half the ordinary length of front, at least 150 of the 52nd fell in less than four minutes. I almost think in less than three, for there was not the slightest check in the advance of the right flank below the average of the old wheeling time. When the 52nd was nearly parallel to the enemy's flank, Sir J Colborne gave the word, 'Charge, charge.' It was answered from the regiment by a loud steady cheer and a hurried dash to the front. In the next ten seconds the Imperial Guard, broken into the wildest confusion, and scarcely firing a shot to cover its retreat, was rushing towards the hollow road in their rear of La Haye Sainte, near to which, according to La Coste's account,[44] Napoleon himself was then standing.

During the charge Sir J Colborne was in front of the left centre, Lieutenant Colonel Chalmers with his cap on the point of his sword in front of the right centre, and Major General Adam, who had galloped up from the 71st, in rear of the centre. Lieutenant Colonel Charles Rowan fell on the left at about the same time that Captain Diggle was wounded on the right. The point at which the left of the 52nd crossed the original line of the left flank of the Imperial Guard was at the highest point of the re-entering angle formed by the projecting tongue of land, and the rise behind which the 52nd had been covered. I convinced myself of this fact the next morning by the manner in which the killed and wounded on both sides were lying.

Although there is reason to believe that the enemy's Second Corps was advanced to cover the left flank of his attack with its own left resting on the hedge of Hougoumont yet no part of it came near enough to menace seriously the right flank of the 52nd Regiment during the whole of the forward movement and charge. This right flank appeared entirely clear of the enemy for at least 300 yards.[45]

In this later version, Gawler has accepted that some Imperial Guard units advanced against Halkett's Brigade and the British Guards. He also states that

---

44. Decoster was a Belgian civilian who, according to his own account, was forced to remain near Napoleon during the battle and provide answers regarding the geography of the locality. His account contains errors within it and it became more egregious with each telling, but there does appear to be an element of truth to his claims.
45. Siborne, The Waterloo Letters, pp 292–4.

Defeating the Third Attack – The Second Column 19.45 to 20.00 Hours

Wellington had ordered the 2/95th to attack the flank of the French column before Colborne ordered the 52nd to advance (following orders by Wellington or not), although being in No.1 Company on the right, he cannot have been an actual eyewitness. He puts Colborne in front of the left wing, but Leeke has him off to the right, warily watching the French cavalry. It would be very strange for Colborne to be absent during such a vital pivot movement, within musket range of the enemy; it is more likely that Colborne went to the right wing only after the Imperial Guard had been overthrown. He is also clear that, having ordered the 71st to conform to the movements of the rest of the brigade, General Adam remained just in rear of the 52nd during its advance. It is interesting that he also believed that there was little or no support for the French attack from their 2nd Corps.

Major Thomas Hunter-Blair, Major of Brigade to General Adam, wrote a couple of letters to Siborne, the first clearly shows his views regarding Gawler's version of events but duly noted that he had altered part of his evidence regarding the cooperation of the 71st Foot in defeating a column of the Imperial Guard:

> Colonel Gawler having acknowledged the error into which he had fallen respecting the 71st Regiment, it appears to me that he has faithfully given the leading features of the position and movements of the Light Brigade, though I am not quite prepared to admit that the 1st Guards, and 2nd and 3rd 95th, may not be said to have cooperated in the repulse of the last attack of the Imperial Guard.
>
> My persuasion is that the summit of our position was partially gained by the Imperial Guard, and I recollect Sir John Colborne telling me immediately after the attack, that he had formed his left company *en potence*,[46] refusing his flank in the apprehension of its being turned.[47]

Captain William Rowan wrote of the movement:

> It appears that my brother was knocked off his horse about the time we wheeled to the left, by the fire from the flank men of the French column and previously to our returning the fire. I enclose herewith a memo from Cross which is quite conclusive as to two or three companies at least having fired into the French column. Cross happened to meet Colonel Chalmers who was a brevet major at the time and like myself officiating as a regimental field officer, in consequence of the very reduced strength of the corps both in officers and men. ... for some time previously to forming line formation, he was the senior officer to the one square and my brother with the other, Sir John Colborne commanding the whole. We all had our horses taken to the rear at either two or three which rendered us less efficient and less able to see what was passing around us.[48]

---

46. En potence – one flank thrown back.
47. Siborne, The Waterloo Letters, p 278.
48. Glover, Letters from the Battle of Waterloo, p 182

It is interesting that all of the officers sent their horses to the rear when they advanced into the front line; evidently, they were seen as too valuable to lose. Later, Rowan wrote in a short autobiography of his life:

> Shortly after this the 52nd Regiment had the good fortune to bear a conspicuous part in what has been considered the Crisis of the Battle. The regiment had been formed into two lines by the right subdivision of each company being formed in rear of the left one, ready to close up and form a line four deep to receive cavalry with the 71st Regiment in column or square on our right and the [2/]95th to protect our left flank. In this formation we continued during our celebrated movement against the flank of the advancing columns of the Imperial Guard, in the midst of which I saw my brother Charles,[49] senior major of the regiment, knocked off his horse by a musket shot, I could only run up to him and express a hope that he was not seriously hurt, when I was compelled to leave him as the regiment was advancing rapidly under a heavy fire. A musket shot passed through my boot, grazing my left ankle bone and causing so much pain I thought I must be wounded, but it was not so.[50]

A short note regarding Lieutenant Mathew Anderson records that:

> At Waterloo, Anderson was with the First Battalion of the 52nd. When Lieutenant Colonel John Colborne (later Lord Seaton), the commanding officer of the 52nd, saw the Imperial Guard advancing in a final push, he ordered Anderson to take a company of about 100 skirmishers to meet the French column, with the 52nd advancing behind them. It was the (apparently unexpected) fire from this company that first caused the halt of the Imperial Guard. The 52nd skirmishers suffered greatly in this attack, and both officers (Anderson and Lieutenant Campbell) were severely wounded, with Anderson having his left leg shot off [actually amputated later]. According to an obituary, Anderson lay on the field for three or four hours; and, while lying there, had his watch, sword, and everything of value about him stolen by a soldier's wife. An English officer, in pity for his sufferings, tried to tramp him to death with his horse, but the sagacious animal leapt over him, and unhorsed its rider. His leg, after he was taken to the infirmary, required to be amputated three different times.[51]

Captain Cross claimed that the battalion halted momentarily having come across French troops holed up in a small copse to the south of La Haye Sainte. This might be assumed to refer to the orchard of La Haye Sainte. It is not feasible that a few companies on the left of the 52nd became engaged with French troops in the orchard, however, given the fact that no one else mentions it, not even the

---

49. Lieutenant Colonel Charles Rowan was a major in the regiment.
50. Mss Personal Reminiscences of Captain William Rowan, Museum of the Oxfordshire Soldier. Ref SOFO 2178.
51. Obituary of Anderson, The Gentleman's Magazine, June 1844, p 669.

2/95th, which would have been fully involved as it stood to the left of the 52nd, this is at least odd. It is possible that they opened fire at French troops who were in a small coppice which was cut down soon after the battle:

> Continuing on as far as a small coppice to the right of La Haye Sainte where the 52nd and Rifle Corps made a momentary halt and opened a fire upon the fugitives, (this halt did not exceed one minute and a half). The 52nd then pursued on along the high ground to the right of the Genappe road leaving a large body of the enemy behind them in this hollow road, which seemed to make it doubtful whether the 52nd had not pushed on too far from the general line without support. The word, 'Halt', was given and at that instant the enemy rushed up out of the hollow road to form on the ground which the 52nd then occupied, but the attempt was very feeble. The 52nd crossed the Genappe road obliquely at this point and continued the pursuit up the hill until they reached two well-formed squares of infantry posted on an eminence. The 52nd without the slightest hesitation charged them in line, the squares fired and then broke. I have a very distinct recollection of these circumstances and in the summer of 1818, I went over the ground and traced out the route of the 52nd as above detailed with the exception of the small coppice which I could not then discover, it might probably have been ploughed up.[52]

Cross reiterated this claim in a memorandum he sent to William Siborne:

> The pursuit was continued by the 52nd and a part of the 95th Rifles into a little copse wood close to La Haye Sainte where those regiments stopped about three or four minutes firing on the fugitives, then resumed the pursuit down into the bottom of the valley, but keeping on the bank to the right hand side of the hollow road, by which means the 52nd got ahead of a great body of the French and again made a momentary halt, and at this instant the fugitives rushed out of the hollow road apparently with the intention of forming on the very ground that the 52nd occupied, and at this instant, Captain Cross called out that they were going to surrender and not to fire upon them, but this proved quite a mistake for the foremost of the enemy commenced firing as they got up the bank, but were unable to make the slightest stand there. The pursuit was resumed by the 52nd across the hollow road, and the regiment subsequently brought up their left shoulders and re-crossed the road and were proceeding at the double march in line to the attack of the three French columns (or squares) posted on an eminence to the right of the Belle Alliance road, and when at the distance of about 150 yards those columns fired and broke, after which the whole French army was in full flight.[53]

---

52. Glover, Letters from the Battle of Waterloo, pp 183–4.
53. ibid, pp 184–5.

It is clear from all the evidence that the 52nd moved directly forward in four-deep line (half companies behind each other – see last page of Appendix II) until level with the head of the column of the Imperial Guard. Then Colonel Colborne ordered No. 5 Company out as skirmishers, whilst the left company (No. 10) wheeled to the left and the other companies re-aligned on it, until the regiment was in line, parallel with the left flank of the French column distant about 150–200 yards. Two or three companies on the left opened fire on the Guard column (it would appear that those on the far right of the line, who took longest to get into formation, did not), causing the French column to halt its advance and the left flank of the French squares in column opened up a very heavy fire of musketry, which brought down large numbers of the 52nd in only a few minutes. The 52nd then charged the French column with the bayonet, which did not stand, but broke and fled towards La Belle Alliance.

The 52nd advance on the French column

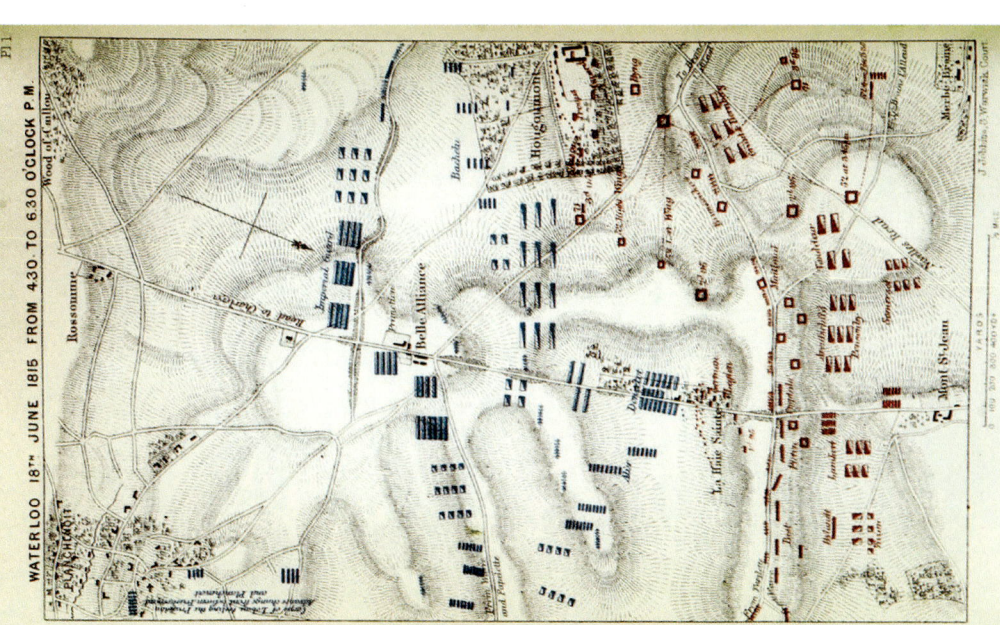

Leek's Map of the position of the forward Squares during the cavalry attacks

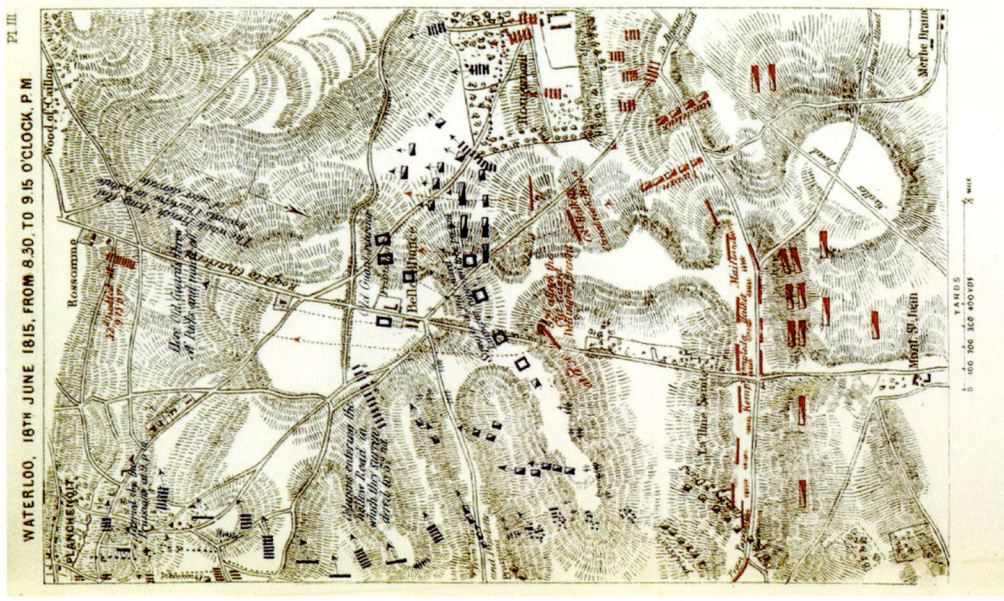

Leek's Map of the advance of the Light Brigade to the French position, note the 71st far to the right

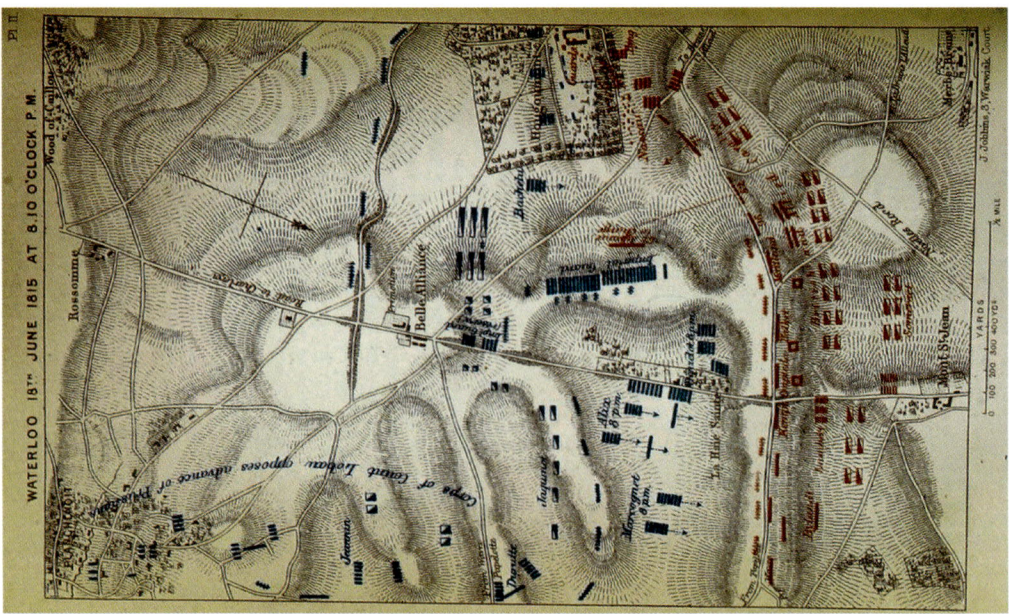

Leek's Map of the movement of the 52nd to attack the Guard column

The 52nd capturing an artillery battery in a lane

Photograph of the same lane today running up to the chaussee, opposite the Wounded Eagle Memorial

Lt General Sir Henry Clinton

Major General Sir Frederick Adam

Lt Colonel John Colborne

Lt Colonel Charles Rowan

Uniforms of the Imperial Guard in 1815 by Knotel

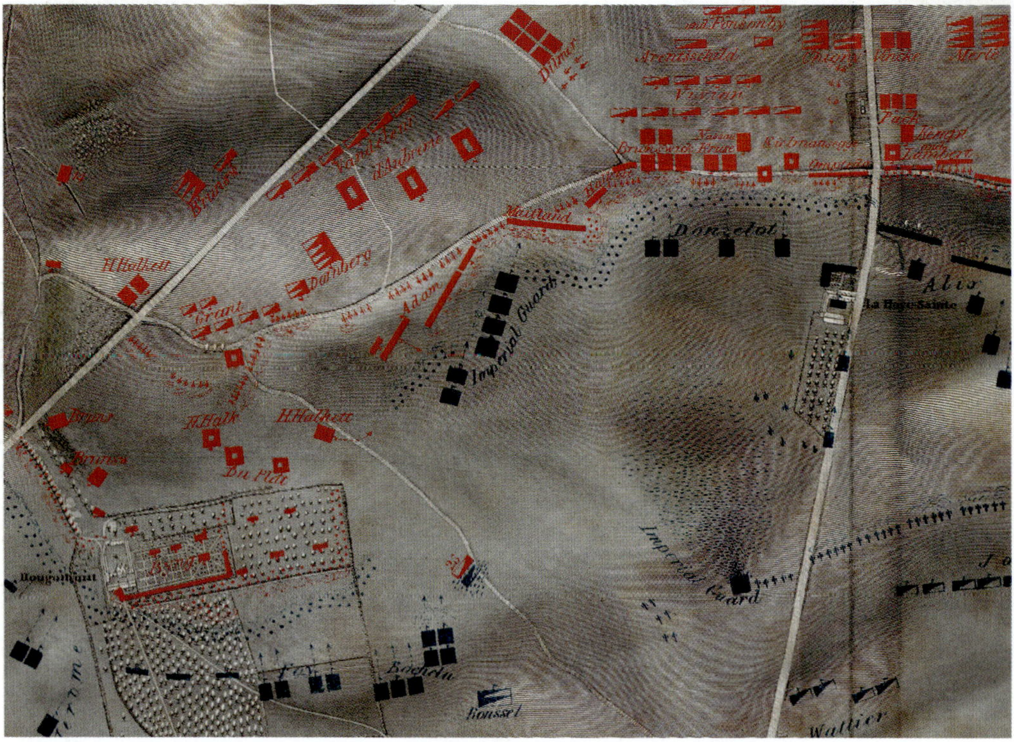

Siborne's version of the attack of the Imperial Guard

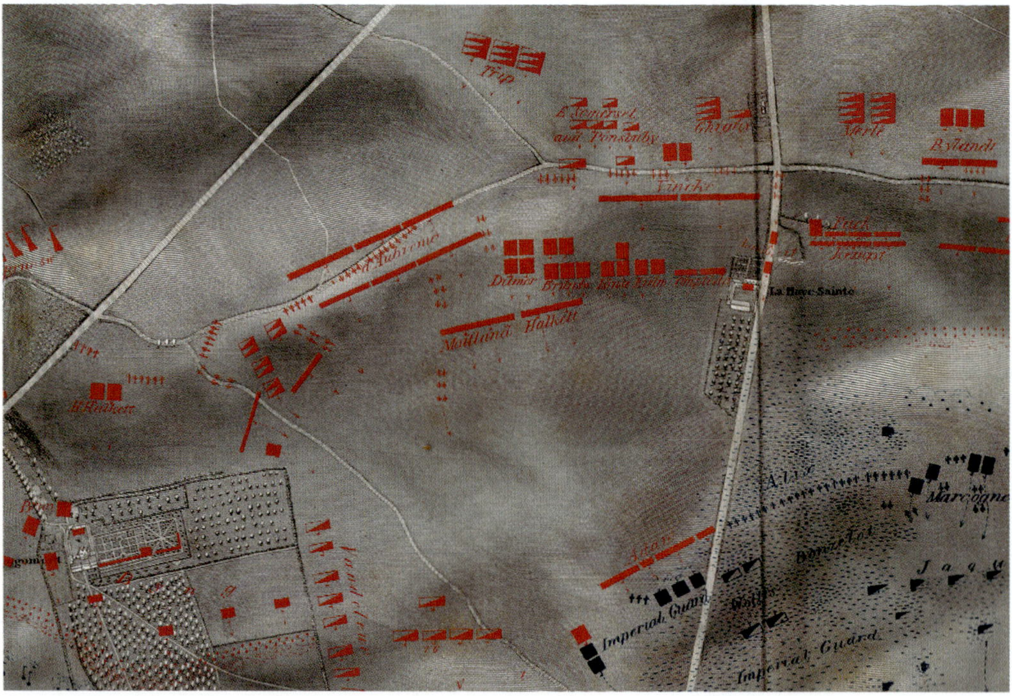

Siborne's version of the advance of the Light Brigade, note that the brigade are shown on the wrong side of the chaussee

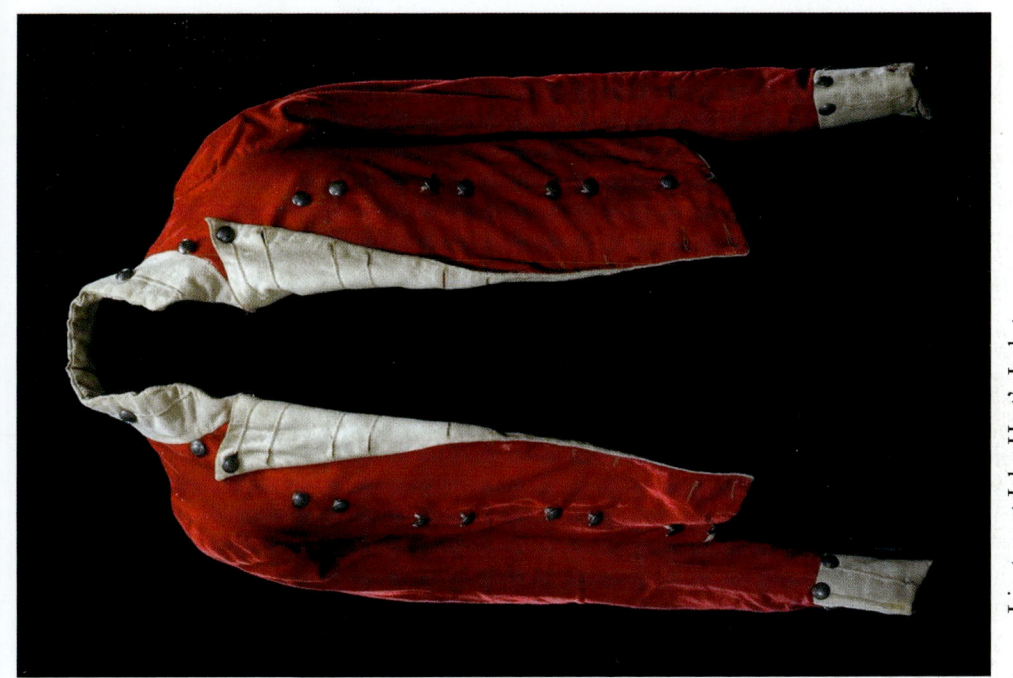

Lieutenant John Hart's Jacket

Lieutenant Mathew Anderson's Jacket

An officer of the 52nd at Paris

Light Infantry Sword

Chapter 12

The Support

What is less clear from the evidence of the 52nd alone, is whether they carried out this manoeuvre entirely alone, unsupported by even the other regiments in the brigade, or not. It is therefore necessary to view the statements of those serving in the other regiments of the brigade. Let us start with the 2/95th Rifles stationed to the left of the 52nd and thus nearer to the head of the French column. Captain Joseph Logan wrote a month after the battle:

> Soon after Bonaparte advanced with his Imperial Guard & commenced a heavy attack. Lord Wellington rode up to me & ordered I should attack them immediately. I marched with the 52nd & 71st Regiments on my right & such a carnage I never before beheld. The firing of guns &c was so great that the man next to me could not hear my orders. After some desperate fighting the French began to retire & you may be certain we stuck to their breasts. That noble fellow Lord Wellington moved on with the 95th & frequently cried out 'Move on my brave fellows'. I feared for his safety; myself I did not care about. My God! Had he fallen what a bitter day it would have been for England. Lord Hill & Sir H Clinton & General Adam were also with us & conducted themselves like heroes.[1]

Logan clearly believed that the brigade manoeuvred as one, but of greater interest, is the fact that he confirms the presence of the Duke, Lord Hill, Generals Clinton and Adam, proving that they all would have observed the movement and concurred with it as any of them could have halted it at any time. Captain George Miller had been wounded shortly before the Imperial Guard advanced but witnessed the attack from a short distance away:

> I had hardly retired to the rear of the position, to get my wound dressed, when I saw the Imperial Guards advancing in a heavy column along the ridge. That is the period you fix upon for your representation of the battle, and I am fortunately able to speak distinctly to it; as the setting sun shone full in the enemy's face, and on the backs of my own regiment. The enemy advanced to the bend of the position, and forced back the left of my regiment, down the eastern slope of the ridge and the right of the one to the left,[2] leaving an opening of between 1 and 200 yards in the line. That appeared to me the most critical period of the battle; as there was only a line

---

[1]. Glover, Waterloo Archive Volume I, p 157.
[2]. The head of the column in this account, struck the line on the right-hand companies of the Guards Brigade and the left-hand companies of the 2/95th.

of Belgians behind, which would probably have made no great resistance, all seemed lost. The advance of the Prussians on the other side however: the resistance he met with towards La Haye Sainte, and perhaps something of a panic, obliged the enemy to give way, when there was certainly no sufficient force in his front to oppose him.[3]

Miller's version is of interest, as it shows the left of the 2/95th falling back so that it was aligned with the 52nd Foot to the right and was therefore parallel with the French column, although separated laterally by about 200 yards. First Lieutenant John Budgen 2/95th also recalled the movement, but had it opening fire when a bit closer:

> Immediately before or during the right shoulder movement of the brigade, the Duke of Wellington rode along our line. I conclude he himself directed the movement. It was the only moment I saw him during the day. He spoke to the men, they cheered him in return. I think the French columns halted in consequence of our movement taking them in flank, and that the most effective fire of the brigade was delivered at a less distance than fifty yards. After receiving it the French column appeared to be in great confusion, and the brigade rushing forward, they immediately gave way without retaining any order or discipline.[4]

First Lieutenant Thomas Smith claimed that they were even closer still when they fired: 'When the 2nd 95th Regiment gave their fire I do not think the final column could have been more than twenty paces from them and which fire well given made most dreadful slaughter.'[5] Second Lieutenant Richard Eyre also wrote to his family:

> The French Imperial Guards and the whole of their infantry advanced and (we flatter ourselves) were met in the most glorious style. The action was now become general and at its height. The fate of the day was at length decided by a charge of our whole army in line four deep. After a conflict which I cannot attempt to describe to you the French Imperial Guards gave way and their whole force were thrown into the utmost confusion.

Private William Aldridge wrote a long statement of his memories:

> The French came up in three columns abreast of each other; they looked like quarter distance columns. Their left was obliquely to his left. They rushed forward three times and came very close to the artillery. The artillerymen left their guns, except two or three who lay down under them. Saw the 52nd move forward to the right of the 2nd 95th and charge those columns. About the same moment Lord Wellington rode up to the 95th and called out, 'Who

---

3. Glover, Letters from the Battle of Waterloo, p 157.
4. Siborne, The Waterloo Letters, p 300.
5. Glover, Letters from the Battle of Waterloo, p 197.

commands the 95th?' Colonel Norcott and Major Wilkins[6] had just been wounded, and at first no officer answered. Then Lieutenant Dixon,[7] who commanded the second company from the right, stepped forward.

Lord Wellington said, 'Order the 95th to charge.' Lieutenant Dixon then saw that Captain Logan, who commanded the right company of the rear line, was in command and gave the order to him. Captain Logan gave the word 'Forward' to the battalion. The enemy gave way. One artilleryman who was lying under the guns jumped up with a match in his hand and let off two or three that were loaded. His comrades afterwards used to call him 'Lord Waterloo.' The left of the 95th passed through the guns. The 95th did not lose a great many men at this time. Joined immediately with the 52nd pursuing the enemy.[8]

Aldridge makes it clear that the Rifles moved forward with the 52nd and interestingly he states that it suffered few casualties in the short firefight, unlike the 52nd, perhaps because it was at an oblique angle to the head of the column, the 52nd being firmly on the flank. It is particularly interesting that he could distinguish three separate columns abreast of each other rather than in column behind each other.

Now we need to look to the 71st, which being on the right, would undoubtedly have had a much more difficult time manoeuvring onto the right wing of the 52nd once that regiment had swung 90 degrees to the left. Its actions did not apparently begin auspiciously as related by Major Egerton of the 34th Foot, an aide de camp to the Sir Rowland Hill:

> On the advance of the 52nd Regiment … I perceived that Sir T[homas] Reynell had faced the 71st to the right about. What was his object in doing so I have never been able to discover, but at this most critical moment of the battle, it appeared to me of vital importance that we should show as good a front as possible. I therefore rode up to Sir Thomas, told him that the Duke had ordered a general advance of the line and requested he would follow the movement of the 52nd, which was immediately done without the slightest delay or hesitation, and the 71st advanced.[9]

This odd movement by Reynell, possibly thinking that the battalion was going to retire in the face of the Imperial Guard, could have deprived the 52nd of essential cover on the right flank, but this momentary error was soon rectified apparently. It is interesting however, that Egerton thought that the general advance had been ordered as soon as the 52nd had overthrown the Imperial Guard. Sir Thomas Reynell unsurprisingly omits to mention this incident, but claims that the battalion was formed very oddly indeed:

---

6. Lieutenant Colonel Amos Norcott and George Wilkins, and Captain George Miller had been wounded by this time.
7. First Lieutenant Francis Dixon.
8. Siborne, The Waterloo Letters, p 302.
9. Glover, Letters from the Battle of Waterloo, p 29.

When all apprehension of further annoyance from the enemy's cavalry had ceased, we took advantage of the ground to display our full front by obliquing[10] in opposite directions, the two wings, and directed our march upon two columns of French infantry, which from the first had appeared at the bottom of the hill. These columns did not wait our approach, but made off.[11]

Captain Samuel Reed also commented, in which he stated that it was in four deep line:

As you particularly mention the hour of seven, I have marked our advance, bringing our right shoulders forward, leaving Hougoumont to our right. In this movement the regiment was formed four deep, supporting the 52nd in a charge on the Imperial Guard, who, I think, were either in square or column. I do not think they were in line.[12]

Ensign Jack Barnett also wrote briefly to his family three days after the battle: 'I can say nothing of the battle, further than that all the old soldiers say they never saw so great a slaughter. Our brigade was charged twice by the Imperial Guards & repulsed them with great slaughter.'[13] He wrote a slightly fuller account to his father a month later: 'We then advanced, 71st in line in the centre, 52nd in square on our left, 3/95th in square on our right, to charge, it seemed to be the last push, for the Duke was in the rear of our regiment & actually gave the word of command himself.'[14]

It is interesting how he portrays his own regiment as the central one. The hard evidence for this is thin, but overwhelmingly favours the fact that the 71st took some time to manoeuvre onto the flank of the 52nd and it therefore was not engaged in the firefight with the Imperial Guard, but followed up the advance of the 52nd, initially being some 200 yards or more behind it, but hurriedly trying to regain its correct station on the right of the 52nd.

Finally, what of the 3/95th? Captain William Eeles wrote a lengthy version of events to William Siborne and it is clear that the two companies initially formed in rear of the 71st and simply followed their movements:

The 71st being on the right, the 52nd close on their left, and I believe the 2nd Battalion 95th on the left of the 52nd and close to the British position, the 3rd Battalion 95th being during this formation in reserve immediately behind the right of the 71st, where they were placed by Sir F Adam.

The brigade when so formed were on a height, or rather a little behind it, being brought considerably forward from the British line, so as to be able to bring their full front on the flank of the French advancing to the attack.

---

10. At an angle neither parallel or perpendicular to the other.
11. Siborne, The Waterloo Letters, p 297.
12. ibid, p 298.
13. Glover, Waterloo Archive Volume VI, p 149.
14. ibid, p 151.

In this order the brigade waited for the advancing enemy. I cannot myself, being at that moment behind the 71st, say what happened, except that after a violent cannonade from the British guns the 3rd Brigade opened a heavy fire and advanced on the line in which they had been placed.[15]

First Lieutenant Dugald Macfarlane of the 3/95th was at Waterloo[16] and recalled:

> About half past 7 in the evening Lord Wellington galloped up to Sir Frederick Adam, and after a moment's interview we [the brigade] were ordered to form a line in crescent, with our flanks well in advance. Soon after we got into position, Marshal Ney, the most renowned soldier in France, came direct upon us at the head of seven battalions of the Old Imperial Guard, that had not fired a shot until then; reserved evidently to break through in our centre and open out in our rear, Napoleon's favourite mode of securing a victory. They fought three deep in their companies and in close columns in rear of their Grenadiers, with a frontage of only thirty men. Our flank battalions were formed two deep,[17] and the 52nd in our centre was obliged to form four deep for want of room. Our strength at this time was about 2,400 men, thus occupying a frontage of about 300 yards, while Ney's seven battalions had only 100 yards frontage, with wide intervals between each phalanx.[18] They charged, drums beating, and cheering '*Vive l'Empereur!*' and when within 150 yards we were ordered to commence a steady fire by volleys of companies, and after seven or eight rounds of those well directed volleys, the whole of the enemy were in utter confusion. Ney's horse was shot under him. He lost his cap; and on foot, sword in hand, he endeavoured to rally his men. This was impossible; they were treading each other down. We were ordered by Sir Frederick Adam to charge with the bayonet, and in a moment about 3,000 of the enemy threw down their arms and rushed in the greatest confusion to the rear. At this moment we were over 100 yards in front of the British line, pursuing this routed multitude with Napoleon's favourite marshal in their midst, and perfect masters of everything in our front.[19]

It is very doubtful that Marshal Ney was here, as he is believed to have been with the troops to the east of the watershed. It is however quite interesting that he estimates that the Imperial Guard column numbered about 3,000 men in total, a much more realistic claim than the 10,000 sometimes mentioned.

The artillery, of course, also played its part in the defeat of the Imperial Guard column. We have already seen the evidence from Captain Bolton's Battery during the attack on the British Guards. Sympher's Troop seems to have withdrawn to re-ammunition before the Guard attack and did not return until after it was

---

15. Siborne, The Waterloo Letters, p 306.
16. He is omitted in Dalton but received a Waterloo Medal.
17. He is in error here. All of the battalions clearly state that they were in four-deep line.
18. This could indicate that they had or were deploying in echelon.
19. Glover, The Waterloo Archive Volume VII, p 164.

over.[20] Further to the right, First Lieutenant John Maunsell of Bean's Troop of Royal Horse Artillery remembered that:

> Major Bean's troop, under my command,[21] was formed on the ridge a good deal to the right of the Brussels road, immediately in front of the Imperial Guards, and continued firing on the advancing columns until our infantry advanced to the charge, when a battalion of the [2/95th] Rifle corps passed through the intervals of our guns.[22]

Major Thomas Rogers commanding a battery, recalled how his five remaining guns were placed just to the left of the 52nd but to the right of Bean's troop: 'The 52nd Regiment being near our right, and our fire taking the advancing French columns diagonally on their left front.'[23] Lieutenant George Maule also of Rogers' Battery gave a bit more detail:

> We ... took ground considerably more to the right, coming to action with three guns (two more being disabled by the loss of horses) at the angle formed by the Guards in line on the left and General Adam's Brigade, 52nd, 95th, 71st, whose right flank had been thrown forward on our right. When there I perfectly remember the French Guard coming up in front, and nearly to our Guards, and their being taken in flank by Adam's Brigade and my guns. [24]

Having read Maule's account, Major Rogers wrote again confirming that although delayed by a shortage of horses, that all five serviceable guns were brought forward and were in position when the Imperial Guard attack occurred. He stated that Maule now agreed, although we only have his statement as proof of that.

We have heard that all the senior officers from the Duke of Wellington down to General Adam were present during this critical moment, so what did they do? Captain Digby Mackworth, aide de camp to Lord Hill describes rather colourfully the approaching storm:

> The cannonade continued without intermission, and about 6 o'clock we saw heavy columns of infantry supported by dragoons forming for a fresh attack, it was evident it would be a desperate and, we thought, probably a decisive one; everyone felt how much depended on this terrible moment. A black mass of the Grenadiers of the Imperial Guard with music playing and the great Napoleon at their head came rolling onward from the farm of 'La Belle Alliance'; with rapid pace they descended the opposite heights, all scattered firing ceased on both sides, our little army seemed to collect within itself, the infantry deployed into line, and the artillery, charged to the muzzle with grape and canister, waited for the moment when the enemy's columns should

---
20. ibid, p 44. Sympher claimed that Bolton's artillery had also retired and may have missed the Imperial Guard attack, despite their claims to the latter.
21. Major Beane was killed and Second Captain Webber had been wounded.
22. Siborne, The Waterloo Letters, p 225.
23. ibid.
24. ibid, p 239.

commence the ascent of our heights; those spaces in our lines which death had opened and left vacant were covered in appearance by bodies of cavalry.

The point at which the enemy aimed was now evident; it was a re-entering angle formed by a brigade of Guards, and the Light Brigade of Lord Hill's Corps, Lord Hill was there in person.[25] The French moved on with arms sloped 'au pas de charge'; they began to ascend the hill, in a few seconds they were within a hundred paces of us, and as yet not a shot had been fired. The awful moment was now at hand, a peal of ten thousand thunders burst at once on their devoted heads, the storm swept them down as a whirlwind which rushes over the ripe corn, they paused, their advance ceased, they commenced firing from the head of their columns and attempted to extend their front; but death had already caused too much confusion among them, they crowded instinctively behind each other to avoid a fire which was intolerably dreadful; still they stood firm, 'La Garde meurt mais ne se rend pas.'[26] For half an hour this horrible butchery continued, at last seeing all their efforts vain, all their courage useless, deserted by their emperor, who had already flown, unsupported by their comrades, who were already beaten, the hitherto invincible Old Guard gave way and fled in every direction.[27]

Captain Orlando Bridgeman, another of Hill's aides de camp recalls how close to the fighting they were:

Our staff were very fortunate, none but poor Colonel Currie,[28] who was shot through the head by a grape shot, & myself were touched, six horses of our staff were shot, Lord Hill had one killed under him, & had several shots through his cloak; I was hit on the left side, just up on the heart, by a grape shot at the close of the day, if it had entered it must have killed me.[29]

He explained a bit more about his lucky escape a few days later:

It was quite at the end of the day about eight o'clock in the evening, I was next to Lord Hill when I was smacked off my horse by a grape shot that struck me directly on my back, it did not enter, if it had, of course it must have killed me, I was carried to the rear.[30]

Major Chatham Churchill, another of Hill's aides de camp, admits that they lost General Hill for a considerable period of time and feared that he was dead. He also recounts a number of personal close calls whilst losing a string of horses:

---

25. This would appear to confirm earlier comments that the head of the column struck the allied line at about the junction of the right of the Guards Brigade and the left of the 2/95th.
26. This is an extremely interesting use of this famous phrase, often wrongly attributed to General Cambronne, General Michel or cited as the invention of a French journalist in late June 1815, but this is from a letter purportedly written the very night of the battle! However, without the ability to view the original it cannot be established beyond doubt that it is not a later addition.
27. Glover, The Waterloo Archive Volume IV, pp 24.
28. Brevet Lieutenant Colonel Edward Currie 90th Foot Assistant Adjutant General.
29. Glover, The Waterloo Archive Volume IV, pp 26–7.
30. ibid, pp 27–8.

> Under cover of this cannonade advanced Bonaparte at the head of his Imperial Guard. Cavalry in a column on the left flank, the Grenadiers of the Guard on their right flank. They advanced most steadily up to our line in the great mass. They halted & commenced firing, their troops were literally mowed down. The fire was so great, nothing could stand. Our guns were moved close up to the flank of their column *foudroyer* [to strike down] with grape into it. Lord Hill moved a brigade (our elite) round the flank. I brought up, six squadrons of cavalry & we made a general charge ...
>
> Currie was killed by a grape shot close to me, Lord Hill in the grand melee with the Imperial Guard, had his horse killed & was rode over. We lost him for an hour & I thought he must have been killed, I saw him at last knocking about [on] a fresh horse ...
>
> I was on my old brown horse, a grape shot went through his body & a round shot struck my hat at the same moment. He fell dead. I was a good deal stunned & could not get from under my horse. The French cuirassiers rode over me, without my hat off, did not wound me. I lay there till the French were licked back. They again rode by me, one of their cuirassiers was killed passing me, I seized his immense horse & with some difficulty got upon him. I rode off & hardly was I clear of them before a round shot struck my horse on the head & killed him on the spot. An officer of the 13th [Light] Dragoons dismounted a man of his regiment & gave me his horse. This was shot in the leg about half an hour after.[31]

General Henry Clinton also wrote to General Thomas Graham of this critical period and an almost identical account to his brother:

> Towards seven o'clock while the fire upon his right was still advancing, Bonaparte saw that he should be exposed to great danger & to the certainty of losing all his guns if he did not disembarrass himself from one of his opponents & having the greater force upon his left (that is opposite to the Duke of Wellington) probably determined him.
>
> He harangued his Guards, who to that time had been in reserve, he pointed out the danger of his position & that his hopes were in them who had so often rendered him great service & that now they might become the defenders & saviours of their country. He increased his artillery, at that time the Duke of Wellington came to the right & though appearances were very favourable, he desired me to strengthen the right as he expected to be attacked by the infantry & cavalry (a French officer had just passed over & had brought the intelligence). The greater part of the division had been engaged excepting two battalions of Hanoverians which were still in reserve & upon the other side of the Nivelles road. The attack, which was formidable as to appearance

---

31. This incident is not recorded so fully elsewhere to the editor's knowledge. Orlando Bridgeman, a fellow aide de camp does confirm that a horse was killed under Lord Hill and that there were a number of shot holes through his cape.

was directed against the First Division's [position?], it was comprised of three masses of infantry (the Imperial Guards). Our Guards advanced to meet it, Adam's Brigade also advanced & brought up their right.[32]

Clinton and his Staff got off lightly, but General Adam received a musket ball in his right leg, although he remained on horseback until the end of the battle, his Brigade Major was also wounded. Evidently, the generals and their staff had been in the very thick of it.

It is clear from all of this evidence that the column attacked by the Light Brigade was heading for the allied ridge at the point where the 1st Guards Brigade met the left of the 2/95th. This also helps to confirm that it therefore cannot be the same column which the 1st Guard Brigade encountered and drove back, as this column had struck the line where the 3/1st Foot Guards was, some 2–300 yards further to the east, they cannot be in any way one and the same. As the Imperial Guard column drew near to the allied crest, the left of the 2/95th was forced to wheel back to form into line with the 52nd Foot, as it manoeuvred onto the flank of the French column. As soon as it was in position the 2/95th, and around three companies of the 52nd, opened fire. This caused the French column to halt its advance and the left of the French squares turned and faced the Light Brigade and began a heavy fire. This took a severe toll on the 52nd of up to 150 casualties in only a few minutes.

As soon as the battalion was in line, Colonel Colborne ordered the battalion forward and the 2/95th conformed with this movement and as it approached the flank of the column, it launched a determined bayonet charge, which the Imperial Guard did not stand against, but turned and fled in a disorganised mass towards La Haye Sainte and La Belle Alliance. As Colborne began this movement, an order arrived from the Duke of Wellington to carry out the very same manoeuvre and this could possibly have led the Duke to presume that they were simply carrying out his orders. The 71st and the 3/95th on the right, were initially confused as to the point of the manoeuvre and were delayed in starting the movement. The 71st received orders to keep formation with the 52nd and it was soon in pursuit to regain its formation. The 71st were too late to fire on the column, but as the 52nd began to march eastward towards the main Brussels chaussee in pursuit of the French Guard, it was forced to temporarily halt to deal with cavalry and the 71st appears to have caught up at this point. The 3/95th were initially in the rear of the 71st but as it began to advance the 52nd and 71st diverged slightly and the 3/95th moved into the gap between the two battalions.

The Duke of Wellington, Generals Rowland Hill, Henry Clinton and Frederick Adam were all in the locality and all were involved in ordering troops up to support the movement. They remained in close contact, except for Hill whose horse was shot, and they were fully aware of the manoeuvres and encouraged them, having ample opportunity to halt the movement if not happy with it.

---

32. See Glover, Correspondence of Sir Henry Clinton Volume 2, pp 121 & 125.

Chapter 13

The Chase 20.00 to 20.45 Hours

The bayonet charge by the 52nd, supported by the 2/95th on its left, caused the last column of Imperial Guard squares to break and flee towards La Belle Alliance. At this point, it may have been natural to have halted the attack and to regroup, to allow the other elements of the brigade to catch up with them and to ensure that they were prepared for any counter-attack by cavalry. However, Colborne, with both General Adam and the Duke of Wellington close in the rear of the regiment, felt emboldened to continue marching perpendicularly across the Allied front, clearing the remnants of the other attacking units off the allied slope. Suddenly, however, cavalry were to be a problem, but they were allied rather than French horsemen. Ensign William Leeke described his memories of these events in great detail:

> The 52nd ... advanced by itself, in the direction of the lower enclosure of La Haye Sainte, towards the Charleroi road,[1] and nearly at right angles with that part of the British position behind which, on the reverse slope, stood Maitland's Brigade of Guards, and Sir Colin Halkett's, Count Kielmansegge's, and Colonel Von Ompteda's Brigades, at a distance from the 52nd varying, as the regiment continued to advance, from 350 to 700 yards.[2] Immediately after the defeat of the Imperial Guard, the 52nd passed over their killed and wounded, who, poor fellows, were lying very thick upon the ground, where I passed on a breadth of about fifty yards; in some places I had to spring over heaps of them lying over each other. One of the 52nd officers, who has now been dead for many years,[3] told me, some time after the action, that an occurrence had taken place as we passed the killed and wounded of the French Guard, which had since given him at times some uneasiness. It was this: As he was advancing in rear of the regiment, he saw a Belgian soldier, who was following us in pursuit of plunder, try to take money from a wounded Frenchman, who begged him to let him keep what little he had; on which the Belgian dealt him a heavy blow on the head with the butt end of his musket, which appeared to kill him, and that he was

---

1. Anyone knowing the geography of Waterloo, will immediately realise that being on the slope running down to Hougoumont, it was impossible to see anything of La Haye Sainte as it is hidden by the watershed which rises between. He is simply indicating the direction taken by the regiment in general terms.
2. This is a wide difference and is pure guesswork by Leeke. If the 52nd followed the route described by Leeke towards La Haye Sainte orchard, then the regiment remained within 2–300 metres/yards of the allied ridge as it marched across the lower slopes.
3. This is likely to refer to Captain James McNair, who died near Glasgow in 1836.

so indignant at this atrocity, that he immediately ran the Belgian through the body with his sword. He asked me what I should have done under the circumstances, and I replied, that I most likely should have done the same; but that I was not sure it was the right thing to do; yet, as the scoundrel had left his own corps in search of plunder, and had under those circumstances taken away life, his own life seemed to be fairly forfeited. I saw a man of the 40th Regiment about the same time, who also was probably on the same sort of errand, and I only mention him, because I observe that in Colonel Ponsonby's account of what happened to him when he was lying wounded on the ground, he mentions amongst other things that a soldier of the 40th came across him late at night, and took care of him till the morning of the 19th. This was probably the same man[4] we had seen earlier in the evening. The 52nd had only got a very short distance from the killed and wounded of the Imperial Guard, when suddenly, through the smoke, it saw a charge of cavalry coming upon its flanks and centre. They consisted of British and German light dragoons, mingled with French cuirassiers, before whom they were retiring at speed. We took them all for the enemy, and they were fired on and [they] lost some men before it was discovered that many of them were English. Some went round the flanks, but many rode at the centre of the regiment, and, when they were about twenty yards off, the line opened about six or eight feet in the centre to let them pass. I thought at the moment that the men were not right in making an opening for those whom we regarded as enemies, and should have received the charge on their bayonets; I, therefore, stood to the front, on the right of the formed line and to the left of the opening, and attempted to draw my sword from the scabbard that I might attack the leading horseman. It was hanging on my left side, hooked up to the waist belt, as officers carrying the Colours do not draw their swords in action, except in cases of emergency.

To my great dismay, the looped sword knot was entangled in the button of the scabbard, and I could not get my sword out, and therefore I instantly took the Colour in both hands with the intention of using it as a lance against the foremost dragoon. The poor fellow was, however, shot dead by our men, and fell headlong from his horse on his back, with his head towards us, about six feet in front of the opening; I then saw by his three stripes that he was a sergeant. The horse passed through the centre of the interval, and, as he was at speed, the stirrups flew out at right angles from the saddle, and the right one nearly struck me in the face. There was then a cry, 'They are English', and the firing ceased. Opposite to the centre of the 52nd, the cuirassiers were seen to draw off in admirable order. On the right, one gallant cuirassier penetrated the line and was cut down, just as he got through it, by the sergeant major.[5] Just clear of the right of our line, an

---

4. Frederick Ponsonby had been wounded at least 500 metres/yards to the west and virtually in the French lines. The chances of it being the very same soldier in the two instances is very low indeed.
5. Sergeant Major Dowdell.

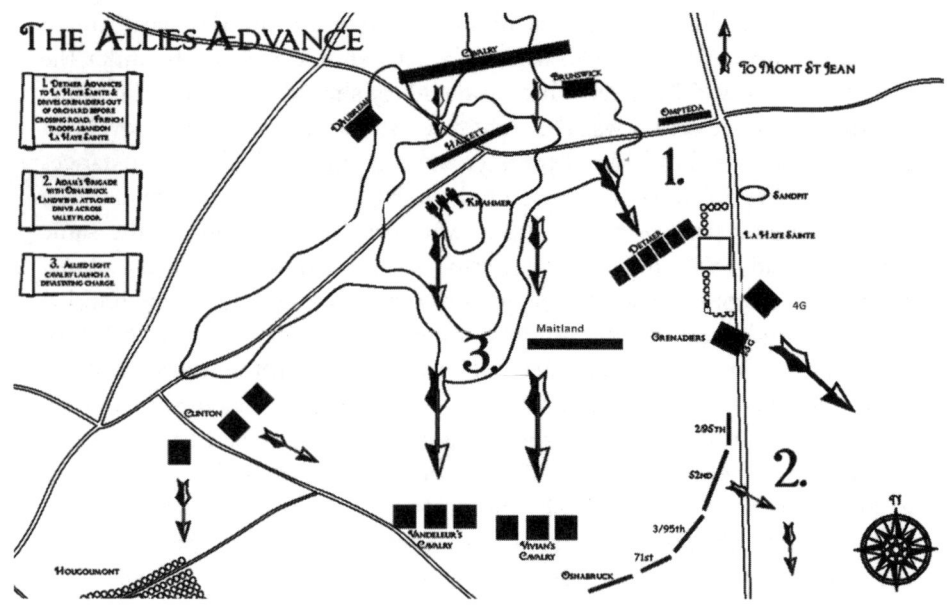

encounter was witnessed between a cuirassier officer and a cadet, (answering to a volunteer in our service) attached to one of the German light dragoon regiments of Dornberg's Brigade. The latter was retreating at speed before his antagonist, with his head down on his horse's neck and his sword over his own neck. The German cadet was watching his opportunity, and on finding himself near his friends, on the right of our line, suddenly pulled his horse up upon his haunches, and dealt the cuirassier a blow across his face; he wheeled round and engaged the cadet in single combat, who managed to strike him again on his face, so that he fell over on one side, and was pierced under the arm and killed.

It was said that some of the 23rd Light Dragoons (and it seems there were German light dragoons with them[6]) had attacked a body of French infantry, probably some of the defeated Imperial Guard, and that being consequently somewhat broken, they were charged by a formed body of cuirassiers, before whom they had to retire, in order that they might re-form. They did good service in engaging the enemy, but when they had to retire, they ought to have ridden round the flanks, and not through the line, of one of their own infantry regiments. I may remark that if all our soldiers, cavalry and infantry, wore the scarlet uniform, these unfortunate mistakes of taking friends for foes would be of less frequent occurrence.[7]

On the subject of these cavalry, Lieutenant George Hall of the 52nd had some pertinent words regarding their uniforms:

---

6. These would have been from the 1st or 2nd Light Dragoons KGL who were brigaded with the 23rd.
7. Leeke, pp 47–9.

The uniform of the light dragoons had just been altered, and they were dressed as the French chasseurs, so it was quite natural that they should receive a volley. I remarked that but few fell in front of the line, but a considerable number in the rear. The coolness of our men in this unfortunate mistake was admirable; in the smoke and noise and confusion, no one knew if his comrade was cut down or not, but there was no thought of dispersing or of lying down for safety; they just faced about and prepared to fire on the supposed enemy in the rear. I believe some did do so before the officers, who had discovered the error, could stop them. Anderson told me that the dragoons who rode through our line, re-formed close to where he was sitting wounded, and that he heard the commanding officer exclaim, in a tone of vexation, 'It's always the case, we always lose more men by our own people than we do by the enemy.' [8]

Colonel Colborne stated in a memorandum that three companies fell back to form square and this caused the regiment to halt to reform, before advancing again:

The three adjoining companies wheeled back to form square.[9] The battalion at this time was under a heavy fire from the Imperial Guards and the regiment was halted for a few minutes to enable the three companies to rectify their line. At this moment, while the three companies were forming up, the Duke was close in the rear, and said 'Well never mind, go on, go on.'[10]

Colonel Colborne makes it clear that the Duke of Wellington was close by and even spoke to him:

At this moment two or three squadrons of the 23rd Dragoons appeared, directly in front of the line of the 52nd, approaching rapidly towards the line. The two companies on the left [right – see below] halted and fired into them, supposing them to be the enemy's cavalry. My horse was wounded: I called out to the Adjutant to stop the fire, and whilst we were rectifying this mistake which had occurred, the only one that had occurred during the day, and which interrupted our march, the Duke of Wellington came to the rear of the left of our line near the two companies which had fired. I said to his Grace, 'It is our own cavalry which has caused this firing.' His Grace replied, 'Never mind, go on, go on.'[11]

Colonel Colborne continued his version of events:

---

8. Leeke, p 50.
9. The short halt when the cavalry came close is known, but previously it has not been clear that three companies began to form square. He does not always state this in his other versions of the advance given at later dates and it is therefore very difficult to be certain as to its accuracy.
10. Glover, Letters from the Battle of Waterloo, p 187. Originally mis-identified as by Cross as in a similar handwriting, but now correctly assigned to Colborne.
11. Siborne, The Waterloo Letters, p 285.

> We continued our advance, which soon brought us under the hill or ascent occupied by the Imperial Guards, and we found ourselves protected from their fire by the hill. Our line, from the badness of the ground and the interruption to which I have alluded [the cavalry] had thrown the two right hand companies into some disorder, and I, suspecting the French cavalry were not far from our right, called out to the officers commanding Nos 1 and 2 Companies to halt and bring up their companies in good line, and whilst I was restraining the disorderly impetuosity of these companies under great excitement, several officers in front, Colonel Churchill and Colonel Chalmers, were cheering and waving their hats and caps in front.
>
> At this time the 71st formed on our right flank, and I ordered the bugles to sound the advance, and the whole line charged up the hill; and on our arriving at the edge of the deep road, the opposite side of which the Imperial Guards had occupied, the 52nd fired, at least most of the companies. We observed the enemy in great confusion, some firing, others throwing away their packs and running to the rear.
>
> Captain Cross called out that the French soldiers near us were going to surrender, but on their continuing to fire on us I ordered the 52nd Regiment to 'pass the road', and the whole passed through the guns and carriages, &c, and we formed columns of companies, our right resting on the road to Genappe. We moved on in column, and passed I think, eighty guns or carriages in about ten minutes after this new formation. No cavalry whatever could be seen on our left, or to the left of the Genappe road, and I am sure that no British cavalry were between us and the French for the last hour of the battle. I think, therefore, that the attacks of our cavalry at this time must have been made by the cavalry which had passed in rear of the 52nd, and to the right of the Genappe road.
>
> I observed smoke and firing towards Plancenoit, and to the right and left of the Genappe road. The 71st did not cross the Genappe road, but moved to the right, as well as part of Sir H Clinton's Division.[12]

Having cleared the cavalry away from its front, the 52nd moved on towards the Brussels/Charleroi chaussee and crossed it before moving on towards La Belle Alliance where three formed squares of the Old Guard were evident. These were undoubtedly the two battalions of the 1st Grenadiers which had been moved forward from Rossomme during the final attack. The third Guard square is less easily identified with certainty, but the most likely candidate is the 1/2nd Grenadiers which we know remained as a reserve to the Grenadier attack near La Haye Sainte and is believed to have retired on its defeat in perfect order. Colborne helpfully wrote a fuller account to William Siborne later:

> They had no reserve formed worth the name of a reserve, all attacks of cavalry or infantry after that moment, were the necessary consequences of

---

12. ibid, pp 285–6.

their flight, and an endeavour to save such part of the crew of the wreck, as could be brought off without incurring further risk. Therefore, however splendid the conduct of any corps might have been after the first flight of the French in reaping the fruits of the victory and in completing the route of the retiring columns; they took no part in the critical affair on the plateau of La Haye Sainte, or plain below it which the left flank of Napoleon's column overlooked. The 52nd in the meantime had proceeded within a short distance of the rising ground on which the French were formed, when a body of British cavalry were perceived in full speed approaching the front of the left company of the 52nd. The officers of the company gave the order to fire, supposing they had come from the enemy's column. The three adjoining companies wheeled back to form square. The battalion at this time was under a heavy fire from the Imperial Guards and the regiment was halted for a few minutes to enable the three companies to rectify their line. At this moment, while the three companies were forming up, the Duke was close in the rear, and said 'Well never mind, go on, go on.' This halt brought the 71st close on the right of the 52nd, which corps had not been so much exposed to the fire as the 52nd. The 52nd then advanced at full speed, the greater part of the French gave way in confusion, but some remained formed close to the deep road running direct from La Haye Sainte to La Belle Alliance. Captain Cross called out 'they are coming over, don't fire',[13] the French however opened a straggling fire, some running across the road and a few remaining till the 52nd were within six or seven yards of them. The whole of the 52nd charged briskly till they were impeded by the deep road, halted for a minute or two till they received the word to pass. They had some difficulty in getting over; when they had passed they formed line and wheeled to the right.

They found a gun on the plateau fully horsed and moved on in line keeping their right on the road, passed La Belle Alliance.... In the meantime the 71st had proceeded towards Rossomme[14] and did not pass the road when the 52nd did. The whole of the Division of Sir H Clinton, the moment the French were observed in retreat and in confusion, had struck to their right towards Rossomme. The 52nd passed about 80 pieces of cannon or tumbrils, within a quarter of an hour after they had passed the Charleroi road from Waterloo.[15]

Each time Colonel Colborne wrote over the intervening years, he unsurprisingly changed his emphasis somewhat over events. Certainly, the incident with the light cavalry occurred whilst marching along the allied front line, the battalion appeared to have crossed the chaussee just to the north of the cutting (which is described as a hill) and advanced with the rest of the brigade, keeping the

---

13. That is passing over to the allied cause.
14. This is incorrect, the 71st did also cross the chaussee.
15. Glover, Letters from the Battle of Waterloo, pp 187–8.

chaussee on its right. Lieutenant Charles Holman, as usual, was a little more circumspect in his comments:

> We followed them up at [the] double quick and passed to the left of the Charleroi road where some of our left coming up, we cut off an amazing number of them. We observed a large body of their cavalry moving on our right, but they did not attempt a charge. We continued following them up, that we came close on their artillery who behaved well, firing until we drove them from their guns. We then took their artillery and baggage from them, as they could not get it off.[16]

General Adam also concurs regarding the advance towards La Belle Alliance:

> The brigade, continuing to advance, crossed the Genappe chaussee, and continued advancing in a direction nearly parallel to that chaussee, which was at some little distance on the right. While advancing, the Duke of Wellington being with the brigade, some battalions of the enemy were re-formed, and appeared inclined to stand. The Duke ordered them to be attacked, but it was suggested to his Grace that the brigade, which from its rapid advance was somewhat loose in its formation, had better be halted and the files closed in. The halt was ordered accordingly, but after a few moments the Duke said, 'They won't stand, better attack them,' and the 3rd Brigade was accordingly again put in motion, and the battalions of the enemy withdrew, and fell into the mass of confusion which existed in our front. These battalions (Imperial Guards) were the last troops of the enemy which had any appearance of order or formation.[17]

Ensign William Leeke has, of course, a great deal more to say:

> Almost immediately after we had become disengaged from the above mentioned cavalry, we suddenly found that some guns on our right, towards La Belle Alliance, were firing grape into the front of the regiment and making some serious gaps in our line. One discharge came into the centre, and the rattle of the grape against arms, accoutrements, and men, was something very different from the roar of round shot, the noise from the explosion of shells, and the whistling and humming of bullets, which we had hitherto been accustomed to. Sir John Colborne, who was not then mounted, anxiously exclaimed, as he went quickly towards the right of the line, 'Where are these guns? They are destroying the regiment.' Lieutenant Gawler, who, after Captain Diggle was wounded, had taken command of the right [No.1] Company, told him they were not far away on the right, and asked if he should take the right section and drive them in; Sir John Colborne told him to do so, and he then wheeled the right section to the right, extended it, and advanced towards them. As soon as the French gunners saw the red coats through the smoke, they immediately limbered up and retired. Gawler

---
16. Holman Lt, Journal for 1815, Royal Green Jackets Museum, Winchester.
17. Siborne, The Waterloo Letters, pp 277.

found a considerable body of French infantry in front of him, at 200 or 300 yards distance, and collected his men and waited for the regiment, which in the meantime had brought its left shoulder rather more forward. When the discharge of grape came into the centre, I saw a man spring behind to take the musket of one who was killed, as his own would not go off. Another man near me said, in an undertone to his comrade, 'the top of —— 's skull was taken off,' mentioning the poor fellow's name, which I do not now recollect. Shortly after, as we were advancing, (there was no halt,) I found about a foot and a half of my Colour pole was very wet with blood, about the height of my shoulder, and that there was blood on the buff cuff of the left sleeve of my jacket. It was not my own blood.

The next morning I found that the thumb of my left hand was black and sore. I think my left hand and the Colour pole must have been struck, without my perceiving it at the moment, by a part of the skull of the man mentioned above, for the contusion could not have been occasioned merely by blood. I believe it was at this time that Lieutenant Holman had three musket balls through the blade of his sword, without being touched himself. I have often seen the sword, and the holes made by the balls are connected with each other, as if they had been made by canister shot; the thick rim of the sword holding the two parts of the blade so strongly together, that Holman used the sword for several years afterwards whenever he was on duty.[18] I have mentioned that Sir John Colborne was on foot when the French fired grape into our line. Just before this, both he and the present Lieutenant General Sir William Rowan, GCB, now colonel of the 52nd, made an ineffectual attempt again to become mounted officers. ... Sir John Colborne's horse was also (afterwards) shot, which led to a laughable scene. On our coming up to an abandoned French gun, with the horses still attached to it, Sir John and I mounted two of the horses, calling to our men to cut the traces, which they were unable to accomplish; and as the regiment was advancing rapidly, we had to dismount and follow as fast as we could. Shortly after we met plenty of horses with empty saddles.

It has been said that the guns which retired with the rear battalions of the second column, and which afterwards, as I have related, fired grape into us, were directed to open fire on the advancing 52nd line by the Emperor himself; but I think it more likely they were directed to take up their ground by General Drouot,[19] who was with the Imperial Guard when they gave way. The Emperor was then on the height above, in front of La Belle Alliance ...

---

18. What is strange regarding this, is that Holman fails to mention this damage to his sword at all.
19. Note by Leeke: It is recorded of Drouot that he always carried a small Bible with him to read, which constituted his chief delight; and he avowed it openly to the persons in the imperial suite, a peculiarity not a little remarkable on that staff, and the admission of which required no small degree of moral courage. Napoleon often placed him in the most exposed positions, so that his situation was full of peril. He was said to be somewhat superstitious, because in action he took care to wear his old uniform of general of artillery, as he had long worn it and had never been wounded. The probability is, that he considered it unwise. to draw the fire of the enemy upon himself by wearing a splendid uniform. He also always dismounted when near the enemy.

At Waterloo he was the 'General aide de camp de l'Empereur.' Directly after the guns were driven in on our right by Gawler, we distinctly saw on our left, 500 or 400 yards up the British position, and on the Hougoumont side of La Haye Sainte, four battalions in column, apparently French, standing with ordered arms. According to all accounts they were too far down the British position to be Dutch Belgians; they certainly were not English.[20] It was thought they were French, and part of Donzelot's Division, who did not know how to get away, and therefore remained quietly where they were until the 52nd had passed. We were then about 200 yards from the Charleroi road, and I think a line in prolongation of our front would on the left have cut the farmhouse of La Haye Sainte, at 300 yards distance, and on our right the south eastern point of the enclosures of Hougoumont, at a distance of rather more than half a mile from us.

The 52nd was then, as before, quite alone, and had these four battalions of Donzelot's Division come down upon our left flank with a regular British charge, they would possibly have prevented the rout of the French army from becoming so complete as it was. The brigades of Alten's Division could not at this time have made any forward movement down a portion of the British position, which they did afterwards, when the Duke ordered the whole line to advance, or we should have seen them. I think the 71st, the right regiment of our brigade, and the left regiment, the 2nd battalion of the Rifles, both of which had been thrown out by the sudden advance of the 52nd, and perhaps the Osnabruck Landwehr Battalion, under Colonel Halkett, were the only British troops which had left the crest of the British position at this time; and we saw nothing even of these till the next morning ... When we were about 200 yards from the Charleroi road, the Prussian round shot, directed either at our line or at the French extreme right, began to strike near us, one about fifteen yards from the centre, but apparently none of them touched the regiment. The Prussians had come up on the right flank of the French from the direction of Wavre and at that time were trying to drive them out of the village of Planchenoit [Plancenoit]; rather later they succeeded in doing so, at an immense loss to themselves. The Prussian guns were more than a mile from us; they soon discovered that we were friends, and ceased to cannonade us. I well remember thinking, when I saw some of these Prussian round shot striking the ground not far from us, that it would be very unfortunate to be killed or wounded just at the close of the action, when the enemy were in full retreat. I think it must have been at a rather earlier period of our advance, that my first thought occurred, of what would become of my soul in case I should be killed; I recollect I quieted the thought at once, by thinking that those who believed in the Saviour, the Lord Jesus Christ, would be saved; and that, as I believed in Him, all would be right if I should be killed that day...

---

20. They were almost certainly Detmer's troops who had driven the Imperial Guard attack off the ridge in that sector and were now reforming before driving the Guards out of La Haye Sainte orchard.

It was about twenty minutes after eight, when Sir John Colborne seeing a considerable body of troops in his front inclined to make a stand, halted the 52nd in the low ground close to the Charleroi road, for the purpose of dressing the line, which had then advanced more than half a mile without any halt from the time it had left the British position. The Regimental Colour and the covering sergeants were ordered out, and Nixon,[21] the acting Adjutant, had just dressed them, when the Duke of Wellington, attended by Sir Colin Campbell, rode up to Sir John Colborne, who was in the rear of the centre of the 52nd, and I heard him say, as I looked back from my position in front of the centre, 'Well done, Colborne! Well done! Go on, don't give them time to rally.' ... The French had then opened fire on our line at about 200 yards distance, and I well recollect that several bullets streaked the ground close to me, many others seemed to whiz very close to my ears, so that I suspected the French were directing more attention than was quite pleasant to me and my Colour. It may however have been principally attracted by the Duke, and Sir Colin Campbell and Sir John Colborne, who were immediately in my rear and about ten paces from me. The colour and the covering sergeants were immediately called in, without the line being dressed, and the regiment advanced and drove off the enemy. It was here that the Marquis of Anglesea [sic], then Lord Uxbridge, rode up to the Duke and said, 'For God's sake, Duke, don't expose yourself so, you know what a valuable life yours is,' and that the Duke replied, 'I'll be satisfied, when I see those fellows go.' Lord Uxbridge was wounded by a grape or musket-shot in the knee. I did not see it, nor was it observed by Sir John Colborne or by any of the officers of the regiment, our attention being engaged by the enemy's troops in our front. Sir Colin Campbell told me, several years afterwards, that, on observing that Lord Uxbridge was wounded, he rode up to him and laid hold of him by his collar and held him on his horse till his aide de camp took charge of him.

These troops, who acted as a rear guard to the French army now retiring in the greatest confusion, were, it is said, three battalions of the Old Guard, a small body of cuirassiers of the Guard, and a few pieces of artillery, probably the same guns which had been driven off by the right section of the 52nd under Lieutenant Gawler. It has been stated and is supposed that the Emperor Napoleon was with these troops. ... From my point of view, I saw in front of us two or three bodies of men on the rising ground before us, but I could not see clearly their formation, for they were either kneeling, or no more of their bodies could be seen than to about a foot below their shoulders, owing to the ruggedness of the ground; they are, however, described by others of the 52nd as having been three squares, with a body of cavalry on their right; they had three guns on their left, which fired a round or two of grape at us. The 52nd did not return the fire of these troops of the Old Guard. On our advancing, the French retired in good order. The

---

21. Lieutenant William Nixon took over as Adjutant when Winterbottom was wounded.

cavalry on their right faced about to cover the retreat of their squares, but, on our pressing on in pursuit, they prudently refused the encounter with our compact four deep line. Only one of their squares retreated by our left of La Belle Alliance and the Charleroi road; and this square the 52nd kept in view for nearly a mile further, until they lost sight of it about a quarter of a mile before it reached the farmhouse of Rossomme, where we brought up for the night.[22]

Lieutenant Gawler wrote of his actions:

The 52nd continued pressing forward; when, from the thick smoke that still hung on the fugitives, a body of horsemen, of which some evidently were cuirassiers, broke furiously upon its front. It had all the appearance of an effort of the French cavalry to cover the retreat, and the whole fire was for a moment concentrated upon it, until some of the headmost horsemen, falling almost on the bayonets, were perceived to belong to the 23rd Light Dragoons, and 1st Light Dragoons, of the German Legion. A murmur ran down the line 'they are English'; the firing ceased altogether, and the cuirassiers, by another effort, might perhaps in such a moment of hesitation have completed their charge by penetrating the regiment, only one however attempted it, who, dashing through the two right companies, was killed in the rear of them by the sergeant major.

Dornberg's exhausted brigade had probably charged the columns which, on the defeat of the Guard, gave way near La Haye Sainte; and having been, when in a state of consequent dispersion, charged in return by the strong reserve of cavalry which the French had in rear of that farm, a part was forced in a lateral direction, through the Imperial Guard upon the unexpected line of the 52nd.

The front of the 52nd was scarcely cleared of the cavalry, when three field pieces, which probably had been attached to the rear of the columns of the Imperial Guard, opened a fire of grape at a distance of not more than 400 yards, in the prolongation of its right flank. The right section wheeled up and drove them off, the rest of the regiment continuing unchecked its close pursuit of the broken masses of the Guard, until it had swept from right to left the whole front of attack, and its left flank was on the hollow in the chaussee to Genappe, in advance of the garden of La Haye Sainte, 800 yards from the ground at which the charge commenced

In its progress, it was not at any time crossed by the fire or charge of any portion of the allied army, with the exception already described.

Thus, at about eight o'clock ended the Grand Crisis of Waterloo. From this period the success of the allies was established beyond a doubt, and their subsequent movements were only directed to complete the victory.

---

22. Leeke pp 50–7.

The smoke had cleared away; some of the fugitives were making an attempt to reform on the other side of the hollow road; but in its evident hopelessness a much more important object was presented, about 400 yards obliquely to the right of the 52nd, in three battalions of the Old Guard, which having formed the rear of the columns of attack, had retired in tolerable order, and now stood in squares, supported by a small body of cuirassiers, on the first rise of their position, not far in the front of La Belle Alliance, on the Hougoumont side of the chaussee. The remainder of the French army (excepting those who a mile obliquely to the left were still obstinately defending Planchenois [Plancenoit] against the Prussians) was seen rushing in total disorganization towards the Genappe road; having broken as soon as the Imperial Guard gave way on Mont St Jean.

The 52nd, bringing up its left shoulders, regained its complete parallelism to the general front of the position, and closing with the 71st, (which during the whole of this time had continued its protecting movement on the right,) the two regiments advanced in line, still four deep, upon the squares of the Old Guard. At this time, no other closed bodies of infantry had advanced from behind the British position; and Vivian's Brigade, the only cavalry in sight, was but just appearing on the summit. Sir John Colborne, observing this distance of support, the strength and attitude of the enemy, and the heavy state of the ground in the valley, (into which, trampled and re-trampled as it had been by twenty thousand horsemen, the sturdy rear rank men sunk at times knee deep,) called out to the 52nd to step short and take breath; but the Duke, who, having galloped up a few moments before, was then in the centre of the regiment, said, 'Go on, Colborne, go on; give them no time to rally;' and, after a hasty correction of the line upon the covering sergeants, all again pressed forward.

The squares of the Old Guard made no attempt to deploy; but, after opening a heavy fire from their front and flanks, as soon as the opposing line drew too near, with great steadiness ceased firing, faced to the rear and commenced their retreat by word of command, the two right squares directly to the rear on the right side of the chaussee, pursued by the 71st and skirmishers of the 95th. The left square, accompanied at first by the cuirassiers, passing obliquely to the left, crossed the chaussee (which was crowded with fugitives) below La Belle Alliance, and then hastened towards Rossomme, along the left side of the road, followed closely by the 52nd Regiment, the two British regiments still in lines four deep. On crossing the chaussee, the cuirassiers fronted as if to charge; but their opponents pressed towards them, presenting their bayonets, unwilling to lose time either by firing or forming square, and the cuirassiers declined the contest.

A hundred yards to the allied left of La Belle Alliance, a hollow road runs nearly at right angles towards the chaussee, up which a column of artillery and infantry from the French right wing was hastily retreating. The square crossed the head of this body, but the high bank concealed the approach of the 52nd until the distance became too small to admit of any but a hand-to-hand contest. The column seemed not sufficiently aware of its desperate circumstances to surrender without hesitation, and for a moment the scene was singularly wild. The infantry, before they threw down their arms, made an effort either at defence or escape; the artillery dashed at the opposite bank, but some of the horses of each gun were in an instant brought down. A subaltern of the battery threw his sword on the ground, in token of surrender; but the commander, standing in the centre of his guns, waved his above his head in defiance. A soldier sprang from the British ranks, parried his thrust, closed with him, threw him on the ground, and keeping him down with his foot, reversed his musket in both hands to bayonet him; when that repugnance to the shedding of blood, which so often rises in the hearts of British soldiers, even under circumstances of personal danger and prudential necessity, burst forth in a groan of disgust from his surrounding comrades; it came, however, in this case too late, the fatal thrust was sped, and the Legion of Honour lost another member. One gun was sharply wheeled round, and discharged into the square of the Imperial Guard by General Adam's aide-de-camp; some hundreds of prisoners were left to those who should come after; and the 52nd pressed on to its first object with so much earnestness, that at a short distance from the farm of Rossomme, the French grenadiers, finding their inability to outmarch their pursuers on equal terms, suddenly halted by word of command, threw off their knapsacks, and thus lightened, quickly disappeared in the closing twilight.[23]

Gawler later altered some of his statement following a heated correspondence with General Hussey Vivian:

By the correction of them, our respective narratives of facts are brought into almost perfect reconciliation. These errors were: First, that in describing 'the first rise' of the French position on which the squares of the Old Guard were posted, I said it was 'not far in their front of La Belle Alliance;' and in the plan attached to the narrative, I have made this 'not far' to be about 350 yards. Whereas, the 'not far' is too narrow a term, and the plan is also incorrect, for an inspection of Lieutenant Siborne's model has convinced me, that 'the first rise' in question is 130 yards nearer to the British position; that is, 480, instead of 350 yards in the French front of La Belle Alliance.

And, Second, that I made the 71st, and part of the 95th, after the attack on the squares, to continue along the right side of the Genappe chaussee, when the 52nd crossed to the left side. Whereas, I am now persuaded, on very solid evidence, that the 71st and 95th, as well as the 52nd, crossed to the left side before reaching La Belle Alliance, thus leaving the whole of the right side open to the subsequent advance of Vivian's Brigade, and to

---

23. Gawler, United Services Journal 1833 Part II, pp 303–6.

its charges upon the enemy in the line of La Belle Alliance. As long as the 71st was supposed to continue close along the right side of the chaussee, it followed of necessity as a matter of inference, that the battalion must have been that which came up with the square charged by Major Howard, near to the chaussee, beyond La Belle Alliance; but the correction of the error in the route of the 71st makes this collision impossible. Some obscurity still remains as to the precise designation of the battalion that overtook the square. It is simply probable that it was one of Colonel Halkett's Hanoverian regiments, as his brigade followed at some distance in support of the advance of Adam's Brigade. Colonel Halkett himself was with the 71st during the attack on the squares of the Old Guard, and at that time, with his own hand, took a French General (I think Cambronne) a prisoner. When the advanced corps of the British attack upon the French position had reached to about the distance of La Belle Alliance, or Primotion, they must have nearly formed a continuous line. On the extreme left, Adam's Brigade with its right on the Genappe chaussee, and its left within one or two hundred yards of the Prussians. In the centre, Vivian's Brigade with its left near the chaussee; and on the extreme right, Vandeleur's just coming up, with its left near the right of Vivian's, and its right moving towards the left of the Bois de Callois, which surrounds the observatory. 'The first rise' of the French position, before referred to, is a very distinguishable point. It is on the western side of the Genappe chaussee, about 530 yards from the south end of the buildings of La Haye Sainte, and 480 yards from the north end of La Belle Alliance. It is a spot of deep historical interest, from these circumstances, that from it Buonaparte watched the progress of the last attack; that towards it the Imperial Guard rushed when it broke into confusion & that from it proceeded the fire by which, during the attack on the squares, Lord Anglesey was wounded; and, if it be really true that Napoleon remained until the squares of the Guard turned, it is further remarkable as the ground on which the two great champions of the destinies of Europe stood in the nearest approach to each other. The Duke of Wellington was with Adam's Brigade during the attack on the squares.[24]

The version he wrote to Siborne later contained a few subtle differences:

Although there is reason to believe that the enemy's Second Corps was advanced to cover the left flank of his attack with its own left resting on the hedge of Hougoumont yet no part of it came near enough to menace seriously the right flank of the 52nd Regiment during the whole of the forward movement and charge. This right flank appeared entirely clear of the enemy for at least 300 yards.

The 52nd continued pressing forward at a hurried pace, until its left was so near the hollow road in front of La Haye Sainte, that an officer of the left

---

24. ibid.

company stepped out to see what the fugitives in it were doing. In its course to this point the coming upon its front of a broken body of Dornberg's Cavalry Brigade at g, and the throwing out of its right section to drive in some guns by which it was enfiladed at about h, occurred, to the best of my recollection and judgment, as already described in my narrative of the 'Crisis and Close, &c'.

The 71st Regiment moved forward to protect the right flank of the 52nd Regiment as described in that narrative, I now think, however, without firing. The two companies of the 3rd Battalion 95th formed line on the left flank of the 71st. The 2nd Battalion 95th followed up on the left flank of the 52nd, but, I think, did not get into line with it until it reached near to the hollow road, and then more as a body of skirmishers than as a line. This battalion of the 95th suffered at some point in its advance a heavy loss This may have been from the French occupying La Haye Sainte. Colonel Halkett's Hanoverian Brigade followed at some distance in support of the advance of Adam's Brigade, and some of the 1st Battalion 95th may have mixed with the 2nd 95th when passing La Haye Sainte. Besides these, I have strong reasons for believing that no other portion of the Duke of Wellington's Army left the British position for a full quarter of an hour after the advance of the 52nd.

Thus ended what may be considered as the second half hour of the last great attack, at rather more than a quarter past eight o'clock. The sun, I think, set before the 52nd reached near to the hollow road twilight was sensibly commencing when it subsequently crossed the chaussee. The position in which Adam's Brigade found and attacked the three squares of the Old Guard covering the retreat was at H H H, instead of being as inserted in the plan accompanying my printed narrative; and I have now reason to think that, at this time, the two companies of the 3rd 95th were between the 71st and 52nd, and that a considerable body of the 2nd 95th were to the left of the 52nd.

I have some reason to think that the 71st formed a two deep line before this attack. The 52nd certainly continued four deep to the close of the day. I very confidently believe that the 52nd crossed the chaussee at K K and the 71st very soon after it. I have not traced the routes of the 52nd and 71st on the east side of the chaussee, because I feel some doubts as to the depth of the sweep which the two regiments described. I feel, however, confident that the square of the Old Guard threw off its knapsacks at about L.[25]

There seems to be common agreement that there were three solid formed squares in front of La Belle Alliance and there has been much speculation as to which battalions they were. It is clear that only three battalions had remained in reserve and had not been involved in any fighting, they were the two battalions of the 1st Grenadiers which had been moved up to La Belle Alliance from Rossomme farm

---

25. Siborne, The Waterloo Letters, pp 294–5.

and the 1st Battalion 2nd Grenadiers, which had remained in reserve during the Grenadier (second) attack. The other battalions which were retreating from their defeat by the Guards (first attack) and the Light Brigade (third attack) attempted to form squares behind the already formed squares but were soon broken gain by the cavalry charges. As the Light Brigade closed towards the formed squares, it began to march away from the field in formation, but slowly disintegrated as it retired. The two Grenadier battalions at Rossomme must have moved forward, as the advancing infantry did not discover further formed squares when they arrived there.

The squares to the east of the chaussee, which the 10th Hussars charged unsuccessfully were most probably the remnants of the Grenadier battalions driven off by Detmer's troops, having been evicted from La Haye Sainte orchard. Leeke particularly makes great claims that the 52nd advanced unsupported by any other troops, while Colonel Colborne states that the other regiments did not regain their positions in line until the temporary halt just south of La Haye Sainte, before they moved on towards La Belle Alliance. So, where do the remaining units of the brigade claim to have been?

Captain Budgen of 2/95th had no doubt that his battalion was on the left of the 52nd throughout and that it deserved full recognition for its part:

> In this charge I am bound to say that the services of the 2nd Battalion Rifle Brigade, then 95th, were as conducive to the result as those of any other part of the brigade, nor could it be otherwise, for from the moment of the charge no check took place, and the advance was at a most rapid pace.
>
> I have a full recollection that after the enemy were broken and running away, the word was given to let the cavalry through, and they passed through our line causing some confusion and breaks in it. After the cavalry passed to the front, the 2nd 95th continued to advance rapidly until it came on some bodies of the enemy posted on some rising ground. A rush was made at them notwithstanding the disordered state of our line from the interruption of the cavalry, and the dreadful miry state of the ground. These, I conceive must have been the rear battalions of the Guard marked at D. The opposition they made was very ineffectual and slight. They were immediately driven off. The 2nd 95th certainly participated in this attack with the rest of the brigade ... I do not think the position at D was quite so close to the high road, as I have no recollection of having passed a road with high banks at that time.[26]

As to why the British Light Dragoons got caught up in the advance of the 52nd, Lieutenant John Banner of the 23rd Light Dragoons has provided us with an explanation:

> Between four and five o'clock in the afternoon of that day, the command of the regiment devolved on Major Latour, who received an order between

---

26. Siborne, The Waterloo Letters, pp 300–1.

five and six o'clock to send part of it towards the centre to the relief of a brigade of guns, which was considerably annoyed by the repeated charges of the French cavalry; and, in obedience with that order, a squadron to which I belonged was dispatched under the command of Captain Cox,[27] who was soon afterwards obliged to leave the field, in consequence of having been previously severely stunned in a charge, by his horse falling upon him. The French cavalry that made the last effort to silence the guns above mentioned were repulsed and driven back by this squadron of the 23rd Dragoons to a square of French infantry, which was found considerably to the front, and behind which the French cavalry took refuge. This square opened a heavy fire on the 23rd Dragoons on their retiring; and in consequence of their experiencing a similar annoyance on approaching the British line, they were induced to move to its flanks.[28]

The 'similar annoyance on approaching the British line' meaning being shot at! Private Aldridge of the 2/95th also confirms that it was very near when the cavalry rode through the 52nd:

Almost immediately after [I] saw a small body of English light dragoons pass to his left and go to the front. Saw these dragoons charge. Saw the French cavalry drive them towards the front of the 52nd. Very soon after this a part of the 95th extended to skirmish.

The French were very thick to his left of a house [La Haye Sainte[29]]. Is sure it was to his left of the house. The 95th were in a rye field, is sure it was a rye field. They lost more men here he thinks, than at any one other time in the day. They then went on with the 52nd to attack some squares or the three French rear guard. They were close to the great road. He knows they were so because he very soon afterwards went down into the great road, and went straight on it until the battalion halted for the night.[30]

It is therefore certain that the 2/95th was on the left wing of the 52nd throughout, but what of the 71st and 3/95th on its right wing? Lieutenant Colonel Thomas Reynell, commanding the 71st, was initially prompted to write to the editor of the *United Services Journal* following the disagreements between Lieutenant Gawler of the 52nd and Sir Hussey Vivian commanding a brigade of hussars, which will be dealt with shortly.

After the deployment from square, the 71st Regiment moved in line, the right wing to the front, the left wing to the rear, forming a third and fourth rank. We passed Hougoumont obliquely, throwing the right shoulders a little forward, as stated by the author of 'The Crisis,' [Gawler] and experienced some loss in the companies nearest to the orchard hedge from the fire of the

---

27. Captain Philip Cox 23rd Light Dragoons.
28. United Services Journal March 1836 pp 360–1.
29. Siborne, The Waterloo Letters, p 303.
30. ibid.

tirailleurs posted there. We had in view, at the bottom of the declivity, two columns of the enemy's infantry; and my object, and I believe the object of every officer and soldier in the corps, was to come in contact with those columns, but they did not wait our approach, or afford us an opportunity of attacking them. I can positively assert that from the time the 71st Regiment commenced this forward movement it never halted, but maintained a steady advance.[31]

This confirms that it moved forward with the brigade but did not come into action against the Imperial Guard, as the 71st found that the column had retired before they were in a position to fire on Napoleon's Guard. Ensign John Barnett of the 71st also recalled being attacked by cuirassiers as it began its advance.

Directly we began to advance, the cuirassiers made a desperate charge on us. Our men never fired a single shot, till they were nearly touching our bayonets, front rank kneeling, they then gave a volley. You heard a scream & saw them fall like leaves, horses with legs shot off limping about, the few who were not killed, faced about & our dragoons who were in rear of us, past by us & cut them down in all directions.

The shout was then universal, we charged them at a steady pace, they formed on the hill in solid square but the bayonet soon drove them to the devil, they threw down their knapsacks & arms, left wagons, horses etc & fled.

The two companies of the 3/95th were initially behind the 71st, but as they moved forward in order to catch up with the 52nd, the 71st apparently moved slightly to the right, leaving a gap between the two regiments, into which the two companies of the 3/95th manoeuvred to maintain a solid line. Captain William Eeles recorded that:

The 3rd Battalion 95th Regiment moved on at the same time, and very shortly, as the 52nd and 71st opened out a little, was formed in line between these two regiments. When the smoke cleared away a little I found that we were moving between both armies, and driving some French before us in the greatest disorder. I was almost immediately ordered out to skirmish with my company, and continued advancing in that manner until some English and German Dragoons, followed by some French, passed along the front of the brigade. At the noise of the advancing horsemen, the company of the 3rd Battalion which was in front, ran in on the other company, which was still between the 52nd and 71st. From that time it continued so to advance in that close and compact order, until the brigade, still formed in line and four deep, came up to three columns of the Old Imperial Guard, which they attacked, and defeated.[32]

---

31. United Services Journal September 1833.
32. Siborne, The Waterloo Letters, pp 306–7.

Eeles clearly believed that the 3/95th and 71st were very quickly up on the right flank of the 52nd and that the brigade was fully formed in line before the light cavalry disrupted the advance of the 52nd. It would appear from the evidence that the brigade was fully formed up again by the time the light cavalry passed across its front or, at the very latest, whilst the 52nd halted for the cavalry to pass. The brigade certainly reached the Charleroi chaussee fully formed up. But what of the rest of the division? General Henry Clinton wrote:

> Their cavalry was still very strong. I supported the attack by a Hanoverian battalion [Osnabruck] at quarter distance, with the King's German Legion in echelon & the 23rd Regiment which formed part of the 4th Division & was placed under my orders. The enemy gave way & was followed across the plain, our cavalry came forward & from this moment there was no check.[33]

We know that Colonel Hugh Halkett followed the Light Brigade with the Osnabruck Battalion and was soon close in the rear of the 71st and then manoeuvred further out to the right in pursuit of an Imperial Guard column which was retiring rapidly. A senior French officer was stunned by a shell exploding near his head and Halkett took the opportunity to capture him, it turned out to be General Cambronne:

> The moment General Adam's Brigade advanced I lost no time to follow with the Osnabruck Battalion (2nd Battalion, Duke of York), then on the left of Hougoumont, of which post I was in command, one of the battalions of my Brigade occupying the wood and two others in the ditches in the rear, other troops occupying the enclosures, &c.
>
> During the advance I sent my Brigade Major, Captain Von Saffe, to bring up the two battalions posted in rear of Hougoumont, but neither he nor the battalions showed themselves. Next day I found that Captain Saffe was killed before having delivered the message. The Osnabruck Battalion soon got in line and on the right of Adam's Brigade. During the advance we were much annoyed by the enemy's artillery. The first company of the Osnabruck Battalion broke into platoons, and supported by the sharpshooters of the battalion, made a dash at the artillery on our right and captured six guns with their horses.
>
> Some hundred yards to our right were some troops of hussars (I believe the 10th). I rode up to them and got them to charge the head of a column of infantry, which was drawing to their left in rear of the French Guards. The charge succeeded admirably and the column dispersed behind some enclosures, after which I saw no more of the cavalry. During our advance we were in constant contact with the French Guards and I often called to them to surrender. For some time I had my eye upon, as I supposed the General Officer in command of the Guards (being in full uniform) trying to animate his men to stand.

---

33. Glover, Correspondence of Henry Clinton Volume II, p 121.

After having received our fire with much effect, the column left their general with two officers behind, when I ordered the sharpshooters to dash on, and I made a gallop for the general. When about cutting him down he called out he would surrender, upon which he preceded me [to the rear], but I had not gone many paces before my horse got a shot through his body and fell to the ground. In a few seconds I got him on his legs again, and found my friend, Cambronne, had taken French leave in the direction from where he came. I instantly overtook him, laid hold of him by the aiguillette, and brought him in safety and gave him in charge to a sergeant of the Osnabruckers to deliver to the Duke; I could not spare an officer for the purpose, many being wounded.

After this I kept in advance of Adam's Brigade;[34] we soon pushed the two French squares upon the mass of their cavalry of all descriptions, who at one moment threatened us in a most vociferous manner. However, after receiving our fire they went off in all directions. About this time, officers were flying in all directions, seemingly with orders from a superior. Some French officers, prisoners. said it was Napoleon. We had the good fortune to take twelve or fourteen more guns of the Guards, in full play on us. On our advance the sharpshooters, supported by a company, were sent among a mass of guns, and by their fire increased the confusion, made many prisoners, and cut the horses from the leading guns… We drove them across the road to Genappe in which direction the Prussians were pursuing & we pushed them as long as we could see. The road was absolutely choked with his artillery, many of the guns & tumbrils horsed. I never saw a more complete rout.[35]

Captain Dreves of the Osnabruck Battalion confirms Halkett's statement:

At about half past 6 o'clock, the battalion moved up to the crest of the ridge and was assigned a position to the right of the battery mentioned earlier.[36] To the left of the battery were battalions of the brigade of the English Colonel Adams; no troops could be observed to the right of the battalion. Opposite our position, very strong enemy columns stood in the background, of which four battalions of the French Guard were nearest to us. These then attacked in columns, while their skirmishers moved up to within a short distance from us. After the skirmishers had been driven back by the English and the battalion's riflemen, the battalion attacked in column in coordination with the English to the left, who advanced in line, against the French columns approaching through a depression in the terrain. After putting up a strong resistance, they began to retreat.

---

34. Having marched directly towards La Belle Alliance rather than the more circuitous route taken by the Light Brigade, the Osnabruck Battalion arrived there before the others.
35. Siborne, The Waterloo Letters, pp 308–9.
36. Bull's and Ramsay's batteries were virtually alongside each other here and it is possible he mistook them for a single strong battery of 12 guns.

As the French Guard retired in some disorder, a French general (whose name, I believe, was Cambronne) was energetically engaged in attempting to halt and reform the battalions. He succeeded several times; but their retiring continued, however, as they were forcefully driven back by our pursuing battalions. Our brigadier, the then Colonel Halkett, had observed that action and, with unequalled intrepidity, rode through the French skirmishers, who covered the retreating columns, to that general and, with great luck, brought him back before the entire line, through the enemy skirmishers, and made him his prisoner, notwithstanding [the man's] forceful resistance.[37]

The retiring Guard still halted several times after that general had been taken prisoner and, by taking every advantage of the terrain, attempted by their fire to stop their pursuers. They eventually had to yield to the forceful advance of the pursuing troops and dissolved into a disorderly mob.

In its pursuit of the enemy, the battalion drove in on four French batteries, one by one, of which two kept on firing. After several rounds of fire from the head of the battalion and from our riflemen, they were seized in our subsequent attack. The third battery was about to retreat and was then taken, and, upon the approach of our battalion, the artillerymen of the fourth battery left their cannon, which were then captured.[38]

The entire Light Brigade reached the Charleroi chaussee a little north of the point where it ran through a deep cutting and having crossed it, the brigade formed line with the right of the 71st touching the road and it then marched towards La Belle Alliance, where three battalion squares of the Imperial Guard stood. Captain Samuel Reed of the 71st recalled that:

> The two regiments formed line, the 52nd still on the left. We here charged three squares of the Guard whom we broke and pursued, crossing the road leading to Genappe, when we brought left shoulders forward, the right of the 71st resting on La Belle Alliance.
>
> Of this I am more positive, as the gun fired there by Captain Campbell Aide de Camp to Sir Frederick Adam, was turned by some men of my own company under the command of Lieutenant Torriano. The French squares having separated, the 52nd pursued what had been their right square; the other two fell to our lot. They retreated by the right of Plancenoit [the French left the village to their left].[39]

What of Du Plat's Brigade, which had stood in squares on the slope behind Hougoumont since 16.00 hours? As the French skirmishers had gained virtually the entire orchard and were firing constantly on the KGL squares, the 2nd Line Battalion KGL was sent into the orchard to push the French back, which was

---

37. The evidence is clear and strong that Cambronne was captured and did not utter the immortal phrase (even this phrase appears to be a later invention). 'The Guard dies but never surrenders.'
38. Glover, Waterloo Archive Volume II, p 69.
39. Siborne, The Waterloo Letters, p 298.

achieved successfully. Due to their heavy losses the 1st and 3rd Line Battalions were amalgamated into one square, with the 4th Line Battalion formed further to the west and they had also retired behind the ridge at 18.00 hours. It is clear from their evidence, that General Henry Clinton rode over to personally order them to support the forward movement by the Light Brigade. Captain Frederick Goeben of the 1st Line KGL wrote that:

> I believe that the main attack by the French Grenadier Guard occurred just as the above mentioned square was being re-formed here and was on the march. After some fighting, it was forced to retreat. Both the battalions [1st and 3rd Line Battalions] united now comprised not quite 350 men under arms, and they marched, formed in a single square, into a valley which was located in front of the right wing of the position, until it was ordered, approximately at d, to advance in a line 4 men deep, which took us, in a straight direction and without encountering any resistance to Belle Alliance. There, enemy artillerymen fired on us from several cannons, and then they rode after their fleeing army.[40]

Captain Leopold von Rettberg also of the 1st Line KGL witnessed the advance:

> [Behind the ridge] we formed square, the 1st and 3rd Battalions again together, and moved against the enemy Guards who threatened our centre. We had advanced some 300 to 400 paces when Lord Wellington rode up and ordered us to form a four deep line and to attack and seize the enemy batteries in front of us. We lost no time in complying with his wishes and moved right into the teeth of the rumblers [*Brummer* – in German]. On arriving at the bottom of the hill where they were posted, we still received some case-shots, but then the enemy artillerymen left their guns, and we shouted 'Victory'.[41]

Captain Albertus Cordemann of the 3rd Line Battalion KGL described the utter confusion as it advanced:

> The concentration that now came into view and the sudden general flight from all positions by the enemy, who until a moment earlier had been so brave, and the abandonment of all who could not get away quickly, that gave the greatest encouragement to our soldiers to advance. How important it was to the Duke of Wellington to pursue the enemy quickly and not to leave him any time may be gauged by the fact that whenever there was a momentary and even justified and excusable delay on the part of a battalion, he was there at a gallop with the order: 'Don't stop! Go on! Straight on!' To see in this manner the rapid movement of the cavalry, artillery, and infantry, in a race, forwards, and to see the enemy fleeing in all directions, was and remains for me a pleasurable and unforgettable vision...

---

40. Glover, Letters from the Battle of Waterloo, p 199.
41. Glover, Waterloo Archive Volume VIII, p 107.

The pursuit of the enemy ordered by the Duke of Wellington was also reinforced and made more mobile at this moment by his troops and horses, which had been less strained. During the first half hour of our advance, between 50–60 abandoned enemy cannon lay behind us on the terrain that we had passed, and a large number of their men were running about leaderless. The rapid and irregular retreat was beyond description, which, as is known, resulted in the complete dissolution of the French army.[42]

The 4th Line Battalion KGL also followed this movement, as did the 23rd Foot, which was also temporarily attached to General Clinton's Division.

Ensign William Leeke gives further detail on the advance of the 52nd along the left of the chaussee, having passed La Belle Alliance in pursuit of the Guard square:

> The infantry they attacked appears to have been one of the squares of the Grenadiers of the Imperial Guard, which had retired just to the right of La Belle Alliance and Primotion, when the square, followed by the 52nd, retired to the left of those houses, and to the left of the Charleroi road. As far as I can make out, this square and another were under Cambronne, and were closely followed, when he came near them, by Colonel Hugh Halkett with the Osnabruck battalion, one of the regiments of his Hanoverian brigade. Halkett had seen the sudden movement of the 52nd, and having sent his brigade-major[43] to order the rest of the brigade to follow, he moved the Osnabruck battalion down the slope of our position from the right of the 71st, and came away to the right of the 52nd, when these squares of the Imperial Guard were attacked by us; Halkett with his Hanoverian battalion got so near to one of these, that he made a dash at General Cambronne, who was at some little distance from the square, and took him prisoner with his own hands. The other square, which Major Howard charged, was farther to the rear of the French position, and more to our right than the square which Halkett was so close to. ... I must now return to the account of the advance of the 52nd in its pursuit of the square of the Old Guard to our left of the Charleroi road. It gradually brought its left shoulders more forward, till opposite to La Belle Alliance the line was exactly at right angles with this road, the British position being about a mile directly in our rear. We passed great numbers of guns and ammunition waggons, which had been deserted in consequence of our rapid advance. Lord Seaton stated that at this time we passed 'no less than seventy-five pieces of French artillery, and that very shortly after the French columns dispersed.' Leaving La Belle Alliance and, farther on, the farm of Primotion on its right, the 52nd advanced in pursuit to the left of the Charleroi road, and at no great distance from it. ...I think it was after passing the farm of Primotion that I remember seeing, on the

---

42. Glover, Letters from the Battle of Waterloo, p 207.
43. The brigade-major was killed before he could deliver his order.

other side of the Charleroi road about 300 yards to our right, a small body of cavalry riding to the charge, probably it was poor Howard's charge, before referred to. Sir Colin Campbell thought, on examining with me a plan of the Field of Waterloo, that this charge took place not far from Primotion; he remembered there were some trees there near to a house, and that it then wanted a quarter to nine by his watch. One hundred yards to the south of the enclosures of Primotion, we being about the same distance to the left of the Charleroi road, the 52nd found itself on the edge of a deep hollow road with steep banks, in which were a large body of French infantry retiring from their right. In the centre it appeared to be a mutual surprise; they threw down their arms in token of surrender, and we rapidly passed through them. In the centre not a shot was exchanged. Captain McNair, however, made the men break some of the French muskets by knocking them against the ground, thinking it unwise to leave so large an armed body of the enemy in our rear, but there was no time for much of this, and probably not more than a dozen muskets were smashed. ...

Near La Belle Alliance, a hollow road runs, nearly at right angles towards the chaussee, up which a column of artillery and infantry was hastily retreating. The square (of the Imperial Guard) crossed the head of this body, but the high bank concealed the approach of the 52nd, until the distance became too small to admit of any but a hand-to-hand contest. The column seemed not sufficiently aware of its desperate circumstances to surrender without hesitation, and for a moment the scene was singularly wild. The infantry, before they threw down their arms, made an effort either at defence or escape. The artillery dashed at the opposite bank, but some of the horses of each gun were in an instant brought down. A subaltern of the battery, threw his sword on the ground in token of surrender; but the commander, standing in the centre of his guns, waved his above his head in defiance. A soldier sprang from the British ranks, parried his thrust, closed with him, threw him on the ground, and keeping him down with his foot, reversed his musket in both hands to bayonet him; when that repugnance to shedding of blood, which so often rises in the hearts of British soldiers even under circumstances of personal danger and prudential necessity, burst forth in a groan of disgust from his surrounding comrades; it came, however, in this case too late, the fatal thrust was sped,[44] and the legion of honour lost another member. On the left flank of the 52nd line, at no very great distance from it, a French officer brought up and formed about a hundred men from the hollow road, apparently with the view of making some attack upon us, but, on this being observed, the left company of the 52nd brought up its right shoulders to drive them in, when they retired back into the hollow road much faster than they came out of it; there was no firing on either side. I was the first up on the top of the opposite bank, and the regiment formed

---

44. This has been lifted directly from Gawler's statement made thirty years previously. See p 153.

on the Colour. It was then getting somewhat duskish, and must have been close upon nine o'clock. At a distance of about 200 yards we observed four French staff officers.

McNair who was on the right of No 4, (his own company, No 9, being in the rear[45]) gave the word, 'No 4, make ready,' when I, who was next to him on his right, begged him to 'let those poor fellows off.' He replied, 'I dare not, I know not who they may be.' He then completed the word of command, and No 4 fired a volley; No 3, on the right did the same.[46]

Leeke mistakenly believed that General Cambronne was with one of the last squares of the Imperial Guard near La Belle Alliance, whereas he commanded a square which had retired further to the west. He does, however, concede that the Osnabruck Battalion was now far in advance of the 52nd Foot as it had taken a more direct march towards the French lines, rather than crossing the chaussee.

It must be added that the 1st Guards Brigade was also ordered to advance, initially marching into the valley floor before reforming and driving towards the French lines. Clearly as we have discussed, it could not possibly have been on the forward slope during the flanking movement of the 52nd as they would have seen each other and more importantly they would have got in the way of each other. Ensign Dirom of 3/1st Foot Guards states:

> At this moment our line was ordered to charge, as I always supposed by the Duke of Wellington himself, who was then immediately in our rear. On our advance the whole of the French columns turned round and made off. Several regiments of light cavalry passed us at full speed in pursuit of the enemy.[47]

Now this comment is very useful, as it indicates that the British Guards were moving forward when Vivian's and Vandeleur's cavalry rode past. Lieutenant Colonel Stanhope of the Guards also wrote that Wellington ordered the advance immediately after the French turned away:

> The first impetus of the French checked, it seems the Duke made up his mind to convert a difficult defence into an attack. Everything advanced and everything before us fled.[48]

Captain John Reeve of the 1st Foot Guards confirms that it marched as far as La Belle Alliance: 'We passed them to the low ground in the direction of La Belle Alliance ... when Sir Felton Hervey adc came to us with an order to halt and form column of companies at half distance which we did.'[49] Major General Maitland

---

45. This would be correct if the 52nd had formed line four-deep by putting the wings of the regiment behind each other, but Colonel Colborne repeatedly states that he used an alternative method by placing half of each company behind the other half.
46. Leeke, pp 61–3.
47. Siborne, The Waterloo Letters, pp 257–8.
48. Glover, Eyewitness to the Peninsular War and the Battle of Waterloo, p 191.
49. Glover, Letters from the Battle of Waterloo, p 160.

confirmed that the Guards halted at La Belle Alliance, to let the Prussian cavalry pass in pursuit:

> The First Brigade, after passing several pieces of ordnance abandoned by the enemy, received orders to halt...The Prussian cavalry advanced along the Brussels road, saluted as they passed, their bands playing 'God save the King', and took up the pursuit.[50]

Ensign Tighe of the 1st Foot Guards makes a very interesting observation when marching across the valley floor: 'On our advance towards La Belle Alliance several battalions of Belgians accompanied us on the left in regular order, having taken no part in the battle.'[51] This must refer to Detmer's and D'Aubreme's Belgians, who had driven off the Imperial Guard squares to the left of Halkett's Brigade. They then cleared the orchard of La Haye Sainte before they marched along the chaussee towards La Belle Alliance, where the Guards saw them.

However, the forward movement of the Guards would appear to have occurred after some delay, perhaps five to ten minutes, allowing the 52nd to have cleared their front. As will be seen in the next chapter, the Guard then moved forward off the ridge before Vivian's Brigade actually advanced.

---

50. Siborne, The Waterloo Letters, p 245.
51. Glover, Letters from the Battle of Waterloo, p 168.

Chapter 14

The Cavalry Assault 20.15–22:00 Hours

As the 52nd, supported by the other battalions of the Light Brigade, drove the column of the Imperial Guard away and began its rapid advance across the battlefield, the British light cavalry was launched against the wavering French lines. Some have claimed that this was the truly decisive movement that finally ended French resistance and turned defeat into a rout, whilst others claim that this attack occurred quite a significant period of time afterwards and that the French were by then already in full retreat, let us therefore look at the evidence. William Leeke of the 52nd stated that:

> Sir Colin Campbell told me that … when the 52nd advanced, the Duke and he went off to our right, which would probably be towards the lower part of the enclosures of Hougoumont, and that some little time afterwards they crossed over some rising ground to their left, where they witnessed the unsuccessful charge by Major Howard and a party of the 10th Hussars upon a body of French infantry, and that the Duke was very angry when he saw them make the attack without having any support. Before he had accompanied the Duke down to the rear of the 52nd and about twenty minutes after we had advanced from the British position, he had taken an order from the Duke of Wellington to Sir Hussey Vivian to bring forward his hussar brigade, consisting of the 10th, 18th, and 1st German Hussars. He met him coming down the slope of the position and Vivian told him his brigade was just behind him. It appears from Vivian's correspondence with Gawler of the 52nd in 1833, that he must have come down the British position, through the interval made by the sudden advance of the 52nd, and that he saw no British troops as he advanced at right angles with the position, either to his right or left, and that his brigade came upon and charged a large body of cavalry somewhere in front of the 2nd French corps. These cavalry were mixed; there were cuirassiers, lancers, and guns with their horses attached. Colonel Gurwood, who had been in the 52nd, but at Waterloo commanded a troop in the 10th Hussars and was wounded, told me that, as he lay on the ground, he saw poor Howard's charge; that Vivian, after the charge of the 10th, observing some formed infantry in front, desired Howard to collect as many men as he could of those who had got into confusion in their charge on the French cavalry and to attack this infantry. This was looked upon as a very desperate service, as cavalry have rarely been known to defeat regularly formed and steady infantry. Gurwood told me that a young officer said to

Howard, 'If I were you, Howard, I wouldn't do it,' and that Howard replied, 'You heard the General's order, and you know my position in the regiment.' The charge was made and repulsed, Howard being killed.[1]

Leeke does not claim to be an eyewitness to these proceedings and indeed there is no earthly way he could have been. However, some have tried to use the statement he records from Colin Campbell as irrefutable evidence that the cavalry did not attack the French lines until a very considerable time after the Light Brigade came into action near La Belle Alliance. This must mean that it is based on the strange assumption that the 10th Hussars advanced alone, without the remainder of General Hussey Vivian's Brigade. This is inferred by Leeke when he describes the futility of Howard's charge, which Colin Campbell claims to have viewed, along with the Duke of Wellington, before they rode up to Vivian, whom they found on the forward slope of the allied ridge and ordered his brigade to advance.

We must therefore investigate what evidence there is from Vivian's Brigade and the other cavalry brigades which advanced. Lieutenant Gawler also attempted to explain the cavalry manoeuvres but was certain that Vivian's entire brigade was in advance.

> On the other side of the road, events were more varied and extensive. Vivian's Brigade of Hussars came up rapidly in echelon of regiments to the assistance of the 71st. The cuirassiers, worn out as they were, and discouraged as they had reason to be, with much devotedness fronted in the line of La Belle Alliance, to protect the squares of the Old Guard, but a squadron of the 10th dashing at them, followed immediately by one of the 18th, they were dispersed in hopeless confusion. The compact battalions of the Old Guard were not so soon routed: a part of the 10th having rallied after the charge on the cuirassiers, found itself under the fire of one of the squares; the men fell very fast, and there was no alternative but instantly to retreat or to charge.
>
> The near approach of the 71st to another face of the same square, decided Sir Hussey Vivian to order the latter. The charge was very gallantly attempted; Major Howard, who conducted it, fell upon the bayonets; some of the grenadiers were cut down by men of the 10th, but even under such circumstances, charged home by cavalry on two faces, (for the 18th immediately followed to the assistance of their comrades,) and under a heavy fire of infantry on the other, the veterans knew too well their strength, and in what their safety consisted, to shrink from the contest: they closed well together, beat off the cavalry with a very destructive fire, and, in spite of the approaching infantry, made good their retreat.[2]

Following a very public correspondence in the *United Services Journal*, with Sir Hussey Vivian, Gawler did amend his own version of events:

---

1. Leeke, pp 58–9.
2. Gawler, United Services Journal 1833 Part II, p 306.

I have sure grounds for stating that, by the correction of them, our respective narratives of facts are brought into almost perfect reconciliation. These errors were: First, that in describing 'the first rise' of the French position on which the squares of the Old Guard were posted, I said it was 'not far in their front of La Belle Alliance;' and in the plan attached to the narrative, I have made this 'not far' to be about 350 yards. Whereas, the 'not far' is too narrow a term, and the plan is also incorrect, for an inspection of Lieutenant Siborne's model has convinced me, that 'the first rise' in question is 130 yards nearer to the British position; that is, 480, instead of 350 yards in the French front of La Belle Alliance.

And, second, that l made the 71st, and part of the 95th, after the attack on the squares, to continue along the right side of the Genappe chaussee, when the 52nd crossed to the left side. Whereas, I am now persuaded, on very solid evidence, that the 71st and 95th, as well as the 52nd, crossed to the left side before, reaching La Belle Alliance. Thus leaving the whole of the right side open to the subsequent advance of Vivian's Brigade, and to its charges upon the enemy in the line of La Belle Alliance. As long as the 71st was supposed to continue close along the right side of the chaussee, it followed of necessity as a matter of inference, that the battalion must have been that which came up with the square charged by Major Howard, near to the chaussee, beyond La Belle Alliance; but the correction of the error in the route of the 71st makes this collision impossible. Some obscurity still remains as to the precise designation of the battalion that overtook the square. It is simply probable that it was one of Colonel Halkett's Hanoverian regiments, as his brigade followed at some distance in support of the advance of Adam's Brigade. Colonel Halkett himself was with the 71st during the attack on the squares of the Old Guard, and at that time, with his own hand, took a French General (I think Cambronne) a prisoner. When the advanced corps of the British attack upon the French position had reached to about the distance of La Belle Alliance, or Primotion, they must have nearly formed a continuous line On the extreme left, Adam's Brigade with its right on the Genappe chaussee, and its left within one or two hundred yards of the Prussians. In the centre, Vivian's Brigade with its left near the chaussee; and on the extreme right, Vandeleur's just coming up, with its left near the right of Vivian's, and its right moving towards the left of the Bois de Callois, which surrounds the observatory. 'The first rise' of the French position, before referred to, is a very distinguishable point. It is on the western side of the Genappe chaussee, about 530 yards from the south end of the buildings of La Haye Sainte, and 480 yards from the north end of La Belle Alliance. It is a spot of deep historical interest, from these circumstances, that from it Buonaparte watched the progress of the last attack; that towards it the Imperial Guard rushed when it broke into confusion & that from it proceeded the fire by which, during the attack on the squares, Lord Anglesey was wounded; and, if it be really true that Napoleon remained until the squares of the Guard turned, it is further remarkable as the ground on which the two great champions of the destinies of Europe stood in the nearest approach to each other. The Duke of Wellington was with Adam's Brigade during the attack on the squares.[3]

Sir Hussey Vivian wrote about his brigade's part in the battle the following day on 19 June 1815:

> The enemy began to give way, I trotted in column of ½ squadrons from the right, round the flank of the infantry in my front & in this manner the brigade proceeded led by the 10th under the heaviest fire of grape & musketry you can possibly imagine, in as good order, intervals as well preserved & as steady, as if at a field day in England. We led for the left of the French where there were two strong bodies of French cavalry (cuirassiers & lancers in each), with a square of infantry in the centre. I directed the brigade to form lines of regiments on their front ½ squadrons, they did it to perfection; this done, with the 10th I charged the left body of cavalry; they went on in the best possible line & at full speed & entered the enemy's line which outflanked & wheeled up to receive them, but was in an instant overthrown & great numbers cut down.
>
> I then ordered the 18th to attack the cavalry on the right of the square & the 10th to rally, which they did to perfection, when I directed Major Howard's squadron, supported by the other two, to charge the square; the gallantry with which they did this is not to be expressed; they were received by a most tremendous fire, but they persisted & cut down the French in their ranks. From this moment, not a shot was fired, every man of the French infantry was either sabred by the 10th or made prisoners by General Vandeleur's Brigade which came up shortly after.[4]

Lieutenant Colonel Henry Murray, commanding the 18th Hussars provides a great deal more information:

> On the Duke of Wellington seeing the success of the charge of Adam's Brigade, he ordered fresh cavalry to check the probable advance of the enemy and to attack the French themselves in front of La Belle Alliance. Lieutenant Colonel Lord Greenock, AQMG of the cavalry, was sent to Vivian with orders for him to move his brigade to its right from its position in the rear of Alten's Division, so as to get clear of the infantry, and then to advance directly to the front by the right of Maitland's Brigade of Guards. A trot now sounded, and our brigade advanced against the cavalry reserves near La Belle Alliance by half squadrons to the right, the regiment following the 10th, the 1st Hussars in rear. Proceeding a short distance in rear of the infantry and parallel to the crest of the position, part of the time over fine

---

3. Gawler, United Services Journal 1835 Part I, pp 303–4.
4. Glover, The Waterloo Archive Volume IV, pp 63–4.

standing corn, we approached Maitland's Brigade, and here the leading half squadron was ordered to wheel to the left through Napier's battery and to lead perpendicularly to the front, and the manner in which Sir H. Vivian led the brigade down, always keeping under the cover of the hill where the ground allowed it, was excellent.

On the occasion just mentioned, the officer commanding this leading half squadron, not correctly catching the word of command, in consequence probably of the noise created by Napier's guns, as also from the shouts of Adam's Brigade, which was following up its triumph, wheeled up to the right instead of to the left. This was rectified by General Vivian in person galloping to the flank of the leading half-squadron, and, with emphasis and a good hearty damn, called out that it was 'towards' and not 'from the enemy' they were to wheel. He took the flank officer's place, and led the column down the hill in the direction he wished to move, and the column thus advanced across the ridge in left front of Vandeleur's Light Cavalry Brigade. We were saluted by the latter with cheers of encouragement, and in a similar manner by Maitland's Brigade, as we passed their flank. As soon as the smoke allowed General Vivian to see the disposition of the enemy's troops in his front, he formed line with the regiment [18th] and the 10th, with the 1st Hussars in support. The moment of the arrival of our brigade was also the moment of Napoleon's last advance, and the fire to which we were exposed, both of cannon and musketry, was very severe... Lord Uxbridge, when on his way to the regiment at this time, was shot in the right leg, and amputation was performed afterwards. After the gallant charge of the 10th General Vivian then, as stated, galloped to the regiment which he found in line and in perfect order. On the front stood two squares of the Grenadiers of the Old Guard, on its left front and much nearer to it were posted artillery and cavalry in advance of the proper right of these squares. This cavalry consisted principally of cuirassiers, the wrecks of entire brigades; nearer to, and partly in rear of the squares stood the chasseurs and grenadiers a cheval of the Imperial Guard, greatly diminished in numbers. It was immediately evident to Vivian that the attack must in the first instance be directed against the advanced artillery and cavalry, and having put the regiment in motion, he placed himself in front of the centre, beside Colonel Murray, for the purpose of putting us into the required direction. He on this said to the regiment '18th, you will follow me,' on which the Sergeant Major Jeffs[5] (afterwards Adjutant of the 7th Hussars) and several exclaimed, 'By Jagus, general, anywhere, to hell, if you will lead us.' He then ordered the charge to sound, when the regiment dashed forward with the greatest impetuosity, and at the same time with as much steadiness and regularity as if they had been at field day exercise on Hounslow Heath. Thus the direction of the charge by the regiment diverged as much to the left as that of the 10th had inclined to the right. Just as our charge commenced,

---

5. Regimental Sergeant Major Thomas Jeffs.

some French artillery coming from their right, and slanting towards the regiment, made a bold push to cross our front at a gallop, but the attempt failed, and we were in an instant among them, cutting down the artillerymen and the drivers and securing the guns. In the next moment we fell upon the advanced cavalry, which we completely dispersed, and then bringing forward our left shoulders we attacked the cavalry and guns that stood more to our right front and near to the right square which was now retiring. This cavalry appeared at first determined to make a stand, and an officer in its front dashed forward and fired at Colonel Murray, but in another moment the regiment was fiercely and dexterously plying their sabres amongst them, and we next charged the Imperial Guard, their cuirassiers and lancers, a regular medley of them all, including infantry and guns, etc., such a scene! The infantry threw themselves down except two squares, which stood firm, but did no good. The sneaking prisoners we had taken hollered 'Vive le Roi.' The Duke said, who saw the brigade charge, 'Well done 10th and 18th.' ... We came to a deep hollow, and on the opposite side was a steep knoll, with a square of infantry very well formed on it. Down this hollow dashed a party of the regiment and up the hill at the square in most gallant style, but were checked and turned by their fire. But for our charge, I am convinced in ten minutes there would have been a good lot of cavalry rallied and squares formed.[6]

After the battle, Captain Arthur Kennedy of the 18th made a familiar complaint:

Our brigade ... most admirably led by Sir Hussey Vivian. This it was, it is said, that [which] decided the day although not a word of it is mentioned in the Duke's dispatch but by referring to the French account you there see it mentioned our regiment advanced to the attack amidst cries of 'No quarter'.[7]

Lieutenant Colonel Lord Robert Manners of the 10th Hussars recalled that the brigade manoeuvred around the British Guard Brigade before advancing:

On the advance of the British army against the enemy's line at the close of the action, the 10th Hussars were wheeled round the flank of the infantry in their immediate front by Sir Hussey Vivian (commanding the brigade) and led by him to the charge. They first encountered a mixed body of the enemy's cavalry ... which they dispersed.[8]

But what of French witnesses of the battle? Sergeant Mauduit of the Imperial Guard wrote:

The Emperor, having no cavalry reserve since it had all been so fatally engaged on the [British] plateau and was dispersed at this critical moment

---

6. Glover, The Waterloo Archive Volume IV, pp 69–71.
7. ibid, p 81.
8. Glover, Letters from the Battle of Waterloo, p 83.

had nothing to oppose the 2,500 cavalry of Vandeleur's and Vivian's brigades, which were moving from La Haye Sainte, except for the four Service Squadrons, and only had time, after having ordered them to charge this cavalry, to put himself under the protection of the square of the 2nd Grenadiers[9]... Alas! What hope did 400 cavalry have against 2,500? They were overwhelmed!

If they had been repulsed, these six English regiments would not have flooded the battlefield and then the Guard infantry would have been able to contain the enemy and rally the army.[10]

It seems clear, that the cavalry was manoeuvred to the right behind the 1st Guards Brigade and then advanced over the ridge at the point vacated by Adam's Brigade. This would mean that it passed to the rear of the Light Brigade as it marched across the valley floor towards the Charleroi Chaussee. As the cavalry then advanced across the shallow valley, it inclined towards the left, heading towards the French ridge just to the west of La Belle Alliance, where they encountered both formed cavalry and artillery and with formed infantry squares in their rear. These French units made a determined stand, but as the hussars of Vivian's and Vandeleur's Brigade further to the right drove at them, the French units turned to flee. Some infantry squares did, however, make a stand and Howard's attack with a squadron of the 10th Hussars failed with severe loss. The French were in many cases already retiring before the hussars attacked, but it is clear that a number of units still maintained a firm front, although in reality they were quite shaky. As many observers state, this could have allowed the French troops to rally behind this façade of stability, and the fact that this crumbled when tested by the hussars' charges, does not mean that the cavalry do not have any claim to have influenced the final rout of the French army. In fact, it provides a strong case for the argument that the advance of the Light Brigade alone was, and could never have been, enough on its own to cause the French line to crumble. The joint effect of both of these shocks, along with the sight of the general advance of Wellington's troops and the clear threat that the Prussians posed to their right rear, undoubtedly combined to break the spirit of the French troops, rather than one single cause

---

9. This would appear to confirm that the 1st Battalion 2nd Grenadiers was one of the three squares of Imperial Guard infantry standing in front of La Belle Alliance.
10. Quoted in Andrew Field's Waterloo, the French Perspective, p 212.

Chapter 15

The Dying Embers of the Day 21.00 to 22.00 Hours

Having advanced beyond La Belle Alliance in pursuit of the few remaining formed squares of the Imperial Guard and having captured the retreating French artillery brigade on the crossroad, the fighting for the 52nd was effectively over, but it continued to advance in the rapidly increasing darkness and confusion. William Leeke describes its movements in detail, but makes a number of incorrect assumptions regarding things he could not possibly have seen:

> The 'cease firing' sounded down the line from the right, and I believe these were the last infantry shots fired at Waterloo. The horse of one of the French officers fell, and we soon lost sight of them. I have thought it was probably Marshal Ney, who thus had his horse shot under him. It tallies with his own account; he speaks of lingering on the field, and of all his horses being shot. When McNair said, 'He did not know who they might be,' he was thinking of Napoleon, and thought it was not right to let him get away, if he could prevent it. It is very possible that the Emperor did form one of this group, for ... he is spoken of as having at the end of the battle been, 'for a moment,' in one of the squares of the Old Guard. Now one of them was retiring before the 52nd, and the other two or three were in our immediate vicinity on the other side of the Charleroi road. He may have been in the square we pursued and have left it when they halted for a moment to throw off their knapsacks. This they were seen to do I think before we reached the hollow road. Being thus lightened they gained on us and we no longer saw them when, from the top of the hollow road, the two centre companies, 3 and 4, fired on the four mounted French officers.
>
> There was no pursuing cavalry on our side of the main road. Vivian's brigade of cavalry came up into line with us, far away to the right, when we were somewhere abreast of Primotion. Vandeleur's Brigade of cavalry came up rather later in pursuit. Halkett, with the Osnabruck Battalion, must have been not very far in our rear, on the other side of the chaussee; and I conjecture from Colonel Reynell's letter that when we were at Primotion, or at the hollow road beyond it, the 71st, one of the two other regiments of our brigade, must have been away on the other side of Vivian's Brigade, in a line with us, but at a distance from us of nearly 700 yards. The 71st, (perhaps the 2nd and 3rd Rifles) and Halkett's Osnabruck Battalion, afforded a most

important support to the 52nd in its single handed attack on the French Imperial Guard, but none of them nor any other regiment of the British or Allied troops were at all engaged with them. As far as I have been able to make matters out, the above-mentioned regiments were the only infantry which advanced that night beyond the low ground between the French and British positions.

The rest of the infantry bivouacked on the lower part of the slope of our own position; the enemy having been fairly routed and dispersed, long before the rest of the British and Allied army passed over the crest of that position. In the advance of the 52nd from the hollow road to the farm of Rossomme, where it halted for the night, it passed at one place within a quarter of a mile of the nearest houses of Plancenoit, but saw nothing of the French who nearly up to that time had been keeping the Prussians in check in that village, and had inflicted severe loss upon them. They had now made off, with the rest of the French army who could get away, in the direction of Genappe and somewhat to their right of it, between it and Maison du Roi. About a quarter of a mile before we reached Rossomme we came upon the knapsacks of the square of the Old Guard. My Colour Sergeant took possession of a havre-sac [sic] and afterwards took from it a loaf, from which he cut a good slice of bread, and offering it to me said, 'Won't you have a slice of bread, Mr Leeke? I am sure you deserve it, sir!' I was very glad of the bread, for I had eaten nothing but one biscuit for more than twenty-four hours; and I was pleased also with the kind and approving words of the sergeant. Shortly after this we reached Rossomme and forming column of companies on the northern side of the farm, we halted in the angle formed by the Charleroi road and the road leading into it from Plancenoit, and piling arms bivouacked there for the night. It was a quarter after nine o'clock.

The farm of Rossomme is three quarters of a mile from La Belle Alliance, and exactly the same distance from the Church of Plancenoit. On this ground we found the straw which the French Imperial Guard had collected for themselves and slept on the night before. The Duke himself must have ordered Sir John Colborne to halt there, for General Adam had not been with us since the defeat of the 10,000 men of the Imperial Guard, but had, notwithstanding he was severely wounded, been away to look after the 71st, who had been so much separated from the 52nd. I did not see the Duke at that time, but I recollect hearing that when he came up to the regiment at Rossomme, he asked Sir John Colborne 'if there was anything he could do for the 52nd', and that Colborne replied he should be very glad if the Duke could send them a barrel of biscuits; which he promised to do ...

Soon after we halted a large fire was lighted, round which the officers stood, and talked over the events of the battle. Whilst we were thus engaged, we heard some cheering away in our rear, near La Belle Alliance, and May,[1]

---
1. Ensign James May of the 52nd Foot.

of the 52nd, coming up shortly afterwards, told us that it proceeded from those who were present when Wellington and Blücher met. One of the first duties attended to when the regiment had piled arms and were lying down in column, was the calling the roll by a sergeant of each company. I observed that in almost every case of absence, some of the men could say what had happened to the man, whether they knew him to be killed or only wounded. We had left, including officers, exactly 206 of our poor fellows on the field of Waterloo. Many of the wounded, I believe, but not all, got into houses at Merbe Braine or at the village of Waterloo.

Major Hunter Blair, our Brigade Major, who was in much concern about General Adam, whom he had not been able to find, came up to me about half an hour after we had halted, when I was near the men, and inquired if anybody had seen General Adam, and stated that he would reward any man who would find the general. This I made known, neither the Brigade Major nor I thinking at the moment that by so doing we were giving an opportunity to any bad fellows, who might be so disposed, an opportunity of quitting the column for the purpose of plundering the killed and wounded they might meet with; I am not aware that any did so; but within half a minute, a man came to me in front of the general, who rode into the bivouac from the direction of Genappe and said, 'Here is General Adam, sir!' Neither Blair nor I thought him entitled to the promised reward, as the general had found the regiment and was within a few paces of it when the man saw him. Adam had conducted himself with great gallantry in front of the 52nd when they took the French Imperial Guard in flank, and evinced his pluck also in not leaving the field, when severely wounded in the leg. As he sat on his horse for some little time near our fire, I heard him say that 'he should never forget the honour of having commanded the 52nd on that eventful day.'

After our arrival at Rossomme I lay down for a few minutes on the flank of No 9 company, and on my saying 'Can anyone give me a drink of water,' I was gratified with the kindness of the men, for there was no getting a supply of water where we were, yet four or five of them, directly they heard me, readily began to pass their canteens towards me. I have always retained a grateful recollection of this little kindness. It is a rule with soldiers to go into action, if they can, with their canteens full of water, for, when a man is severely wounded, the desire for water is sometimes almost intolerable. I shall have to relate an instance of this presently. About three quarters of an hour after we had halted at Rossomme, the first column of the Prussians, by whom the pursuit was to be taken up, arrived from Plancenoit. As they marched round the column of the 52nd from Plancenoit into the Charleroi road, they broke into slow time, and their bands played, 'God save the King.' A mounted officer, who rode up the bank, and passed along the flank of the column, which was lying down, pulled up and asked me in French 'if that was an English Colour;' (I still kept it in my possession, to give some poor tired fellow a little rest before he was placed on sentry over it). On my replying that it was, he let go his bridle, and taking hold of the Colour with both hands, pressed it to his bosom, and patted me on the back, exclaiming, 'Brave Anglais.'

Some few of the Prussian soldiers passed up the bank and along the flank of our column with strings of three or four horses each, which they had picked up between Plancenoit and Rossomme. They were apparently horses taken from the French guns and ammunition waggons. One man, to whom I spoke, I found very ready to part with a couple of horses for a few francs. Probably then thinking he would have considerable difficulty in conducting his prizes very far, in the confused state of the roads by which the Prussians were to advance, may have had something to do with his willingness to part with them at so small a price. I had no defined object in the purchase, except that I thought it unfair that the Prussians should walk off with all the horses they came across, whilst we got none of them for our portion of the spoil. I took one of the horses for myself, and the other as a mess horse for the officers of the company. It turned out to be a very useful purchase; for half the officers of the regiment lost the whole of their baggage and baggage horses, in the confusion which prevailed during the whole of the 18th on the road between Waterloo and Brussels. The officers of McNair's company were amongst the unfortunate sufferers. In a pocket on one of the saddles I found a quart bottle of brandy, which I suppose the Prussian soldier had not discovered. I do not think I tasted any of it myself, but I have no doubt it was properly appreciated by some of the more experienced officers, in the absence of anything else to drink or to eat. Major Chalmers had a small straw hut constructed for himself just large enough to cover the upper half of his body. I took the liberty of lying down at the back of it with my head near to his and my legs stretched out in a contrary direction. I slept soundly and sweetly that night from eleven till about half past two. How many thousands, within the space of two miles from us, British, Hanoverian, Brunswick, Nassau, Dutch, Belgian, Prussian and French, who bid as fair for life as any of us on the morning of the 18th, were now sleeping the sleep of death or lying desperately wounded on the field of Waterloo amidst what Marshal Ney described, as 'the most frightful carnage he had ever witnessed!' ...

Probably the whole amount of the loss on both sides during those three days would be about 75,000 men. Almost all the 52nd wounded officers were very 'severely wounded'. The late Lieutenant General Sir James Frederick Love, then a brevet major, was wounded in the head in our attack upon the columns of the Imperial Guard. On falling, he lay on the ground stunned, for some moments; and, on recovering, he put his finger into the wound, and, in his confusion, it appeared to him to go straight down into his head, and, feeling convinced that no man could recover with such a wound, and seeing the 52nd advancing, he ran after them, thinking that he would die with his regiment, instead of lying to die where he was. He, however, after making the trial, had to succumb. He remained on the ground and there received another severe wound in the foot, besides two other slight wounds. There was some serious intention at one time of taking off his leg, but Bell,[2] the eminent surgeon who wrote one of the 'Bridgewater Treatises', to whom he was known and who had received some attention from him in the Peninsula, hearing that he was lying badly wounded at the village of Waterloo, went to see him, and by his advice the operation was delayed and the limb was saved. Sir J F Love had two brothers in the 52nd,[3] and they, hearing that their brother was severely wounded, obtained leave from Sir John Colborne, after the action, to go back and look for him. As people are so apt to do in the night, they completely missed their direction, and after wandering about for a considerable time, till they were regularly knocked up, they determined to remain for the night at a farmhouse which they had come to. Here the people, who were very glad of their protection, were very kind to them; and after getting something to eat, they had just laid themselves down on some straw in the large kitchen, when there was a loud knocking at the great gates of the farm, and, on these being opened, in stalked three grenadiers of the Imperial Guard with their firelocks and with bayonets fixed. They would not have been pleasant opponents perhaps for two young officers, but on the elder Love saying to them 'Vous etes prisonniers?' they very gladly acquiesced in the proposal, and their firelocks having been placed against the corner of the room, after a little time the five wearied soldiers, who had so lately met in mortal strife, were lying side by side on the same straw, and there slept together till daylight. The French soldiers, no doubt, were most thankful for the protection thus secured to them; for soldiers of a defeated army can never feel quite sure that their lives will be spared by any of their enemies whom they may fall in with; and I suspect the French were that night especially, to make use of an elegant expression recently imported from Cambridge, 'awfully afraid' of the Prussians.

Soon after the 52nd had halted at Rossomme, the present Sir William Rowan, then a brevet major, received permission from Sir John Colborne to go and look after his brother, the late Sir Charles Rowan, KCB, who had been wounded. After passing beyond La Belle Alliance and the ground beyond it, he found Maitland's Brigade of Guards between the British and French positions, with their arms piled, he thought. He fell in with an officer of the 1st Regiment of Guards, whom he knew; whilst he was speaking to him Sir John Byng rode up and asked 'Who is that?' and on the officer replying, 'It is Rowan

---

2. Sir Charles Bell came over from Britain to assist in caring for the wounded after news of the battle reached London. The Bridgewater Treatises were published under the auspices of the Reverend Francis Egerton, Earl of Bridgewater, who left in his will a sum of money to be held at the disposal of the president of the Royal Society of London. Eight works were produced, Sir Charles Bell producing No. 4.
3. It is quite noticeable how many apparent siblings served in the 52nd Foot at this time. The brothers of Captain James Love were Lieutenant George Love and Ensign Frederick Love.

of the 52nd, Sir,' Sir John said, 'Ah, we saw the 52nd advancing gloriously, as they always do.' Sir John Byng, in the early part of the action, commanded the Brigade of Guards, composed of a battalion of the Coldstream and one of the 3rd Guards, which was posted in and to the rear of Hougoumont. When General Cooke was wounded, Byng succeeded to the command of the whole division of the Guards, and was with Maitland's Brigade when the 52nd attacked the Imperial Guard and advanced in the manner described by him in such glowing terms. Now this conversation happened about a quarter past ten o'clock, two hours after the 52nd had crossed the whole front of the right wing of the British army, 300 yards and more below the crest of the position; and the fact that Maitland's brigade was still at that late hour below the French position, helps to confirm the idea I have before advanced that scarcely more than four infantry regiments and two brigades of cavalry, Vivian's and Vandeleur's, advanced over the low ground towards the French position on the evening or night of the 18th of June, notwithstanding all that has been said about the Duke's advancing his whole line in support of those troops. I suppose that the greater portion of the British and Allied troops left their stations on the reverse slope of our position, and sought out for themselves ground on which to bivouac, more free, than that on which they had been stationed, from the melancholy sight of the slain and from the groans of the wounded and dying. I fear it was an unavoidable necessity that many of the wounded should be left for the night on the field of battle. One of the 52nd officers who was ordered on duty to Brussels the next morning, on passing over the ground by which we had advanced, was called upon by name by some of the 52nd men, who had been lying wounded all night, to get something done for them. He was unable to assist them, but at a very early hour a strong fatigue party was sent out from the regiment to place them under the care of the surgeons. Another fatigue party was sent out to collect the arms belonging to the regiment. I think by far the greater number of the wounded on our side were removed into houses at Waterloo, Merbe Braine, and other villages, before it became dark on the evening of the 18th. Sir William Rowan proceeded to Waterloo and there found his brother and all the 52nd wounded officers, except Anderson, in the same house.[4]

Leeke makes a few claims in his version of events, which need to be examined. He claims that most or all of the remainder of the brigade were, by the time that it reached Primotion, several hundreds of yards off to the right. This has been clearly shown to be completely wrong, with the rest of Adam's Brigade in fact being in close attendance. He went further and stated that the Osnabruck Battalion was just behind the battalion and was its only support (distant as it was), whereas we know that this battalion had remained to the right (west) of the chaussee and was at least level with the 52nd if not ahead, but off to the right. He then went even further by claiming that these few troops, along with Vivian's

---

4. Leeke, pp 63–72.

The Dying Embers of the Day 21.00 to 22.00 Hours

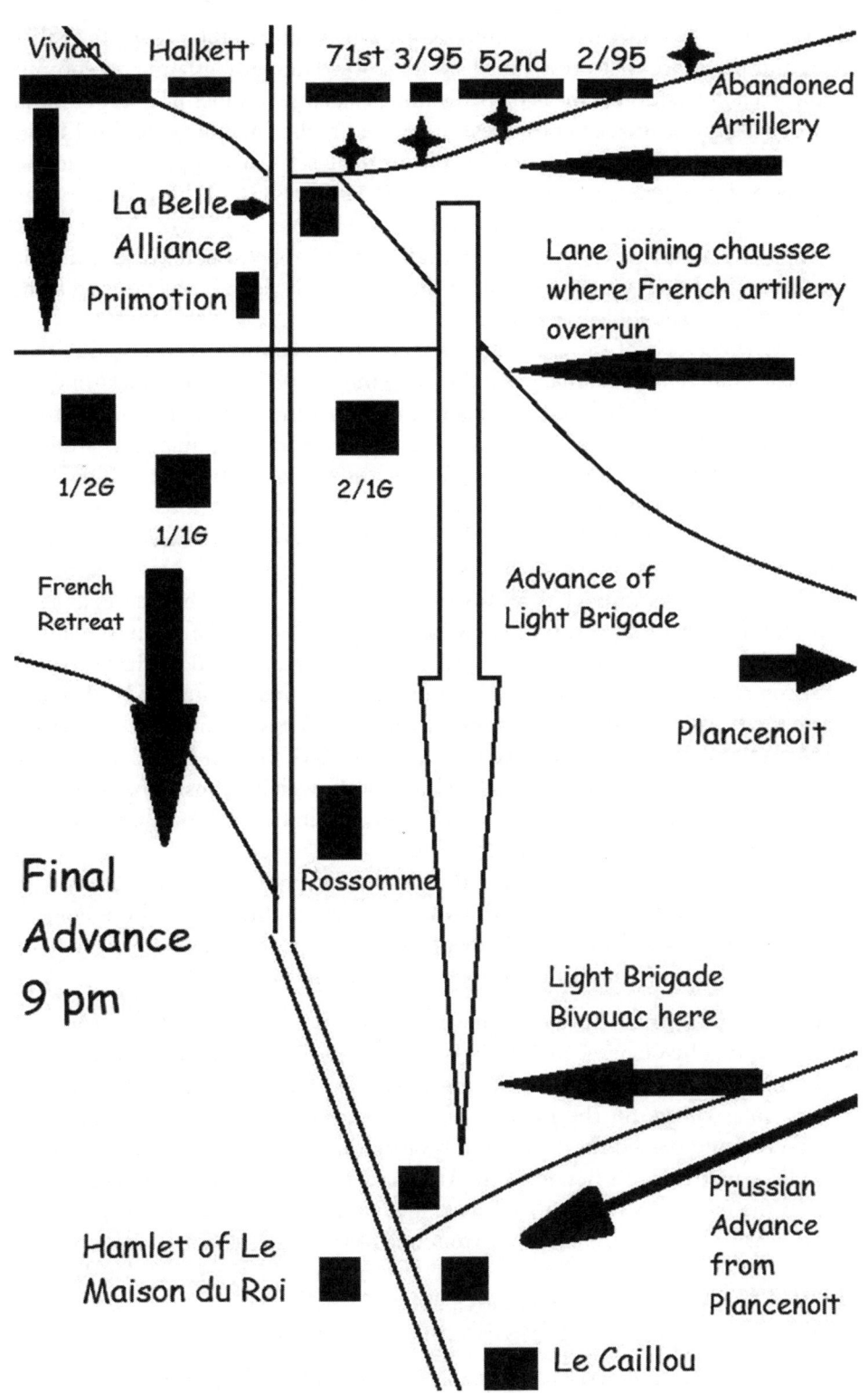

and Vandeleur's cavalry, were the only troops which entered the French lines that night and therefore that these four battalions were the only infantry to encamp on the French position. This is palpably untrue, a large number of infantry units recorded that it bivouacked near Rossomme that night, including the 23rd Foot, 1st, 2nd, 3rd and 4th Line Battalions of the King's German Legion, while the 1st Guards Brigade, 28th Foot and 8th Line Battalion KGL encamped at or near La Belle Alliance. Evidence for this is plentiful: Captain Goeben of the 1st KGL writing that: 'We pursued the French fugitives until approximately the region of Rossomme, and then we bivouacked for the night on the left side of the road from Brussels to Genappe'.[5]

Lieutenant Hesse of the 2nd Line Battalion KGL confirmed this, stating that the amalgamated light company battalion and the 2nd KGL 'at 9 o'clock [pm] we met at La Belle Alliance.'[6] Major Mejer of the 4th Line Battalion KGL claimed to have gone further, leaving 'Le Caillou on the right, we marched straight through the fields and bivouacked in the grounds of a nearby farm.'[7] The 23rd Foot bivouacked about 300 yards from La Belle Alliance.

It is also questionable how long the brigade was encamped near Rossomme before the Prussians joined them and took over the pursuit. Leeke estimates that it was at Rossomme for three quarters of an hour before the first Prussians arrived, this seems like an inordinately long time. Following the premise that the 52nd had driven off the Imperial Guard at 20.00 hours, it could not have arrived at Rossomme before 21.00 hours, this would therefore make it nearly 21.45 hours before the Prussians arrived at this spot. Plancenoit is only 20 minutes away from the Brussels chaussee, therefore we are asked to believe that the Prussians did not advance from Plancenoit until nearly 21.30 hours, which seems to be much too late, given that we know that the French front around La Belle Alliance was in complete rout no later than about 20.30 hours.

Given that General Adam appeared from the direction of Genappe, it is very likely that he had been forward with the Duke of Wellington as the following statements will show. Undoubtedly, because he was heavily fatigued, Lieutenant Holman wrote a little more abruptly than usual in his journal, that:

> Just at dark, while busily employed in the pursuit, a Prussian corps commanded by General Bulow cut in on our left, by which means we again cut off a number of prisoners. We joined company at 10pm, we halted close to a small village on the main road, where we soon made fires to warm ourselves and passed the evening in hearing the Prussian's account of their exploits and [re]counting our own. At ½ past 10 Lord W[ellington] coming from the front,[8] halted and paid us a fine compliment on the behaviour of our brigade. I cut a French horse from one of the guns, as did several other

---

5. Glover, Letters from the Battle of Waterloo, p 199.
6. ibid, p 201.
7. ibid, p 209.
8. This confirms that Wellington proceeded far to the south of Belle Alliance and presumably also met Blücher far to the south.

officers of the brigade, fancying it would be much better to continue the pursuit in the morning mounted than on foot, particularly after three such fatiguing days.[9]

It is interesting that Holman agrees with Leeke's timing for the arrival of the Prussians at nearly 22.00 hours. However, when Colonel Colborne wrote to William Siborne, he seemed to indicate that the Prussians arrived almost simultaneously with the 52nd at the junction near Maison du Roi:

> At the junction of the Genappe road and the road leading, I believe, from Wavre to Nivelles, the skirmishers of the 52nd and the advance of the Prussians under General Bulow mixed. When we passed this point it was nearly dark. We halted a few hundred yards from it, and the whole of General Bulow's Corps passed our right on the road leading to Genappe. The Duke of Wellington, on returning, I suppose, from Belle Alliance, passed the left of our column and enquired to halt for the night.[10]

He also wrote similarly to William Siborne that 'they'

> Were joined by the skirmishers at the head of Bülow's corps, that shortly after that came obliquely from the left… The skirmishing or attack that took place in the retreat from Rossomme or Plançenoit, the 52nd took no part in; they halted when the evening closed. Bülow's Corps in column passed the 52nd after the regiment had halted. The writer has never been on the ground since, but he is positive, as far as his memory can be relied on, that these facts are correctly stated, and it is thus certain that no corps whatever passed between the 52nd and the French, from the time the 52nd moved on the flank of the French, for the 52nd were under a heavy fire the whole time and were opposed to the moment they touched the Charleroi road. When they were formed to the left of the Charleroi road, no corps was near them. The only corps of cavalry near the 52nd or the French column during this attack was the regiment of cavalry that moved in the direction of the left company of the 52nd.[11]

From these sources, it is clear that this road junction is the one where the main Brussels to Charleroi chaussee is met by the Chemin de la Maison du Roi, which leads directly to the centre of Plancenoit village. William Rowan also recorded that:

> Our brigade continued to advance against everything opposed to it, passing the wreck of the French army, guns, ammunition waggons, soldiers who had thrown away their arms &c &c, until we reached the elevated ground beyond Rossomme, overlooking Maison du Roi, being then and for some time previously, considerably in front of the allied troops. As it was getting dark,

---

9. Holman Lt, Journal for 1815, Royal Green Jackets Museum, Winchester.
10. Siborne, The Waterloo Letters, pp 286–7.
11. Glover, Letters from the Battle of Waterloo, p 188.

the Duke rode up to us and ordered the brigade to bivouac for the night on the ground on which it then stood. I immediately obtained permission to go to the rear to look after my brother Charles. With much difficulty I found him about midnight in a house in the village of Waterloo, to which many of the wounded of the regiment and several French officers had been conveyed, it was a miserable night for us all. The following morning I accompanied my brother into Brussels, remained there that day and only in the morning of the 20th, I started to rejoin my regiment, which I reached in the afternoon, having passed over the field of battle, which still presented a horrible spectacle.[12]

Digby Mackworth, aide de camp to Lord Hill described these final moments with his usual flourish:

The battle was over, guns, prisoners, ammunition wagons, baggage, horses successively fell into our hands; night and fatigue compelled us to halt, we halted on each side of the Genappe road, and in a short time we saw numerous columns of Prussians advancing along in pursuit of the enemy, each column cheered us in passing, the officers saluted, and many embraced us; never was witnessed a more enthusiastic moment; we felt amply rewarded for the exertions of the day. We retired to take a little most welcome repose while the Prussians continued the pursuit without intermission, and thus ended this ever memorable day.[13]

His 'in a short time' seems more realistic, making the Prussian arrival at Maison du Roi at around 21.15 hours. Lieutenant Gawler accepted that the final attacks were made by both British infantry and cavalry:

The loss sustained from the compact square of the Old Guard was, however, avenged by repeated and effectual charges of Vivian's Brigade, now strengthened by the remains of Vandeleur's, upon broken masses of fugitives of all arms, on the ground between Rossomme and Mon Plaisir, and for three miles farther, to the neighbourhood of Genappe.

The village of Planchenois [Plancenoit], eight hundred yards to the left of Rossomme, had been the main object of the attack of the Prussians, from about half past four o'clock pm, when their two leading brigades first got into action. This post, however, which then became the French extreme right, was effectually maintained by the eight battalions of the Young Guard and a part of the 6th Corps, until the mass of the French army, driven before the British advance, passed along the high road in its rear, when they also retired, and soon after broke into confusion. The 52nd, 71st, and the head of the Prussian columns met just beyond the farm of Rossomme; and at the same moment the Duke of Wellington and Marshal Blücher riding up

---

12. Mss Personal Reminiscences of Captain William Rowan, Museum of the Oxfordshire Soldier. Ref SOFO 2178.
13. Glover, The Waterloo Archive Volume IV, p 24.

together from La Belle Alliance, the Prussians were ordered to continue the pursuit; and the British advance of infantry, strengthened by the three battalions of the 95th, halted on the spot for the night.

The main body of the allied army had advanced in lines from the position of Mont St Jean, about the time that the squares of the Old Guard turned before the attack of Adam's Brigade. The greater part of the cavalry pushed forward in support of its advanced brigades to the neighbourhood of Genappe. The infantry halted in the line of La Belle Alliance. The remains of the several divisions then spread over the ground to search out their bivouacs among the wounded and the dead, and night closed upon the FIELD OF WATERLOO.[14]

Lieutenant John Hart wrote only briefly of the action, but gave interesting details of the wounds of the various officers:

> We then continued our charge and drove the French Grenadiers about 2 miles, when Napoleon was seen rallying them on top of a hill. We charged again with 2 companies and drove them off, Nap[oleon] and all and after having driven them away, we took up our quarters for the night and slept sound after the fatigue of the day. I have not heard of our loss, but I will tell you that of our regiment killed, 1 Ensign, J Nettles, shot through the heart by an 8 pounder; wounded 1 Lieutenant Colonel Rowen [Rowan] contusion from a spent ball; 1 Major, Love, musket ball through head and foot; 1 Captain, Diggle, grape through head, not expected to live; Lieutenant Winterbottom, head; Lieutenant Campbell, groin; Lieutenant Dawson, lungs; Lieutenant Cottingham, chest shot off; Lieutenant Anderson, leg amputated; rank and file 218.[15]

His estimate of the killed and wounded was slightly over estimated. However, his acceptance that the cavalry had proceeded as far as Genappe was in direct variance with others from his own regiment. Now, let us take a look at what the other regiments say regarding the last movement of the day. Private William Aldridge of the 2/95th stated that:

> Just before they halted they came to a village, through which they skirmished; it was full of French artillery. Halted at the other end of the village on the right hand side of the great road, near a large pond of water.[16]

Poor Second Lieutenant Richard Eyre of the 2/95th was wounded just as it stopped to encamp, he must have been one of the last casualties of the battle:

> We now came to an immense hill where we found the consternation of the routed enemy so great that all classes of them, dragoons, infantry and artillery were mixed in one immense and confused mass. The greater part

---

14. Gawler, United Services Journal July 1833 p 306.
15. Lieutenant John Hart's letter dated 20 June 1815.
16. Siborne, The Waterloo Letters, p 303.

of their infantry threw down their packs and arms to be able to mount the hill they were then endeavouring to get over. Those we came up to ran into us as prisoners. Our lines then shortened pace to allow our cavalry and light troops to make a flank movement and get round to the other side of the hill, by this we succeeded in taking a great number of prisoners, a great part of their artillery and the whole of their provision and ammunition wagons. It however gave us some hard work as the part of the French army we had cut off fought hard with the idea of joining their companions who were better at running than themselves. In this however they were foiled, and in this last movement (about half past nine at night) which gloriously concluded a well and hard fought day, I was fortunate enough to get wounded! A musket ball entered just below the wrist in my left hand, the bones leading to my thumb and forefinger are a good deal smashed, the ball is still in my hand. Some leather and velvet which was driven in from my sleeve and glove have been already extracted but there is too much inflammation to allow them to cut out the ball. I am however assured that there is no danger of losing the hand and that I shall in great measure recover the use of it. I have now given you a [full?] description of the fight and shall conclude by saying a little more of myself. When I was wounded it was dark, my friend Drummond[17] (who you have heard me mention) got a man of the band to assist me to the rear in quest of a surgeon but after wandering as far as my strength would allow me I found the attempt to find one useless and therefore got the man who was with me to search for some blankets among the packs of the unfortunate fellows who were pretty thickly scattered about us and after getting well wrapped up laid down for the remainder of the night. In this situation I suffered the most excruciating pains. In the early part of the fight I was struck in the left knee by a piece of shell; whilst I kept myself in motion I felt very little from the blow which did not penetrate but after I had lain some time on the ground it gave me an immensity of pain as it was much swollen and perfectly stiff.[18]

Captain Reed of the 71st states that the battalion halted to the right of Plancenoit:

In front of which village we bivouacked for the night. We were here passed by a body of Prussian light cavalry, their music playing God Save the King. The first and second companies of the 71st were stationed in the village [Maison du Roi], where we found a park of seventy-two pieces of artillery which the enemy had abandoned.[19]

Lieutenant Colonel Thomas Reynell commanding the 71st, confirms the location, with a great deal more information. It proceeded,

---

17. First Lieutenant George Drummond, 1st Battalion 95th Rifles.
18. Glover, The Waterloo Archive Volume III, pp 116–7.
19. Siborne, The Waterloo Letters, pp 298.

> ... until it reached the village of Caillou [Maison du Roi], against the walls of which were deposited a considerable quantity of arms, as if abandoned by the soldiers composing the enemy's two columns. It was becoming dark at this period, and after scouring the village of Caillou [Maison du Roi], we retired to a field to the right of it, where we bivouacked for the night, near to our friends the 52nd. I do not recollect to have seen in our advance anybody of [allied] men, cavalry or infantry, to our front, but the two columns of the enemy; nor do I know that there was any on our right flank so much advanced as we were.[20]

First Lieutenant Macfarlane of the 3/95th was certain that the brigade was together when it drove the last French battalions from in front of La Belle Alliance:

> The left of the 2nd Battalion Rifle Brigade had now reached the high road a little below La Belle Alliance, and shooting the horses of the enemy's artillery, flying to the rear, blocked up the road, and thus secured about eighty guns of Count Reille and Count d'Erlon's corps. About 2,000 of the enemy, under General Cambronne, were posted in front of La Belle Alliance to cover the retreat. They got panic struck and adding disaster to confusion, fled with the Old Guard. Cambronne was taken prisoner by Lieutenant Colonel Hugh Halkett and we drove this routed mass a short distance beyond La Belle Alliance, when the Prussians took up the pursuit. It was now getting dark. We were halted and ordered to take ground to our right and slept upon the field, where Count d'Erlon's men had bivouacked the night before.[21]

Finally, we have the statement of Captain Eeles of 3/95th, who confirms that the,

> 3rd 95th again extended, and followed, as fast as they were able, accompanied by the 71st Regiment, still in line and four deep, the retiring French, until they came near some houses, which I believe to have been the farm of Rosomme. I then, having been for some time in command of the 3rd Battalion, thinking that the enemy would make a stand, under cover of the houses, checked the advance of the riflemen, and having drawn them close together, prepared to act in concert with the 71st Regiment. There was, however, no enemy to attack. They had all gone off in the dusk of the evening, and the 71st and 3rd Battalion 95th bivouacked for the night on the right of the wood.[22]

Colonel Halkett claimed that he and the Osnabruck Battalion had proceeded on another 2 miles (3 km) with the Prussians, halting at the northern end of Genappe:

---

20. ibid, p 297.
21. Glover, The Waterloo Archive Volume VII, p 164.
22. Siborne, The Waterloo Letters, p 307.

> I had followed the enemy on the Genappe road, where I met the Prussians, and moved on with them to some houses on the left of the road near Genappe, which houses I occupied during the night, the battalion being much knocked up, and not seeing any redcoats in the rear. Soon after we halted, I sent the major of the battalion with a company into Genappe to see what was going on.[23]

It is doubtful however, whether it actually marched as far as Genappe, Halkett being the only one to claim so. Indeed, Major von Dreves claims that he was ordered to command the advance guard, not the battalion commander, Lieutenant von Munster. He records:

> The battalion pursued the enemy jointly with English and Prussian troops, eventually intermingled with them, on and along the side of the Genappe highway, until about 10 o'clock at night. The remnants of the battalion gathered near some houses, probably Maison du Roi or Le Caillou. The battalion was unable to continue its advance further, due to the extraordinary exertions on this day. Having thus become separated somewhat from the other troops, I was charged at 11 o'clock at night by the brigadier, the then Colonel Halkett, with a reconnoitring assignment, with as many of the battalion's men as I was able to put on the road. I undertook this with the greater part of the remnants of the battalion in the direction of Genappe. While faced with great difficulties due to the extreme exhaustion of the troops and the darkness of night, I executed this assignment to the satisfaction of the brigadier.[24]

This confirms that a sizeable reconnaissance was carried out as far as Genappe, but the battalion actually halted for the night in the area of Maison du Roi also. It also confirms that the brigade had acted in close cooperation throughout and was not separated from the Light Brigade by hundreds of yards as Leeke claimed.

---

23. ibid, pp 309–10.
24. Glover, The Waterloo Archive Volume II, p 70.

Chapter 16

The Morning After – 19 June

Although the company rolls had been completed the previous night when it halted, it was only the following morning when some idea of the regiment's losses could be ascertained and parties sent back to the battlefield to help the wounded onto waggons to carry them to hospital in Brussels and to bury the dead. William Leeke lists the casualties exactly as recorded in the regimental record which is still held in the archives of the Museum of the Oxfordshire Soldier. The following was the return of the casualties of the 52nd at Waterloo:

Killed
Officers 1 (Ensign Nettles) 1 Sergeant and 36 Rank & File

Wounded
1 Major (Brevet Lieutenant Colonel Charles Rowan – Slightly),
2 Captains (Captain and Brevet Major J F Love – Severely & Captain Charles Diggle – Severely),
5 Lieutenants (Lieutenant and Adjutant John Winterbottom – Severely, Lieutenant Charles Dawson – Severely, Lieutenant Matthew Anderson – Severely, Lieutenant George Campbell – Severely & Lieutenant Thomas Cottingham – Severely)
10 Sergeants and 150 Rank and File

This figure of one Officer and 37 Other Ranks killed and eight Officers and 160 Other Ranks wounded tallies exactly with Leeke's previous assertion that its losses totalled 206 and it is obvious that he referred to this table when he wrote his version of events.

However, Leeke wrote forty years after the event and had the benefit of referring to what should presumably be exact figures calculated long after the battle. In fact, Leeke's claims that the men seemed to know the fate of almost every man, does appear to be largely backed up by the official Return accumulated for the army immediately following the battle,[1] which actually states the losses of the 52nd Foot at 199 in total, which is not too far removed from the final accepted figure of 206.

These figures however, comprising of one Officer and 16 Rank and File killed, with eight Officers, eight Sergeants and 166 Rank and File wounded shows no 'missing'. Given the situation when the Return was compiled this is pretty accurate, although it does not explain how two sergeants and five privates who were clearly wounded, were simply lost in the accounting between these two sets of returns and were not even shown simply as 'missing'. That must be put down to the understandable exhaustion and confusion surrounding the undoubtedly cursory company musters carried out in the dark that night.

---

1. Published in Siborne's History of the Waterloo Campaign, p 564.

	Killed					Wounded					Missing					Total
	Officers	Quarter Masters and Sergeants	Trumpeters & Drummers	Rank & File	Horses	Officers	Quarter Masters and Sergeants	Trumpeters & Drummers	Rank & File	Horses	Officers	Quarter Masters and Sergeants	Trumpeters & Drummers	Rank & File	Horses	
1st Battalion 52nd	1			16		8	8		166							199

This however does not tally exactly with the Return found in General Henry Clinton's papers for the losses of the 2nd Division and reproduced in part opposite and cannot be the source for the official figures used by Siborne.[2]

This third set of Returns comes up with a third number of casualties, this time totalling nine Officers killed and wounded (which is reported consistently throughout), but the Other Ranks now total 205 killed and wounded.

The only other Return [See Appendix 5] we have, shows that the battalion had 35 men sick in May 1815 and 205 sick in June, but this increase of 170 cannot simply be put completely down to the wounded from the battle, as we would also expect some men to have recovered during this month and returned to the ranks, whilst others would have fallen sick, especially during such a period of intense marching in terrible conditions and with little in the way of regular food or supplies.

This goes to show how incredibly difficult it is to be exact with the losses sustained in any action, the three muster totals varying in excess of 10 per cent of the total, a not insignificant margin of error.

It is therefore clearly impossible to be completly accurate as to the wounded totals for any regiment, as the three-monthly Muster Returns reported to Horse Guards (with monthly confirmation muster checks within) do not, unfortunately, often differentiate between sick in hospital with illness and those in hospital with battle wounds. It has been shown by recent investigation of Army hospital returns at Brussels and Antwerp in 1815, that regiments could expect to receive approximately 60 per cent of those wounded and who lived to get medical attention in a hospital, later returned to the regiment, fit to serve again. Only 10 per cent of those who got to hospital died and on average 30 per cent survived, but were so badly injured as to preclude them continuing to serve with their regiment and were sent home for service with a veteran battalion, or more often, discharged with a meagre pension.[3]

We can however, be far more accurate with those that were killed or died later of their wounds as this was specifically detailed when 'discharged dead' from the Muster Rolls.

---

2. Glover, Correspondence of Sir Henry Clinton Volume 2, pp 105–6.
3. See M. Crumplin & G. Glover After the Glory, for further detailed analysis.

1. Killed.

Regiments	Killed General Staff	Colonels	Lt. Colonels	Majors	Captains	Lieutenants	Cornets/Ensigns	Staff	Troop Quartermasters	Sergeants	Drummer/Trumpeter	Rank and File	Total	Horses
1/52nd Foot							1					16	17	
71st Foot							1			1		23	25	
2/95th Foot										2	1	31	34	
3/95th												3	3	

2. Wounded.

Regiments	Wounded General Staff	Colonels	Lt. Colonels	Majors	Captains	Lieutenants	Cornets/Ensigns	Staff	Troop Quartermasters	Sergeants	Drummer/Trumpeter	Rank and File	Total	Horses
1/52nd Foot		1		1	2	5				8	1	182	199	
71st Foot			1		4	8				7	3	150	174	
2/95th Foot			2		2	10				6	2	171	183	
3/95th			1	1		2				1	1	34	40	

Losses by Company in Battle Order (excluding officers)+

Other Ranks	Killed	Died of Wounds	Wounded Discharged	Wounded but Returned to duty	Total Losses
1 Diggle	0	4	3	11	18
2 Love? *	1	1	2	10	14
3 Langton?* (Young absent)	3	4	3	12	22
4 P Campbell	5	2	3	13	23
5 Anderson (Brownrigg absent)	1	3	6	21	31
6 Chalmers?#	2	4	4	16	26
7 Rowan?#	0	10	4	7	21
8 Cross (R Campbell absent)	0	0	6	12	18
9 McNair	2	3	2	7	14
10 Shedden	0	5	7	11	23
Total Battalion	14	36	40	120	210
Percentages of Casualties	6.7%	16.7%	19.5%	57.1%	100%

+ All officer casualties have been omitted because we cannot apportion the majority of the junior officers to a specific company.

* It has proven impossible to be certain which company Love or Langton commanded, Nos 2 or 3. The losses per company are correct, however.

It has proven impossible to be certain which company Chalmers or Rowan commanded, Nos 6 or 7. The losses per company are correct however.

As can be seen, although there was some variance in the numbers of killed and wounded per company, the variance is not particularly significant. Although, it could be argued that the centre companies (Langton, P Campbell, Anderson and Chalmers?) and the left company (Diggle's) suffered a higher level of casualties, which does perhaps indicate that the losses were predominantly caused by the Imperial Guard, which was more closely engaged with the left of the battalion as it swung through ninety degrees before charging. Anderson's company was sent out in advance as skirmishers and clearly suffered the highest number of casualties as a consequence. Despite a lower overall casualty rate in No 7 Company (Rowan's?), this company suffered by far the most fatalities at nearly 50 per cent of its casualties. Such anomalies sometimes defy explanation and clearly serve to indicate the folly of trying to analyse casualty rates unless particularly marked. For further details of the killed and wounded please refer to Appendix 2.

Four men are recorded as having been absent from the ranks during 18 June and were later court martialled (Regimental) for it. These included Sergeant Richard Cox, Corporal Jonathan Moliment and Private John Baird of Captain Love's company and Corporal Henry Moore of Lt Colonel P. Campbell's company. All four were later convicted and sentenced to receive 300 lashes each. In all cases this sentence was remitted to an unspecified period of confinement. Sergeant Cox was also reduced to the ranks, but Corporal Moliment would appear to have avoided this further sanction.

The troops that morning were roused with daylight in case of an attack and then settled down to cook what little scraps they still had, or could find in the nearby houses and packs of the corpses surrounding them, until the commissariat waggons finally arrived with supplies. They were under orders to march that day in pursuit of the French and had to prepare themselves and their kit for the challenges still to come on the long march to Paris, some 168 miles (275 km) away.

Holman, a Peninsular War veteran, wrote only a brief note in his journal, reporting the earliest estimates of regimental casualties, which was to prove to be a bit of an exaggeration and claimed the capture of 76 cannon, but he did readily admit that the regiment's losses were very light for what it had achieved:

> Our loss was trifling compared to the work done [by] it. One officer killed E Nettles,[4] 1 Lieutenant Colonel,[5] 1 major,[6] 1 captain,[7] 5 lieutenants[8] [wounded] and about 270 rank and file killed and wounded.[9] Sent out a party with an officer to mark the guns taken by the brigade, which I have heard were 76 pieces.
>
> Marched at daybreak about 3 miles on the main road, where we halted. At 5 [pm] marched thro[ugh] Nivelles on the main road to the little village of Herrigue about 4 leagues, no baggage arrived, various reports of its having been plundered by the native troops. We bivouacked here and one British division passed to our front. Found that the enemy had retired by the main road to Charleroi.[10]

William Leeke, who was new to war and therefore found everything a great novelty, wrote much more fully:

> At daylight on the 19th all were stirring. It was some time before we left our bivouac at Rossomme, perhaps an hour or two. On the opposite side of the Charleroi road was a battalion of the 95th Rifles, whom we had not seen the night before; probably they were the 2nd battalion of the 95th, who belonged to our brigade, and had come up some time after we had halted for the night. About a third of a mile from the 52nd bivouac, near the farm of

---

4. Actually Ensign William Nettles 52nd Foot.
5. Lieutenant Colonel Charles Rowan 52nd Foot
6. Major William Rowan 52nd Foot
7. This would be Captain James Love, but he was also a major in the army.
8. Lieutenants John Winterbottom, Charles Dawson, Mathew Anderson, George Campbell and Thomas Cottingham.
9. Siborne shows 190 rank & file killed and wounded.
10. Holman Lt, Journal for 1815, Royal Green Jackets Museum, Winchester.

Rossomme to the south east, is the house in which Bonaparte is said to have slept on the night of the 17th.[11] On the other side of the Charleroi road, we found at some little distance some dead bodies, and swords and cuirasses which had been thrown away. This would be the ground over which some portions of Vandeleur's and Vivian's cavalry brigades must have passed in pursuit the night before. In one place were a number of letters strewn about which appeared to have been taken from the dead body of a French officer; they were the letters of a young lady in Scotland, to her husband, a French officer, who had recently left her to join the French army. They were just the tender affectionate letters which a young loving wife would write to a husband under such circumstances. I well remember the following sentence in one of them, 'How I pity the poor English.' Portions of these letters were listened to with great interest by several officers who were present, and all felt distressed at the thought that such a bitter cup of sorrow awaited the poor young widow. It was observed that one of those present took a peculiar interest in the writer of these letters; he frequently spoke of them, and of her afterwards, and it turned out that he had taken down her name and address, and that on his going on leave to Scotland some time after, he determined to go to the place in which she lived and to make enquiries about her. The sequel of the story is, that he was somewhat disappointed to find, that she and her husband were living most happily together. The husband had only been severely wounded at Waterloo and had lost his letters ...

The Scotch officer died many years ago.[12] On moving from Rossomme, we passed through the burning village of Maison du Roi, about a quarter of a mile off, and joined the 71st on the other side of it. The 52nd remained for several hours on the morning of the 19th near Maison du Roi, before they marched to Nivelles. Meat was served out, and the men cooked. I recollect having there first eaten 'beefsteaks fried at the end of a ramrod'. My servant brought some water for us to drink from a pond in which he said there were the dead bodies of two French soldiers, and that he could not find any other water. Some of our men had some orders and other things, which they had picked up on the field of battle; probably the men had belonged to one of the fatigue parties sent out to take up any of our wounded who had remained on the ground all night, and to collect arms belonging to the regiment. I bought a pair of brass barrelled pistols from one of the men. In a field about two hundred yards off, to the left of the chaussee, I found a French ammunition waggon, and supplied myself with some cartridges, which fitted my pistols, for the purpose of putting an unfortunate horse, that had had its leg shot off, out of its misery. I did not succeed very well, as the horse, whenever I pulled the trigger, so suddenly moved his head

---

11. Le Caillou.
12. This almost certainly refers to Captain James McNair who resided at Greenfield near Glasgow and who died there in 1836.

that my aim did not take effect. Two Prussians coming up from Plancenoit, one of them a sergeant, shot the horse for me. After this I rode forward to a hamlet nearly half a mile in advance.[13] I took three or four canteens with me to see if I could not get some water fit to drink; but one of our men whom I desired to fill them for me, told me when I was leaving the place afterwards, that he had filled them with beer, which he thought better than water. I remained in a farmhouse at this place for some time, as there were several wounded men filling all the lower rooms, to whom I and some of our men tried to render some little services. One was a man of the 7th Hussars who had received seven wounds when that regiment charged the French lancers, just to the north of Genappe, on the afternoon of the 17th. He described to me the manner and order in which he had received his wounds, all of which I do not distinctly recollect; but several of them, though not all, were lance wounds, inflicted whilst he was lying on the ground. There appears to have been much of this unnecessarily cruel work of piercing those lying on the ground wounded, carried on by the French lancers at Waterloo. ... This 7th Hussar man, who had not till then been discovered and visited by any surgeon, was, whilst I was at the place, taken away by his own regiment. How he had got so far away from the ground on which he was wounded I do not know; but I think the distance from Genappe must have been nearly two miles. I had some hope that the man would recover.

On the other side of the fireplace, on a bed or mattress, lay a poor fellow belonging to the Grenadiers of the French Guard. He had, I thought, a fatal wound from which the bowels protruded. When he saw one of our men washing the wounds of the hussar, he begged that he would bring the water to him also; and on this being done, he eagerly seized the basin, and quenched his burning thirst by drinking deeply of the bloody water which it contained.

On my return to the regiment, with my canteens hanging on each side of my saddle, and my pistols stuck through the straps which fastened on my boat cloak in front of me, I saw our general of division, Sir Henry Clinton, and some of his staff coming towards me. He looked all the more formidable from a fashion he had adopted of wearing his cocked hat, not in the usual way, 'fore and aft,' but with the small ends over either shoulder. I thought I must look so much like a marauder, that I was rather ashamed of being seen by him. I soon disposed of my pistols by pitching them over a hedge on my right, never to see them again, and thus freed from the chief appendage I was ashamed of, I passed the general without attracting his particular attention. Whilst I was away, a French ammunition waggon was blown up not far from the regiment, and two men of the brigade were killed. I think one belonged to the 71st and the other to the 95th Rifles. They were on the top of the waggon, hacking at it with a hatchet or bill hook to get some wood

---

13. Probably Maison du Roi.

for cooking. I am not sure that it was not the same ammunition waggon from which I had been helping myself to cartridges some little time before.

When the regiment fell in for the march to Nivelles, an inspection of knapsacks took place and several things were thrown away with which some of the men had encumbered themselves. We formed square either before or after this inspection, and some men were paraded as prisoners, who had fallen out drunk at Braine le Comte on the morning of the 17th, in consequence of getting access to some wine vaults in that town, and had thus missed being with their regiment at Waterloo. Sir John Colborne addressed them, and said he should forgive them, as he considered it was a sufficient punishment for them that they had been absent from their regiment 'when they had the honour of defeating the Imperial Guard of France, led on by the Emperor Napoleon Bonaparte in person.'[14] We supposed then, from what the French chef d'escadron had reported, that the Emperor was with his Guard when we attacked them; but it afterwards appeared from the French accounts that it was not so, and that after they had marched past him in the low ground between the two armies, he had gone back to the French position, from which he only retired with the squares of the Old Guard.

I believe it was between twelve and one o'clock on the 19th,[15] when we left our ground near Maison du Roi, and marched to Nivelles, which, by the road we took, was about nine miles off. We had now fairly started on our triumphant march to the French capital, and all were in the highest state of delight at our glorious victory, in the gaining which the 52nd had been fortunate enough to take such a leading part, and in our glorious prospect of immediately entering France, and eventually Paris itself. We bivouacked about a mile beyond Nivelles, on the left of the chaussee, and about a hundred yards from a beautiful little stream, at which we washed our hands and faces, not having been able even to wash our hands since the morning of the 16th. Hearing that there was an opportunity of sending letters to England, I got some paper from the Colour Sergeant of the company, and wrote two short notes, one to my mother and sisters, the other to a kind friend much interested in the 52nd.

The unfortunate explosion of a caisson is confirmed by a number of witnesses, but some, like Private Thomas Knight of the 2/95th Rifles, were certain that the men killed were from the 71st and 52nd:

Whilst here, being ill off for firewood, one of the 52nd and 71st, followed by others, went with choppers to the bottom of the hill to break up a large

---

14. Private Thomas Rielly or Riley was marked as having fallen out on the march on 16 June, he missed Waterloo, but is recorded as being on duty on 25 June 1815 and continued serving with the regiment. Private James McCardle is also shown as having fallen out on the march on 16 June, he missed Waterloo, he was invalided to England on 24 October 1816 and discharged to pension on 21 November 1816.
15. Holman states that it was much later, around 17.00 hours.

ammunition waggon, which the French had left; and, one mounting on the top, while the other was on the wheel, were chopping away, unaware of its being loaded, when a spark catching the powder, the 52nd man on the top was blown into the air, and the other was knocked to the ground, with one side completely singed. Hearing the report, we ran down, and lifting the poor fellow up, carried him to the doctor, who rubbed him with oil. Returning to collect the splinters, and looking about, I stooped down to pick up what I supposed to be a piece of wood, but was startled to find that it was a man's foot, all black with powder.

We then searched for the rest of the body, and discovered it all but one foot, it being an awful sight, we dug a hole, and buried it; we then demolished the remainder of the waggon.[16]

Private Knight would appear to be in error, however, in stating that one of those killed was from the 52nd as there is no record of any man of this regiment being killed on 19 June. Indeed, Lieutenant William Gavin of the 71st states that three men were killed, all being from his own regiment:

We remained on our ground and received half allowance of rum. The whole face of the country was covered with the wreck of the French army. Three of our regiment in search of plunder opened an ammunition wagon filled with cartridges. On finding it of so little value they let the iron-bound cover suddenly fall, by which a spark emitted and communicated to the powder, and blew the unfortunate men to atoms. Corporal Sims, who had served with us at the Cape of Good Hope, Corunna, and all the battles in the Peninsula, and escaped the dreadful slaughter of the day before, was shot by a drummer, who playfully presented a French firelock at him, which he picked up from the field of battle, not knowing it was loaded. On the field lay a wounded French officer, who applied to me to assist him. I requested of a few Belgian boors, who were stripping the dead, to carry him to a farmhouse in sight, to which they consented on my taking charge of their heap of spoil till their return. They placed him on two muskets, and four of them took him off. As soon as I saw them near the house I abandoned my charge, and in a second their heap of plunder disappeared.[17]

Leeke's letters home have unfortunately been long lost, but we do have Colonel Colborne's brief letter written to his step-sister, Miss Fanny Bargus from near Nivelles:

You will be anxious to hear of us, of the most severe conflict I have ever witnessed and I think it will be the most important in the result. William Leeke is well.[18] The infantry behaved nobly and the 52nd as usual.

---

16. Leach, Men of the Rifles, pp 34–5.
17. Glover, The Diary of William Gavin 1806–15, pp 132.
18. Ensign William Leeke 52nd Foot was a cousin.

I have only time to write you these few lines. You will be surprised at the Gazette, we have lost some of our most valuable officers. My kind regards to your mother and nana. Your affectionate brother, J Colborne.[19]

Tupper Carey, the commissariat officer assigned to the 2nd Division, wrote regarding the problems of transporting his supplies without adequate protection from marauding Prussians. He was particularly critical of Colonel Colborne, for refusing to supply guards:

> They began to plunder the biscuit convoy most unceremoniously, and I had great difficulty in preventing it. Perceiving some troops to our right I rode up to them and found they were a part of our division; the 52nd Regiment, commanded by Sir John Colborne (now Lord Seaton), moving across the country towards Nivelles. I applied to him for a guard to protect the convoy, but he refused it with some unmeaning excuse, and I was therefore left to my own resources to get out of the difficulty as well as I could. The Prussians kept moving by us occasionally, and I would most certainly have been plundered by them of the best portion of the biscuit, had it not been for the opportune arrival of a detachment of our German cavalry (the King's German Legion). The commanding officer, seeing my dilemma, immediately ordered some of his men to draw their swords and accompany the convoy, and thus we moved on to Quatre Bras through Genappe. I there beheld, in addition to many other debris of the French Army, Napoleon's carriage on the spot where it had been overtaken and plundered. Around it were Prussian soldiers scraping and sifting the ground, in consequence of a report that some diamonds had fallen from their settings in the night scramble. When once past Quatre Bras we fortunately saw no more of the Prussians, and jogged on quietly until we reached Nivelles, not, however, before night fall, but in time for a most acceptable distribution to the troops.[20]

Others began to turn their minds to report writing, Lieutenant General Henry Clinton would have received reports from each of his brigade commanders, to enable him to write to Lord Hill as corps commander. Clinton's report was dated at Nivelles on the evening of 19 June.

> My Lord,
> I have the honour to report to your lordship that the conduct of the Second Division during the action of yesterday is as such as to entitle it to the approbation of your lordship and to that of the commander of the forces, the steadiness with which the young Hanoverian Brigade under Colonel Halkett sustained the effect of a lasting cannonade during the several hours which that brigade continued to be in reserve, would have been creditable in veteran troops.

---

19. Glover, The Waterloo Archive Volume VII, pp 163.
20. Glover, The Waterloo Archive Volume VI, p 240.

From the moment at which the 2nd Division was called upon to take a more active part in the action by relieving some of the corps in the first line, the good conduct of the whole could hardly be surpassed.

The brigade of Colonel Du Plat was the first employed in this manner, and it was not long before its valuable commander received a dangerous wound, which will long deprive the army of the benefit of his services. It then fell to Major General Adam's Brigade to take its share of the same honourable service, the manoeuvre in which the several regiments, the 52nd Regiment under Colonel Sir J Colborne, the 71st under Colonel Reynell, and the 2nd and 3rd 95th under Colonel Norcott and Lt Colonel Ross[21] have discharged their duty was witnessed & admired by the whole army. It was late in the day when I brought forward the brigade under the command of Colonel Halkett, the activity with which this move was performed by every battalion of the brigade, the regularity of its movements and the correctness of its formations under a destructive cannonade were very praiseworthy in these young troops, the Salzgitter Battalion under Major Hammerstein I employed by reinforcing the post of Hougoumont, at that moment vigorously attacked, and the Osnabruck Battalion under Lt. Colonel Count Munster advanced with the first line, while the battalions of Bremervorde and Quakenbruck under Lt Colonel Count Schulenburg and Major Baron Bussche continued in reserve as a support to the right of the line where the handsome repulse of the enemy's last attack by the Imperial Guards, afforded the opportunity to become ourselves the attacking body, so judiciously taken advantageously of by Major General C Adam's Brigade under your lordship's immediate direction. I directed Colonel Halkett to reinforce the attacking line with the Osnabruck Battalion under Lt Colonel Count Munster and I added to it the brigade of the German Legion, the command of which had now devolved upon Lt Colonel Wissell, the 23rd Regiment under the command of Major Dalmer[22] in consequence of Lt Colonel Sir H W Ellis[23] being wounded, advanced as a support to the right of the attack. The gallantry with which this service was performed, by every corps which had the good fortune to be employed in it I am sure attracted your lordship's notice, and I think without claiming too large a share of merit for these several corps. I may say that the result of these noble efforts greatly contributed to the complete success of this glorious day. Though the whole of the artillery and numerous trophies taken from the enemy, may belong in consequence to every corps engaged, as the effect of their exertions, I must report that the enemy was driven from four pieces of cannon which he was attempting to carry off upon the right of the Genappe road, by the Osnabruck Battalion which also during its advance got possession of two pairs of Colours.

---

21. Lt. Colonel John Ross.
22. Major (Lt. Colonel in the army) Thomas Dalmer.
23. Lt. Colonel Sir Henry Walton Ellis.

Major Sympher's troop of horse artillery and Captain Bolton's [Artillery] Brigade conducted themselves entirely to my satisfaction, the service has lost an excellent artillery officer in Captain Bolton, who was killed near the close of the day after usefully exerting himself during the whole of it. Major Sympher's troop followed in support of the cavalry until the darkness put an end to the pursuit of the enemy.

The brigade of the 4th Division commanded by Colonel Mitchell[24] having been placed for the moment under my orders, I am happy here having to make the same favourable report of the conduct of every corps composing this brigade, the 51st Regiment under [blank – Lt Colonel Mitchell] having been most usefully employed during the whole of the day with one squadron of the 15th Hussars in keeping in check a considerable body of the enemy's cavalry supported by infantry which menaced our right and the 14th Regiment under Lt Colonel Tidy[25] having acted as a support to the 51st Regiment and latterly as a support to the right of the post of Hougoumont. I have also to acknowledge the assistance which I had from Lt Colonel Sir Jeremiah Dickson[26] the Assistant Quarter Master General and from Captain Bentinck acting as Assistant Adjutant General as well as from the officers of my personal staff. I beg that your lordship in making your report to the commander of the forces will have the enclosed letter from Major General Adam laid before his Grace. H C.[27]

The report makes it clear that Clinton was very pleased with the performance of all of his troops, especially the raw Hanoverian troops. He does, however, make special mention of the movement of Adam's Brigade against the Imperial Guard. Clinton duly gives full recognition of the movement and its importance, even forwarding General Adam's report to Lord Hill, despite the fact that he says the manoeuvre was 'so judiciously taken advantageously of by Major General C Adam's Brigade under your lordship's immediate direction'. This is a questionable assertion, as we know that Hill did not order the movement and may well not have seen it, having had his horse shot and falling heavily to the ground around this time.

Lord Hill spent that night collating his Divisional reports, to complete his own Corps report for the Duke of Wellington. Hill completed and despatched his report at 08.00 hours on 20 June before he marched from Nivelles:

My Lord Duke,
 Although your Grace witnessed the conduct of that part of the troops under my command which had the good fortune to be employed in the action of the 18th instant, still I think it my duty to transmit the accompanying report from Lieutenant General Sir H Clinton, commanding the 2nd Division, and

---

24. Brevet Colonel Hugh Mitchell, 51st Foot.
25. Brevet Lt. Colonel Francis Tidy.
26. Lt. Colonel Sir Jeremiah Dickson was a permanent Assistant Quarter Master General.
27. Glover, The Correspondence of Sir Henry Clinton in the Waterloo Campaign, Volume 2, pp 112–3.

beg leave to express my entire concurrence with the Lieutenant General's sentiments respecting the gallant conduct of the troops on this occasion.

I have also the satisfaction of reporting to your Grace the good conduct of Lieutenant Colonel Webber Smith's Troop of horse artillery, which acted with my corps during the day.

I have also to mention the steady conduct of the 3rd Division of the troops of the Netherlands, under the command of Major General Chasse, which was moved up in support of Major General Adam's Brigade, to repulse the attack of the Imperial Guard. The brigade of Belgian artillery also deserve my best thanks for their steady conduct and well directed fire during the last mentioned attack.

I particularly remarked the firm manner with which two battalions of Brunswick infantry, commanded by Major Proestler and Major Holstein (formed in squares in support of the artillery), received the repeated attacks of the enemy's cavalry.

I cannot conclude this report without expressing my particular thanks to Lieutenant Colonel Sir C Broke, and to Lieutenant Colonel Sir Noel Hill, to Major Egerton, Major Churchill, and my personal staff, as well as to Captains Lord C Fitzroy and Hillier and their respective departments. I have the honour to be, my Lord, your Grace's most humble servant, Hill.

Enclosure: Lieutenant General Sir H Clinton to Lieutenant General Lord Hill.[28]

Lord Hill's report is brief, particularly with regard to Adam's Brigade, but this he openly admits, was because he was simply forwarding General Clinton's letter as an enclosure and that the Duke was also an eyewitness to these events. It is clear however, that he <u>did not</u> send General Adam's report on as an enclosure.

In a subsequent report Clinton listed three officers from each of his battalions, who were recommended for brevet promotion. In the 52nd Foot, the following officers were recommended:

<u>52nd Regiment</u>
Brevet Lieutenant Colonel Chalmers[29]
Captain C. Diggle[30]
Lieutenant & Adjutant J. Winterbottom[31]

Henry Clinton's wife, then at Brussels, wrote a candid letter home from the initial reports heard from the battlefield:

> Your friend General Adam whose leg is wounded was brought in yesterday in a cart very feeble, but is doing well, his Brigade Major Blair also wounded

---
28. Gurwood, The Duke of Wellington's Dispatches 1799–1815, Volume 12, p 544.
29. Brevet Lieutenant Colonel William Chalmers received this brevet on 18 June.
30. Captain Charles Diggle was severely wounded at Waterloo.
31. Winterbottom was not allowed his brevet as it was not usual to grant to officers of this rank, promotion by brevet.

in the arm slightly, came in with him. I know scarcely any particulars of the action but an officer told me today that the 2nd Division had been highly distinguished, from the commencement of the action at 12, although in reserve, they were exposed to the heavy cannonade, at 3, I believe earlier, they were brought into action & engaged till 11 at night in pursuit, the last attack of the enemy having been completely repulsed at 8. About 6 there was a very nervous moment, the enemy got possession of some strong ground & their cavalry was formidable. It was this I suppose that induced Henry to order all his baggage to Brussels. Between 11 & 12 that night after my having put up the best way I could 11 of his horses & a mule in my stables, coach house & yard, also the horses of some of his Staff, a friend received what he considered certain intelligence that my poor fellow was wounded so he hurriedly came & ordered off 3 servants & horses with blankets, I knew nothing of this till the morning although I was up till 2 expecting him every minute, I suppose General Adam had been taken for him. Some wounded soldiers of the 52nd report that Henry was much pleased with their regiment & made them very happy by riding up to thank them after the action. The young Hanoverian Brigade was under Halkett behaved I am told admirably, they took 12 pieces of cannon & Halkett took himself a French general officer. Of the Germans I have not yet been able to pick up anything except that they were equally engaged with the rest & that Du Plat who we much like is well. I have seen Allix & young Lascelles this morning,[32] they left Henry in the morning well at Nivelles, they have to come to look for their baggage & horses, great loss has been sustained amongst all the officers in consequence of an alarm given by the Belgians running away, when the bat men even at the gates of this town thought the enemy at their heels, abandoned their horses & baggage & saved themselves, all this without the slightest cause for alarm.[33]

Susan confirms that Henry Clinton thanked the 52nd after the battle, and others describe Hill and Wellington also thanking them. It is therefore abundantly clear that the regiment's movements had been fully observed and appreciated. However, the thanks were clearly given to every battalion of the brigade, Ensign Barnett of the 71st noting that: 'The regiment was thanked on the field, by Sir H Clinton & Lord Hill & I heard General Adam says he would rather have commanded the regiment than have been a king. This was in the heat of the battle.'[34]

Lord Hill apparently addressed the entire officer corps of Halkett's Brigade at Nivelles: 'Lord Hill desired me to collect the officers of the Brigade round him, on which occasion he paid them a handsome compliment.'[35]

---

32. Captain Charles Allix, Adjutant and Captain Charles Lascelles, 1st Foot Guards, the latter was wounded.
33. Glover, The Correspondence of Sir Henry Clinton, Volume 2, p 114.
34. Glover, The Waterloo Archive Volume VI, p 151.
35. Siborne, The Waterloo Letters, p 310.

Chapter 17

The March on Paris 19 June–5 July

The march to Paris saw little serious fighting for the British troops and does not really impinge on our understanding of the Crisis of the Battle of Waterloo. There are however, a number of incidents on the march and on arrival at Paris, which do indicate something about the capability, morale, discipline and renown of the 52nd Foot, following its actions at Waterloo, which are certainly of relevance. The number of men who deserted or fell out of the march on the way to Paris was very high, reaching a rate of at least one every day (19 in 17 days). It is noticeable however, that few of these were officially recorded as desertions on the Returns quoted at Appendix 3, but this could also be true for other regiments, with those returning later possibly being omitted, in an attempt to hide the problem. This might well be an area worthy of further research in the future. In the absence of General Adam, Colonel Colborne temporarily commanded the Light Brigade, until Adam returned after it arrived at Paris.

Cantonments of the 52nd Foot on the road to Paris

19 June	Herrigue near Nivelles
20 June	Estinne au Mont
21 June	1 mile from Bavay
22 June	Cateau Cambresis
23 June	Cateau Cambresis
24 June	Cateau Cambresis
25 June	Joncour
26 June	Beauvoir
27 June	Roye
28 June	Petit Grevecoeur
29 June	Clermont
30 June	La Chapelle
1 July	Jardin de Paris near St Denis
5 July	Bois de Boulogne
8 July	Lead the Army into Paris

Susan Clinton had mentioned the baggage at Brussels, but a large part of the officers' baggage was reported stolen by Belgian cavalrymen during the confusion of the battle. This later transpired to be wholly untrue, it had been stolen by some of the officers' servants who were from the 52nd Regiment. Lieutenant Holman, who had been sent to Brussels to help organise the efforts to deal with all of the

The March on Paris 19 June–5 July 219

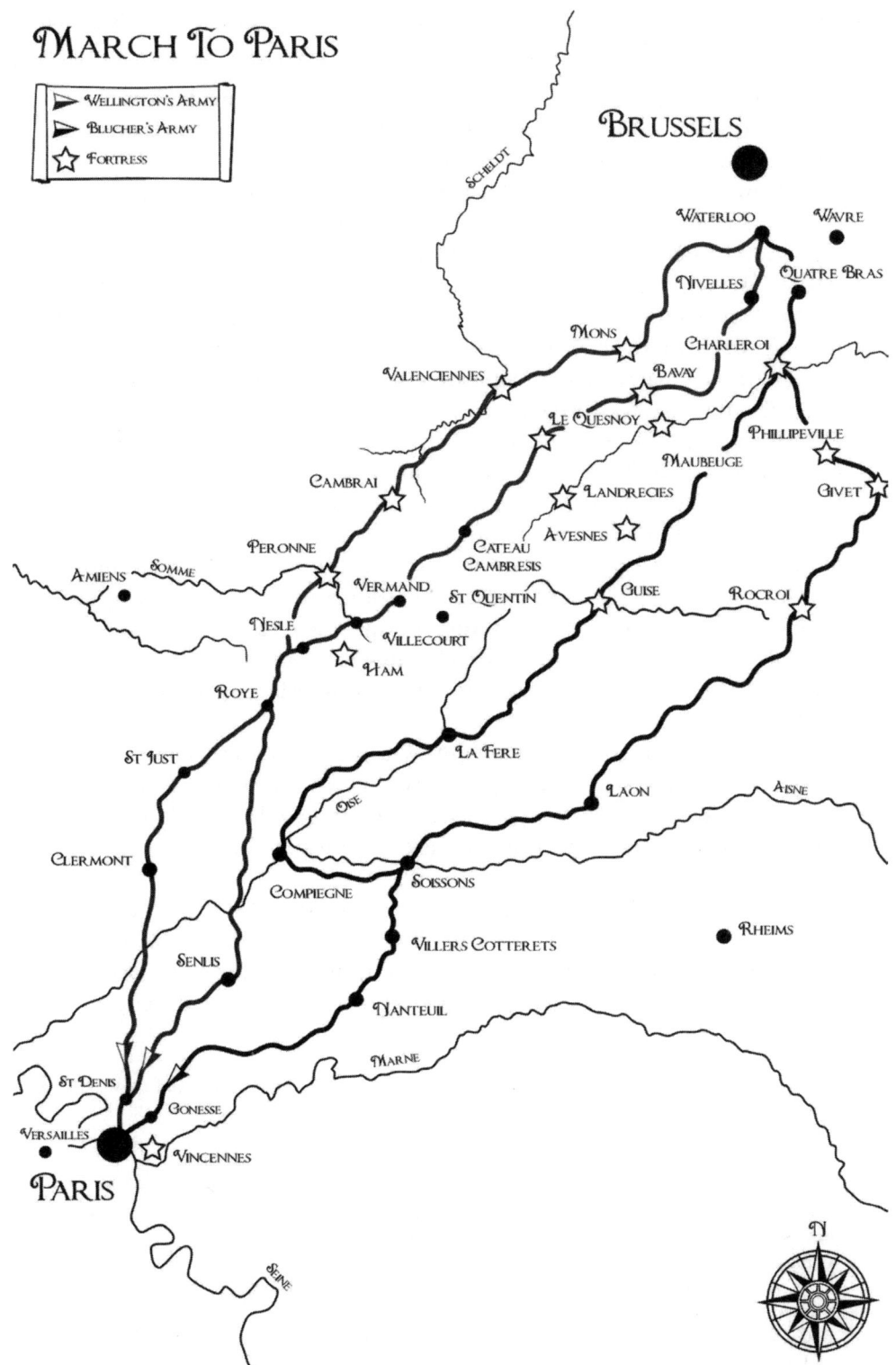

wounded, was one of the first to discover the truth and recorded the subsequent investigation in his daily journal:

> 16th August – Lieutenant Campbell told me of his having made Private Pat Kibby[1] of Major Love's[2] company, batman to Colonel Rowan[3] prisoner, on the suspicion of desertion and of having stolen Colonel Rowan's mare.
>
> At 9am went to the Provost Guard to see the prisoner, who would not confess anything about the mare. At 7pm encountered Privates John Ellson and Scattergood[4] of No.4 Company [P Campbell's], servants, with Private Greig[5] of No.9 Company, servant to Captain McNair,[6] prisoner under escort of an Hanoverian Guard for deserting with the companies beasts and making away with them as well as the officer's baggage. Returned with him to the Provost Guard when he confessed there were some things of Captain McNair's at the Hotel d'Angleterre.
>
> 17th August – Went at 10am with Lieutenant Campbell and prisoner to the Hotel d'Angleterre where we found two trunks, the property of Captain McNair, which I took to my quarters. We then went to the house of one De Wight [Witt?] in Pelican Street, where Greig had been living. On searching an outhouse we found two portmanteaus broken open empty, two oil case baggage covers and a bed belonging to Lieutenant Young [Yonge] and Griffiths.[7] On my return the prisoner Kibby confessed, he had sold Colonel Rowan's mare for 15 Napoleon's[8] to Mr Hillen, No. 576 Place St Michael, immediately sent the Provost Martial [Marshal] [to] claim her.
>
> 18th August – Prisoner Greig confessed there were still some articles at the house of De Wight [Witt?]. We went down and he produced a few shirts and other articles which were sent to Campbell. I ordered De Wight [Witt?] to be confined in the Provost Guard for the night. Received Colonel Rowan's mare.
>
> 19th August – Reported the whole to Major Evatt,[9] who would not interfere, I then called on the mayor and told him I had confined the man as I knew not at that house where to find any of the police of the town. Ordered the prisoner De Wright [Witt?] to be given up to the police of the city.

---

1. This was Private James Kibby of Major Love's Company. The June muster roll shows that he deserted on 18 June 1815.
2. Major (Captain in the regiment) James Frederick Love 52nd Foot
3. Lieutenant Colonel Charles Rowan 52nd Foot.
4. Private John Ellson and Edward Scattergood of Captain P. Campbell's Company
5. Private Charles Gregg of Captain McNair's Company. He deserted on 17 June. He was later court martialled and sentenced to serve abroad for the remainder of his life.
6. Captain James McNair 52nd Foot.
7. Lieutenants William Crawley Yonge and John Rogers Griffiths 52nd Foot.
8. A Napoleon was a gold coin worth 20 Francs.
9. Major George Evatt, 55th Foot, he had superseded Colonel Jones as Commandant of Brussels on 25 July 1815.

20th August – This morning a Commissary of Police came to my quarters and took down my deposition against De Wright [Witt?] and asked me if I meant to prosecute him, which I assured him I did.

21st to 31st August – Several days with the judges about the prosecution of De Wight [Witt?] who at last adjudged him to 2 years hard labour and confinement.[10]

William Leeke is able to provide further detail of later proceedings against Kibby:

The baggage of half the officers of the 52nd was entirely lost, and it was reported that it was plundered on the 18th, on the road to Brussels, by some foreign cavalry, who were running away from the action.

We afterwards learnt the true fate of the baggage of some of the officers. Two of the batmen, of which the man having charge of the string of horses belonging to McNair's company was one, reached Brussels, and had the rascality to pass themselves off as wounded English officers, having managed to rig themselves out with the officer's clothes which had been entrusted to them; they managed to obtain billets from the proper authorities. This was not likely to last long, when there were upwards of 170 wounded officers and men of their own regiment in Brussels, besides the officers and men who had been sent there to look after the wounded; so in the course of three or four weeks they were denounced to the officers, and I recollect our man was sent up to the regiment, and tried by a general regimental court martial, and was sentenced to be transported for seven years. Amongst the clothes which this man had not got rid of, and he had sold the greater part of the things, there were articles of clothing discovered belonging to all the other officers of McNair's company except myself. After the court marshal [sic] I asked him how this happened to be the case, and he told me that in the great confusion which there was amongst the baggage, it was almost impossible for one man to take care of a string of four or five horses, and that much baggage was lost in consequence; that my horse was the last, and that he saw a Belgian peasant cut the rope which fastened him to the horse before him; that he could not leave the leading horse, and that whilst he was loading his firelock to have a shot at the Belgian, some increased confusion took place, and the man succeeded in getting off with my horse and baggage. Very possibly this account was correct. I forget what became of the other delinquent, but he was not tried at the same time with our batman.[11]

The march to Paris was particularly uneventful for the Light Brigade and Leeke continues by giving some details of the actions of the 52nd Foot on arrival outside Paris:

---

10. Holman's Mss Journal, The Green Jackets Museum, Winchester.
11. Leeke, pp 144–5.

On the 1st of July, when we were not many miles from Marshal Moncey's chateau, the 52nd first saw Paris, and the splendid dome of the Hospital of the Invalides in the distance. It was a beautiful day. The regiment moved off the road to the right to a rising ground, called the Jardin de Paris, finding large quantities of fruit trees covering an immense extent of ground. Here they looked down on St Denis, rather towards the left, and the hill of Montmartre, between them and the French capital.

Montmartre appeared very rugged and to be strongly fortified, and our feelings got on to the war establishment again, as we fancied we might very probably have to storm this not very pleasant looking fortified hill on the morrow. It was when we arrived at the Jardin de Paris that we first saw the French troops again after their defeat at Waterloo, they having sent out from St Denis along the high road a few skirmishers to fire at one of the English videttes. It was not a very pleasant post for him to be on sentry in, as he had some thirty or forty fellows blazing away at him for some considerable time at a distance of about 250 yards. As he walked his horse up and down on his post, he occasionally returned the fire of the skirmishers by giving them a shot from his carbine. Sir John Colborne, who had commanded the brigade since the action, Adam and Reynell being wounded, sent down a party of the 71st, who drove the French skirmishers off. I remember we very much enjoyed the ripe currants and cherries on the slope to the right below our bivouac. At the bottom of the slope, about half a mile off, I found a deserted village, in which there were a great number of gentlemen's houses completely plundered, and every atom of furniture destroyed in the most wanton manner by the Prussians, mirrors and chests of drawers, &c, &c, were smashed to atoms. This was the first time that we had come across the Prussian line of march. They were determined to retaliate upon the French civilians all the suffering and cruelty they had experienced at the hands of the French soldiers in bygone years.

On the 2nd of July the 52nd were alone at Argenteuil on the Seine. Here we found the village had been plundered by the Prussians. Three of them who had to turn out of the village, when we arrived there, not being well pleased at being interfered with, did us the favour, when they had proceeded about two or three hundred yards on the road, to send three musket balls whistling through our bivouac; they rather astonished us, but did no harm; and I think the fellows were not followed and punished. In the afternoon of the 2nd McNair's company crossed the Seine in boats and took possession of and loopholed a gentleman's house on the other side, to protect the formation of a pontoon bridge across the Seine; the French troops being about a mile off, but not shewing themselves. The next morning another company of the 52nd joined us, and pushed on an officer and some men to a village in front, from which a few French soldiers hastily retired as they entered it. ... Napoleon having abdicated and fled, by which, amongst other arrangements, it was agreed that there should be a suspension of arms, that the French army opposed to us should evacuate Paris in three days, and retire behind the Loire, and that, within the same space of time, all the barriers of Paris and also Montmartre should be given up. The English and Prussian commissioners, Colonel Hervey and Baron Muffling, were fired at in the streets of Paris, shortly after entering it by the Barrier of Villette; which might have led to very disastrous consequences, but an ample apology was made by the Prince of Eckmuhl and the French commissioners charged with the execution of the convention, and the affair was passed over.

On the afternoon of the 3rd of July the 52nd crossed the Seine on the pontoon bridge, and proceeded to the bridge of Neuilly. We observed places along the side of the road where the Prussians and French were buried who had been killed there, I think, the day before. Sir John Colborne had received orders to cross the bridge of Neuilly; but the French refused to retire from the strong barricade, which had been built across the centre of it. The two front companies of the 52nd (10 and 9) were advanced a very short distance in front of the column of companies, on the road by the side of the river, with fixed bayonets. Sir John Colborne coolly took out his watch and allowed five minutes to the French commander in which to give up the bridge or to have it stormed; in two or three minutes it was given up, some few men coming over and shouting '*Vive le Roi!*' The village of Neuilly, within a short distance of one of the barriers of Paris, was occupied, and the 52nd passed the night in the walled graveyard of that place. The only things I recollect as occurring on that night were the getting some bread and cheese in a cabaret; and, with the assistance of one of the officers, getting late at night a truss of hay for our horses out of the hayloft belonging to a gentleman's house, which was either deserted, or the inhabitants declined to 'show up'.

On the morning of the 4th of July, we saw the last of the French troops, two videttes close to the gate of the graveyard, having two English videttes within twenty paces of them and a French infantry picket about half a mile off on the road to Paris. They soon retired, and the French army began to evacuate Paris that day, and, I think, it was on the same day, that the National Guard of Paris relieved the guard of the troops of the line at the Barriere de l'Etoile. The 52nd proceeded to the Bois de Boulogne, to the right of the road from Neuilly to Paris and remained there till the 7th. On the 5th Montmartre was given up to the English, and on the 6th, I believe, some of our brigade took possession of the Barriere de l'Etoile.

On the morning of the 7th of July General Adam's Brigade (52nd, 71st, and 95th) had the honour of entering Paris by the Barriere de l'Etoile. They marched down the centre of the road leading through the Champs Elysees, to the Place Louis Quinze, (now the Place de la Concorde) and the Tuileries. A brigade of artillery, with lighted matches, was posted close to the barrier on either side of the chaussee. It was a proud and happy moment, when, with bands and bugles playing, we thus took possession of and entered, the capital of France. At least I am sure it was the proudest moment of my life, when I found myself riding down the centre of the avenue of the Champs Elysees, bearing in triumph, into the enemy's capital, that same 52nd Regimental Colour which I had the honour of carrying to victory on the eventful and glorious day of Waterloo. The whole brigade halted and piled arms in the Champs Elysees, to the right of the main road and between it and the Seine, and not far from the Place Louis Quinze. These were the British troops which occupied the French capital; almost the whole of the rest of the Allied army remained in the Bois de Boulogne, although some were at Montmartre. Before the 52nd band was dismissed, Sir John Colborne ordered it to play '*Vive Henri Quatre*,' one of the principal Royalist tunes, but it did not appear to attract any number of people... The 52nd, in the course of the morning, crossed the main road and encamped on the other side of the Champs Elysees, leaving the 71st and 95th on the side nearest to the river, and throwing its sentries forward about 140 yards to the low rail separating the Champs Elysees from the Place Louis Quinze... Close to the large open space in which the 52nd encamped there was a decent restaurateur's. There were several of these places, and also dancing houses, in different parts of the Champs Elysees.

Either the day after we entered Paris, or on the following day, No 9 and No 10 companies of the 52nd were ordered to encamp nearer to the Place Louis Quinze, and near to where the Quarter Guard already was, close to the wall of the Duke of Wellington's garden. The cords of the officers' tents were close to the short palings, which fenced off about ten feet of garden ground between them and the wall. My tent was against the little gate in the palings which led to the garden door, and close up to it, so close that one day, about a week or fortnight after we arrived, I heard somebody floundering about and stumbling over the cords, and, on looking out, found it was the Duke himself, who sometimes, but not often, came out that way. He desired that the tent might be moved a few feet forward. The whole brigade remained encamped in the manner I have mentioned till the 2nd of November, a period of nearly four months.

Lieutenant Colonel W[illiam] Rowan of the 52nd was made commandant of the first arrondissement of Paris. We, who belonged to No 9 and No 10, considered ourselves as an especial guard to the Duke. There was a Sergeant's Guard at the entrance to the courtyard of his residence, in a short street leading out of the Place Louis Quinze. ...

The King, Louis XVIII, reached Paris on the 8th of July, the day after we entered the city. I was present in the Tuileries on the afternoon of the day of his arrival, and I think no one could have desired to have a greater display of enthusiasm and loyalty than was manifested on the occasion of his presenting himself to the people on one of the balconies of the Tuileries looking towards the Champs Elysees. There must have been from fifteen to twenty thousand persons assembled. When the King came forward there was a cry for the people to take their hats off, which almost all appeared to do, and, being tall, I had a good view over the whole assembled people. I was in the midst of the crowd, and whilst they knocked off the hats of one or two obstinate fellows near me, they treated me with marked civility, one patting me on the back, as the Prussian officer did on the night of the Battle of Waterloo, and calling me '*Brave Anglais.*' As an officer in uniform I of course kept my cap on. I saw two other English officers at a distance in the crowd.[12]

Others noted the 8 July as a special day for the regiment, William Rowan noted that:

The Duke made his formal entry into Paris on the 8th of July our brigade only accompanied him. At the Barriere de L'Etoile he and all his Staff placed themselves in front of the 52nd, and with band playing, Colours flying and such, we marched down the Champs Elysees, the 52nd taking up its bivouac close to the Duke's residence, where it remained as his body guard until the end of October.[13]

Lieutenant Shaw, who had missed Waterloo on Baggage Guard would appear to have escaped sanction for the loss of the officers' baggage, rejoined the regiment before Paris:

On the 5th we were encamped in the Bois de Boulogne. On the 7th, having put laurels in our caps by order, we marched through the Champs Elysées, and halting close to the Place Louis XV. bivouacked. There were very many young officers, almost boys, with the regiment. The place was crowded with inhabitants to see the army pass in review, and we joined as spectators.[14]

Adam's Light Brigade had been given the singular honour of leading the British Army into Paris and of maintaining guard at the Duke of Wellington's headquarters, while the Foot Guards and everyone else encamped in the Bois de Boulogne. The column proceeded down the Champs Elysees left to the front, meaning that the 2/95th led, followed by the 52nd, then the 71st and at the rear the 3/95th. At this time, such honours were taken very seriously indeed and it was a potent symbol of Wellington's approval of the actions of Adam's Brigade at Waterloo, that it was given this role, even over the 1st Foot Guards. However, there is some circumstantial evidence that Colborne sought permission for the 52nd to lead the column but was refused. If he did ask, he cannot have been surprised that the Duke maintained a precedent which he had established in 1808. Leeke continues with a few of the highlights of its stay in the city:

---

12. Leeke, pp 148–153.
13. Glover, Letters from the Battle of Waterloo, p 180.
14. Shaw, pp 47–8.

There was no regular officers' mess whilst we were in Paris, but the officers of each company messed together in one of their tents and I remember that I continued to be the caterer and a very inexpensive mess it was, for we none of us cared much about eating and drinking. A considerable number of the Parisians visited our camp from the first, and some of them I know were ladies belonging to superior Bonapartist families; such confidence had they in the discipline and good behaviour of the British soldiers. Crowds of persons came to see us play at cricket, which we sometimes did in the 52nd. It was a game to which the French were unaccustomed, and one speech which was overheard was that, 'no wonder the English were not afraid of cannon balls, when they could so fearlessly meet and stop those dreadful cricket balls coming towards them with such terrific force.' It was a current report at Paris, that the Emperor had said, that 'at Waterloo the English squares had stood like walls, and the French cannon balls could make no impression on them.' Out on the same open place on which we played at cricket, beyond the 52nd encampment, our regular drill was carried on, and as I had done very little in the way of drill before the campaign commenced, I had much to learn after we reached Paris. I perhaps was the only British officer who had the honour of finishing his drill in the French capital. We had many spectators who, of course, were much interested in the light infantry movements, and the bugle sounds. We had some forty men who had to go through the same amount of drill that I had. The 52nd drill instructors were always required to be most particular in the marching drill, from the goose step upwards; and it was to this great attention paid to the balancing of the body in marching, and the avoiding of all flourishing of the foot as it came to the ground, that we used to attribute the good marching of the 52nd, and especially their beautiful advances in line, for which they were very remarkable in my 52nd days...

About ten days after our arrival in Paris, Sir John Colborne (Lord Seaton) very kindly invited me to dine with him at his lodgings, or billet, somewhere to the left, in a line with the principal entrance of the Tuileries from the Place Louis Quinze, and in the street leading down past the end of the Rue de la Paix. I met there only three or four of the senior officers of the regiment and I well recollect his telling me, before them, that I might consider myself one of the most fortunate fellows in the whole army; for I had only been in it two months, and had, in that short space of time, not only taken part in the glorious action at Waterloo, but had also been present at the taking of the capital of France. I kept no journal at that time, and not till about four years afterwards, and then only occasionally during the next four or five years, so that in describing the circumstances that occurred at Paris and elsewhere, I have to trust to my memory, which I have good reason to think is particularly retentive and accurate. ... I was at the Louvre once or twice when this taking down and packing the pictures was going on; whether or not I was there on duty I do not recollect, but I remember seeing a fatigue party of the 52nd there. There was no particular excitement observable amongst the French on that occasion. But about that time the 52nd remained fully accoutred and ready to fall in at a moment's notice, for eight and forty hours, and on one of those two days, we were marched up, and remained for two or three hours on the Place Louis Quinze, in front of the gates of the Tuileries; I think it was when the Austrians were taking down the horses dedicated to the sun from the top of the gateway leading into the Place du Carrousel. They had been taken from Venice. It was expected that much discontent would be manifested by the French, and perhaps some violence on that occasion. Each horse was taken away separately, and was escorted by a whole regiment of Austrian dragoons. I was the orderly officer on the day that the last horse was removed and was sent that evening by Sir John Colborne to report to General Adam, who had recovered from his wound and taken command of the brigade again, that all had passed off quietly.[15]

After a couple of weeks in Paris, Henry Clinton reviewed the 52nd Foot. His report was good overall, but he made a few unexpected comments (the underlining is mine to highlight it):

Champs Elysees, 17th July 52nd Regiment
Field Officers 1, Captains 8, Subalterns 30, Sergeants 47, Drummers 20, Rank & File 755

This battalion is in good serviceable order, the excellent system introduced by Sir J Moore continues its influence, indeed it has been in its full practise under its present good commander Sir J Colborne. The arms, ammunition & appointments are in good order, and as long as there is only a question of successful fighting however severe, the complaint may be this regiment will do its duty <u>but in case unhappily this regiment shall be employed in assaulting a place or in any service in which its subordination shall be called in question to support the authority of its officers, all its good qualities will be of little accord. There is in this respect, a laxity of discipline which is very disgusting</u>, an officer of whatever corps or rank receives from a soldier of this regiment no acknowledgement of respect. Upon a march, they used in the presence of this officer the most disrespectful language, nor do the officers pay the least attention to these instances of disrespect & insubordination, for the sake of security I would rather have in other respects a less efficient corps.[16]

The 52nd Foot was one of a handful of regiments heavily criticised in a General Order for the failure to complete a Return, warning that failure to complete the

---

15. Leeke, pp 157–8.
16. Glover, The Correspondence of Sir Henry Clinton in the Waterloo Campaign Volume 2, p 164.

Return would lead to the arrest of the respective commanding officer! When one realises that only four of these battalions were at Waterloo and the rest would be sending in Nil Returns, it looks even worse.

Headquarters, Paris 1 September 1815
No.1 The following regiments have not sent in the explanation required by the Secretary at War letter of the 28th July 1815 inserted in the General Orders of the eighth of last month.[17]

21st Regiment	1st Battalion
27th Regiment	1st Battalion
27th Regiment	3rd Battalion
37th Regiment	2nd Battalion
39th Regiment	1st Battalion
40th Regiment	1st Battalion
41st Regiment	1st Battalion
44th Regiment	2nd Battalion
52nd Regiment	1st Battalion

No.2 If the explanations are not immediately transmitted to the Adjutant General the Field Marshal will be under the necessity of ordering that the officers commanding the several regiments shall be placed in arrest.

On 2nd September, Henry Clinton exercised the Light Brigade and was again highly critical of Sir John Colborne:

---

17. This refers to: War Office 28 July 1815, to Field Marshal the Duke of Wellington:

    My Lord, His Royal Highness the Prince Regent having taken into his most gracious consideration the distinguished bravery displayed by the non-commissioned officers and soldiers of the British forces of the glorious victory lately gained near Waterloo by the army under your Grace's command and His Royal Highness being desirous of testifying in a marked manner the sense entertained by him of their serving upon that occasion, has been most graciously pleased that hence forward every non-commissioned officers, trumpeters, drummers and private men who served in the Battle of Waterloo or in the actions which immediately preceded it, shall be borne upon the muster rolls and pay lists of their respective corps as 'Waterloo Men' and that every Waterloo man shall be allowed to count two years' service in virtue of that victory in reckoning his service for increase of pay or for pension when discharged.

    It is however to be distinctly understood that this indulgence is not intended in any other manner to effect the conditions of their original enlistments or to give them any right to their discharge before the expiration of the period for which they have engaged to serve.

    I request that your Grace will communicate these, His Royal Highness's gracious orders to the British army under your command & that you will at the earliest opportunity transmit to me a list of the several corps to which this order may be considered by your Grace to apply; with accurate Muster Rolls containing the names of all the Waterloo men in each corps, such Muster Rolls being to be preserved in this office as a record honourable to the individuals themselves and as documents by which they will at any future time be enabled to establish their to the benefits of this regulation.

    I have the honour to be &c Palmerston

I exercised the Light Brigade without the Barriere de Neuilly. The 78th Regiment is improved, <u>the 52nd is seen to great disadvantage under Sir J. Colborne, he knows nothing of manoeuvring and seems to higher himself upon gaining no information on instruction by means of any superior officer</u>. This day the two brigades of British heavy cavalry exercised on the Plain des Sablons.[18]

Such comments, given the renown of Sir John Colborne and the 52nd Foot, may appear to be unfounded and perhaps based on pettiness, however General Adam also reported in similar vein a month later:

Inspection Report of the 1st Battalion 52nd in the Champs Elysees, Paris 26 October 1815

The regiment is in very good order, moves very well, is remarkably pliable and handy, and well versed in the manoeuvres prescribed.

The officers are zealous, attentive and intelligent. The captains are in general a particularly good body of officers; and I have seen no body of subaltern officers so generally well instructed, or who do their duties more exactly. I have every reason to believe that perfect unanimity and good understanding exist in this battalion, a great esprit de corps, and a strong feeling for the reputation of the regiment. Lieutenant Winterbottom is one of the most active, zealous, intelligent of officers in his station I have ever seen, of exemplary gallantry and coolness in action.

The sergeants and corporals are a respectable body of men in their appearance and general conduct, for the most part well instructed and active in their field duties, and, I believe, pay every attention to maintain and promote good order. In their mode of doing duty on guard there is an air of alertness.

The buglers are perfect in their soundings, and the best I know.

The numbers of the musicians are not limited according to regulation. No corps I have ever met with attends to this rule. They are trained to and fit for the ranks.

The privates are on the whole a fine body of men, have every appearance of health, and are remarkably smart and cleanly. They are individually well trained, and do their duty with much exactness and attention. I have not had occasion to observe much drunkenness amongst the men; <u>but with regard to their good behaviour, the Court Martial Return does not bear a favourable testimony</u>. Something, however, in extenuation may be found in the situation of the corps so close to Paris, and the men not accustomed to the temptations of a licentious metropolis. Yet riotous or disorderly conduct publicly has not since under my command been observable.

The arrangements in companies are well attended to, the gradations of duties and the chain of subordination well defined and observed.

---

18. Glover, The Correspondence of Sir Henry Clinton in the Waterloo Campaign Volume 2, p 196.

The men live well, although messes are not established. Every man cooks for himself in the small tin he carries, for this battalion has no camp kettles. Previous to the last campaign it was permitted to deliver them into store, and the experiment has been successful; at least, the proportion of sick has not exceeded that of those corps in the brigade who had camp kettles. The supplies are all drawn from the commissariat. No officer's mess has been established. The necessaries supplied are of good quality and are charged at reasonable prices. No complaints have come to my knowledge, and I do not believe any to exist.

<u>The number of court martials (90) held since my last report is very considerable</u>. Confinement is substituted to a considerable degree for corporal punishment, but a resort to other modes of chastising misdemeanour might be more frequent, and would be advantageous.

The hospitals have been kept in excellent order. Proportion of sick small. Deaths few. The Surgeon, Mr Gibson, is capable, zealous and attentive; and the assistant surgeon competent.

Sixty rounds of ammunition are in possession of each man, and the arms are clean and in excellent order.

The battalion is an excellent corps; and the system upon which it has been formed is superior to that of regiments in general, both as to discipline and interior regulation, as well as instruction, both of officers and men. In some points the original system has been deviated from or relaxed, but still much exactness remains.

An excellent spirit amongst the officers as far the reputation of this corps is concerned, and an habitual exactness in all duties is particularly observable.

<u>Sir John Colborne governs his regiment with a firm hand, but an inclination to deviate from established rule, and a desire of independence of his superior officers, is perhaps one of the causes why a sort of exclusive spirit exists in the battalion.</u>

The body of men is good, but they require a strong hand to keep them in order, and value themselves more than they should.

The men are generally so well drilled individually, that though their movement is not equal to what it was formerly, yet a very little good practice would restore it. Though an officer of superior merit and ability, <u>Sir John Colborne is not a very expert drill.</u>

Taking it all in all, the 52nd 1st Battalion may with justice be deemed one of the finest corps in the service.[19]

There does seem to be a belief that the soldiers of the regiment were too full of their own reputation and that they displayed an arrogance beyond their station. The criticism of Sir John Colborne is quite a shock, however such views in two independent assessments, by very experienced senior officers cannot be easily

---

19. Light Infantry Chronicle of 1914.

brushed aside. Is it possible that his extended period away from the regiment had led him to neglect his basic drill and manoeuvring?

Another inspection by General Henry Clinton on 13 February 1816 praises the regiment but once again makes a comment regarding its general insubordination and Colborne:

> 52nd Regiment of Foot – This is so fine a body of men that out of 900, there are only two men at all exceptionable as to their fitness for service & these were as from accidents, but if this regiment is superior in efficiency, <u>it is greatly deficient in a very important quality, viz insubordination, there is an air in these men generally which bear very much the character of mutinous spirit, they require different means of making some stand from Colonel Colborne, excellent, as in some respects he is, to manage them</u>.[20]

A further review by Henry Clinton in 1816 at Therouanne on 19 April praises the regiment in every way, which he admits he could not find fault with. The sting in the tail however, was his comment that the present commanding officer, Lt Colonel Charles Rowan, had got the regiment under better order than Sir John Colborne ever had!

> 52nd Regiment – Field Officers 1, Captains 7, Subalterns 24, Sergeants 58, Buglers 22, Rank & File 861.

> This regiment has no pioneers, it seems this part of the establishment was taken from it when it was made a light regiment. Lt Colonel Rowan[21] who has commanded the regiment during the last 4 months, is a reliable commanding officer, it bears the mark of great attention having been paid to its wellbeing since my inspection of it in July last. In the most minute inspection I am able to make, nothing appears to give rise to a single infraction, the number in each company either exactly agrees with the state or the commander is ready to explain the reason of any deviation. The arms, accoutrements, ammunition, all are in good order, the clothing though old & worn out is still made to look well, <u>this regiment performs all its movements with expedition & accuracy, in this it is seen to much greater advantage under Colonel Rowan than under Sir J Colborne</u>. It is so healthy that out of 955 rank & file there are only 32 sick, including present & absent & convalescent. Another striking superiority in this regiment over most if not all regiments in our army, is in the appearance & qualities of the whole of the officers. The late Sir J. Moore has bequeathed a valuable legacy to the British army in this proof of the excellence of the system which he introduced.[22]

Other less savoury events regarding the discipline of the regiment also occurred in Paris. William Leeke explained how a 52nd man, had refused the orders of an officer of the 81st Foot when on detachment in May. The officer was court

---
20. Glover, The Correspondence of Sir Henry Clinton in the Waterloo Campaign Volume 2, p 239.
21. Lt. Colonel Charles Rowan.
22. Glover, The Correspondence of Sir Henry Clinton in the Waterloo Campaign Volume 2, p 259.

martialled at Paris for striking the soldier and cutting him, but was very publicly acquitted of all charges. The soldier, a Private James Raw, was then court martialled himself, found guilty of mutiny and sentenced to death by firing squad. The regiment was paraded on three sides of a square to watch the execution, but he was reprieved by the Duke of Wellington at the very last second. Such very public trials, published in General Orders, did nothing to improve the reputation of the regiment for ill-discipline.[23]

On Monday 15th April 1816, Sir Henry Clinton recorded attending another court martial on a man of the 52nd, for murder: 'I went to St. Pol to preside at a court martial upon a corporal of the 52nd Regiment for murder, which was got through in less than 2 hours.'[24]

From this comment, it might appear that he was quickly convicted. In fact, Corporal James Maskell was quickly found 'Not Guilty' and released. Unfortunately, no details of the case have yet been uncovered. My thanks to Zack White for helping me identify both men.

William Leeke itemises its later movements during the Army of Occupation:

> On the 2nd of November 1815, we broke up our agreeable encampment in the Champs Elysees, and went into quarters at Versailles.
>
> About the middle of December 1815, the 52nd marched from Versailles to St Germain.
>
> The 52nd marched from St Germain, I think, on Christmas day 1815, towards the cantonments which they were to occupy in the Pas de Calais.
>
> About the beginning of February 1816, we reached our cantonments in the north of France. The regiment occupied six-and-twenty villages. They were within a circle of which the ancient town (now only a village) of Therouanne might be considered as the centre.

The regiment remained in these cantonments for the next two years, with annual marches to Valenciennes each autumn for a Review and sham fight before returning. In 1818 it proceeded to Valenciennes once again, but then remained there as the garrison, whilst the remainder of the Army of Occupation sailed home. It eventually marched out on 19 November and embarked at Calais on 25 November, arriving at Ramsgate the following day. The 52nd was the very last regiment to return from France after the Waterloo campaign.

---

23. Full details of this case can be found at Appendix 9.
24. Glover, The Correspondence of Sir Henry Clinton in the Waterloo Campaign Volume 2, p 252.

Chapter 18

The Rancour of Jealousy

The Duke of Wellington returned to his quarters in the village of Waterloo physically and emotionally exhausted and his attempts at getting some rest was disturbed by Doctor Hume in the early hours, who came to him to inform him of the death or maiming of dozens of close colleagues and personal friends. In the poor light of his bedroom Hume could not see Wellington's face, but he could feel his tears falling on his arm. The Duke was clearly emotionally broken by this battle and his comment that 'thank God, I don't know what it is to lose a battle; but certainly nothing can be more painful than to gain one with the loss of so many of one's friends' simply reflected the melancholy that overwhelmed him following such terrible carnage.

Despite all of this, the Duke was up at dawn, sitting at his desk to write a despatch for the Prince Regent, declaring the victory, which he did not name, but heading his paper as usual 'Headquarters Waterloo' and the name stuck, over 'Mont St Jean' as the French termed it, or 'La Belle Alliance' as the Prussians preferred, both of which were more correct geographically. Having finished a draft, Wellington rode to Brussels and having checked it over one more time, before giving it to his aide de camp Major Henry Percy, to carry to London.

Wellington was renowned for his terse battle reports, which barely covered the salient facts of the battle and rarely singled out individuals or regiments for specific praise.[1] His Waterloo despatch was no different and many hoping for a mention were to be bitterly disappointed.

His description of the actual battle is particularly short, dealing more with the operations that culminated in the Battle of Waterloo and those of his Prussian allies, than any detailed account of the battle itself. Indeed, d'Erlon's attack and the stout defence by his heavily outnumbered infantry on his left wing is completely ignored, beyond a brief mention of the subsequent charge of the British heavy cavalry and the capture of many prisoners and one [sic] eagle.

The subsequent huge French cavalry attacks on the allied right centre receives no comment and the final defeat of the Imperial Guard only receives a cursory

---

1. The number of regiments mentioned fell throughout Wellington's wars. At Busaco in 1810 he picked out no fewer than 22 regiments for praise; at Fuentes d'Onoro in 1811 he mentioned 16; at Salamanca in 1812 only two regiments are named; at Vitoria in 1813 again only two; at the Pyrenees in 1813 he did mention 15 regiments but this describes operations over some five days; at the Nivelle he did not mention any regiments specifically, at the Nive in 1813 he mentions 2 and at Toulouse in 1814 he mentioned six. In his Waterloo Despatch covering both Quatre Bras and Waterloo he mentioned seven regiments.

mention, which does not even hint at the Imperial Guard being involved at all. There is no mention of either Maitland's Guard Brigade, Adam's Light Brigade or Chasse's troops, nor indeed are the subsequent charges of the British light cavalry brigades alluded to. Indeed, it is perfectly fair to say that Wellington really pleased no one with his despatch. The only mention of the Guards was in relation to the defence of Hougoumont, which does get a short paragraph, but of course Wellington personally viewed it as the key to his entire position, no matter what some recent historians think of that.

So having written so little on the battle itself, how was it that Lord Bathurst was standing up in Parliament only five days after the battle, announcing that the Imperial Guard had been defeated by the British 1st Foot Guards and prompting the Prince Regent to announce that he was renaming the regiment the 'Grenadier Guards' in commemoration?

Henry Bathurst, the 3rd Earl Bathurst, was Secretary of State for War and the Colonies. His eldest son, Henry Lord Apsley, was in Brussels as a civilian in June 1815, and another son, Seymour, was an Ensign in the 1st Foot Guards and served at the Battle of Waterloo. Henry wrote to his father from Brussels on 19 June and he probably had the letter sent in the official despatch bag, and it certainly would have been in London by 22 June. This letter has been readily available to anyone who wanted to find it in Bathurst's correspondence. In it Apsley states:

> I saw Seymour before I went to bed and also Algernon Greville; he is safe. I took him a bottle of brandy this morning to comfort him after three nights bivouacking without baggage ... The Duke has forgot to tell you in his despatch that the French not only left all their cannon, baggage etc, but that they threw away their arms and knapsacks. Such a sight as the field of battle was never seen. Bonaparte had a scaffolding built out of cannon shot for him, but when the battle went against him, the prisoners say he led the Imperial Guard in person. He was met by the 1st Regiment of the Guards, which threw them quite over. Seymour was in this affair.[2]

The mail would easily be in London from Brussels within three days and on 23 June Earl Bathurst stood up to announce the great victory in Parliament. Within his long speech of thanks, he announced that:

> Towards the close of the day, Bonaparte himself, at the head of his Guards, made a desperate charge upon the British Guards, and the British Guards instantly overthrew the French.[3]

The similarity between his son's letter and Bathurst's speech makes it clear where he got the information from. The answer was simple and as can readily be seen, it was not via any top secret message sent from Wellington and delivered by Percy

---

2. Glover, The Waterloo Archive Volume VII, p 266.
3. Hansard The Parliamentary Debates from the Year 1803 to the Present Time Volume 31, p 973

(by hand or even verbally for greater secrecy) as some have tried to claim, it was far more ordinary than that. In July 1815 the Prince Regent issued a proclamation naming the 1st Foot Guards, 'Grenadier' in recognition of its having defeated the French Grenadiers of the Imperial Guard. It read:

War Office 29 July 1815[4]

The Prince Regent, as a mark of his Royal approbation of the distinguished gallantry of the Brigade of Foot Guards in the victory of Waterloo, has been pleased in the name and on the behalf of His Majesty, to approve of all the Ensigns of the three regiments of Foot Guards having the rank of Lieutenants, and that such rank shall be attached to all the future appointment to ensigncies in the Foot Guards, in the same manner as Lieutenants of those regiments obtain the rank of Captain.

His Royal Highness has also been pleased to approve of the 1st Regiment of Foot Guards being made a regiment of Grenadiers, and styled 'The 1st or Grenadier Regiment of Foot Guards' in commemoration of their having defeated the Grenadiers of the French Imperial Guards upon this memorable occasion.

Whilst encamped in the Bois de Boulogne at Paris in early August, the Guards would have received news of this Royal proclamation with great pride, but the Light Brigade also heard the news and were almost certainly not so enamoured, with the 52nd particularly believing that they deserved to receive at least a share of the honours, if not to receive them all.

To the ensigns of the 52nd Foot, the implementation of 'double rank'[5] for ensigns in the Guards battalions particularly rankled with them and certainly caused William Leeke to feel aggrieved and to fight the case for the 52nd for the rest of his life. I say 'probably' as the evidence in 1815 is very scant indeed, with lieutenants Holman and Hart, being the only officers to record their thoughts contemporaneously and neither mention any dispute with the Guards at all, which I think is very telling.

Observant readers may have noticed that neither Wellington nor Lord Apsley had mentioned that they had defeated the Grenadiers of the Imperial Guard and Earl Bathurst did not say this in his speech to Parliament, so where did that claim come from?

A number of officers of the 1st Foot Guards actually wrote directly to the Duke of York immediately after the battle (many dated 19 June). This is explained by the fact that the Duke of York was then Colonel of the 1st Foot Guards and officers were obviously 'toadying' up to him. One such letter, emanating from Lieutenant Colonel the Honourable James Stanhope stated:

---

4. The London Gazette issue 17045, p 1537.
5. Guards officers then held a rank in the regiment and were classed as one rank higher within the army, always making them the senior officer over any line officers of the same regimental rank. This had always been the case for officers of the rank of lieutenant or higher, but not previously for ensigns.

> The most gratifying event of the whole day was the desperate attack, made about seven o'clock by the Imperial Guard, headed by Buonaparte in person. His Grenadiers attacked the Guards, and had soon cause to find they would not sup in Brussels.[6]

Such letters to the Duke of York, brother to the Prince Regent are undoubtedly the reason that the Prince decided to rename the Grenadier Guards in recognition of its feats. No evidence for a campaign to gain honours for the Guards has ever been linked to the Duke of Wellington, indeed the Duke had no affiliation with the regiments of Guards. Indeed, Wellington spent the whole of the war complaining at his inability to retain or influence in any way the deployment of battalions, he was always moaning that he was merely at the whim of Horse Guards. To claim that Wellington secretly sought honours for the Guards over the Light Brigade is simply wrong. No letters on such matters have ever materialised in his own files of correspondence or of any of his recipients and any attempt to claim that their absence proves that there was a 'cover up' right at the heart of government has simply no basis in fact whatsoever.

Other subsequent claims which are aimed to give substance to these conspiracy theories will be dealt with in the following chapter, but here we must discuss the consequences of this royal recognition of the Guards and the acrimonious debate it engendered which still rankles within certain quarters of the two regiments to this day.

In the early afternoon, Sir George Cooke commanding the 1st Division, was wounded and Sir John Byng took overall command. He was therefore an eyewitness but did not take command of the First Guard Brigade, which was, of course, commanded by Maitland.

> About four o'clock the command of the division devolved upon me, and, having rode over to see the First Brigade, just at the time the attack was made by the enemy's cavalry, I had an opportunity of witnessing the steady manner in which they received the several charges made to their front.
>
> I had also to witness the gallantry with which they met the last attack made by the Grenadiers of the Imperial Guard, ordered on by Buonaparte himself, the destructive fire they poured in, and the subsequent charge, which, together, completely routed the enemy. A second attempt met with a similar reception, and the loss they caused to the French, of the finest troops I ever saw, was immense. I beg you, Sir, to understand that my presence or advice to General Maitland never was required; I merely stayed with him as an humble individual, when the assistance of every one was required. His own judgment and gallantry directed everything that was necessary.[7]

Sir John Colborne did write in later years that he had discussed the 'Crisis' with Major General Sir John Byng at Paris, who then commanded the entire Guards Division:

---

6. Glover, The Waterloo Archives Volume I, p 133.
7. Glover, The Waterloo Archive Volume IV, p 144.

> Sir John Byng mentioned to me, at Paris, that he observed our movement in front of his brigade, and that at this time his brigade had no ammunition left. Lord Hill mentioned to me also that he was near the Brigade of Guards when he observed the 52nd moving across the plain, that some men of the British Guards were retiring, that he ordered them to advance, waving his hat to them.
>
> I think, therefore, that this was the time when a portion of the Imperial Guards halted to fire on the 52nd, and that immediately after this halt the British Guards charged, and made their forward movement. It appears to me evident, if this statement be correct, the movement of the 52nd took place some time before any forward movement was made by the Guards.
>
> I have been particular in stating many unimportant occurrences, because I am persuaded several absurd blunders and stories have originated from the movements of the 52nd, and General Adam's Brigade, having been misrepresented.[8]

There are hints from some of the Guards that they were short of ammunition and that some men were using French cartridges they picked up from the corpses but claims that Lieutenant Colonel Stanhope was sent off to desperately find ammunition are incorrect. He makes it clear that he was sent off to find horses to drag off some abandoned artillery pieces in its front, well before the Guard attack began and returned (having failed in the task) as it occurred.

However, Lieutenant Colonel Henry Rooke, who was actually in the 3rd Foot Guards, but acting as Assistant Adjutant General to the division confirms that:

> I was not with the First Brigade at the moment he [Siborne] particularly refers to, and therefore I cannot positively answer the question he seems most anxious about. I had left them about two minutes previous to that. The division was in want of ammunition. Two or three officers had been sent to order it up but could not find it and Sir John Byng wished me to go, as I knew where it was placed. Before I got back the attack had been made and the brigade had since advanced.[9]

Colborne's claims are backed by William Leeke, who wrote that he recalled that:

> Shortly after the 52nd reached Paris and were encamped in the Champs Elysees, Sir John Colborne gave us the following account of what Sir John Byng had said, on meeting him a day or two before. He said, 'How do your fellows like our getting the credit of doing what you did at Waterloo? I could not advance when you did, because all our ammunition was gone.' Some little time afterwards, when Sir John Colborne met Byng, and tried to lead him to speak on the subject again, he found him quite disinclined to do so. Many years afterwards, I think it was in 1850, when I was dining with Lord Seaton in town, one of his sons requested me to try and draw his father out

---

8. Siborne, The Waterloo Letters, p 287.
9. Glover, Letters from the Battle of Waterloo, p 158.

to talk about Waterloo, saying that he often told them about his other battles, but they could not get him to speak much about that.

I took an opportunity of asking him if he recollected much about Waterloo, and I suppose I particularised the charge of the 52nd on the Imperial Guard, for I remember he said, 'Did you ever hear what Sir John Byng said to me at Paris?' I replied that I had a very distinct recollection of it; but that I should be very much obliged if he would repeat to me what Sir John Byng had said, in order that I might see, if my recollection of it exactly tallied with his. Lord Seaton then gave me the account of what passed on the two occasions of his meeting Byng, just as I have related it above, and exactly as I remembered to have heard it from him five and thirty years before in the camp at Paris.[10]

This certainly backs up Colborne's claim and I have no reason to doubt its authenticity. There is, however, a major difference between being completely out of ammunition and requiring a replenishment before that situation occurred. No eyewitness from the Guards complains of seriously running out of ammunition, it would seem that they were low rather than completely out of it. Indeed, until the initial request was sent out in late 1830 by William Siborne, to officers who were at Waterloo for information on where their regiments had stood and what they were doing at the time of the 'Crisis', there was little discussion of these matters. It was however, like opening Pandora's Box and all of that pent-up anger and frustration was unleashed on this poor unsuspecting captain, who was then only trying to produce a model.

Siborne was soon embroiled in the claims and counter claims from the Guards, the 52nd and Vivian's cavalry, all suddenly demanding the lion's share of the accolades for the overthrow of the Imperial Guard and the subsequent rout of the French army.

All of them were trying to remember events from more than fifteen years ago, many having significant incidents deeply embedded in their memories, but with little certainty as to the exact timing or even sequence of these events. This undoubtedly engendered discussion between former colleagues and in time no doubt, many of these distant memories became rearranged and altered by these discussions and eventually morphed into hard fact and certainty, although questionable as to its correctness.

These agreed views than became entrenched and a virulent correspondence began with Lieutenant Gawler's *The Crisis and Close of the Action at Waterloo, by an eyewitness,* published in the United Services Journal No. 56 for July 1833. Unfortunately, the lengthy article sought to claim all of the laurels for the 52nd and sought to deny the validity of the claims of all other regiments, even those within the Light Brigade. Realising the inflammatory nature of the article, the editor allowed Sir Hussey Vivian the opportunity to counter it in the same edition. This sparked a heated debate of course, with articles from Banner of the 23rd Light Dragoons and Reynell of the 71st amongst others being published

---

10. Leeke, p 80.

in subsequent journals, questioning these assertions. Finally, after two years of wrangling, Gawler published *A Correction of some points in 'The Crisis of Waterloo'* in the Journal for March 1835, which seems to have placated most with a version which gave others at least some of the laurels. This did not stop a number of people writing to Siborne privately, however, ranting at such claims. Here are a couple of these, to give a flavour. Sir Hussey Vivian, who was determined to see the exploits of his cavalry properly recorded, wrote: 'Truth is history, and history without truth does not deserve the name; and I am anxious for the sake of the gallant men I commanded, that one day at least the truth may be known.'[11] Whereas Captain Arthur Shakespear of the 10th Hussars was a little more heated:

> What do the Guards say to this statement, because if true, the 52nd take all credit from them – as Major Gawler says, they charged across their front!
>
> His arrogating for the 52nd all the glory of the crisis, deserves severe handling. Those who served under you, will feel thankful for the part you have taken, in defending the brigade, and indeed other regiments, entitled to share the honour of the day.[12]

In fact, the response from members of the Guard was particularly muted, this could be because they had already been given many of the victor's laurels and did not want to reignite the argument. Although the arguments had now largely died away, the rancour never left and it has been given new life periodically.

William Leeke's *The History of Lord Seaton's Regiment*, published in 1860, made no bones regarding his distaste for Gawler's compromise and vehemently argued once again for the 52nd to receive all of the accolades for defeating the Imperial Guard and routing the French army single-handedly. He sought the evidence from other surviving officers of the regiment to back his claims. As I have explained throughout this volume, some of his claims have been shown to be incorrect or exaggerated, but that his general narrative was honest and in agreement with many established facts. However, the refusal to accept that any other corps, even those of his own brigade, should share any of the glory has, and rightly, should be challenged. It is a good attempt at an honest account, but is undoubtedly too heavily biased by regimental loyalties, which blind it to some incontrovertible truths.

The *Origin and History of the First or Grenadier Guards*, published in three hefty volumes by Lieutenant General Sir F. Hamilton in 1874 certainly sought to reimpose the 1st Foot Guards as the prime cause of the defeat of the Imperial Guard, whilst generously accepting that the Light Brigade shared some of the glory. By this time of course, Leeke was no longer living, to continue the debate.

An uneasy truce therefore remained for the next century, with neither regiment claiming all of the glory, but both quietly assuming that their own regiment deserved the greater plaudits, whilst trying to avoid another huge public argument.

---

11. Siborne, The Waterloo Letters, p 160.
12. Glover, Letters from the Battle of Waterloo, p 93.

Chapter 19

Investigating the Claims

This relative peace was shattered once again in 2005, when the first of two volumes was published, which not only claimed all of the glory for the 52nd, but also began to expound a huge conspiracy theory in which the Duke of Wellington knowingly sought to deny the regiment the glory and instead actively sought to give it all to the Guards, for his own means. A second volume published in 2014 continued this same theory, but interestingly, it abandoned almost all of the original arguments provided as evidence for the conspiracy, but replaced them with new and even more explosive claims.

Conspiracy theories are almost impossible to investigate entirely, and notoriously difficult to refute, simply because the evidence that is missing/lost over the centuries is so easily used to back up claims that they have been destroyed in a cover up. Lack of evidence becomes proof of the highest order in its own right.

This however, for a historian, cannot be seen as good history. That is not to say that there was no conspiracy, but that the evidence that we do have must be properly analysed and evaluated, whilst personal motives must be critically assessed.

My role as a military historian is to attempt to remove the gaping holes we have in much of our knowledge, using the primary sources we do have, to work out what the missing documents probably said from the hints contained in other documents. The views of eyewitnesses have to be carefully assessed, taking into account the length of time after events that it was written, and assessing the motives and intentions of the author to establish their overall reliability. Comparing numerous accounts, although they always vary in some aspects, there is usually a thread of commonality which allows the correct version of events to be surmised, but this always has to be subjective. It is impossible to be cast iron certain regarding anything we read or surmise from it, but history has to be based largely on corroborative accounts and the blanks filled in with likelihoods based on years of research on how people at that time usually dealt with such situations. It is surprisingly reassuring that in most cases they thought and acted very similarly to ourselves, times were very different, but we as human beings have not changed that markedly.

Some of the claims that are used to back the conspiracy theories, have been fully investigated at the appropriate point in this volume, but many of the claims are not directly related to the actual events on the battlefield on that fateful day in June 1815 and need to be investigated separately. I have previously investigated a number of the claims in the original 2005 volume and it is noticeable that most of these claims were quietly dropped without comment in the 2014 version. I have, however, chosen to repeat them here although I have fully updated them, as these old claims often linger and, although fully discredited, have an amazing ability to rise again, like a phoenix from the ashes.

I hope that I have described fairly and without favour the role of the 52nd in the battle and the honest achievements of each other regiment involved. I do believe that the 52nd were unfairly treated in the aftermath of the battle, but were they caught up in part of some grand conspiracy? I'm not so sure. Let us look at the actual evidence for and against.

1. Has the battlefield been materially altered by the building of the Lion Mound and if so, where?

We do know that for the construction of the Lion Mound between 1822 and 1826, earth was removed from the allied ridge, but to what extent and exactly what was removed?

It is sometimes stated that the site of the Mound was chosen to represent the exact spot where the Prince of Orange was wounded around the time of the Crisis, but it was actually constructed simply on the best spot for ease of construction. The position chosen was a natural plateau area which extended for about one hundred yards to the south of the track running along the ridge line and then it descends slowly all the way across the valley towards La Belle Alliance, forming a ridge or watershed between La Haye Sainte and Hougoumont. This means that even on horseback, anyone situated at the one location cannot see anything of the other. Claims that this plateau area was removed to construct the Lion Mound are completely unfounded, the plateau forming the perfect base to build upon. This area is therefore virtually as it was at the time of the battle except for the mound being added on top.

The Lion statue stands at 43m tall (141 feet) on a circular column of brick, which supports its weight and provides a solid core for the earthen ramp raised around it, which has a circumference of 520 metres. It is calculated that 287,000 cubic metres of earth were taken from the allied ridge to construct it.[1]

Looking at the Gordon monument today, perched high above the surrounding land, it can be seen how much earth was removed from the southern side of the allied ridge between the crossroads and the Lion Mound. Surveyors have suggested that some three to four metres of soil have been removed from the allied ridge south of the road running along the crest line up to the crossroads and this, with possibly smaller amounts taken from the area just north of the mound, would have supplied all of the soil needed for the monument. The allied ridge to the west of the mound was not changed at all and neither was the ground to the east of the crossroads.

Changes to levels here have been affected over two hundred years by soil erosion, which has accelerated with intensive farming. It is calculated that up

---
1. Taken from a full RTK GPS survey produced for Channel 5 Television in 2003.

to 1.5 metres of earth has washed from the ridges and has been deposited in the bottom of the valleys, making both heights and troughs much less pronounced than they would have been two hundred years ago.

Conclusion – The battlefield has only been majorly altered on the forward slope, where up to four metres of soil was removed from the area to the immediate east of the Lion Mound right up to the crossroads and very little alteration was made to the rest of the battlefield. Subsequent soil erosion over two centuries has however removed 1 metre off the tops of the ridges and raised the valley floors by up to 2 metres since 1815.

2. Did Wellington both See and Approve the Movement of the 52nd?
It is claimed that Wellington was behind the First Brigade of Guards when the 52nd made its flank movement and that he therefore downplayed the role of the 52nd as he was not personally involved.

Wellington was certainly behind the Guards when they drove back the first attack of the Imperial Guard and Leeke is a witness to a host of skirmishers (disbanded squares?) of Imperial Guardsmen running down the face of the ridge. The Guards apparently pursued these for a short distance before returning to the ridge line on the appearance of another column to its right. Wellington was now free to observe what occurred and to react to it.

Captain Logan and Private Lewis of the 2nd Battalion 95th are both witnesses to the fact that Wellington personally ordered it to follow the movement of the 52nd. General Adam had sent Major of Brigade, Thomas Hunter Blair to enquire what Colborne intended to do and it is certain that he approved and immediately ordered the 71st and 3/95th to support it. We have further evidence that Wellington then rode down to the KGL battalions at Hougoumont and ordered them to further support this movement as witnessed by 1st Line Battalion KGL.

In one of Colborne's accounts of the battle he even admits that the Duke sent an order to attack the Imperial Guard column about the time that he decided to order the advance himself:

> A strong company of the 52nd was sent to skirmish in front, and to fire into the Imperial column. At this moment General Adam came to the 52nd from the 71st and desired the 52nd to move on. The Duke it appears at the same time, had sent Colonel Percy to the 52nd to move on, the 52nd however were already in motion, its right flank totally unprotected, and marched off in two lines [four ranks] well formed and covered by the skirmishers commanded by Lieutenants Anderson and Campbell, who had directions to push on, and to look to the whole battalion as their support.[2]

This means that Wellington had to be close enough to see the movement and fully approved of it. Because he had sent an order for it to charge the column, he may well have honestly believed that they were reacting to his order rather than doing so of their own volition.

---

2. Glover, Letters from the Battle of Waterloo, p186.

Conclusion: Wellington was close enough, that if he had wanted to, he could have cancelled the movement very quickly. In fact, the Duke appears to have appreciated the movement very quickly and approved of it. The evidence shows that he also personally ordered up all the other units he could find in the vicinity to support it.

3. Were the corps and divisional senior officers, namely Lord Hill and General Clinton, absent from this part of the front and therefore played down the significance of the actions of the 52nd?

We have two eyewitnesses, both Hill's aides de camp, that Lord Hill was in the vicinity when the 52nd advanced and indeed was so close to the action that his horse was shot, by which he took a heavy fall, and he was believed to have been killed for some time. Sir Henry Clinton was also near enough to have witnessed the movement and we know that he rode over to personally order Halkett's Hanoverian Brigade forward (although only the Osnabruck Battalion actually received the order, because the officer carrying the message was then killed).

Conclusion: Every senior officer in this sector of the battlefield was in the vicinity of the Imperial Guard attack and quickly became apprised of Colborne's movement and readily ordered up units to fully support it. In fact, they attempted to get not only the entire 2nd Division on the move in support, but as much of the 4th Brigade as possible in addition.

Indeed, Clinton's private letters, written immediately after the battle, were more effusive regarding the performance of Du Plat's and Halkett's Hanoverian troops. It would appear that the manoeuvre was fully supported by Clinton but was not regarded by him as anything especially outstanding for experienced British troops and simply expected it of them!

4. Why did Colborne and the remainder of the Light Brigade move directly towards the chaussee across the valley floor?

Having driven the Imperial Guard column away, we know that some of the French soldiers fled along the track which is still there today, towards La Belle Alliance. There are two obvious reasons for that, in that it took them directly back towards their Guard reserves and of course travelling on the track would be quicker for them than marching through the fields of crops.

The fact that the Light Brigade chose not to follow this route is therefore something that needs to be addressed. It is clear that not all of the Imperial Guards moved off in that direction, some being pushed directly eastwards and some (probably from the rear of the column) appear to have retired more directly to the south. Given this fanning out of the routed fugitives, what motivated Colborne to continue eastwards?

Claims that he aimed for La Haye Sainte and could see French troops massed here, could only have been written by someone who has never been on the battlefield. It is perfectly obvious when there, that when the 52nd defeated the Guard column they were in quite a deep trough and even those officers on horseback, could see nothing beyond the watershed, which rises at a steady incline from the valley floor. The obvious answer therefore was that Colborne was aware that some French forces including artillery were still in operation near the plateau area and could be seen along the ridge line of the watershed. A move across the valley would therefore threaten the line of retreat of these troops and cause them to pull back. Only once over the ridge of the watershed, would their situation as regards to La Haye Sainte become apparent and the troops were then made to enter the chaussee between La Haye Sainte orchard and the deep cutting some 400 yards to the south of the farm. This was the only place where they could cross the chaussee without having to scramble down steep embankments and then ascend the other side and thus maintaining their organisation.

It must also be reiterated, that we know that both Wellington and General Adam were close to the rear of the brigade and if the line of advance had not been to their liking, they could have easily altered it. The fact that there is no evidence they did so makes it clear that the direction of movement was fully sanctioned (if only by silence) and was the most militarily-sound option.

Conclusion: The movement of the brigade along the valley floor was designed to relieve pressure on the troops in the centre, by threatening the rear of the French troops still pressing the allied line here. The decision regarding exactly where was the best place to join the chaussee was only decided once over the crest of the watershed.

5. Did the movement of the Light Brigade onto the chaussee just south of La Haye Sainte cause the French defenders to abandon the farm?

This is an additional claim that has recently arisen to further enhance the claims of the 52nd to have been the chief architects of the final defeat of Napoleon's army.

Such claims have arisen from the obvious fact that the movement of the Light Brigade into the French rear on the chaussee would undoubtedly have unnerved the defenders and almost certainly caused those Frenchmen still struggling on the allied ridge to think again and to begin to fall back. This is supported by the evidence of Captain Leach of the 1/95th who wrote:

> A very short time (a few minutes only I think) before Picton's Division joined in the general advance against the French position, the French suddenly evacuated the farmhouse and retreated in haste; and this, I conclude, was in consequence of the total repulse of the Imperial Guards, and the forward movement of a part of the Duke of Wellington's right wing. [3]

I think it not improbable that some troops may have fled from La Haye Sainte at this point and we know certainly that the remnants of the Imperial Guard were ousted from the orchard by Detmer's brigade soon after, so Leach may well have

---

3. Siborne, The Waterloo Letters, p 367.

seen these fugitives. It must also be noted that he states that the general advance occurred only minutes later. But was La Haye Sainte abandoned because of the Light Brigade? When Sir John Lambert's Brigade took over the farm complex during the general advance it is stated that:

> When the general advance was ordered ... I do not recollect that the enemy made any stand at the Haye Sainte; all that could get away retired, leaving it full of wounded, and many prisoners were made there.[4]

This indicates that many troops were still holed up there and only retired on the general advance, so it is clear that they had not abandoned it wholesale when the Light Brigade passed, or even after Detmer's troops cleared the orchard. This is confirmed by Captain Simpronius Stretton of the 40th Foot, who recalled that:

> When the British line moved forward, the 40th drove the tirailleurs from the rising ground in its front, and occupied it; at the same time the 27th, with the grenadiers of the 40th, took possession of La Haye Sainte, in which they made prisoners of a general officer and a party of the enemy.[5]

Conclusion: The advance of the Light Brigade weakened the defence of La Haye Sainte, but it was not abandoned by the French and small parties of unwounded French troops were captured within, as well as numerous wounded at the general advance.

6. Were many of the killed and wounded of the 52nd Foot actually caused by British cannon fire?

It has been claimed, because the 2/95th had to pass through the guns of Beane's Troop Royal Horse Artillery during its advance and that the artillerymen were seen to fire a few of their cannon at the Imperial Guard as the Light Brigade advanced, that the majority of the losses of the 52nd occurred from this fire rather than that of the Imperial Guard. This is what the modern army calls a 'blue on blue' incident. The evidence for this is based on the account of Private Aldridge of 2/95th who stated that:

> The French came up in three columns abreast of each other; they looked like quarter distance columns ... saw the 52nd move forward to the right of the 2nd 95th and charge those columns. About the same moment Lord Wellington ... said 'Order the 95th to charge' ...one artilleryman who was lying under the guns jumped up with a match in his hand and let off two or three that were loaded. The left of the 95th passed through the guns.[6]

It is interesting that he claimed he saw three columns abreast of each other i.e. deployed. Lieutenant Maunsell of Bean's Troop confirms that it was his guns that: 'continued firing on the advancing columns until our infantry advanced to

---

4. ibid, p 393.
5. ibid, p 401.
6. ibid, p 302.

the charge, when a battalion of the Rifle Corps passed through the intervals of our guns.'[7]

This confirms that the guns fired for as long as possible on the column and stopped when the riflemen passed through and moved in front of it. There is also no reason to disbelieve that Aldridge witnessed a gunner fire off three cannon BEFORE the column passed in front of the guns.

As the 2/95th mirrored the movement of the 52nd and was able to advance with it, being on the innermost point of the pivot and did not have to march anywhere to get into position, there is no reason to believe that the 52nd was further in advance of it and therefore in front of the cannon when they were fired. A detailed study of the casualty rates by company show that the left companies of the 52nd did not suffer any more casualties than the right, this proves that the artillery firing on the left of the regiment did not cause any appreciable loss, if any. However, the clearest evidence that the 52nd was not struck down by its own cannon, is simply the fact that not one individual in the regiment, in the battery, or the 2/95th claims or even hints that it may have happened. Leeke accounts completely for its losses, which he puts at 150 men killed and wounded, purely to the fire of the Imperial Guards. Leeke is not the sort of man to gloss over such a catastrophic incident, particularly as it would have shown his regiment in an even greater light, having been mauled by his own side!

The one mention that Lieutenant Colonel William Rowan's horse was shot at around this time by 'grape shot' must be taken with a large pinch of scepticism, as no one had any opportunity to examine the horse minutely or extract the ball to ascertain its size. A musket ball fired close range into the vitals of a horse could bring it down just as effectively. It is also surprising how far cannister (grape was only fired at sea where they used iron cannon; as the iron balls scoured the inner chamber of brass cannon, damaging them) balls could fly. No French cannister rounds are known to have been fired within three hundred metres of Hougoumont or at the farm complex, yet 'Waterloo Uncovered' have unearthed a few French cannister balls in the walled garden.

Conclusion: Absence of even a single hint that the 52nd was struck by cannister shot fired by its own side, means that any such claim is groundless and nothing but pure speculation. Given the number of casualties suffered at this time, any possibility of allied guns having inflicted such carnage on their own troops would certainly have engendered a mention at the very least.

7. Was the Imperial Guard column, which was defeated by the Light Brigade, escorted by artillery?

It is generally accepted that each of the French columns of the Imperial Guards were escorted by a few artillery pieces on their right flank. The Imperial Guard units that advanced towards the plateau area certainly appear to have had artillery with them and the allied troops in this area suffered heavily from close range

---

7. ibid, p 225.

cannister fire. If cannon had escorted the column attacked by the Light Brigade, such positioning would however have prevented the artillery from being used against the 52nd as its own Imperial Guard was in the way.

However, some doubt must be cast over whether this column did have artillery with it. It is not mentioned by anybody, either French or Allied, in any of the numerous accounts of the 'Crisis'. Given the sudden collapse of the French column and its immediate hurried retreat to the southeast, they would have had to retreat straight through these guns. Such heavy weapons were not very manoeuvrable on boggy ground and it would not have been possible for the guns to turn around and retire at anywhere near the same rate as the infantry of the Imperial Guard. They would therefore have been left very vulnerable to being taken as a complete unit or the cannon themselves would have had to have been abandoned. Despite this no eyewitness from the Light Brigade mention capturing or even seeing any French artillery as they advanced, until they approached La Belle Alliance.

Conclusion: The fact that there is no mention of cannon being captured or even pursued soon after the defeat of the Imperial Guard column, it appears highly unlikely that they were escorted by cannon at all.

8. Was the general advance only ordered some fifteen to twenty minutes after the attack by the Light Brigade?

An attempt has been made to identify where and when the Duke of Wellington went during the 'Crisis' and it has been calculated from these supposed events that the general advance was not ordered by Wellington until at least fifteen minutes after the advance of the 52nd. This thereby helps to confirm that the general advance had no bearing on the final defeat of the French and was no more than a symbolic march across the battlefield, so as to capture the enemy's ground, confirming the victory.

It would appear from this scenario that, following Uxbridge's wounding, the Duke of Wellington rode west along the valley floor, to ensure that there was no danger from that quarter, before eventually arriving back on the allied ridge to personally order the general advance. This is claimed to be proof that the advance was heavily delayed.

Eyewitness accounts are very unclear on this subject, but almost all talk of an immediate or pretty much so, advance. Byng, however, estimated that there was a ten-minute delay, but he is virtually alone in claiming this. In fact trying to assess an exact time of the general advance is frankly impossible, but we can make a good approximation.

We do know that Vivian's cavalry was launched across the valley, having moved right to find a space in the line vacated by the infantry. This is assumed to be the space vacated by the Light Brigade and near to Hougoumont, but is that correct?

We know that the 1st Guard Brigade was ordered forward as part of the General Advance, which it did. The question is whether the Guards moved before or after Vivian's cavalry rode forward.

The clear answer is that the brigade had already marched forward into the valley, as Vivian's cavalry clearly remember riding past it on the floor of the valley, where the Guards had halted to reform, before marching east to join the main chaussee. We also know that Vivian's cavalry arrived on the French ridge, earlier than the Light Brigade got to La Belle Alliance as the infantry witnessed the poorly organised charge of the 10th Hussars on a nearby square.

Working backwards, the 52nd would have taken approximately 20 minutes to proceed from its start point near Hougoumont to La Belle Alliance even at the quick march. The cavalry would have taken five minutes to move to the right and form up after the general advance was ordered. Moving at a canter and riding on a more direct path, they must have taken about 10 minutes to get to the French lines and therefore probably passed the British Guards Brigade at about one third of the way across the valley, when the cavalry were still some five minutes from the French lines.

It would have taken the Guards 10 minutes to get this far into the valley after the order to advance was given, therefore the order for the general advance must have occurred no more than five minutes after the 52nd defeated the Imperial Guard column.

To make this easier to comprehend, let us put this in tabular form:

0.00 hours: The 52nd drive the Imperial Guard column away and begins its march towards the chaussee and then heads for La Belle Alliance

0.05 hours: The general advance is ordered, the Guards set off immediately into the valley, Vivian's Brigade moves to the right and manoeuvres through the guns before advancing

0.10 hours: Vivian's cavalry begins to canter across the field directly towards the French lines

0.15 hours: Vivian's cavalry pass the Guards Brigade halted on the valley floor.

0.20 hours: Vivian's cavalry strike the French squares, as the Light Brigade approaches close to La Belle Alliance.

This timing is in complete agreement with almost all of the eyewitnesses, who talk of immediacy. Not one eyewitness (other than Byng) complains of a long delay or pause, which they surely would have done, if held back when raring to attack.

Wellington was an extremely experienced general, he recognised that the French were unsteady and anticipated that a general advance, in support of the attacks of the Light Brigade and the light cavalry, would tip the balance. Even so, the complete rout that then occurred was almost certainly beyond his wildest hopes.

As to the issue of Wellington's movements and therefore his ability to personally order the general advance, there is no mystery here. Wellington was regularly described as completely alone or with only one foreign officer in attendance on him during these anxious moments. Wellington's staff had indeed been decimated during the battle, but many staff officers were still readily available to him. It is almost certain that they were absent because they had been sent away to order the various corps and divisional commanders to order their troops forward, there was no need for him to do it personally, allowing him the freedom to ride around the field as he wished.

The romanticised image of Wellington raising his hat on the ridge, ordering his army forward, is a Victorian myth, it did not happen.

Conclusion: The general advance was ordered less than five minutes after the success of the Light Brigade. It was purely designed to overwhelm the already shaky French forces and to destroy their morale, in this it worked spectacularly. The infantry involved in the general advance did not actually become engaged in much fighting, but it was certainly in close support and substantially increased the perceived threat. The infantry, therefore, can claim to have had a major influence on the total overthrow of the French army, but not alone.

9. Did Wellington suppress General Adam's After Action Report?

It is claimed that the report written by General Adam regarding the actions of the Light Brigade was ignored by the Duke of Wellington and that it was somehow lost, as it is not in the archives. This is therefore used to indicate that Wellington actively suppressed or even destroyed the report which, it is presumed, was very supportive of the case for the 52nd or at least the Light Brigade.

Henry Clinton mentioned the report by Adam and attached it to his report to Lord Hill. It is very noticeable however, that Lord Hill's report to the Duke of Wellington only mentions attaching Henry Clinton's report. His letter dated 20 June 1815, Nivelles 08.00 hours begins:

> My Lord Duke, Although your Grace witnessed the conduct of that part of the troops under my command which had the good fortune to be employed in the action of the 18th instant, still I think it my duty to transmit the accompanying report from Lieutenant General Sir H. Clinton, commanding the 2nd Division, and beg leave to express my entire concurrence with the Lieutenant General's sentiments respecting the gallant conduct of the troops on this occasion.[8]

As he does not mention enclosing General Adam's report, it would appear that it was never sent to the Duke. This means that it has been lost from Lord Hill's papers (the majority of which are unfortunately lost to us) not Wellington's papers as claimed.

This would have been quite normal procedure, reports being made out to the next senior officer and only rarely passed on with the report to the next in seniority. Therefore, a brigade commander's report even being forwarded to a corps commander was quite a rare occurrence. It was virtually unknown for a

---

8. See Supplementary Despatches, volume X p 544.

letter to be passed up three levels of command, all the way to the commander in chief of the army. In fact, I have yet to find another instance of this happening.

General Adam was in bed recovering from a leg wound on 19 June, having remained to the end of the battle on horseback despite his injuries and having been transported to Brussels on a farm cart the following morning being described by Susan Clinton as 'very feeble'. Clinton had however, received Adam's report before that evening, which then allowed him to forward it to General Hill that same night. It is difficult to imagine that this report was particularly long or detailed and if it had contained anything particularly contentious would it have been forwarded?

It's subsequent loss is highlighted as being particularly suspicious, as though it might have contained earth-shattering evidence to prove the entire conspiracy theory, and yet at another point, the author actually admits that it may not have contained anything important at all anyway, but it is then still held up as a possible 'smoking gun'.

This all assumes that we have no other contemporary accounts from General Adam which show his honest opinions of the battle, untainted by later influences. It is claimed that his later writings could easily have been heavily influenced by Wellington's version of events.

However, it so happens that we do have contemporary evidence from General Adam. The author spent a considerable amount of time trying to find a copy of Adam's report in Clinton's, Hill's and the Wellington papers, without success. However, this search led him to the National Records of Scotland, which kindly put the author in direct contact with a descendant of General Adam, who retains a large number of files of his personal correspondence in his private collection, including three particular letters.

These include a letter incredibly written half an hour before the battle started, which begins: 'It is believed we shall have a General action this afternoon – it is now eleven.' The second is a letter dated 22 June 1815, enclosing a letter of 19 June, partly written by the wounded Frederick Adam, and the third is a description of General Adam's Brigade's part in the Battle of Waterloo, dated 24 June 1815.

The owner prefers at present to keep the letters private and has unfortunately declined to allow the author to publish them, or even to see them. I believe however that Adam's views did not alter significantly to his later writings. He praised his Light Brigade as a whole rather than picking out specific regiments.

Conclusion: Lord Hill did not forward Adam's report to Wellington, because Clinton's report covered the same information and it added nothing material to it. There is therefore no evidence of a suppression of evidence by the Duke of Wellington and the only conclusion that can be reached is that there is No 'Smoking Gun'.

10. Was the 52nd's entry into Paris designed to placate it and was its long service in the Army of Occupation designed to keep it away from the British public?

When the troops arrived at Paris, only one brigade of the Duke's allied army received the honour of marching down the Champs Elysees escorting the Duke, with Colours unfurled and bands playing. This was the Light Brigade with the 52nd following the 2/95th as per seniority. The Light Brigade was also the only allied body to encamp on the Champs Elysees and given the honour of mounting guard over Wellington's headquarters. If Wellington had wished to honour the Guards Brigade over everyone else, would they not have expected this honour to be bestowed upon them?

As to the troops who remained as part of the Army of Occupation until 1818, it is a fact that along with the 1/52nd, the 4th, 71st and 79th Foot also remained in France until the end of 1818, were all these other regiments being kept out of the way as well? Henry Clinton remained in command of the 2nd Division throughout, was he also being silenced?

It is perfectly clear that Wellington had very little influence over the choice of regiments he had with him and often complained about his inability to influence such matters. The Duke of York and Horse Guards protected this privilege very tightly indeed.

Conclusion: The honour of being the only British brigade to march into Paris was clearly a very significant honour and a clear sign to everyone, of Wellington's pleasure with the performance of this brigade. The subsequent glory awarded to the 1st Foot Guards was not instigated nor sought by Wellington, this was very much the work of its colonel the Duke of York, and the Prince Regent who had soon convinced himself that he had actually been at the battle!

The fact that the regiment remained in France until 1818 was nothing to do with any attempt to silence them (it certainly did not silence its claims to the laurels of victory), as has been seen, a number of other regiments who fought at Waterloo remained throughout the entire period of the Army of Occupation.

There was a clear attempt to honour the brigade during the prestigious ceremony of occupying Paris and there is absolutely no evidence of an attempt to keep the regiment from Britain for any other reason than duty.

11. Did Wellington suggest the Waterloo Medal to glorify his achievements and argue against the issue of the Military General Service Medal to ensure the battle's ascendancy over all others, with both the military and public?

The idea for a Waterloo Medal for all men who served at Waterloo or Quatre Bras did emanate from the Duke of Wellington. He wrote to the Duke of York on 28 June stating that:

I… beg leave to suggest to your Royal Highness the expediency of giving the non-commissioned officers and soldiers engaged in the Battle of Waterloo, a medal. I am convinced it would have the best effect in the army; and if that battle should settle our concerns, they will well deserve it.[9]

His brother, William Wellesley-Pole, who was Master of the Mint, took up the idea enthusiastically and by 11 July he was writing to the President of the Royal Academy for designs to be submitted for a large medal in gold for the Allied sovereigns and a small medal in bronze for all officers and soldiers. The design chosen for the smaller medal was actually submitted by Mr Wyon, the Chief Engraver of the Mint. The order was eventually altered and the final Waterloo medal was produced in fine solid silver and the name of each individual was stamped into the rim, establishing the pattern for all future British medals. The medal does immortalise Wellington's name on the reverse, but there is absolutely no evidence that the Duke had any say in the design at all.

It has been stated that when the Duke of Richmond brought forward the idea of a medal for officers who had served in the Peninsular War in 1845, the Duke of Wellington argued against it. This has then been used to claim that the Duke wanted to avoid granting medals for that war, as it would diminish his victory at Waterloo. Given that he was the hero of both conflicts such an attitude would be a little strange as it would surely only heighten his esteem, not diminish it. His argument actually centred on the fact that a general issue to all ranks had up until then, only occurred on three occasions of supreme national need, the first of which had been Waterloo. If there was to be a medal for services, then it should not be a Peninsular medal, as that precluded the issue of medals to those who served in Egypt or at Maida and of course to the Royal Navy. He finished with the words 'If you take the step now proposed, you must take others' i.e. to cover all of these various important services as well.[10] This is hardly a resounding attempt to stop any other general issue of medals to all ranks, given by 1845 there had already been three such medal issues.

Conclusion: The Duke was more concerned that the parliamentary discussion on medals was particularly for the Peninsular War only and only for officers. His belief was that it must (if any issue be made) be general to all ranks, must cover the other campaigns and must also include the actions of the Royal Navy. This is hardly the act of a man trying to maintain the renown of 'His' victory at Waterloo over everything else.

12. Did Wellington use Alava to propagate 'His' version of Waterloo and did Alava later use this to blackmail the Duke?

General Alava had become a trusted friend of the Duke during the many years they worked together in the Peninsular War, whilst Alava served at the Duke's

---
9. Gurwood, Wellington's Dispatches Volume XII, p 520.
10. Hansard Parliamentary Debates (Lords) 21 July 1845 pp 717–729.

headquarters as his Spanish liaison officer. This friendship was renewed in 1815 by sheer fluke, as Alava had just been appointed the Spanish Plenipotentiary to the Court of the King of the Netherlands, but was still at Brussels awaiting his credentials before he could see the king, when the campaign began. There is no evidence that he was present at the Battle of Quatre Bras, but it is likely that he remained in Brussels. Alava joined Wellington unofficially and remained with headquarters during the 18 June and witnessed the Battle of Waterloo, one of a handful of men to witness both Trafalgar and Waterloo.

He remained in Brussels when the armies subsequently marched into France and having received his credentials, soon travelled to the Hague to present himself to the king. Alava wrote two letters during the campaign to the Spanish Secretary of State, Don Pedro Cevalles. The first dated 16 June has been lost (no copy of it can be found in his papers in Madrid, but he refers to it in his second letter). It is clear that this letter announced the invasion of Belgium by Napoleon's forces on 15 June and was sent off before news was received that the battles of Quatre Bras and Ligny had been fought.

His second letter was dated 20 June 1815, and it gives a very broad-brush description of the campaign and ends with Wellington leading the British Guards to victory over the Imperial Guard, and with no mention of the Light Brigade.

There is however, absolutely no evidence that Alava was influenced by Wellington in regard to what he wrote. Wellington had no reason to believe that Alava's letter would ever be made public, indeed it wasn't until 13 July that it was published in Madrid, the previous letter never being published. Even then, Wellington could never have imagined that the British press would republish it in English at a later date.

Claims that Wellington could have sought to use this way of getting 'His' version of events into the public domain, via such a circuitous route, are extremely tenuous at the best. Even those suggesting this as a possibility have realised how tenuous the proposition is and have even gone so far as to suggest that Alava may have sent a cutting to the *Times* newspaper to ensure that it was picked up and published!

Wellington's later financial support for Alava can only be seen as an open-hearted gesture to a long standing friend, there is absolutely no evidence of extortion. Wellington was often generous to his friends when in serious financial difficulties, such as in the cases of Gurwood and his own brother Richard. The fact that Alava eventually fell out of favour with Wellington was because he was too eager to gossip, which the Duke found distasteful. Their relationship, however, only cooled, it was not severed.

Conclusion: Any suggestion that Wellington colluded with Alava to get 'His' version of Waterloo published in the British press are too far-fetched to deserve serious scrutiny. There is not a shred of evidence to support the claim and the Duke had, had he wished, too many easier avenues to achieve such an aim.

13. Did Wellington fail to praise Uxbridge and purposely set him up for a fall?

It is well known that the cavalry commander, the Earl of Uxbridge, did not serve in Spain and Southern France with Wellington because of the awkwardness of the situation. Uxbridge had eloped with Wellington's brother Henry's wife in 1809, causing a huge scandal, as can be imagined. Uxbridge was therefore not sent out to serve with Wellington, although he never refused him.

In 1815 Uxbridge was appointed to Wellington's army in Belgium. When Wellington was asked about the situation, he replied laconically, 'Well he won't run off with me!' Whether they liked each other, nobody really knows, but the evidence is that both worked well together professionally.

Wellington was always renowned as a bit of a control freak, but there is ample evidence that by the time of Waterloo, he had mellowed somewhat and trusted some of his senior officers more. It is within this background that their relationship at Waterloo must be seen.

Claims that the appointment of Uxbridge to the command of the entire allied cavalry, a significant sign of trust by Wellington, was actually an abdication of all responsibility for their future failings is to put it mildly, far-fetched. The British cavalry, it would be fair to say, had a very mixed reputation in Spain and certainly had seen only limited success. This was particularly evident when in large formations, where expert command and control was essential. However, to claim that Wellington was absolving himself of all blame in advance for the poor showing of the cavalry and was therefore protecting his own reputation, is frankly absurd. Such an abrogation of his duty would simply not have been contemplated by Wellington.

Wellington's failure to impart his battle plan to Uxbridge, stating only that they must defend and react to Napoleon's attacks, is not further evidence of this absolution as claimed, nor is his reputed comment when Uxbridge lost his leg proof of his dislike for him – particularly as it is certainly a fable, Uxbridge nor anyone else knew that it was serious enough to cause him to lose his leg for many hours.

The Duke of York, a close friend of Uxbridge, was not overly friendly with Wellington and he certainly criticised him for failing to give Uxbridge due praise after Waterloo. However, when Wellington was silent about individuals, it was usually for a different reason. The Duke was to admit later in life that he did not praise enough, but although caustic towards certain individuals to their face, he rarely wrote terrible comments about individuals in official reports. He avoided open criticism of individuals, but in this case he had much to criticise Uxbridge for, hence most likely the lack of praise.

The attack of the Heavy cavalry had been successful in stopping d'Erlon's attack, but lack of self-control led to their own annihilation as an effective force for the remainder of the battle. There are also many reported comments from Uxbridge during the battle, regarding the refusal of part of his light cavalry to charge home when the French cavalry were milling around the squares.

Wellington also watched the useless charges against solid squares of French infantry at the close of the day, costing the lives of numerous gallant, but perhaps foolish, officers.

Conclusion: The relationship between Uxbridge and Wellington may well have been strained but was always professional. Claims that Wellington was such a narcissist that he set Uxbridge up to take the fall in the case of defeat, does not bear the least scrutiny, with his well-known characteristics of service and loyalty to the crown and the army.

14. Did Wellington actively refuse to discuss the merits of the 52nd's movements? Does this prove that he suppressed the evidence?

Wellington does appear to have been very cagey about talking about the action in detail in later years. For example Colonel Bentham wrote:

> 'I met Gurwood in London about 1828 [...] and I asked him why he never drew the Duke out about the catastrophe [crisis] at Waterloo. He said that he had repeatedly made the attempt, but that it was a subject which always created great impatience. On the last attempt the Duke said 'Oh! I know nothing of the services of particular regiments: there was glory enough for us all!'[11]

Rumours of his having been taken by surprise by Napoleon on 15/16 June 1815 had soon surfaced and a great number of units were extremely unhappy with their lack of a mention in the Waterloo Despatch. What of Picton's Division standing against d'Erlon? Vivian's and Vandeleur's light cavalry charges at the end of the battle? The heroic defence of La Haye Sainte by Major Baring? To name but a few who did not get a mention.

As early as 1816, Wellington was not actually trying to dissuade all attempts to write a history of the campaign but cautioning against trusting the words of individuals. On 28 April, he wrote to a Mr Sinclair:

> The people of England may be entitled to a detailed and accurate account of the Battle of Waterloo, and I have no objection to their having it; but I do object to their being misinformed and misled by those novels called 'Relations', 'Impartial Accounts' &c &c, of that transaction, containing the stories which curious travellers have picked up from peasants, private soldiers, individual officers &c &c, and have published to the world as the truth.[12]

Writing to William Mudford only a few days later, he again cautioned on the use of popular accounts:

> I have long ... felt myself under the necessity of declining to give my consent that any work should be dedicated to me, with the contents of

---

11. Letter of Colonel Bentham dated November 1853 quoted by Leeke.
12. Wellington, Supplementary Despatches of the Duke of Wellington, Volume 10, p 507.

> which I am not previously acquainted; and you will readily believe that I feel this necessity in a stronger degree in regard to a history of the Battle of Waterloo than I should do upon any other subject. More accounts have been published of that transaction than of any other that for many years has attracted the public attention; and those who have written them have thought they possessed all the necessary information for the purpose when they have conversed with a peasant of the country, or with an officer or soldier engaged in the battle. Such accounts cannot be true; and I advert to them only to warn you against considering them as any guide to the work which you are about to publish. [13]

He also cautioned that it would be very difficult to accurately recount the events of the battle, writing in August 1815 to Mr Croker:

> The history of a battle is not unlike the history of a ball. Some individuals may recollect all the little events of which the great result is the battle won or lost, but no individual can recollect the order in which, or the exact moment at which, they occurred, which makes all the difference as to their value or importance.

Wellington may not have wanted anyone to look too closely at the battle for many reasons, but one reason was certainly the fact that he was concerned that any deep analysis might find evidence that not everyone had performed well at the battle. Wellington in fact, did everything he could to protect people's reputations after the battle, only occasionally complaining in private letters. On 21 December 1815, he wrote privately to Earl Musgrave, Master of the Ordnance, explaining his displeasure of the artillery at Waterloo:

> I had a right to expect that the officers and men of the artillery would do as I did, and as all the Staff did, that is to shelter in the squares of the infantry till the French cavalry should be driven off the ground, either by our cavalry or infantry. But they did no such thing; they ran off the field entirely, taking with them limbers, ammunition, and everything: and when, in a few minutes, we had driven off the French cavalry, and had regained our ground and our guns, and could have made good use of our artillery, we had no artillerymen to fire them, and, in this point of fact, I should have had no artillery during the whole of the latter part of the action if I had not kept a reserve in the commencement.

What he did not do, was to wash such dirty washing in public, in fact he made it clear that many reputations might suffer severely if they dug too deep and he had no intention of allowing such to occur.

Conclusion: Wellington does appear to have been tetchy over requests to discuss the battle and was against any attempt to write a thorough

---

13. ibid, p 508.

history of the campaign. This is likely to have partly been because he did not want his own actions questioned, particularly regarding his poor showing on 15/16 June rather than his own actions on the 18th.

He was also acutely aware that many great men's reputations might be damaged if the truth came out. The author has certainly discovered instances of officers failing to carry out orders; others departing the field early or being very tardy in their arrival; and some who undoubtedly showed cowardice. Indeed, a number of officers were allowed to quietly resign their commissions after the battle to avoid such an embarrassment, whilst there is clear evidence that some major misdemeanours were quietly swept under the carpet in the euphoria of the victory.

Wellington loyally avoided too close a scrutiny of these events for this very reason. However, despite his aversion to attempts to write the campaign history, accusations that Wellington actively blocked such attempts (as per the supposed campaign against William Siborne) have been generally shown to be well wide of the mark. See the author's *Letters from the Battle of Waterloo* for full details on that conspiracy theory.

15. Were Wellington's relationships with Napoleon's mistresses and collection of Napoleana evidence of excessive triumphalism?

Wellington just like Napoleon, liked women, and when he was in Paris, it is claimed that he had sexual relationships with at least two of Napoleon's former conquests. One who certainly caught Arthur's eye was the famous contralto, Giuseppina Grassini who had formerly been a lover of Napoleon and was known as '*La chanteuse de l'Empereur*' [the singer of the Emperor]. Now turning forty, she still possessed a radiant beauty that certainly attracted Arthur and she was often to be seen on his arm at all of the great functions he was invited to. Indeed the Countess de Boigne recorded that:

> I recall that on one occasion he decided to make Grassini, then in possession of her favours, the queen of the evening. He placed her on a raised sofa in the ballroom and never left her side. He had her served first before anyone else, arranged everyone so that she could dance, gave her his hand to take her into supper first, sat her next to him, and finally paid her the kind of attention normally granted only to princesses.

He also showed much attention to the 27-year-old Mademoiselle Georges, real name Marguerite Weimer, who was the star of the *Theatre Francais*. She had also been a former lover of Napoleon and later famously compared the two great men, stating that: 'The duke was by far the most vigorous/stronger.' However, her claims cannot be substantiated and if she did go with the Duke, she had only recently stopped entertaining Tsar Alexander I, as she had given him an illegitimate daughter, Maria Parijskaia, in March 1814.

But to claim that Wellington pursued these ladies in order to outdo Napoleon in some way, is very far-fetched as he certainly never intended these relationships to become public.

As to Wellington's small collection of Napoleana, it has to be understood how he obtained most of them. His most famous (and completely unavoidable) piece is the huge statue of Napoleon as *Mars the Peacemaker* by the artist Canova which stands to this day in the stairwell of Apsley House in London. Much is made of the fact that Napoleon hated it and that it had been hidden away, therefore Wellington was using it, it is claimed, to degrade the French Emperor. In fact, this statue was given to the Duke by the Prince Regent as a present in 1817 and was placed in the stairwell, as the only place in the whole house tall enough to take it and there it has remained for two centuries. It is not known what Wellington thought of the gift, but he could hardly not put on display such a conspicuous present from his sovereign.

Napoleon's sword was also a gift, this time from Marshal Blücher, whilst the sixty-six Napoleonic flags were a gift from King Louis XVIII. Most of the items in the collection turn out to be extravagant gifts, not personal purchases by the Duke.

Conclusion: Wellington did not set out to collect pieces of Napoleana, but was gifted them. Indeed Wellington throughout his life was complimentary of Napoleon's abilities on the battlefield, often saying that his presence was worth forty thousand troops. He was, however, not an admirer of Napoleon as a man. Wellington's penchant for beautiful women, some of whom had already attracted Napoleon, and the employment of Napoleon's cook are however hardly signs of triumphalism over his adversary.

16. Did Wellington use the Reverend Gleig to ruin Siborne financially?
The Reverend George Gleig (an ex officer of the 85th Foot and a Peninsular man) published a popular history of the Battle of Waterloo in 1847, three years after William Siborne's very successful *History of the War in France and Belgium in 1815*. Siborne's work in two volumes and an accompanying map volume, was based on the research he had carried out for his models, which had unfortunately turned out to be a financial disaster. This was largely because of Siborne's decision to entrust everything to a third party, indeed his financial acumen has been shown to be woeful throughout. The book did sell well and two editions were published before Gleig's work appeared, so most people who wished to have a copy had ample opportunity to purchase one, if they could afford it.

Gleig however, sought to produce a slimmed down version of the battle and to sell it at a price that was accessible to the masses. His single volume history did sell very well, but it is clear that it plagiarises significant parts of Siborne's original work. Undeterred, Siborne revised his *History* following further correspondence engendered by the original publication. He published his third edition in 1848, a year before he died.

Suggestions that Gleig was 'persuaded' by Wellington to bring out this cheaper edition to undercut sales of Siborne's book and to financially ruin him, are not backed up by any evidence of any kind. By the time Gleig's book had been published, Siborne's book had been selling for three years and had gone through two full editions already, it was indeed a major financial success, which put Siborne's finances back on an even keel. Gleig's book appeared far too late to undercut sales of this work and the poorer sales of Siborne's third edition simply follows the age-old publisher's maxim – that every edition sells half of the previous one.

Gleig later fell out with Wellington and in later life he was certainly very critical of the Duke. His *Life of Arthur, Duke of Wellington* appeared in 1865, when both Siborne and Wellington were dead and unable to challenge him. He was therefore free to make claims without worrying about being sued. His claims that two officers (including Gurwood) were pushed into committing suicide by the Duke have been dealt with elsewhere in this volume, but he certainly had ample opportunity to divulge his great secret regarding the Duke's campaign to ruin Siborne – if there had been the slightest grain of truth in it. The fact that he did not speaks volumes in itself.

Conclusion: Wellington did not use Gleig to publish in an attempt to financially ruin Siborne.

17. Were the generals who commanded in the 2nd Corps silenced by honours?

It is claimed that a greater number of honours were bestowed upon those officers who would need to be silenced to avoid the supposed unfair treatment of the 52nd becoming public knowledge. The names of the officers so rewarded include Uxbridge, Hill, Clinton, Maitland and Adam. Why Uxbridge and Maitland are included, who could not gain any advantage personally or for their corps, by favouring the 52nd's claims, is very unclear.

Robert Burnham and Ron McGuigan[14] clearly show that no officer gained a baronetcy after Waterloo, three officers received the Knight Commander of the Bath for Waterloo, (Cooke, Maitland and Adam) and one got the Knight Grand Cross, (Kempt). These were however personally awarded by the Prince Regent.

Regarding the Thanks of the Houses of Parliament, twenty officers were actually granted this distinction, all were at least brigade commanders at Waterloo.

The claims even go so far as to suggest that the unfair award of foreign medals was part of this, the issue of which was in the prerogative of those various monarchs. How Wellington was supposedly able to influence these awards has not been established however.

With regard to the Order of Maria Theresa, 23 officers were granted it, either as a Commander or a Knight, amongst them were Uxbridge, Hill, Clinton (Byng and Adam were not – although the conspiracy theorists claim they were), but they were also granted to Colborne and Reynell.

---

14. *The British Army Against Napoleon* by Robert Burnham and Ron McGuigan, Barnsley 2010.

Regarding the Russian Orders of St George, St Wladimir, or St Anne, officers gained one of them, nobody gained two or three. In total 66 officers gained one of them, in one of the three classes of each award. Amongst the recipients were indeed Uxbridge, Hill, Clinton and Adam, but so again were Colborne and Reynell.

Regarding the Netherlands Order of Wilhelm, there were 24 recipients including, Clinton and Maitland. Finally, regarding the Bavarian Order of Maximilian Joseph, there were 11 recipients, these included none of the specific listed officers, but did include Norcott of the 95th.

Conclusion: With regards to honours granted by the Prince Regent or even Foreign honours granted by their own Heads of State, there is absolutely no evidence that any officer gained a significantly higher number of awards than others. There is no clear evidence therefore that these awards had been manipulated by anyone, including the Duke of Wellington, to influence people.

18. How soon did the Prussians reach the Brussels/Charleroi Chaussee and where did Wellington and Blücher meet?

The exact time when the Light Brigade drove off the last Imperial Guard column cannot be ascertained with any real accuracy, but it may have been around 20.15 hours or a little later and it was nearly 20.45 hours before it arrived at La Belle Alliance just before sunset, which would have been due at 21.00 hours GMT. There are no mentions of Prussian soldiers being met on the road, beyond odd skirmishers, as the Light Brigade marched south. Leeke and Holman both claim that the Prussians did not enter the chaussee at Maison de Roi from the Ligny road until around 21.45 hours.

This would be consistent with the French defenders remaining in Ligny and abandoning its defence at around 20.45, just as the French defence line crumbled, allowing the defenders to clear through Maison du Roi before the Light Brigade arrived there. The eyewitnesses in the Light Brigade do not mention large numbers of French troops coming from their left, so they must have cleared through the village of Maison du Roi before their arrival.

We also know that Ziethen's troops were driving up the road from Papelotte to La Belle Alliance and as the French defence crumbled, they were able to rapidly move on their objective, but can we estimate their time of arrival? We know that they arrived after the Light Brigade had moved through there around 20.45 and indeed, we know from officers of the 1st Foot Guards that they had also arrived here before the Prussians, which would put us beyond 21.00 hours.

As Maison du Roi is a thirty-minute march from La Belle Alliance the Light Brigade would have arrived there around 21.15. If the Light Brigade eyewitnesses are correct in saying that the first Prussians they saw arrived at 21:45 hours and came from Plancenoit rather than from La Belle Alliance, then Ziethen's troops must have arrived at La Belle Alliance after 21.15. They had been ordered to lead the pursuit and immediately marched south on the chaussee, so there was no real delay once on the chaussee, yet they did not pass the Light Brigade until after 22.00 hours.

So, where did Wellington and Blücher actually meet? It is probably true to say that we may never know for sure, as Wellington believed it occurred further south near Genappe. General Gneisenau stated that it was at La Belle Alliance and that Marshal Blücher suggested it as a good name for the battle but was rebuffed by Wellington. Gneisenau is unfortunately not a reliable witness, particularly when he wants to portray people in a certain light, and it is clear that he did not like or trust Wellington. Unfortunately, many who claim to have seen the meeting couldn't have been there and many who possibly were are quite vague as regards the specifics. Wellington certainly rode forward towards Genappe and they could have met near there around 21.45 to 22.00 hours. If it occurred at La Belle Alliance it must have been after 22.00 as Wellington made his way slowly back to his headquarters at Waterloo. The likelihood is that it was somewhere to the south of La Maison du Roi as that is where the main force that had been struggling for Plancenoit and where Blücher had concentrated his efforts, joined the chaussee. Blücher also rested that night at the inn at Genappe, so it is quite possible that Wellington was correct that they met near there.

Conclusion: The victory of Waterloo was very much a combined effort and all nations involved share the glory. The exact time specific units actually reached the main chaussee around La Bell Alliance is purely speculative and ultimately unimportant to the overall result, but it is certain that the Light Brigade and British cavalry pushed through to Rossomme before the Prussians entered the chaussee at any point.

19. As Wellington rode back to Waterloo after the battle, was he in a black mood or desperately sad?

It is clearly almost impossible to read into the mind of anyone, but especially such an enigmatic character as the Duke. The claim has been made that Wellington was not sad at the loss of life, but angry and frustrated, at having to concoct a 'cover story' to protect 'His' version of Waterloo as he wanted it to be seen; with him personally leading the Guards to victory. His black mood was apparently due to the knowledge that he would have to work extremely hard to ensure that 'His' version was the only one that would gain credence and to do this he must play down the parts performed by the 52nd Foot and the Prussians.

The evidence from those around him that night and the following morning shows clearly that he was deeply affected by the heavy loss of life and injury (far worse than anything else he had personally witnessed in all his campaigning) and the death of so many personal friends. In fact, their description of his mood is very much akin to psychological trauma[15] in modern parlance.

A quote of his from the first twenty-four hours after the battle makes his personal feeling of melancholy abundantly clear:

---

15. For those who question this assertion, some of the symptoms can be shock, difficulty concentrating, anger, irritability, mood swings, guilt, shame, self-blame, withdrawing from others, feeling sad or hopeless.

> My heart is broken by the terrible loss I have sustained in my old friends and companions and my poor soldiers. Believe me, nothing except a battle lost can be half so melancholy as a battle won: the bravery of my troops hitherto saved me from the greater evil; but to win such a battle as this of Waterloo, at the expense of so many gallant friends, could only be termed a heavy misfortune but for the result to the public.

That night, Surgeon Hume felt the Duke's tears on his hand as he read out the list of the dead and wounded. This was not a man scheming to enhance his reputation by subterfuge, it was an honest reaction to the awful truth which swept over him. The adrenalin and nervous energy of the battlefield had turned into shock and genuine horror at the butcher's bill he was in part responsible for and this clearly temporarily overwhelmed him. It was, however, a temporary state and it began to pass during the next few days, as the never-ending workload distracted him. However, he was being nothing but genuine when he said: 'I pray to God I have fought my last battle.'

Conclusion: Wellington was in shock over the enormity of the death and destruction he had just witnessed, he was not in any condition for scheming. There is clear evidence of his melancholy and no evidence of anything else.

20. Is it true that Clinton's Report lacked any comment on the actions of the 52nd due to the fact that he was ignorant of events?

Leeke claims that Clinton had not been near the regiment throughout the day as he had been busy with the rest of his division. He says that Clinton's diary:

> May appear to carry weight with it, is of no weight at all, because he can only have received it as one of the reports current in the Army on the 19th of June and afterwards. Clinton could not have seen what the 1st Guards did at Waterloo, for the right of his command was two-thirds of a mile from the right of the Guards, and all his troops except Adam's Brigade, were stationed at that time to the rear of Hougoumont[...]
>
> Clinton therefore, was fully employed in that important portion of the battlefield, and it was often mentioned in the 52nd, that he was never seen amongst them at Waterloo; much less could he have seen what happened to the 1st Guards.[16]

However, the evidence from Clinton's diary and letters show clearly that he did witness the attack and only then rode to the Hanoverian troops to send them forward in support of the Light Brigade.

Conclusion: It is clear that Clinton was in the vicinity, he saw the manoeuvre and acted quickly to support the attack. Although I have much sympathy with the claims of the 52nd, one has to be honest and

---

16. Leeke.

conclude that Clinton was not so much interested in the individual actions of one regiment but saw that the decisive movement by most of his division was of much greater importance.

21. Did the 52nd advance alone without support and therefore deserve all of the laurels on its own?

It has been shown clearly, that despite its claims to the contrary, the 52nd did not advance alone. The 2/95th moved with it immediately and the 71st and 3/95th followed quite quickly after but were initially 100 yards or so behind. They had caught up by the time the 23rd Light Dragoons rode across the 52nd, causing them to halt for a minute or two. Claims that the 71st then deviated so far from the 52nd that there was a large gap measuring several hundred yards have been proven to be incorrect. In fact they remained within 100 yards or so of each other, the gap being filled by the 3/95th. The Osnabruck battalion also drew close to its right and even got slightly ahead of it, by following a more direct route.

Conclusion: There is no doubt that the 52nd played a significant role in the defeat of at least a significant part of the Imperial Guard. Its advance across the valley towards La Belle Alliance also undoubtedly played a very significant part in the collapse of the final French defence and that it therefore deserved greater recognition beyond the army than it actually received.

There is also, however, no doubt that the Guards Brigade did defeat another column of the Imperial Guard and that the attack by the light cavalry also played a very significant part in the complete collapse of the French army.

The claim that the 52nd drove the French army beyond La Belle Alliance completely unsupported is shown to be false. It was fully supported by the rest of the brigade, which marched with it in formation and was supported by other elements of the 2nd Division as well.

22. Was Gurwood hounded into a premature death by the Duke, because of his determination that his version of events could not be challenged?

Colonel John Gurwood had entered the army as an ensign in the 52nd Foot in 1808. He commanded the 'forelorn hope' at Badajoz and despite being wounded, captured General Barrie, the governor. Soon after he transferred to the cavalry, initially serving with the 9th Light Dragoons, but later transferring to the 10th Light Dragoons. He was appointed an aide de camp to General Henry Clinton in 1815, but fell out with him and served at Waterloo with his regiment. It is difficult to know who was at fault, as Clinton was certainly a difficult man to work for, but Gurwood had already fallen out with another senior officer in Spain, so it would appear that he might also have been an awkward man.

Gurwood was not particularly well known to Wellington. After carrying out a diplomatic mission to Portugal and Brazil in 1825–6 with Sir Charles Stuart, on his return, Gurwood was posted to the West Indies. He came to the Duke's attention and on his return from the West Indies in 1830. He prepared the Duke of Wellington's General Orders for publication and, with his sanction, published them in 1832. The Duke loved reading over these old orders aloud and Gurwood took the opportunity to suggest that he edit the Duke's official despatches. This was agreed, but it soon grew into a project to publish all of the Duke's outbound wartime correspondence and it eventually became a 12-volume set covering his campaigns from 1799–1818, published between 1837–9 (with an accompanying index volume) to great acclaim. The work was however very onerous, putting great stress on Gurwood, causing him to become an insomniac. The Duke retained editorial control of the project, to ensure that nothing would be published which could hurt individuals or upset foreign governments and the process of indexing the series was purgatory. Names and occasional dates were redacted but generally the majority of his correspondence was published. Gurwood became his Private Secretary during this period.

Gurwood had a very public spat with Colonel William Napier, who challenged him over his role at Ciudad Rodrigo in his *History of the Peninsular War*.

The Duke became aware of Gurwood's frail mental health and financial worries and did much to gain him well-paid sinecures and signed over all rights to the profits from the publishing of his despatches to him. In fact the evidence shows clearly that Wellington did what he could to help and support Gurwood, but there is no denying that he was a hard task master.

Gurwood took his wife and children to the seaside for Christmas in 1845, but on Christmas day he put a cut-throat razor to his own throat and committed suicide (a not uncommon practice at this time for gentlemen who could not cope with life).

The Reverend Gleig, a former soldier and wannabe biographer of the Duke, although his work heavily plagiarised others, wrote many years after Wellington's death, that the Duke had caused Gurwood's death. He cited stories that the Duke had learnt that Gurwood was keeping a private record of their conversations for future publication, causing him to castigate him for his underhand ways. This claim has resurfaced recently again as evidence, it is claimed, of Wellington's determination to stop anyone unearthing the truth about the 52nd at Waterloo.

Gleig however, was a terrible scandal monger and a very unreliable witness, he even blames the Duke for causing another officer to take his own life in 1813, despite the fact that a very simple check of the facts shows that the officer did not commit suicide at all, but carried on a successful career for many years after.

A study of all of the evidence regarding Wellington's involvement in both officers' deaths was made by the eminent historian John Hussey in the *Journal of the Society of Army Historical Research* Vol 80 No.232 (2002) pages 98–109. In it he concluded that there was not one shred of evidence that the Duke had a hand in Gurwood's death (the other officer he proved had never died by his own hand), indeed the evidence was clear that Wellington had done everything to help him when he realised that he was unwell.

As to the story regarding Gurwood keeping secret notes on conversations with the Duke, this has a basis in fact. However, the Duke only learnt of these papers AFTER Gurwood's funeral, when the Duke, who was undoubtedly very angry, wrote harshly to his widow over what he viewed as a betrayal. He was eventually calmed by strong assurances that the papers had been destroyed.

Conclusion: Claims that Wellington caused Gurwood's death in an effort to protect his version of the Battle of Waterloo have absolutely no creditability at all. The Duke was undoubtedly a hard task master, but he also cared for those around him and tried to help them financially. This is a particularly nasty claim which has no basis in fact.

Chapter 20

Overall Conclusion

We have investigated every conceivable aspect of the attack of the Imperial Guard and have concluded that both the British and French accounts can be brought broadly into agreement. The Imperial Guard attack was launched in a hurry and piecemeal. Initially the four battalions of the Chasseurs of the Middle Guard marched forward in column of squares and deployed just as they arrived at the allied ridge line, where the two battalions of the 1st Foot Guards (less the two light companies in Hougoumont) engaged them in a fierce but short firefight, before driving them off with the bayonet. A little while later two battalions of the Grenadiers of the Middle Guard drove onto the allied ridge just to the west of La Haye Sainte and supported by artillery, decimated the already shaky troops in the vicinity (up to 10,000 Brunswickers, Hanoverians, Nassau and British) driving them back, until reinforced by Chasse's Netherlands troops. The advance of Detmer's Brigade with the bayonet, almost certainly coupled with the knowledge that the attack further to the west had failed and that allied troops were threatening its retreat, caused it to retire precipitately. Seeing that the Chasseur battalions were being driven back, three reserve battalions advanced to cover their retreat in column of squares, causing the advancing British Guards to retire back up the allied ridge. Lieutenant Colonel Colborne, on his own initiative began to move his regiment forward and pivoted it, so as to position it on the flank of this final column of Imperial Guard. Despite taking some heavy casualties from the musketry of the Imperial Guard, a few companies of the 52nd opened fire while the other companies hurried themselves into position and they then launched a bayonet charge, against which the Imperial Guard did not stand, but turned and fled. Wellington had ordered the manoeuvre, but Colborne had anticipated it. Wellington and all the senior officers of the corps were nearby and sent off orders for other units to support the 52nd in its advance and it was not long before the brigade was formed up and moving as one unit.

Some have sought to make this manoeuvre onto the flank of the Guard as something of a wonder and is used to prove the superiority of the 52nd over any other regiment, which of course ignores the fact that the rest of the Light Brigade followed suit. What I find most telling however, is that very few eyewitnesses to the manoeuvre even bother to comment on it. It was a manoeuvre that was well executed, but far from unknown before, Colborne having witnessed a very similar scenario played out at the Battle of Maida in 1806 by the 20th Foot.

Wellington, recognising that the French troops were now showing clear signs of being very close to breaking point, ordered the Light Brigade to drive on and almost simultaneously ordered a general advance of his whole line, in support. The advance of the Light Brigade now combined with Vivian's, Vandeleur's and Dornberg's cavalry brigades striking into the French lines, along with Prussian forces pushing on from the east, finally caused the French army to collapse in total rout.

As can be seen by this brief overview, a large number of troops played some part at least in the defeat of the French troops. Amongst them, the 52nd and the rest of the Light Brigade performed a conspicuous and vital part within this, but they did not do it all alone. The overall conclusion must be that although the 52nd was not recognised officially as much as it perhaps should have been for its conspicuous part in the defeat of the French army, this appears to have been more an accident of circumstances rather than a concerted effort to prevent it receiving their full portion of the acclaim due them.

The claims published by members of the 52nd in later years were well meaning and they certainly prove that the regiment deserved greater recognition for its achievements. However, it is clear that in their valiant efforts to gain greater recognition for their own part in the victory of Waterloo, they overstated their case, unfairly downgrading the part performed by other units within the Light Brigade, the British Guards and the British light cavalry, in order to further their own renown. Massively overstating the numbers defeated by the 52nd did not help the cause either. The 52nd and the Light Brigade defeating around 3,000 Imperial Guardsmen and some supporting troops, was no mean feat, but claims of defeating 10,000 are simply flights of fancy. This was unfortunate and unnecessary, causing a great deal of offence and creating bitter rivalry between different corps, the repercussions of which are felt even to this day and hence the need for this further in-depth investigation.

Colborne eventually became aware of the numerous discrepancies even between the accounts of the different officers of his own regiment. This simply emphasised their inability to have even a moment during the events described to take real stock of what was actually occurring around them. In a confidential letter written to William Siborne, he requested that he destroy his memoranda as it just added to the discord, something he was painfully aware of:

> I send you my explanations, persuaded that we of the 52nd, who have so freely given our notions of the results of the movements towards the close of the action, were little qualified to furnish correct information on the subject of the general operations of our army, in consequence of our whole attention having been absorbed by the movements which we were actively engaged in carrying into effect, and that you, you have had access to the evidence of officers posted in every part of the field, must be enabled to form a just conclusion as to the grand features of the battle.
>
> I met in town with several officers of the 52nd who were near me at the close of the action, and as they all differ materially in their accounts of it, I beg you will destroy the confidential statement which I forwarded to you,

and which I drew up after being acquainted with your earnest desire to collect information on certain points, under the impression only that some of the details mentioned by me might tend to confirm other accounts in your possession.[1]

Nine years later, Colonel Colborne wrote to Lieutenant Yonge of his fears that his regimental officers would not do any good by publishing their versions of events:

> I fear it may be the intention of Bentham, or some of our 52nd friends, to bring before the public the exploits of our corps and its officers. Nothing can be more disagreeable or create more jealousy than thrusting continually before readers the claims, or supposed merits, of particular corps of officers long after the events, to be discussed or recorded, as a tribute to their exertions. It does no good to individuals or generals, and such notices are very properly considered as puffs, or as published for some interested motive.[2]

With regard to the Duke of Wellington, it is clear that he resisted all attempts to rewrite his despatch with a better history of the battle in later years to protect the reputations of many who had not performed as well that day, as they might have. Indeed Colonel Colborne understood Wellington's view when in Paris in July 1815:

> I heard the Duke of Wellington say at his own table at Paris in 1815, 'Let the Battle of Waterloo stand where it does; we are satisfied'. He knew that the first impressions given could not be removed easily, and that the merit of the English army being brought into an authorised controversy would become depreciated by the advocacy of some and the jealousy of others.[3]

That is what Wellington tried to avoid for the rest of his life. He knew that too thorough an investigation would cause divisions and highlight the failings of a number of individuals and regiments, his view was no more or no less than 'to let sleeping dogs lie'. The suggestion that Wellington deliberately favoured other regiments, actively sought to conceal or destroy evidence to the contrary and bought the silence of everyone around, is both completely unsubstantiated and a terrible slur on a national hero which must be refuted without reservation. No man is perfect and Wellington certainly had many flaws in his character, but these were not them.

In conclusion, it must be clear from this thorough investigation of the evidence, that there was more than enough glory for all of the victors of Waterloo to share but that the 52nd surely deserved its full share and did not get it.

However, the final verdict must be, that there was no conspiracy to rob the 52nd Foot of its well-deserved laurels.

---

1. Moore-Smith, The life of John Colborne Lord Seaton, p 410.
2. ibid, pp 415–6.
3. ibid.

Appendix I

Company Numbers

While carrying out research on the records of the 52nd Foot I have discovered a great deal of confusion over the allocation of officers and men to company numbers and it is necessary to explain this.

The basic company system of the British battalion during the Napoleonic wars was to have ten companies running from right to left, No.1 Company (also usually designated the Grenadier company) on the right of the line, eight centre companies numbered Nos 2 to 9, and No.10 company on the left of the line (also usually designated the Light company). In Light Infantry battalions, such as the 52nd all ten companies were light infantry, so there were no special designations for companies 1 and 10.

When the 1st Battalion of the 52nd served in Belgium during the Waterloo campaign the Muster Rolls show the individual companies of the men numbered 1–10 as expected and at the end of the Three Monthly Muster Return, the ten captains of companies are listed almost in seniority order with their company number. As can be seen by comparison with the Army List of seniority for the 1st Battalion, they nearly match exactly, except for No. 5 Company, where Kenneth Snodgrass has been changed for James McNair. This would appear to have occurred because Snodgrass had been severely wounded at the Battle of Orthez in 1814 and was unable to serve. As Snodgrass had not officially left the regiment, McNair was temporarily put in his place, but he was left at No. 5 in the list although junior to all of the other company commanders.

Robert Campbell, Brownrigg and Young are emboldened on the list as not being at Waterloo and their three companies were commanded by the next three senior officers, Captains Langton, Cross and Lieutenant Dawson. This makes perfect sense so far, although confusingly the Waterloo Medal Roll lists them in a different order and the Waterloo Prize Money Roll lists them in a different order again.

The Waterloo Medal Roll List in fact shows the official officers in command of companies but now places McNair at the bottom as the most junior, whereas the Waterloo Prize Roll shows the actual company commanders present at Waterloo but not in seniority order.

270 The Great Waterloo Controversy

June Muster Rolls	Seniority by Army List	Waterloo Medal Roll Companies	Waterloo Prize Money Roll Seniority
1 Patrick Campbell	Patrick Campbell	Patrick Campbell	Patrick Campbell
2 **Robert Campbell**	**Robert Campbell**	**Robert Campbell**	William Chalmers
3 William Chalmers	William Chalmers	William Chalmers	William Rowan
4 William Rowan	William Rowan	William Rowan	James Love
5 James McNair	**Kenneth Snodgrass**	**Robert Brownrigg**	Charles Diggle
6 **Robert Brownrigg**	**Robert Brownrigg**	Charles Diggle	John Shedden
7 Charles Diggle	Charles Diggle	John Shedden	George Young
8 John Shedden	John Shedden	George Love	James McNair
9 James Love	James Love	**George Young**	Edward Langton
10 George Young	**George Young**	James McNair	John Cross
	James McNair		
	Edward Langton		
	John Cross		
	Charles Dawson		

As you can see, there is a good deal of confusion with all of these lists, but at least they all agree as to who was present and who commanded a company at Waterloo. All the Returns of individual soldiers show their company number and these all correspond with company commanders as listed in the June Muster Roll.

However, what I have recently discovered is that these company numbers in the Musters are purely administrative and bear no resemblance to the company number of the company in which they served on the battlefield!

I found a number of memoirs, including Lieutenants Gawler and Holman and Ensign Leeke, who occasionally identify certain officers and the companies they were actually assigned to in the line and from this I have been able to complete the following incomplete list of companies.

June Muster Rolls	Actual Line Company	Other officers known to be attached to Company			
1 P Campbell	1 Diggle	Gawler	Hart		
2 **Robert Campbell**	2 Love or Langton?				
3 William Chalmers	3 Love or Langton?				
4 William Rowan	4 P Campbell	Dawson	Holman		
5 James McNair	5 Anderson	G Campbell	F Love		
6 **Robert Brownrigg**	6 Rowan or Chalmers?				
7 Charles Diggle	7 Rowan or Chalmers?				
8 John Shedden	8 Cross	Ogilvie			Nettles
9 James Love	9 McNair	Hall	Yonge		Leeke
10 **George Young**	10 Shedden	Scoones	Ripley		Hayes

We know that Love and Langton commanded companies in the right wing, but it is unclear which of companies 2 and 3 (the only two unallocated) they each commanded with any certainty. We also cannot identify with accuracy which company Rowan and Chalmers commanded, but we know that they commanded companies 6 and 7 between them in the left wing.

P Campbell was absent until about 16.00–17.00 hours and the company was commanded by Dawson in his absence. R Campbell was absent, and his company was commanded by Cross. In the absence of Young, Langton commanded his company

In the absence of Brownrigg (who had been appointed Deputy Adjutant General in Ceylon in 1814), Lieutenant Anderson commanded his company as there were no more captains to fill the gap. A number of recent books on the regiment at Waterloo state that Anderson commanded No 10 company, but my research has shown that Leeke's statement that he commanded No 5 company is correct.

Right Wing

Anderson	P Campbell	Langton?	Love?	Diggle
5	4	3	2	1

Left Wing

Shedden	Mc Nair	Cross	Rowan?	Chalmers?
10	9	8	7	6

As can be seen, the actual positions of companies in the field bear absolutely no relation to the administrative company number given to them in the Muster Rolls, making it incredibly difficult to be certain where officers or men actually were in the line of battle. This however, makes perfect sense. When the regiment was inaugurated, presumably the highest ranking officers by seniority were put in order to command the companies. When they were superseded they were more than likely replaced by a very junior officer, unless they exchanged, but it would be very inconvenient and a major disruption, to have to move all of the officers of the regiment around to keep the sequence of seniority going correctly. It was much easier and less disruptive, given the frequent number of officer exchanges or replacements, to simply put the new officer into the company that had become vacant without worrying about the order of seniority. Only in the administrative Returns was the order of seniority important and therefore the companies were numbered differently here. Clearly, for military historians however, establishing the true position of companies in the line is of paramount importance.

Unfortunately, I have not discovered any regimental paperwork which lists the companies as they actually appeared on the battlefield, so it is only the luck of finding odd mentions in memoirs and regimental histories which help.

I have therefore played safe, referring to Captain …'s company as well as company numbers where know in the text of this book to try to avoid confusion.

Appendix II

Named Casualties of the 52nd Foot at Waterloo

Killed in Action 18 June

	Ensign William Nettles		Single

Company Commander	Rank and Name	Born	Occupation	Enlistment
Love's No.2 Company?	Private George Hodges	Faversham, Kent	Carpenter	11 December 1811
Young's No.3 Company?	Private George Gibbs 2nd	Henfield, Middlesex	Labourer	17 October 1799
	Private Richard Pearson	Sittingbourne, Kent	Labourer	6 December 1813
	Private Joseph Shipley	Gateside, Durham	Cordwainer	17 October 1799
P Campbell's No.4 Company	Corporal Peter Gorman	Goshill, King's Lynn	Labourer	13 April 1804
	Private Richard Bull	Andover, Hants	Labourer	3 October 1812
	Private William Harrington	Oxham, Kent	Labourer	1 April 1812
	Private Michael Kilty	Roscommon	Tailor	10 May 1805
	Private Barnaby Price	Cavan	Weaver	10 May 1804
Brownrigg No.5 Company	Corporal Samuel Collis	Resden, Herts	Labourer	8 June 1805
Chalmers No.6 Company?	Private George Robb	Forfar	Sadler	2 January 1807
	Private Henry Whicker	Barton Stacey, Hants	Labourer	16 December 1813
McNair No.9 Company	Private William Fairman	Gilding Kent	Labourer	5 April 1814
	Private John Pratt	Manchester, Lancaster	W[heel] Smith	1 April 1813

Appendix II 273

Died of Wounds

Company Commander	Rank and Name	Born	Occupation	Enlistment
Diggle No.1 Company	Sergeant William Busswell	Kettering, Northampton	Master Tailor	DoW 21 June 1815
	Private James Inscow			Dow 24 June 1815
	Private Robert North	Hamilton	Labourer	DoW 22 July 1815 Brussels
	Private Daniel Pray	Rumbland, Down	Labourer	DoW 2 July 1815 Brussels
Love No.2 Company?	Private Andrew Milton	Dunbar North Britain	Weaver	DoW 18 June 1815
Young's No.3 Company?	Corporal William Withall			Died at Brussels 19 June 1815
	Private James Chapman	Theakston Northampton	Labourer	DoW 1 July 1815
	Private Thomas Fogarty	Queens county	Cordwainer	DoW 1 July 1815
	Private James Neagle	Cork	Labourer	DoW 4 July 1815 Brussels
P Campbell's No.4 Company	Sergeant Charles Clark	Contellan, Argyle	Labourer	Died 30 July 1815
	Private Patrick Flanagan	Kilarney, Cavan	Labourer	DoW 13 July 1815 Brussels
	Private Samuel Topping	Limerick	Miller	DoW 14 July 1815 Brussels
Brownrigg No.5 Company	Private Richard Bence	Somerset	Labourer	DoW 18 June
	Private Hugh Dorning	Antrim, Londonderry	Weaver	DoW 29 June 1815 Brussels
	Private Charles Murphy	Derry	Labourer	DoW 30 June 1815
Chalmers No. 6 Company?	Private George Bell	Northwick, Chester	Cordwainer	DoW 4 July 1815
	Private Henry Harding			DoW 24 June 1815
	Private Thomas Jones	Caernarvon	Shoemaker	DoW 24 June 1815
	Private Thomas Vittey	Leeds, Yorkshire	Labourer	DoW 1 July 1815 Brussels
Rowan No.7 Company?	Sergeant William Williams			DoW 24 June 1815

Company Commander	Rank and Name	Born	Occupation	Enlistment
Rowan No.7 Company?	Private James Dickenson	Wigan, Doncaster	Labourer	DoW 11 July 1815 Ostend
	Private Anthony Grogan	Killoney, Wexford	Labourer	DoW 10 July 1815
	Private William Marshall	Appledore, Kent	Labourer	DoW 25 June 1815 Brussels
	Private Thomas Matthews	Rugby	Labourer	DoW 14 July 1815 Antwerp
	Private James Meyer			DoW at Brussels 24 March 1816
	Private Jonathan Rogers	Galway	Labourer	DoW 24 June 1815
	Private William Simms			DoW 24 June 1815
	Private James Williams			DoW 24 June 1815
	Private Jonathan Wilson	Stafford	Locksmith	DoW 5 July 1815
Mc Nair No.9 Company	Private John Conroy	Conna, Queens	Labourer	DoW 9 July 1815
	Private William Dighton	Bucks	Baker	Died 14 September 1815
	Private James Gould	Hatford, Fife	Labourer	DoW 30 June 1815
Shedden No.10 Company	Private John Jones 1st	Caernarvon	Labourer	DoW 23 July 1815 Brussels
	Private John Jones 2nd	Birmingham, Warwick	Bitt maker	DoW 18 June 1815
	Private Patrick McCarthy	St Catherine, Dublin	Weaver	DoW 3 July 1815
	Private Richard Pierce	Gillingham, Kent	Labourer	DoW 14 July 1815 Brussels
	Private John Sumner	Preston, Lancashire	Weaver	DoW 18 June 1815

Wounded who were Invalided

Company Commander	Rank and Name	Born	Occupation	Enlistment
Diggle No.1 Company	Private John Black	Kent	Labourer	Invalided to England 13 September
	Private Robert Ratcliffe			Invalided to 2 Batt 29 Oct 1815
	Private Thomas Roberts	Hatfield	Labourer	Invalided to England 13 September
Love No. 2 Company?	Sergeant Dennis Rice	Cork	Labourer	Invalided to England 13 September
	Private Adam Holmes	Derby	Labourer	Invalided to England 13 September
Young No.3 Company?	Private Malachi Caulfield	Galway	Labourer	Invalided to England 13 September
	Private Michael Moreley			Invalided to England 29 Oct 1815
	Private William Sewell	Essex	Butcher	Invalided to England 29 August
P Campbell No.4 Company	Private Richard Blackborough	York	Labourer	Invalided in England
	Private Clark Burblow	Somerset	Cooper	Invalided in England
Brownrigg No. 5 Company	Sergeant James Whitehead	Porth	Weaver	Invalided in England
	Corporal Robert Hood	Edinburgh	Weaver	Invalided to England 13 September
	Private William Allen	Birmingham	Brass Founder	Invalided to 2nd Batt 29 Oct 1815
	Private Joshua Atkinson	York	Labourer	Invalided in England
	Private James Davis	Lidagavey, Antrim	Joined 11 May 1805	KIA 18 Jun Later found to be only wounded
	Private John Leonard	Fermanagh	Weaver	Invalided to England 13 September

Company Commander	Rank and Name	Born	Occupation	Enlistment
Chalmers No.6 Company?	Corporal Alexander McPherson	Renfrew	Weaver	Invalided in England
	Private William Clark	Derby	Shoemaker	Invalided to 2 Batt 29 Oct 1815
	Private John Whitaker			Invalided to 2 Batt 29 Oct 1815
	Private John Wood	Kent	Labourer	Invalided to England 31 August
Rowan No.7 Company?	Corporal James Clarke	Surrey	Labourer	Invalided to England 13 September
	Private Edward Bowman	Somerset	Labourer	Invalided to England 13 September
	Private Henry Boxall	Kent	Sawyer	Invalided to England 13 September
	Private David Francis	Warwick	Glass Cutter	Invalided to England 13 September
R Campbell No.8 Company	Corporal William Smith	Surrey	Tanner	Invalided to England 13 September
	Private Robert Blacklock	Antrim	Weaver	Invalided to England 13 September
	Private William Dixon			Invalided to 2 Batt 29 Oct 1815
	Private Hugh Gaddis	Monaghan	Weaver	Invalided to England 10 August
	Private James Hagan			Invalided to England 24 Oct 1815
	Private Thomas Weightman	Nottingham	Bridle maker	Invalided to England 10 August

Company Commander	Rank and Name	Born	Occupation	Enlistment
Mc Nair No.9 Company	Private Charles Hock	Hants	Labourer	Invalided to England 13 September
	Private Stephen Smith			Invalided to 2 batt 29 Oct 1815
Shedden No. 10 Company	Private James Hickman	Hants	Tanner	Invalided to England 13 September
	Private Alexander Hinds			Invalided to England 24 Oct 1815
	Private Arthur Dillon	Galway	Tailor	Invalided to England 13 September
	Private James Marlow			Invalided to England 29 Oct 1815
	Private James Plant	Chester	Cotton Spinner	Invalided in England
	Private Thomas Vaughan	Roscommon	Labourer	Invalided to England 13 September
	Corporal Thomas Venable	Kent	Labourer	KIA 18 Jun Later found to be only wounded – survived – Invalided to 2 Batt 29 Oct 1815

Wounded Officers

Lt Colonel Charles Rowan – slightly (a contusion from a spent ball)
Major William Rowan – slightly (Musket ball in elbow)
Captain Charles Diggle – severely (grape shot wound in head)
Major James Frederick Love – severely (Musket ball in head and second in foot)
Lieutenant / Adjutant John Winterbottom – severely (shot in the head)
Lieutenant Charles Dawson – severely (Shot in the lungs)
Lieutenant Matthew Anderson – severely (Left leg amputated)
Lieutenant George Campbell – severely (Shot in the groin)
Lieutenant Thomas Cottingham – severely (Chest wound)

Wounded who eventually recovered and returned to battalion

Diggle
No. 1 Company
   Sergeant Thomas Archer
   Private Joshua McCombe
   Private Henry Cockerton
   Private Thomas Craig
   Private Frederick Cratter
   Private Willowby France
   Private Thomas Frost
   Private Thomas Ganley
   Private Matthew Hague
   Private Samuel Hardy
   Private George Paxton

Love
No. 2 Company?
   Sergeant John Bastable
   Corporal Valentine Gregory
   Corporal James McMasters
   Private Elias Adley
   Private John Davis
   Private William Jones
   Private James Levell
   Private Edward McCann
   Private John McDermott
   Private Andrew Milton

Youngs
No. 3 Company?
   Corporal William Withall
   Private Ralph Booth
   Private James Calverly
   Private James Chapman
   Private Titus Cummerford
   Private John Farrow (see deserted 23 June 1815)
   Private Samuel Gorman
   Private John Kay
   Private John Keogh
   Private John Kelly
   Private George Nelson
   Private George Savage

P Campbell
No. 4 Company
   Corporal Denis Rice
   Corporal Michael Rutledge
   Private John Butler
   Private James Day
   Private James Dayton
   Private Edward Dowling
   Private Anthony Dyer
   Private Patrick Flanagan
   Private Thomas Goulding
   Private Thomas Johnston
   Private Robert Lane
   Private Edward Scattergood
   Private George Wynyard

Brownrigg
No. 5 Company
   Sergeant John King
   Corporal William Delicate
   Corporal William McKenzie
   Private Richard Bence
   Private William Davis
   Private James Davis
   Private Hugh Dorning
   Private James Duffey
   Private John Duggen
   Private Thomas Fahey
   Private John Fitzgerald
   Private Charles Fuller
   Private John Graham
   Private Patrick Layden
   Private John Lester
   Private Francis Lillywhite
   Private James Sanders
   Private James Sheran
   Private Samuel Walker
   Private Patrick Ward
   Private Edward Wilson

Chalmers
No. 6 Company?
   Corporal Robert Wood
   Corporal Peter Senior
   Private George Bell
   Private Patrick Burke
   Private William Child
   Private William Foster
   Private Richard Gadd
   Private Henry Harding
   Private Henry Hawood
   Private John Johnston
   Private John Long
   Private William Martin
   Private John Masters
   Private Allen Pearson
   Private James Riley
   Private Thomas Vittey

Rowan
No. 7 Company?
   Sergeant William Williams
   Private Jonathan Cadman
   Private Joshua Dickeson
   Private Samuel Hill
   Private William Marshaw
   Private James Meyers
   Private James Williams

Appendix II   279

R Campbell
No. 8 Company   Sergeant Robert Ginn
                 Corporal John Owers
                 Private William Bellamy
                 Private Henry Brierly
                 Private George Gurr
                 Private William Maddon
                 Private Francis Mayne
                 Private Hugh Martin
                 Private John McLaughlin
                 Private John Scully
                 Private John Wilmore
                 Private Michael Wood

Shedden
No. 10 Company   Sergeant George Innis
                 Private William Blacklock
                 Private Patrick Cox
                 Private William Dray
                 Private John Gilman
                 Private James Hickman (see deserted)
                 Private Patrick McCarty
                 Private Jonathan Stopford
                 Private Jonathan Summer
                 Private Thomas Watson
                 Private John Wilson

McNair
No. 9 Company   Corporal Henry Gilpin
                 Private John Conroy
                 Private Richard Hunt
                 Private Robert Jones
                 Private Thomas Lucas
                 Private Samuel Wellington
                 Private Charles Winch

Casualties	No.10 Shedden	No.9 McNair	No.8 R Campbell (Cross)	No.7 Rowan?	No.6 Chalmers?	No.5 Brownrigg (Anderson)	No.4 P Campbell (Dawson)	No.3 Youngs? (Langton)	No.2 Love?	No.1 Diggle	Total Battalion	Percentage of Total
Killed in Action	0	2	0	0	2	1	5	3	1	0	14	6%
Died of Wounds	5	3	0	10	4	3	2	4	1	4	36	18%
Total Killed	5	5	0	10	6	4	8	7	2	4	51	24%
Wounded & Invalided	7	2	6	4	4	6	3	3	2	3	40	19%
Wounded Recovered	11	7	12	7	16	21	13	12	10	11	120	57%
Total Wounded	18	9	18	11	20	27	15	15	12	14	159	76%
Total Casualties	23	14	18	21	26	31	23	22	14	18	210	100%
Percentage of total	11%	7%	9%	10%	12%	14%	11%	10%	7%	9%	100%	

Note: Although the casualty rates per company were similar throughout, with only a narrow range of 7–14 per cent casualties per company, there are some noticeable discrepancies worth highlighting. No.8 company did not suffer any deaths but still incurred a pretty average loss overall. No.5 company suffered the highest casualty rate of all, and this is almost certainly because they were sent out as skirmishers against the Imperial Guard. However, the casualty figures do help to establish whether the four deep line was formed with wings behind each other (Leeke/Gawler) or half companies placed behind each other (Colborne/Rowan) as although overall the two wings suffered almost exactly half of the casualties each, company 1 and 2 suffered less casualties than companies 6 and 7, which would have been in the rear of 1 and 2 if Leeke and Gawler were correct. This would be very unlikely and therefore points towards Colborne and Rowan being correct with each half company being behind each other.

Appendix III

Known Desertions from 52nd Foot December 1814–December 1815

From the evidence from the 1st Battalion, it can be seen that desertions were higher than average despite some not being prosecuted for desertion (i.e. those having dropped out on 16/17 June and missing Waterloo). On the march to Paris, the desertions became almost daily. It can also be seen that desertion rates varied significantly by company, with companies 2 & 3 accounting for nearly half of all desertions, whilst two other companies (5 & 6) suffered no desertions at all.

Desertions

Company Commander	Individual	Comments/ Occupation	Dates Absent
Love	Private Henry Holland	At Waterloo	Deserted 12/12/14 rejoined 2/1/15
Love	John Quinn	Weaver, Tyrone At Waterloo	Deserted 20/12/14
?	George McMahon	Not at Waterloo	Deserted 27/12/14
?	William Callaghan	Not at Waterloo	Deserted 3/1/15
Shedden	James Hickman	Wounded at Waterloo	Deserted 7/1/15 rejoined 12/5/15
?	Cornelius Mahoney	Not at Waterloo	Deserted 26/3/15 rejoined 22/4/15
?	Jonathan McNulty	Not at Waterloo	Deserted 9/5/15
Love	Patrick Wall		Deserted 11/5/15 rejoined 25/5/15 Deserted 16 June–23 June 1815
Rowan	Private Terence O'Neal	Tailor, Antrim	Deserted (Not at Waterloo)
McNair	Private Charles Gregg	Not at Waterloo	Fell out 16 June Deserted 17 June to 17 July 1815
Love	Private Thomas Rielly	At Waterloo	Fell out 16 June
R Campbell	Private James McCardle		Fell out 16 June

Company Commander	Individual	Comments/ Occupation	Dates Absent
P Campbell	Private James Coffey		Deserted 17 June to 16 July 1815
Shedden	Private Francis Bass	Not at Waterloo	Fell out 17 June
Young	William Scott	At Waterloo	Deserted 19 June 1815
Rowan	Private Jonathan Chewcraft	At Waterloo, Sussex	Deserted 21 June 1815
Love	Private Thomas (or James) Kibby Labourer	Devon	Deserted 23 June 1815 (Not at Waterloo)
Young	Private John Farrow	Labourer, Aindow, Yorks	Absent 25 June – Deserted 13 July 1815
?	Daniel Cooper	Labourer, Kent	Deserted 27 June 1815
Love	Private Michael Kielley	Labourer, Cavan	Deserted 28 June rejoined 24 Sept 1815 (discharged to service abroad for life 24 Jan 1816 by sentence of court martial). At Waterloo
?	Thomas Darby		Deserted 3 July 1815
Young	Private Jonathan Mowby	Labourer, Tidmarton, Oxford	Deserted 11 July 1815 (At Waterloo)
Young	Private John Farrow	At Waterloo	Deserted 13 July 1815
Young	Private William Bartle	Brass Founder, Worcester	Deserted 28 July & Rejoined 9 Aug 1815
		Not at Waterloo	Deserted 30 Sept & Rejoined 12 Aug 1816
Diggle	Private Thomas Vickers	Potter, Stafford	Deserted 28 July Rejoined 30 August 1815
	Not at Waterloo		
Love	Private James Hanlon	Labourer, Galway	Deserted 31 July Rejoined 12 October 1815
		At Waterloo	
Young	Private William Halfpenny		Deserted 2 August, rejoined 30 August
Mc Nair	Private Henry Brand	At Waterloo	Deserted 24 August rejoined 30 Jan 1816
P Campbell	Private Thomas Johnston	Weaver, Tyrone	Deserted 30 Sept 1815 (At Waterloo)
Rowan	Private Terence O'Neal	Not at Waterloo	Deserted 14 October 1815

Desertions by Company (where known) – December 1814–December 1815

1 Diggle	1	3%
2 Love?	7	25%
3 Langton? (Young absent)	6	21%
4 P Campbell	1	3%
5 Brownrigg	0	0%
6 Chalmers?	0	0%
7 Rowan?	3	10%
8 Cross (R Campbell absent)	1	3%
9 McNair	2	7%
10 Shedden	2	7%
Unknown Company	6	21%
Total Battalion	29	100%

List of those known to have fallen out on the march to Paris (including desertions)

Date	Company	Individual
19 June	P Campbell	Private Patrick Curran
	P Campbell	Private Thomas Stanley
20 June	P Campbell	Private John Dunstead
	P Campbell	Private Robert Smith
	P Campbell	Private Daniel Campbell
	P Campbell	Private William Hunt
	P Campbell	Private Isaac Prince
	P Campbell	Private Edward Sales
	?	Private Francis Milton
	Shedden	Private John Daniels
	?	Private Thomas Hamill
	R Campbell	Private William Jackson
	Chalmers	Private William Goldsmith
	Brownrigg	Private Thomas Dunster
22 June	R Campbell	Private Dennis Leddy
25 June	Diggle	Private John Davis
27 June	Mc Nair	Private John Moody
28 June	Love	Private Michael Kielley
2 July	R Campbell	Private Francis Dawson

Falling out on the march by Company (where known) – 19 June–5 July 1815

1 Diggle	1	5%
2 Love?	1	5%
3 Langton? (Young absent)	0	0%
4 P Campbell	8	43%
5 Brownrigg	1	5%
6 Chalmers?	1	5%
7 Rowan?	0	0%
8 Cross (R Campbell absent)	3	16%
9 McNair	1	5%
10 Shedden	1	5%
Unknown Company	2	11%
Total Battalion	19	100%

Given that the causes of falling out on the march can be quite numerous, it is very noticeable that there is no correlation between desertion rates by company and for those that fell out on the march.

Appendix IV

Soldiers on Command etc. in June 1815

Sgt Hugh McCurrie (P. Campbell) Baggage 2nd Division
Pt John Hayden (R. Campbell) Ostend with prisoners
Pt Francis Watts (Diggle) Brussels – hospital orderly
Pt William Barnett (Chalmers) Servant to General Adam
Pt John Butcher (Diggle) Servant to Captain Diggle
Pt Thomas Cook (Diggle) Servant to General Adam
Pt George Coves (P. Campbell) Servant to Lt Cottingham
Pt Edward Dee (Diggle) Servant to Winterbottom
Pt Thomas Ewell (Diggle) Servant to Captain Diggle
Pt William Fisher (Love) Servant to Major Love
Pt Robert Hill (P. Campbell) Servant to Lt Farron
Pt Thomas Lee (Young) Servant to Captain Yorke
Pt Edward Pheasant (Chalmers) Servant to Lt Anderson
Pt James Price (P. Campbell) Servant to Earl of March
Pt John Smith 1st (Love) Servant to Major Love
Pt Uriah Watkinson (R. Campbell) Servant to Lt G Campbell
Pt William Wilson (P. Campbell) Servant to Lt Dawson
Pt Henry Anderson rejoined from PoW 8/1/1817!

Appendix V

Comparison of Battalion Returns April–July 1815 Adam's and Maitland's Brigades

Month	Effectives	Effectives as %	Total Sick	Sick as %	On Command	Total Other Ranks	Dead, since last return	Deserters	Sent Home
May 1815	986	95.54	35	3.39	11	1032	0	2	0
June 1815	793	77.59	205	20.06	24	1022	17	0	0
July 1815	797	78.91	180	17.82	33	1010	14	0	0

71st Foot 1st Battalion

Month	Effectives	Effectives as %	Total Sick	Sick as %	On Command	Total Other Ranks	Dead, since last return	Deserters	Sent Home
May 1815	781	96.42	22	2.72	7	810	0	0	0
June 1815	593	76.52	150	19.35	32	775	36	0	0
July 1815	720	81.91	144	16.38	15	879	2	0	0

95th Foot 2nd Battalion

Month	Effectives	Effectives as %	Total Sick	Sick as %	On Command	Total Other Ranks	Dead, since last return	Deserters	Sent Home
May 1815	568	97.09	14	2.39	3	585	0	0	1
June 1815	350	63.52	168	30.49	33	551	31	0	0
July 1815	399	70.49	151	26.68	16	566	3	0	0

95th Foot 3rd Battalion

Month	Effectives	Effectives as %	Total Sick	Sick as %	On Command	Total Other Ranks	Dead, since last return	Deserters	Sent Home
May 1815	180	94.74	5	2.63	5	190	0	0	0
June 1815	127	68.65	43	23.24	15	185	2	2	0
July 1815	290	58.94	51	10.37	151	492	4	0	1

1st Foot Guards 2nd Battalion

Month	Effectives	Effectives as %	Total Sick	Sick as %	On Command	Total Other Ranks	Dead, since last return	Deserters	Sent Home
May 1815	924	90.86	60	5.90	53	1017	1	1	0
June 1815	552	59.68	361	39.03	12	925	73	0	0
July 1815	637	64.47	321	32.49	30	988	9	0	0

1st Foot Guards 3rd Battalion

Month	Effectives	Effectives as %	Total Sick	Sick as %	On Command	Total Other Ranks	Dead, since last return	Deserters	Sent Home
May 1815	980	94.50	42	4.05	15	1037	0	0	0
June 1815	562	58.12	400	41.37	5	967	74	0	0
July 1815	686	64.72	347	32.74	27	1060	16	0	33

Please note the very low total of official deserters against the known deserters for the 52nd Foot.

Appendix VI

Number of Regimental and General Courts Martial (by Company) held on members of the 1st Battalion 52nd Foot in 1815

1 Diggle	8	6%
2 Love?	13	11%
3 Langton? (Young absent)	13	11%
4 P Campbell	29	23%
5 Brownrigg	8	6%
6 Chalmers?	6	5%
7 Rowan?	10	8%
8 Cross (R Campbell absent)	11	9%
9 McNair	10	8%
10 Shedden	6	5%
Unknown Company	10	8%
Total Battalion	124	100%

Again, there is no evidence of any correlation between the number of desertions, numbers falling out on the march and the overall number of courts martial per company. Lieutenant Colonel P. Campbell's Company is significantly higher regarding numbers of those falling out on the march and those court martialled, but the one inevitably led to the other. Most of these incidents of absence were short term and very often caused by drunkenness. The number of desertions may have been interpreted as a sign of unhappiness in the companies, however although Love and Langton's companies suffered nearly half of all desertions that year, they only accounted to 11 per cent of the total number of courts martial that year, which is higher than average, but not inordinately so. The number of courts martial for a year is however exceptionally high and would indicate a high level of ill-discipline in the regiment.

Year	Total Number of Court Martials	Number where punishment was remitted in part or in full	Percentage of Punishments remitted	Commanding Officer
1815	124	96	77%	Colonel Rowan/ Colonel Colborne
1816	25	14	56%	Colonel Rowan
1817	18	1	6%	Colonel Rowan
1818	33	24	73%	Colonel Rowan/ Colonel Colborne

Lieutenant Shaw claimed in his journal, that Colonel Colborne readily commuted sentences imposed by courts martial on the promise of future good behaviour, whereas Colonel Rowan in his absence rarely commuted sentences and the rate of offences dropped significantly. But does the data support this claim? There certainly were a very large number of courts martial in 1815, when Colonel Colborne personally commanded the regiment from May until December, but of course this was when they were involved in fighting and marching, giving the men greater opportunity for crime and of course absconding. The number of courts martial and the levels of ill-discipline was obvious to his seniors and was commented on in their reports. It is difficult to judge from 1815 alone, therefore. For the whole of 1816, 1817 and the first half of 1818, Colonel Colborne was on extended leave, taking his wife on the 'Grand European Tour'. It can be clearly seen that Colonel Rowan oversaw a significant reduction in the numbers of courts martial and a clear moving away from the policy of the wholesale remitting of punishments. It can of course be argued that the troops were more settled in cantonments and this had a major effect on the reduction of ill-discipline. However, the situation is most markedly demonstrated in 1818, where Rowan commanded until Colborne returned in June 1818. The number of courts martial in the second half of the year nearly quadrupled and the rate of remitting sentences reached a very high level indeed. It would therefore seem that Lieutenant Shaw's claims can be verified. It may be difficult for us today to admit that leniency and compassion towards the rank & file in the Georgian army, although an admired trait, failed to maintain discipline, but the evidence would appear to prove the case beyond doubt.

Splitting the commands within years				
Year	Total Number of Court Martials	Number where punishment was remitted in part or in full	Percentage of Punishments remitted	Commanding Officer
Jan–April 1815	2	2	100%	Colonel Rowan
May–Dec 1815	122	94	77%	Colonel Colborne
Jan–June 1818	7	2	29%	Colonel Rowan
June–Dec 1818	26	22	85%	Colonel Colborne

Details of Courts Martial included in General Orders 1815

GO 24 May 1815

No.23 At a General Court Marshal held by virtue of a warrant and in pursuance of an order from field marshal the Duke of Wellington KG commander of the forces &c &c at Ath on the 17th day of May 1815 whereof Colonel Du Platt of the 4th Line Battalion KGL was president and Captain Glasse of the 95th Regiment Ass Deputy Judge Advocate. Lieutenant Scott of the 52nd Regiment was arraigned upon the following charge, viz.

For neglect of duty when in command of a detachment on its route from Ostend to Audenarde by leaving or absenting himself from the said detachment when at or near Ghent, on or about the morning of the 25th April last, thereby impeding the public service and causing great irregularity in the march of the said detachment which by devolving to the charge of Corporal Hinton of the 52nd Regiment was moved to Brussels instead of the proper place of its destination.

Opinion and sentence

The court having maturely & deliberately weighed and considered the whole of the evidence adduced against the prisoner together with what he has stated in his defence is of opinion that he is guilty of the crime laid to his charge, in as much as he absented himself from his detachments for a short time at Ghent on the morning of the 21st of April last and the same being in breach of the Articles of War do in consideration of all the circumstances attending the case and the anxious endeavours made use of by Lieutenant Scott to rectify his error do sentence the prisoner to be reprimanded in such a manner as the commander of the forces thinks proper. Which opinion and sentence has been confirmed by His Grace the commander of the forces.

GO 14 June 1815

No.4 After a General Court Martial held at Ath on the 17th and continued by adjournments to the 23rd of May 1815, by a virtue of a warrant from H[is] G[race] the Duke of Wellington KG & GCB Commander of the Forces &c of which Colonel Du Platt 4th Line Battalion Kings German Legion was president & Captain F Glasse of the 1st Battalion 95th Regiment, Acting Deputy Judge Advocate. Private William Montgomery of the 52nd Regiment was tried on the following charge, viz.

'For desertion from his regiment or party when encamped at or near the town of Vera in Spain on or about the 7th of August 1813.'

Opinion and Sentence

The court having maturely and deliberately weighed and considered the evidence against the prisoner and what he has stated in his defence, together with his acknowledgements of the crime laid to his charge are of opinion that he is guilty of the said crime, being in breach of the Articles of War & sentence him the prisoner, Private William Montgomery of the 52nd Regiment to receive a punishment of 1,000 lashes, at such time and place as the Commander of the

Forces may direct. Which opinion and sentence His Grace the Commander of the Forces has been pleased to approve and confirm.

> Headquarters, Paris 14 August 1815
> To Field Marshal the Duke of Wellington

My Lord Duke,

The Judge Advocate General having submitted to the Commander in Chief the proceedings of a General Court Martial held for the trial of Captain Taylor of the 81st Regiment together with his report thereon of which I herewith enclose a copy & likewise a letter from your Grace dated 1st instant HRH directs me to express to your Grace his regret that the award of the court was not framed in terms more decisively declatory of the perfect acquittal of Captain Taylor grounded on the circumstances which demanded his interference, which unfortunately occasioned the infliction of the wound on Private James Raw 52nd Regiment.

On reading over the proceedings the Commander in Chief observes that certain men of the detachment under Captain Taylor's command presumed to declare that they would not obey him or any other officer except those of the regiments to which they immediately belong. HRH cannot but consider this a very great aggravation of the crime of which they are guilty & one for which they should be brought to trial, nor can he suppose that any soldier can be so ignorant of his duty as to imagine that it is not equally incumbent on him to obey the order of any officer under whose command he may be placed to whatever regiment the officer may belong.

If however your Grace should be of opinion that such an opinion is entertained by any part of the troops under your command the issue of a General Order explicitly and decidedly condemning so erroneous and so dangerous a principle.

GO 19 October 1815

No.3 At a General Court Martial held by virtue of a warrant and in pursuance of an order from Field Marshal His Grace the Duke of Wellington KG, Commander of the Forces &c&c at Boulogne, near Paris, on the 16th day of October 1815, whereof Lieutenant General Sir Henry Clinton GCB was president and JG Harris Esquire, Deputy Judge Advocate, Private James Raw of the 52nd Regiment was arraigned upon the following charges, viz

1st 'For beginning mutiny in a detachment of His Majesty's Forces of Foreign Service at Sass in Flanders, on or about the 14th day of April 1815'.

2nd 'For mutiny in using violence against Captain PC Taylor of the 81st Regiment in command of a detachment of His Majesty's Forces, at Sass in Flanders on or about the day above mentioned'.

3rd 'For mutiny in disobeying the lawful commands of Captain PC Taylor his superior officer at the time and place above mentioned'.

Opinion & Sentence

The court having considered the several charges exhibited against the prisoner, Private James Raw 52nd Regiment and the evidence produced in support of the same, and also the evidence produced by the prisoner in his defence, do find him Private James Raw, guilty on the said several charges exhibited against him, and do therefore sentence him Private James Raw 52nd Regiment to be *shot to death* at such time and place as the Commander of the Forces shall direct and appoint.

No.4 Which opinion and sentence has been confirmed by the Commander of the Forces.

No.5 The sentence of the General Court Martial on Private James Raw of the 52nd Regiment is to be carried into execution on Monday the 23rd instant, under the direction of the Assistant Provost Martial attached to the 2nd Division of infantry, and in presence of that division paraded for that purpose.

No.6 The proceedings and sentence of the above General Court Martial are to be read at the head of every regiment in this army.

GO 6 January 1816

No.12 Horse Guards 27 December 1815
To Field Marshal His Grace the Duke of Wellington KG

My Lord Duke,

Having laid before the Prince Regent the proceedings of a General Court Martial held at Paris on the 20 September 1815, and reassembled on the 7 October following for the trial of Private Charles Gregg of Captain McNair's company of the 1st Battalion 52nd Regiment, who was arraigned on the undermentioned charges, viz.

1st For desertion on or about the 18th of June 1815.

2nd For making away with or losing through neglect his arms, accoutrements, ammunition and blanket.

Upon which charge the court came to the following decision:

'The court having duly considered the evidence adduced against the prisoner, together with what he has said in his defence, is of opinion that he the prisoner, Private Charles Gregg is guilty of both the charges preferred against him, which being in breach of the Articles of War do by virtue thereof adjudge, that the prisoner, Private Charles Gregg, enlisted for unlimited service, shall serve as a soldier for life in any regiment or regiments or corps, in any country abroad or otherwise as His Majesty shall think fit.'

I am to acquaint your Grace, that His Royal Highness was pleased in the name and on the behalf of His Majesty, to approve and confirm the finding and sentence of the court. I am, my Lord Duke, yours Frederick, Commander in Chief.

No.16 27th December 1815
To Field Marshal His Grace the Duke of Wellington KG

My Lord Duke,

Having laid before the Prince Regent the proceedings of a General Court Martial held at Paris on 29 September 1815 and reassembled on the 23rd October following, for the trial of Private Michael Kielly of the 1st Battalion 52nd Regiment who was arraigned upon the undermentioned charge, viz 'For desertion on or about the 28th June 1815', upon which charge the court came to the following decision.

The court having duly weighed and considered the evidence adduced against the prisoner, Private Michael Kiely, together with what he has said in his defence, is of opinion that he is guilty of the crime laid to his charge, and do adjudge, that the prisoner, Private Michael Kielly, enlisted for service in the 52nd Regiment, shall serve His Majesty as a soldier for life, in any regiment or regiments or corps, and in any country, or place or places abroad, or otherwise as His Majesty may think fit.

I am to acquaint your Grace that His Royal Highness was pleased in the name and on the behalf of His Majesty, to approve and confirm the finding and sentence of the court. I am, my Lord Duke, yours, Frederick, Commander in Chief.

Appendix VII

General Adam's Wound

We know that General Adam was wounded in the leg but that he remained on his horse and remained on the battlefield until the fighting was over. Having dismounted he could not get back on a horse and we know from Susan Clinton that he was brought into Brussels on 19 June on a cart, looking very pale. He was, however, able to write a report to Henry Clinton that day and Clinton certainly had received it that same evening at Nivelles, allowing him to forward it to Lord Hill. Recently however, claims have been made that he was struck in the knee, which would have undoubtedly left him with a permanent stiffening of the joint and a pronounced limp. We are fortunate to have recently discovered his medical report,[1] which I now append to this work.

Report No. 137.

General Adam

Musket ball entered at A right leg, passed between the bones & is lodged & two fragments of cloth pantaloon were extracted by a counter opening, in the calf of the leg.

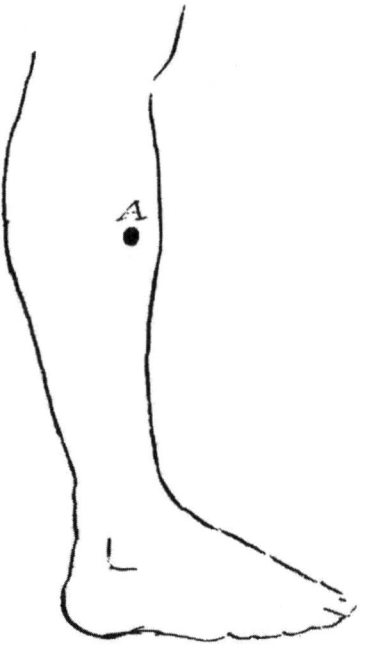

> The patient was Major General Frederick Adam. It seems that the tibia and fibula (the two bones in the leg that the ball passed between) may have been intact – this was fortunate. Also it was commendable that the portions of pantaloons were successfully removed. These were a potent source of sepsis, although, admittedly, a senior officer's overalls (trousers) would likely be cleaner than a private soldier's! Counter incisions were made on the opposite side to the wound or original incision, often as an additional drainage procedure. Adam retained his leg and survived until 17 August 1853.

---

1. Published in Waterloo, After the Glory, by Gareth Glover and Michael Crumplin.

Appendix VIII

Deployment of the Imperial Guard Battalions at Waterloo

Like many Waterloo enthusiasts, I have read numerous accounts of the actions of the French Imperial Guard at Waterloo and have found that almost every one differs in at least some details from the next. This is not surprising due to the large number of eyewitness accounts which seemingly cannot agree. The only thing that all historians of the battle do agree on was that there were 23 battalions of the Imperial Guard infantry at Waterloo, although some believe that two of these battalions were formed as one, so we do not have full unanimity even here. To illustrate these differences of opinion, without judging anybody's version better or worse than any other, I list below firstly the 'Classic' historians' views of how each battalion was deployed and then follow it with all of the main modern historians who have attempted to solve it. As can readily be seen, some things are not contentious at all, but the role of others are viewed very diversely indeed.

Source	1/1G	2/1G	1/2G	2/2G	1/3G	2/3G	4G	1/1C	2/1C	1/2C	2/2C	1/3C	2/3C	1/4C	2/4C	1/1T	2/1T	1/3T	2/3T	1/1V	2/1V	1/3V	2/3V
Petit	R	R	S	P	F	H	F	L	H	P	B	F	F	FC	FC	P	P	P	P	P	P	P	P
A F Becke	R	R	P	S	F	H	F	L	S	P	S	F	F	FC?	FC?	P	P	P	P	P	P	P	P
Henry Lachouque	R	R	S	P[1]	F	H	F	L	S	P	H[2]	F	F	FC	FC	P	P	P	P	P	P	P	P
John Ropes	R	R	P?	B?[3]	F	F	F	L	P	P	B	F	F	FC?	FC?	P	P	P	P	P	P	P	P
William Siborne	R	R	P?[4]	S?	F	F	S	L[5]	S	P	P	F	F	S	S	P	P	P	P	P	P	P	P
Henry Houssaye	R	R	P	S	F	H	F	L	S	P	S	F	F	FC	FC	P	P	P	P	P	P	P	P
Andrew Uffindel	R	R	P	S	F	S	F	L	S	P	S	F	F	F	F	P	P	P	P	P	P	P	P
Alessandro Barbero	R	R	P	S	F	S	F	L	S	P	S	F	F	FC	FC	P	P	P	P	P	P	P	P
Peter Hofschroer	R	R	F	F	F	H	F	L	H	P	F	F	F	F	F	P	P	P	P	P	P	P	P
Mark Adkin	R	R	P	S	F	H	F	L	S	P	S	F	F	FC	FC	P	P	P	P	P	P	P	P
Gordon Corrigan	R	R	F	F	F	F	F	P	F	L	F	F	F	FC	FC	P	P	P	P	P	P	P	P

1. In his Waterloo book, he has the battalions of the 2nd Grenadiers the other way around. This is how he has them in Anatomy of Glory.
2. He states 'Sent to the left flank by Morand' p 490
3. Ropes only states that a battalion was in Plancenoit and the other near La Belle Alliance without stating which was exactly where.
4. Siborne does not specify which battalion of 2nd Grenadiers was in Plancenoit.
5. Siborne has this battalion at Le Caillou and in the second attack – however, he omits to mention 2/2 Grenadiers and I presume that he meant that these took part in the secondary attack – not 1/1 Chasseurs.

	1	2	3	4	5	6	7	8	9	10	11	12	13	14	15	16	17	18	19	20	21
David Chandler	R	R	P	?6	F	R	F	L	?	P	?	F	F	FC	P	P	P	P	P	P	P
John Hussey	R	R	P	S	F	H	F	L	P	S	S	F	F	FC	P	P	P	P	P	P	P
Andew Field	R	R	B	P	F	H	F	L	B	P	B	F	F	FC	P	P	P	P	P	P	P
Jacques Logie	R	R	S	P	F	S	F	L	S	P	S	F	F	FC	P	P	P	P	P	P	P
Pierre de Wit	R	R	B7	P	B	H	B	B	B	P	B	F	F	F	P	P	P	P	P	P	P
John Franklin	R8	R	T	P	S	H	S	L	T	P	T	F	F	F	P	P	P	P	P	P	P
Tim Clayton	R	R	S	P	F	H	F	L	H	P	S	F	F	FC?	P	P	P	P	P	P	P
Hamilton–Williams	R	R	S	P9	F	H	F	L	S	P	S	F	F	FC	P	P	P	P	P	P	P
Paul Dawson	R	R	P	T10	S	T	S	L	T	P	T	F	F	F	P	P	P	P	P	P	P

Key

G=Grenadiers, C=Chasseurs, T=Tirailleurs, V=Voltigeurs
L = Le Caillou, P=Plancenoit, B= In the valley in front of La Belle Alliance, F=First Wave Attack, S=Second Wave Attack, H= Near Hougoumont Orchard, R=Reserve at Rossomme, C=Battalions Combined, [?] = Historian admits they are unsure.

6. David Chandler does not specify any role whatsoever for these three battalions marked [?] Presumably he felt that they stayed in reserve somewhere south of La Belle Alliance.
7. Pierre de Wit states that only the four Chasseur battalions advanced to the attack and that none of the others moved beyond the low ground between the two armies and only became involved when the allied forces attacked them.
8. John Franklin's map appears to show these two battalions at La Belle Alliance, but the text confirms that they were at Rossomme
9. On page 338 he says the 1/2G and on page 340 he states the 2/2G were in Plancenoit, but he later puts 1/2G in the secondary attack – I have therefore ignored page 338 as a typographical error.
10. Paul Dawson believes that Major Golzio was in charge of 1st battalion, hence it was 1/2G in Plancenoit. See p. 402.

It has to be admitted, that even I have made a previous attempt at solving this issue, but given further information which has since come to light, I wish to try to produce the most accurate theory yet, based on all of the available evidence.

Which Guard Battalions can we be certain where they deployed?

Looking at the above list of battalions of the Imperial Guard, it seems that the deployment of 11 of the 23 (or 22 – see later) battalions can be identified with very great certainty as all historians place these units in the same location.

The 1st and 2nd Battalions of the 1st Grenadiers were kept as a reserve in the area of Rossomme.

General Petit, who commanded 1st Grenadiers states: 'The 1st Regiment of Grenadiers formed ... two squares ...The 2nd Battalion to the right of the main road ... dominating the small track which ran between the village of Planchenoit and the main road. ... The square of the 1st Battalion formed on the left of the main road, on the height that the Emperor had first occupied.'[1]

The 1st Battalion 1st Chasseurs remained in the vicinity of Le Caillou throughout as a guard at headquarters

Whilst the 8 battalions of the Young Guard – that is the 1st and 2nd Battalions of the 1st and 3rd Tirrailleurs and the 1st and 2nd Battalions of the 1st and 3rd Voltiguers were all deployed in Plancenoit to hold the village against the Prussian advance.

We can place these with great certainty, we now only have to deal with the other 12 battalions

Which other battalions were sent to Plancenoit later?

Almost all historians agree that two further battalions were later sent to bolster the Young Guard and to drive the Prussians back out of Plancenoit but cannot agree as to which battalions were involved. So, what is the evidence?

The first battalion which is almost universally accepted to have been in Plancenoit was 1st Battalion 2nd Chasseurs. The evidence for this deployment comes from Brigadier Pelet who commanded 2nd Chasseurs, who says 'General Morand said to me "Go with your 1st Battalion to Planchenoit [sic], where the Young Guard has been beaten."'[2] If anyone should know, it would be him, and there seems to be little contention regarding this battalion. This however is not true of the other battalion deployed there.

We know for certain that a battalion of the 2nd Grenadiers was also deployed in the Plancenoit area, but which one has divided historians quite evenly and a number, such as Ropes and Siborne avoid stating which battalion was sent at all. So what is the evidence? Pelet of the 2nd Chasseurs states: 'Whilst the 1st battalion of the 2nd Chasseurs were throwing themselves against the Prussians, the 1st Battalion of the 2nd Grenadiers under the orders of Lieutenant Colonel Golzio, received the order to support it.'[3] Now, the naming of the commander

---
1. Andrew Field Waterloo p185.
2. Andrew Field Waterloo the French Perspective p178.
3. ibid.

of the battalion as Golzio is very useful, but according to Mark Adkin, Golzio commanded 2nd Battalion of the 2nd Grenadiers, not the 1st Battalion as stated by Pelet.

Paul Dawson confuses the issue even further in his recent book, as he uses the following quote from General Christiani commanding 2nd Grenadiers twice, but in error gives two different translations. 'On page 337 he states: "I received the order to send a battalion of the regiment into the village, that was to the right, behind the position I occupied...It was M Golzio, head of the 1st Battalion of the regiment that went on this mission." Whereas on page 402 he states "I received the order to send a battalion of the regiment into the village, that was to the right, behind the position I occupied...It was M Golzio, head of the 2nd Battalion of the regiment that went on this mission."'

Paul goes on to make it clear that he believes that the 1st Battalion fought at Plancenoit, and backs this up by quoting de Mauduit, although de Mauduit was in the 1st Grenadiers and was not a witness to the deployment. The other witnesses quoted to support this statement really prove nothing either way.

Andrew Field provides the same quote and translates it as 'Between five and six pm, ... I received the order to send a battalion of the regiment into a village situated to the right rear of the position that I occupied, to chase away the Prussians ... I gave this mission to M. Golzio who commanded the second battalion of the regiment.'[4]

The only way to end this confusion of what General Christiani said was to view the original source. Having done so I can confirm that it definitely states that 'Between five and six pm, perhaps later, I received the order to send a battalion of the regiment to the village situated to the right rear of the position that I occupied to drive off the Prussians who had come to seize it. It was M. Golzio, chief of the 2nd Battalion of the regiment that I tasked with this mission', but the clinching sentence has unfortunately been omitted by them both, as he continues: 'Finally, towards 7pm I think, I left with the 1st Battalion that remained to me, to go to join the Emperor who was to the left of the road, a little distance from the position that I had previously left.'

As he commanded the other battalion personally, we can be certain therefore that Golzio did command the 2nd Battalion 2nd Grenadiers and that it was this battalion that was deployed in Plancenoit. This is further confirmed by Pigeard[5] who says in *Composition de la Garde impériale à Waterloo:*

2e Grenadier Maréchal-de-camp baron Christiani,
1er bat. Chef de bataillon Martenot de Cordoux,
2e bat. Chef de bataillon Golzio [Ref 1064. S.H.A.T Xab 68 à 74].

No other battalions of the Guard were sent to Plancenoit. Therefore, we can be certain that they were the 2nd Battalion 2nd Grenadiers and the 1st Battalion 2nd Chasseurs.

---

4. ibid.
5. Pigeard, *L'Armée napoléonienne*, p 272

So how many battalions did Napoleon have available to attack Wellington's ridge with?

Ignoring the 1st Battalion 1st Chasseurs, which could not leave headquarters unguarded, Napoleon had a maximum of 12 battalions available (if the 4th Chasseurs formed as two battalions, rather than one as stated by Petit).

Their roles have been exhaustively reviewed in this volume, but this will provide an overview.

1st Battalion 1st Grenadiers	Old Guard	Held in Reserve
1st Battalion 1st Chasseurs	Old Guard	Held in Reserve
2nd Battalion 1st Chasseurs	Old Guard	Third Attack
1st Battalion 2nd Grenadiers	Old Guard	Held in Reserve
1st Battalion 2nd Chasseurs	Old Guard	Third Attack
1st Battalion 3rd Grenadiers	Middle Guard	Second Attack
2nd Battalion 3rd Grenadiers	Middle Guard	Third Attack
4th Grenadiers	Middle Guard	Second Attack
1st Battalion 3rd Chasseurs	Middle Guard	First Attack
2nd Battalion 3rd Chasseurs	Middle Guard	First Attack
1st Battalion 4th Chasseurs	Middle Guard	First Attack
2nd Battalion 4th Chasseurs	Middle Guard	First Attack

Conclusion

I believe that we can for the first time, now finally establish exactly where each of the Imperial Guard battalions were towards the end of that fateful day and their roles. I believe they are as opposite:

Source	1/1G	2/1G	1/2G	2/2G	1/3G	2/3G	4G	1/1C	2/1C	1/2C	2/2C	1/3C	2/3C	1/4C	2/4C	1/1T	2/1T	1/3T	2/3T	1/IV	2/IV	1/3V	2/3V
My Latest Interpretation	R	R	B	P	S	H/T	S	L	T	P	T	F	F	F	F	P	P	P	P	P	P	P	P

Sources used in this summary:

Petit – *General Petit's Account of the Waterloo Campaign*
A F Becke – *Napoleon & Waterloo*, London 1936
Henry Lachouque – *Waterloo*, London 1972, and *The Anatomy of Glory, Napoleon and His Guard*, London 1997
John Ropes – *The Campaign of Waterloo*, New York 1916
William Siborne – *History of the Waterloo Campaign*, London 1848
Henry Houssaye – *1815 Waterloo*, London 1900
Andrew Uffindel – *On the Fields of Glory*, London 1996
Alessandro Barbero – *The Battle, A new History of the Battle of Waterloo*, London 2005
Peter Hofschroer – *1815 The Waterloo Campaign, The German Victory*, London 1999
Mark Adkin – *The Waterloo Companion*, London 2001
Gordon Corrigan – *Waterloo, Wellington, Napoleon and the Battle that Saved Europe*, London 2014
David Chandler – *Waterloo the Hundred Days*, Oxford 1980
John Hussey – *Waterloo the Campaign of 1815 volume 2*, Barnsley 2017
Andrew Field – *Waterloo the French Perspective*, Barnsley 2012
Jacques Logie – *Waterloo the 1815 Campaign*, Stroud 2006
Pierre de Wit – Website http://www.waterloo-campaign.nl/
John Franklin – *Waterloo 1815* (3 Volumes), Oxford 2015
Tim Clayton – *Waterloo Four days that changed Europe's Destiny*, London 2014
Hamilton-Williams – *Waterloo New Perspectives, The Great Battle Reappraised*, London 1993
Paul Dawson – *Waterloo the Truth at Last*, Barnsley 2018

Appendix IX

Private James Raw's Execution

Ensign Leeke wrote a long piece in his work *Lord Seaton's Regiment at Waterloo* on the case of a soldier of the 52nd. With the help of my friend Zach White, who has been compiling a huge database of General and Regimental Court Martials during the Napoleonic Wars, we have been able to identify all of those involved in the case and can tell the whole story here. Leeke wrote:

> A very sad and exciting business occurred, whilst we were at Paris, in connexion with the mutinous behaviour of one of our own men, when coming to join the army with detachments under the command of a captain and other officers belonging to other regiments; I think I recollect the circumstances very clearly, they were these: Several of the men of these detachments had got drunk, and this man, when ordered by Captain [Philip Taylor 81st Foot] to be silent, or to perform some duty, refused to obey, as he was not a 52nd officer, and swore at him, calling him a d[amned?] d[evil?]; the officer drew his sword, and cut the drunken mutineer very severely across the shoulder. For this the officer was afterwards brought to a court martial and honourably acquitted. The Duke of Wellington, on reading the proceedings of the court martial, ordered the 52nd soldier to be brought to a general court martial for mutinous conduct towards his superior officer; he was accordingly tried, found guilty, and condemned to be shot. The Duke, who always felt the vast importance of upholding the discipline of the army, determined that the sentence should be executed. I saw at a little distance, not far from my tent, an interview between the Duke and Sir John Colborne, which I had reason to believe was connected with this man's execution. The Duke had come into our camp from his garden door, and as Colborne almost immediately joined him, I fancy the interview had been arranged before. The Duke, who generally appeared a person of very quiet demeanour, seemed on this occasion to speak with some considerable earnestness, and Colborne, who was most anxious, as we all were, that the man's life should be spared, was equally energetic. The conversation did not last more than seven or eight minutes, and I did not learn the result, until the order for the execution appeared in orders. I think the next morning, the regiments of the brigade marched to some ground near the walls of Paris, to see the sentence carried into effect.

The first reference to this case was published in General Orders in a letter sent to the Duke of Wellington on behalf of the Prince Regent by Lord Palmerston:

General Orders Headquarters, Paris 14 August 1815
To Field Marshal the Duke of Wellington

My Lord Duke,

The Judge Advocate General having submitted to the Commander in Chief the proceedings of a General Court Martial held for the trial of Captain Taylor of the 81st Regiment[1] together with his report thereon of which I herewith enclose a copy & likewise a letter from your Grace dated 1st instant HRH directs me to express to your Grace his regret that the award of the court was not framed in terms more decisively declatory of the perfect acquittal of Captain Taylor grounded on the circumstances which demanded his interference, which unfortunately occasioned the infliction of the wound on Private James Raw 52nd Regiment.

On reading over the proceedings the Commander in Chief observes that certain men of the detachment under Captain Taylor's command presumed to declare that they would not obey him or any other officer except those of the regiments to which they immediately belong. HRH cannot but consider this a very great aggravation of the crime of which they are guilty & one for which they should be brought to trial, nor can he suppose that any soldier can be so ignorant of his duty as to imagine that it is not equally incumbent on him to obey the order of any officer under whose command he may be placed to whatever regiment the officer may belong.

If however your Grace should be of opinion that such an opinion is entertained by any part of the troops under your command the issue of a General Order explicitly and decidedly condemning so erroneous and so dangerous a principle.

This was a strongly worded letter and highly unusual in its strident support of the proceedings of Captain Taylor whose actions were being very publicly approved of. This was followed by a further General Order in October, promulgating the results of a General Court Martial on Private James Raw:

General Orders Headquarters Paris 19 October 1815

No.3 At a General Court Martial held by virtue of a warrant and in pursuance of an order from Field Marshal His Grace the Duke of Wellington KG, Commander of the Forces &c &c at Boulogne, near Paris, on the 16th day of October 1815, whereof Lieutenant General Sir Henry Clinton GCB was president and JG Harris Esquire, Deputy Judge Advocate, Private James Raw of the 52nd Regiment was arraigned upon the following charges, viz

1st 'For beginning mutiny in a detachment of His Majesty's Forces of Foreign Service at Sass in Flanders, on or about the 14th day of April 1815.'

2nd 'For mutiny in using violence against Captain PC Taylor of the 81st Regiment in command of a detachment of His Majesty's Forces, at Sass in Flanders on or about the day above mentioned.'

3rd 'For mutiny in disobeying the lawful commands of Captain PC Taylor his superior officer at the time and place above mentioned.'

Opinion & Sentence
The court having considered the several charges exhibited against the prisoner, Private James Raw 52nd Regiment and the evidence produced in support of the same, and also the evidence produced by the prisoner in his defence, do find him Private James Raw, guilty on the said several charges exhibited against him, and do therefore sentence him Private James Raw 52nd Regiment to be shot to

---

1. Captain Philip Taylor of the 81st Foot.

death at such time and place as the Commander of the Forces shall direct and appoint.

No.4 Which opinion and sentence has been confirmed by the Commander of the Forces.

No.5 The sentence of the General Court Martial on Private James Raw of the 52nd Regiment is to be carried into execution on Monday the 23rd instant, under the direction of the Assistant Provost Marshal attached to the 2nd Division of infantry, and in presence of that division paraded for that purpose.

No.6 The proceedings and sentence of the above General Court Martial are to be read at the head of every regiment in this army.

This court martial is confirmed by General Henry Clinton who wrote in his journal that he sat on it 17–18 October 1815. However, Ensign Leeke wrote of the execution day:

> The regiments were drawn up so that each occupied one side of a large square, the man to be executed being placed in the middle of the fourth side of the square with his coffin behind him, and the firing party, consisting I think, of a sergeant and twelve rank and file, a few paces in his front. The Brigade Major, or some other staff officer, then rode forward and read the charge against the soldier, the finding of the court martial, and the sentence. When this was done, an aide de camp, the bearer of a reprieve, rode into the square; I think it was an order from the Duke, granting the man a pardon, and stating, amongst other reasons for doing so, that it was partly in consideration of the high character of the regiment to which he belonged, that the Duke was induced to take this course. I have an idea that some of us were aware the night before that the man would be pardoned, but the man himself, and the men of the regiment and of the brigade generally, expected the execution to take place. I met him close to the camp, in the course of the afternoon, walking with one of the men, and I recollect that the poor fellow sobbed as he passed and saluted me. I cannot quite bear in mind whether I spoke to him or not; but I am sure I must have shewn him, in some way, how much I felt for him. [2]

It was not the next day as Leeke remembered it, as General Clinton wrote in his journal on 23 October:

> My division paraded to put in execution a soldier of the 52nd Regiment who had been sentenced to be shot for mutiny, this was rendered as solemn as possible & appeared to have an effect on the soldiers, after seeing the proceedings & his terror to the sermon close to his coffin & his grave, I communicated to him the pardon of the commander of the forces.[3]

Private James Raw was reprieved his execution at the very last moment and he was discharged to pension in June 1816.

---

2. Leeke, pp 170–1.
3. Glover, The Correspondence of Sir Henry Clinton in the Waterloo Campaign Volume 2, p 207.

Bibliography

Unpublished Manuscript Material
Hart Lt J, *Letter written to his father dated Estien au Mont 20 June 1815* National Army Museum reference 1981–11–84
Holman Lt, *Journal for 1815*, Royal Green Jackets Museum Winchester
Batty Ens R, *Letter dated Bavay 21 June 1815*
Powell Ens H, *Letter dated near Binche 20 June 1815*
SOFO 6388, *Journal of the 52nd 1811–1823 by Surgeon JB Gibson* Museum of the Oxford Soldier
SOFO 6566, *Historical Record & Record of Services 52nd Foot*, Museum of the Oxford Soldier
WO12/6253, General *Muster Books and Pay Lists, 1st Battalion 52nd Foot 1815–16*, National Archives
WO25/1282, *Muster Master General's Index of Casualties &c 52nd Foot 1797–1816*, National Archives
WO25/1850, *Casualty Returns 1st Battalion 52nd Foot 1809–16*

Published Articles
Davout A, *Journal of General Pelet at Waterloo*, Carnet de la Sabretache Paris 1903, Pages 33–54.
Gawler G, The Crisis and Close of the Action at Waterloo, United Services Journal 1833 part 2, pp 299–310.
Moore Smith, *General Petit's Account of the Battle of Waterloo*, The English Historical Review, Volume XVIII, Issue LXX, April 1903, Pages 321–326
Oxford LI, Colours of the 52nd at Waterloo, *Chronicle of the Oxford & Bucks Light Infantry 1895* pages 144–5.
Oxford LI, Extracts from General Adam's Brigade Orders, *Chronicle of the Oxford & Bucks Light Infantry 1905* pages 207–214.
Oxford LI, Extracts from General Adam's Brigade Orders, *Chronicle of the Oxford & Bucks Light Infantry 1906* pages 193–209
Oxford LI, Colonel Cross' Account of Waterloo 1821, *Chronicle of the Oxford & Bucks Light Infantry 1914* pages 133–4
Yonge, The 52nd Regiment, *The Christian Remembrancer, Vol 54 July-Oct 1867*, pages 239–285

Published Books
Abbott P, *'Every Implement of Destruction was used against us'*, Private 2015
Anonymous, *Army Lists*, Various
Chair Somerset de, *Napoleon's Memoirs*, London 1948
Crosse RB, *A Short History of the Oxfordshire and Buckinghamshire Light Infantry 1742–1922*, Aldershot, 1925
Dawson P, *Waterloo: The Truth at Last*, Barnsley 2018
Eaton C, *The Battle of Waterloo… By a Near Observer vols 1 & 2*, London 1817
Field A, *Waterloo: The French Perspective*, Barnsley 2012
Field A, *Grouchy's Waterloo*, Barnsley 2017
Franklin J, *Waterloo Hanoverian Correspondence*, Ulverston 2010
Franklin J, *Waterloo Netherlands Correspondence*, Ulverston 2010

Glover G, *Letters from the Battle of Waterloo: Unpublished correspondence by Allied Officers from the Siborne Papers*, London 2004
Glover G, *A Guards Officer in the Peninsula and at Waterloo, The letters of Captain George Bowles Coldstream Guards*, Godmanchester 2008
Glover G, *Eyewitness to the Peninsular War and the Battle of Waterloo, the letters of Lt Col James Stanhope 1803–25*, Barnsley 2010
Glover G, *The Diary of William Gavin, Ensign and Quarter Master of the 71st Highland Regiment 1806–15*, Godmanchester 2013
Glover G, *Waterloo, Myth & Reality*, Barnsley 2014
Glover G, *The Correspondence of Sir Henry Clinton in the Waterloo Campaign, Volumes 1&2*, Godmanchester 2015
Glover G, *Waterloo: The Defeat of Napoleon's Imperial Guard*, Barnsley 2015
Glover G, *The Waterloo Archive volumes I to VI*, Barnsley 2010–14
Glover G, *The Waterloo Archive volumes VII to VIII*, Godmanchester 2019
Glover G, *A Light Infantryman with Wellington: The letters of Captain George Ulrich Barlow 52nd and 69th Foot 1808–15*, Warwick 2018
Gourgaud Baron, *Talks of Napoleon at St Helena*, Chicago 1903
Gourgaud Baron, *The Campaign of 1815*, London 1818
Gronow R, *Reminiscences of Captain Gronow*, London 1862
Hamilton FW, *The Origin and History of the First or Grenadier Guards Volume III*, London 1874
Hansard T, The Parliamentary Debates from the Year 1803 to the Present Time - Volume 31, London 1815
Haythornthwaite P, *The Armies of Wellington*, London 1984
Leach J, *Men of the Rifles*, Milton Keynes 2010
Leeke Rev W, *The History of Lord Seaton's Regiment (The 52nd Light Infantry) at the Battle of Waterloo 2 volumes & addend*, London 1866–71
Miller D, *The Duchess of Richmond's Ball 15 June 1815*, Staplehurst 2005
Moore Smith GC, *The Life of John Colborne, Field Marshal Lord Seaton*, London 1903
Moorsom W, *Historical Record of the Fifty-Second Regiment (Oxfordshire Light Infantry) from the year 1755 to the year 1858*, London 1860
Park & Nafziger *The British Military, System and Organization 1803–1815*, Cambridge Ontario 1983
Sale N, *Wellington's Waterloo Secret*, Witney 2005
Sale N, *The Lie at the Heart of Waterloo, The Battle's Hidden Last Half Hour*, Stroud 2014
Shaw, Col. C, *Personal Memoirs and Correspondence of Colonel Charles Shaw, KCTS &c, Volume I*, London 1837
Siborne HT, *Waterloo Letters*, London 1891
Summerfield & Law, *Sir John Moore and the Universal Soldier. Vol 1 The Man, the Commander and the Shorncliffe System Of Training*, Godmanchester 2016
Summerfield & Law, *Prelude to Waterloo, Adam's Light Brigade in the Netherlands (1813–15)*, Godmanchester 2015
Swinton Hon Mrs J, *A Sketch of the Life of Georgiana, Lady de Ros*, London 1893
Verner R, *Reminiscences of William Verner (1782–1871) 7th Hussars – SAHR Special Publication No. 8*, London 1965
Wellington Duke of, *Supplementary Despatches, Correspondence and Memoranda of Field Marshal Arthur Duke of Wellington, KG*, London 1862
—— Edited by His Son, *The Duke of Wellington KG. Volume 10*.
Yonge WC, *Memoir of Lord Seaton's Services*, Privately published London 1853